Jews and Baseball

VOLUME 1

ALSO BY BURTON A. BOXERMAN
AND BENITA W. BOXERMAN

Ebbets to Veeck to Busch:
Eight Owners Who Shaped Baseball (2003)

Jews and Baseball

VOLUME 1

Entering the American Mainstream, 1871–1948

BURTON A. BOXERMAN
and BENITA W. BOXERMAN

Foreword by Martin Abramowitz

McFarland & Company, Inc., Publishers
Jefferson, North Carolina, and London

LIBRARY OF CONGRESS CATALOGUING-IN-PUBLICATION DATA

Boxerman, Burton Alan, 1933–
Jews and baseball : / Burton A. Boxerman and Benita W. Boxerman ;
foreword by Martin Abramowitz.
v.   cm.
Includes bibliographical references and index.
Contents: v. 1. Entering the American mainstream, 1871–1948.

ISBN-13: 978-0-7864-2828-1
(illustrated case binding : 50# alkaline paper) ∞

1. Jewish baseball players—United States—Biography.
2. Jews—Cultural assimilation—United States.
3. Baseball—Religious aspects—Judaism.
I. Boxerman, Benita W.   II. Title.
GV865.A1B645   2007   796.3570922—dc22   2006034478

British Library cataloguing data are available

Cover art: Hank Greenberg ©2006 Arthur K. Miller; www.artofthegame.com

Manufactured in the United States of America

*McFarland & Company, Inc., Publishers
Box 611, Jefferson, North Carolina 28640
www.mcfarlandpub.com*

We dedicate this book with love
to our children and grandchildren:
Sanford, Cynthia, Hannah and Robert,
Arlene, Leonard, Benjamin and Matthew,
our inspiration at all times.

And to our animal friends,
Chuckles, Paco, and the late Samson,
who never complained
no matter how many walks they missed.

Acknowledgments

We are deeply grateful to many people who provided time, knowledge, and materials as we researched, wrote, and acquired pictures for this book. Many are referenced in the notes and bibliography, but we want to give special recognition to the following:

Steve Gietschier, Director of Historical Records, *The Sporting News*, for his guidance, advice, and patience.

Martin Abramowitz, whose baseball cards, Jewish Major Leaguers, were our authority for determining who was Jewish; he honors us by writing the foreword to this book.

Al Rosen, former American League MVP and long-time Giants executive, who granted a lengthy and fascinating telephone interview which confirmed many of our theories about conditions for Jews in the majors after 1948.

Harry Danning, former Giant catcher and, at the time, the oldest living Jewish player, who, shortly before he passed away, answered our letter about the decades after Hank Greenberg.

Ross Baumgarten, former pitcher for the Chicago White Sox and Pittsburgh Pirates, who also responded to our query and wished us well.

The families and associates of a number of our subjects, who provided photos, documents, and a liberal amount of time for interviews, including: Harriet Block, widow of Cy Block; Marina Lee, daughter of Andy Cohen; Neal Ross, nephew of Andy and Syd Cohen; Ray Sanchez, *El Paso Herald* sportswriter, who closely followed the careers of Andy and Syd Cohen; Daniel Yates, grandson of Dan Daniels; Dave Danning, nephew of Harry and Ike Danning; Evelyn Eisenstadt, widow of Harry Eisenstadt; Helen Ann Meltzer, daughter of Emil Fuchs; Joseph M. Solomon, son of Mose Solomon; and Professor Irwin Weil, son of Sidney Weil.

The staffs at numerous public and private libraries and archives who opened every available resource on our behalf, especially the American Jewish Archives in Cincinnati, the Boston Public Library, the Cincinnati Public Library, and the Saul Brodsky Jewish Community Library in St. Louis.

The staff at the Baseball Hall of Fame in Cooperstown, the ultimate resource for all baseball historians, and particularly John Horne, Photo Sales, who expertly, cheerfully, and patiently helped us in our research.

Steve Steinberg, noted baseball author and good friend, who selflessly shared leads, offered guidance, and generously gave us permission to use his photos as needed.

Dave Garino, associate and long-time friend, who helped with chapter titles and gave encouragement.

Jeff Leen, Pulitzer Prize-winner journalist, *Washington Post*, and Burton's former student, who provided a marvelous photo of Shirley Povich.

Our friends and associates, who always seemed genuinely interested in the progress of our book, even those who had to take on extra duties as deadline time drew near.

The staff at the Society for American Baseball Research (SABR) for graciously and quickly filling all our requests for hard-to-find documents.

Finally, we wish to thank the most unselfish, helpful group of people we have ever encountered—the members of SABR—who shared anything we asked for and often volunteered information and resources they hoped would be useful.

All the information aided us in our research; however, we take full responsibility for any errors.

Burton A. Boxerman
Benita W. Boxerman
St. Louis, Missouri
Fall 2006

Table of Contents

Foreword
by Martin Abramowitz

How do we explain the fact that the last ten years or so have seen an unprecedented flowering of interest in Jews in baseball? Think about it: David Spaner's seminal essay and list in *Total Baseball*; Peter and Joachim Horvitz's reference book, *The Big Book of Jews in Baseball*; two sets of Jewish Major Leaguers baseball cards; a Hall of Fame two-day commemoration of "American Jews in America's Game"; and now this long-awaited history by the Boxermans. Meanwhile, the Jews in Sports websites have flourished, and Shel Wallman and Ephraim Moxson have faithfully produced—and found an audience for—bi-monthly updates in their *Jewish Sports Review*.

What's going on?

We're probably looking at a few factors coming together to produce this sudden interest: the new respect for ethnicity and origins in American society; the notched-up fascination with baseball statistics generally; the cyberspace revolution that has made it easier for those few of us who have been totally carried away with this subject to stay in touch with each other and to recruit fresh troops; the baseball industry's own "marketing" success in enveloping the sport in the heart-warming mistiness of memory and nostalgia for a supposedly simpler time; the growth of the sports memorabilia and sports card industry.

The Boxermans' fine book suggests at least two other factors at play. One is the extent of Jews' contributions to the game—certainly on the field, but also as pioneering owners and general managers, as statisticians, as sportswriters, as coaches and minor-league managers.

The second factor is a bit more elusive. It has to do with what the association of two words (*Jewish* and *baseball*) meant to two or three generations of American Jews in the first half of the twentieth century, and what it has come to mean in the first years of our own century. From the 1870s to the late 1940s, baseball meant "America." The Jews who labored in its vineyards were figuratively as well as literally playing America's game; they were "making it" in America—making a living, and a name—demonstrating that a Jew could also be a successful American.

The Jews who paid to watch, or who hovered around radios, bars, and sports pages as fans of the game, were absorbing America, being absorbed by America, and contributing to America. It's no surprise that Solomon Schechter, the long-time chancellor of the Jewish Theological Seminary and the leader of Conservative Judaism, told his students that if they wanted to be successful as rabbis, they needed to understand baseball!

While the connection between Jews and baseball may indeed be a metaphor for the Jewish experience in America, this book is not a sociological treatise. Rather, it is first and foremost a highly readable and well-documented contribution to baseball history. So, for example, the stories of the early generations of Jewish ownership in Cincinnati, and of Barney Dreyfuss in Pittsburgh and Andrew Freedman in New York, contribute to our understanding of the origins and the structure of the game as we know it. Just as, for instance, John McGraw's continual search for Jewish ballplayers in New York is also a story of the New York Giants.

It's all here—the owners, the scribes, the beginning of baseball statistics, the brushes with anti–Semitism. And there are the players—the turn-of-the-century pioneers, the name-changers, the cup-of-coffee players. There are the stories of the deadball-era hurler veterans like pitchers Erskine Mayer and Barney Pelty, known as the "Yiddish Curver"; Moe Berg, the journeyman catcher, Princeton graduate, and sometime spy; the All-Stars Buddy Myer and Harry "The Horse" Danning; and of course the superstar and "credit to his people," Hank Greenberg.

What's also here, woven into the text and texture of the book, are the answers to such questions as: Who was the first Jewish pitcher? What Jewish pitcher had the lowest career ERA? Who gave up Babe Ruth's last American League homerun? Who was "The Rabbi of Swat"? How many sets of major-league brothers were Jewish?

This book is a delightful and instructive addition to any baseball library, and an immediate classic for those of us for whom the words *Jewish* and *baseball* go together like gefilte fish and horseradish.

Martin Abramowitz, Ph.D., is president of Jewish Major Leaguers, Inc. (www.jewishmajorleaguers.org)

Prologue

This is a book about the love affair between baseball and American Jews—a passion that many historians feel is unique in how deeply Jews have identified with the game. Many reasons have been given for the strong attraction baseball exerted on this group.

The most accepted reason is that baseball was the means for many Jews to enter the American culture. Baseball also served as proof that they had succeeded. A Jew who could play baseball and knew its finer points had truly become part of the greater community.

Some historians have speculated that baseball represented the ultimate American ideal and a way of expressing the common rebellion of youth. The drama and mystique of the National Pastime and, for some, the challenge of defying immigrant parents who disapproved of their children's obsession with baseball made the game even more appealing.

In addition, baseball, a game founded on statistics and history, had great intellectual appeal. For many Jews, studying and debating the meanings of sacred texts were traditions handed down for generations that seemed "old country" in America. What could be better for the American Jew than to modernize these traditions by focusing on baseball instead? Reading about baseball and then discussing its philosophy, and arguing the best strategies and the merits of individual players, soon became a favorite activity reminiscent of early Jewish scholars, but updated for the new world.

But the love affair of Jews and baseball was not one-sided. Jews not only benefited from baseball but baseball benefited from the contributions of many Jews. The most visible participants were the Jewish players, including a few truly outstanding ones, who not only contributed to their teams but in some cases became heroes to the Jewish community. Although there is no question that the total number of players is smaller than might be expected in a game so highly esteemed, Jews have contributed to baseball in a number of other ways. Jews not only were—and are—among the most devoted of baseball fans, but many Jews have dedicated their lives, and sometimes their fortunes and reputations, to shaping and improving the game. Jewish club owners and executives, Jewish sportswriters, Jewish coaches, statisticians, baseball clowns, and even manufacturers of the baseball itself have all played a part in making the game what it is today and will likely be in the future.

The love affair is documented in this book through the stories of some of the people who have been part of this relationship. We chose them to demonstrate the diversity of the love between Jews and baseball and how this love was affected by the events and issues of their times. Because this book is not intended to be an encyclopedia, we selected only individuals who illustrate a particular theme, break new ground, or are distinctive in some way. We also considered only players authenticated as Jewish by Martin Abramowitz, president, Jewish Major Leaguers, Inc.

Finally, we limited the scope of the book to the first eight decades that Jews were involved with professional baseball, beginning with the debut of the first Jewish professional player and ending in 1948. It is an appropriate year to stop for a number of reasons. World War II, where Jews proved that they would and could fight for the United States, had ended. The German and Eastern European communities had merged into a single Jewish-American community, and the State of Israel had been founded. Although anti–Semitism was still apparent in many areas, it was becoming less acceptable to the majority of Americans and far less a factor in major league baseball. But perhaps most importantly for this book, 1948 marked the end of the playing career of Hank Greenberg, the Jewish superstar most responsible for making baseball a better place for his contemporaries and those who would come after him.

Although Greenberg's popularity seemed to legitimize the historical link between Jewish players and baseball, as King Kelly's had the Irish decades before, the relationship would grow more complex, and the storylines more varied. *Jews and Baseball: Volume 2, The Post-Greenberg Years, 1949–2006* will show that the involvement of Jewish men and women in major league baseball deepened, in the clubhouse and especially in the ranks of leadership, at a time when questions about labor relations, race, and ethnicity pushed the game toward crisis.

1. From the Beginnings

The development of baseball as a unique American sport and the establishment of a thriving Jewish-American community were essentially parallel movements during the nineteenth century.

Our understanding of early baseball is still taking shape. Historians, having long since conceded that baseball's antecedents are British (not, as the Mills Commission found in 1908, American), have lately argued about its relationship to rounders—and even whether "baseball" is in fact the name that sport was first known by.[1] And John Thorn, David Block and others have qualified our praise of Alexander Cartwright, still widely credited with devising a set of rules and regulations in 1845 that incorporated the basic elements of the game: a diamond-shaped infield with bases 90 feet apart, a pitcher's box 45 feet from home plate, nine men on each side, three outs per team per inning, nine innings, and various ways a batter could be out.[2] Most do agree, however, that in 1846 the first recorded baseball contest took place between Cartwright's Knickerbockers and the New York Baseball Club at the Elysian Fields in Hoboken, New Jersey.[3]

Other clubs outside New York City soon adopted the New York version of baseball, but it was still a game played by amateurs. In 1857, representatives from 25 amateur teams in the northeast attended a convention to discuss rules and other baseball matters and the following year the first organized baseball league, The National Association of Base Ball Players, was formed. Although the league supported itself by occasionally charging fans for admission, the players were not paid.

Interest in baseball increased during the Civil War as Union soldiers carried the game to other parts of the country by playing baseball in their army camps. Soon even the Confederate soldiers began to play. Baseball was quickly becoming the national pastime. By 1865, there were more people playing baseball than ever before. At the annual convention of baseball teams in 1868, delegates from more than 100 clubs attended.[4]

In the early 1860s, ballpark owners were making money by regularly charging admission to games. Players began to pressure owners for a share of the profits, forcing the National Association of Base Ball Players to change its policy in 1868 to legally allow players to accept payment. The following year, 1869, the Cincinnati Red Stockings officially announced that it would have an all-salaried professional team, becoming the first to publicly acknowledge what had been happening "under the table" for years. Later that year, the professional Red Stockings team toured the country, winning 60 games without a loss.[5]

Not surprisingly, just a year later, professional players outnumbered amateurs in the NABBP and the remaining amateurs left the league. On March 17, 1871, the National Association of Base Ball Players became the National Association of Professional Base Ball Players.[6] But the Association was short-lived as fans stayed away from the games because of the presence of gamblers and the sale of liquor.[7]

The National League of American Base Ball Teams replaced the National Association following the 1875 season. Run by businessmen rather than players, the National League saw what had happened to its predecessor and banned alcohol at games, did not play on Sundays, and, in an attempt to "keep out undesirables," charged fans 50 cents to get into the parks. Still in existence today, the National League is considered the first "officially" credited major league.[8]

By 1882 some teams found the restrictions imposed by the National League so onerous that a competing professional league, the American Association, was founded. Known as the Beer and Whiskey League, the American Association charged only 25 cents admission, played on Sundays, and allowed liquor to be sold at games.[9]

Obviously, the American Association had a financial impact on the National League, for in the fall of 1883, the National League sought a truce with its rival. This 1883 National Agreement recognized the American Association as a major league and called for teams in both leagues to honor each other's player contracts. In other words, the American Association adopted the National League's reserve clause, which bound a player to the team that had him under contract until the team released him.[10]

The players, of course, were unhappy about the agreement between the two leagues and in 1884 attempted unsuccessfully to form their own league. In 1890, disgruntled players made a second attempt to form a rival league, the Players League. Promised a profit-sharing plan, the elimination of the reserve clause, and the right to purchase stock in their own clubs, some of the biggest stars of the American Association and the National League signed up. The National League fought back by scheduling games on the same dates as the Players League, bribing PL players to jump ranks, and threatening to withdraw advertising from any newspaper which supported the Players League. Faced by such opposition, the Players League went bankrupt after one season. The National League lost money in the Players League War of 1890, but the war was worse for the American Association. The following year, when four of its best teams—St. Louis, Louisville, Baltimore, and Washington—joined the National League, the American Association ceased to exist. From 1892 until the founding of the American League almost 10 years later, the National League was baseball's sole major league.[11]

Coinciding with the development of baseball during this period was the founding of a Jewish ethnic group that would play a significant role in the game and in other aspects of American culture.

A few Dutch and German Jews immigrated to the colonies well before the American Revolution and by 1820, nearly 4,000 Jews were living in the United States. During the following two decades, the number of Jews in America increased to 15,000 and then surged to 50,000 by 1847, as Jews, like their non–Jewish counterparts, left Europe to better themselves economically and avoid political oppression.[12] By the eve of the Civil War, two million German-speaking Europeans, including 150,000 Jews, had come to the United States.[13]

Most of the Jews, as well as the non–Jews who came to the United States from Germany and Ireland during the first half of the nineteenth century, were poor and from small towns. But the Jewish immigrants differed in two respects that helped them succeed in the New World. The Jews were peddlers and middlemen rather than farmers, because these were the two chief occupations they were allowed to pursue in Europe. And even the poorest Jew usually could read. Most began by reading only the Hebrew prayer book, but in Europe, German soon replaced Hebrew, and in the United States, English quickly replaced German.[14]

These Jews could not have arrived at a more opportune time. America wanted immigrants to fulfill its "manifest destiny" of extending the United States boundaries westward to the Pacific. Moreover, America was becoming urbanized, creating markets to exchange what the farmers produced for what the cities manufactured. The demand for middlemen in America was at an all-time high and, since the Jews who were arriving from Central Europe were experienced in buying and selling, their opportunity to get rich was never better.[15] For many Jews, peddling was a temporary vocation. As soon as they had accumulated the necessary capital, they changed from wandering salesman to "respected" retail-store owner.[16]

Almost all of these Jews were of Central European origin and most settled in large cities along the Atlantic Ocean and in small towns in the Northeast, the South and the Midwest, where organized baseball was already being played and enjoyed.

Anti-Semitism was not a major problem for the 150,000 German Jews in America prior to the Civil War. Because they were so few in number compared with the 1.7 million Irish and 1.3 million Germans, Jews were rarely the targets of American "nativist" groups. In fact, a small number of Jews even joined the nativist movement.[17]

Following the Civil War, however, the image of the Jew changed. As Jews suddenly began to accumulate wealth, but had not yet, in the opinion of "established" Americans, developed conventional manners or dress, the Shylock image of the Jew began to appear. Jews were now considered ostentatious, vulgar, pushy and unscrupulous.[18] In contrast to later times when Jews were perceived as a threat to American security, this criticism was aimed only at the Jewish "way of life." German Jews decided that they could change this perception by attempting to "fit in" or assimilate with American culture.[19]

Some Jews in the United States attempted to assimilate into American society by becoming involved in politics and other civic life.[20] But many German Jews found an easier and quicker road to acculturation and assimilation: participation in the new national pastime—baseball.

2. The Earliest Jewish Professional Players

During the nineteenth century, when baseball was becoming popular in the U.S., the Jewish population was still relatively small, and during this period, only six Jews played professional major league baseball. Of these six, only two were good enough to establish credible major league careers. But the first Jewish professional baseball player—Lipman Pike—was one of the best and most popular players in baseball for more than 20 years, from the late 1860s into the late 1880s.

Lipman Pike

Lipman Emanuel Pike was born on May 15, 1845, in New York City—the same year and in the same city where Alexander Cartwright developed his rules for baseball. Pike was one of four sons of Emanuel and Jane Pike, Jews of Dutch origin, a group that had been living in New York prior to the American Revolution. When Pike was still a youngster, the family moved to Brooklyn, where baseball was played on vast stretches of empty land. Boaz Pike, Lipman's oldest brother, was the first to play baseball on an organized team.

One week following his Bar Mitzvah, 13-year-old Lipman Pike appeared in his first recorded baseball game. He and Boaz played together on a number of amateur teams prior to 1866. In 1866, although the practice was not yet legal, Lipman Pike accepted $20 a week to play third base for the Philadelphia Athletics, becoming one of the earliest acknowledged professional baseball players, and certainly the first Jew to play baseball professionally.[1]

From 1867 to 1870, Pike played for three teams in addition to the Philadelphia Athletics—Irvington, New Jersey, the New York Mutuals, and the Brooklyn Atlantics. In 1871 Pike left the Atlantics to accept the position of player-manager for the Troy Haymakers of the National Association of Professional Baseball Players. This made him not only the first professional Jewish ballplayer but also the first professional Jewish manager.[2] Pike played in the National Association for five years, one each with Troy and Hartford, two with the Lord Baltimores, and his final season in the Association in 1875 with the St. Louis Brown Stockings.[3]

During his five seasons in the National Association, Pike was known both for his hitting and his speed. Nicknamed "the Iron Batter," he compiled a .321 average in 160 games, and played both the outfield and the infield.[4] Pike was also a home run champion, winning the slugging title four of his five years in the Association by hitting a total of 16 home runs. His best year was 1872, when he clouted seven round trippers for the Lord Baltimores, accounting for 20 percent of all 35 homers hit in the National Association that year. (These were the years when the baseball consisted of a cover wrapped loosely around a rubber-centered ball of yarn. It would be 1910 before a ball with a cork center would add new life to the game.)[5]

Pike was also a speed demon on and off the base paths. In August 1873, while a member of the Lord Baltimores, Pike accepted a $250 wager to race a horse—a fast trotter named Clarence—in a 100-yard dash. The race, held at Baltimore's Newington Park, attracted a crowd of about 400 people at 25 cents a head. There they witnessed Pike, clad in tights rather than his baseball uniform, run the distance in 10 seconds, defeating Clarence by four yards.[6]

Pike's 1875 season with the St. Louis Brown Stockings marked the end of the National Association and Pike went with the team to the National League as that League's first Jewish player. Pike hit .323 with 19 doubles for the Brown Stockings in 1876.[7] The next year he moved to the National League's Cincinnati Red Stockings as player-manager for the opening weeks of the season,

Lipman Pike was the first Jewish professional baseball player. He debuted in 1871 with Troy of the National Association. He then played in the National League four years and one year in the American Association. In 1877 his four home runs for Cincinnati of the National League were enough to lead the league that year (courtesy Transcendental Graphics).

becoming not only the first professional Jewish manager, but also the first one in major league baseball. He was also the home run leader again in 1877 with four. Pike played 31 games for the Red Stockings in 1878 and finished the year with the NL's Providence Grays.[8]

From 1879 to 1881 Pike played for six non–National League teams. He returned to the National League in 1882 to finish his major league career with the Worcester, Massachusetts, Ruby Legs. Unfortunately, it was not a pleasant ending. The Ruby Legs, one of the worst teams in the National League, made Pike the scapegoat to justify its poor performance, even though he had played only five games for the team. The Worcester manager accused him of not playing his best and insisted that the National League place Pike on its first blacklist for insubordination and for not playing up to his potential.[9] Although the ruling was decidedly unfair, it did not appear that anti–Semitism played any role in the incident.

Pike announced that he was permanently retiring from baseball. During the time between the 1881 season and his games with the Ruby Legs, Pike had gone into the haberdashery business in Brooklyn as his father had done years earlier. The business was now successful and the store had become a gathering place for local baseball men.

Despite being "permanently retired," in 1887 the 42-year-old Pike decided to return to baseball as a member of the New York Metropolitans of the American Association. After only one game, he retired again, but he remained in baseball by umpiring in both the National League and the American Association.[10]

Pike died suddenly of heart disease in 1893 at the age of 48. Toward the end of his playing career, the *New York Clipper* had praised Pike's abilities, calling him "a very hard hitter ... a sure catch, a remarkably fast runner, and singularly graceful in all his movements."[11]

The *Brooklyn Eagle* noted in Pike's obituary, "Many wealthy Hebrews and men high in political and old time baseball circles attended the funeral services of the late Lipman E. Pike.... Reverend Dr. Geismar, pastor of Temple Israel, conducted the services and paid fitting tribute to the exemplary life led by the deceased."[12]

The Sporting News noted, "...the passing of "Lip" Pike, one of the greatest sluggers who ever batted for Cincinnati."[13] *The Sporting News* also attested to Pike's off-the-field qualities, stating, "Pike was one of the baseball players of those days who were always gentlemanly on and off the field—a species which is becoming rarer as the game grows older."[14]

Two honors came to Lipman Pike in the years following his death. Francis Richter, editor of *Sporting Life*, selected Pike as an outfielder on his 1870–1880 All Star Team.[15] In 1936, 43 years after his death, Lipman Pike received one vote in the first election for the Baseball Hall of Fame.[16]

Although Lipman Pike was without a doubt the outstanding Jewish player of his era, the other five Jews who played baseball in the nineteenth century also are worth noting.

Nathan Berkenstock

Nathan Berkenstock, born in 1831 in Philadelphia, was the second Jewish professional player and, at the age of 40, the oldest player in the league at that time. He was also the only major league player born before 1835. A retired amateur, and one of the team's founders, he played in one game for the Philadelphia Athletics in 1871—that year's final National Association championship game between the Athletics and the Chicago White Stockings. A wild swinger who would go after anything near the plate, Berkenstock got no hits, but did make the final put out in the game, which the Athletics won.[17]

Berkenstock was also active in the management of the team, and remained an officer of the club after his retirement from active play.[18] He died on February 20, 1900, at the age of 68.[19]

Jay Pike

Jacob Emanuel (Jay) Pike was another "one game wonder" in the major leagues. When he entered baseball, he and his older brother, Lipman, became the first of five pairs of Jewish brothers to play in the majors before 1948. Jay was born after the Pike family moved to Brooklyn. After umpiring for the National Association in 1875, Jay Pike finally got his major league opportunity when he appeared in one game for the Hartford Dark Blues on August 28, 1877. The game, played in Brooklyn, where the Dark Blues played all their home games, pitted Hartford against his brother's team that year, the Cincinnati Red Stockings. Lipman had one hit in the game and scored his team's only run, as the Dark Blues defeated the Red Stockings 5 to 1. For that one day, Jay was his brother's equal at the plate, also getting one hit in his four at bats in the majors.[20]

Jake Goodman

Six-foot, two-inch first baseman Jake Goodman, like Nate Berkenstock, was a native of Pennsylvania. Born in Lancaster on September 14, 1853, he made his major league debut on May 2, 1878, with the Milwaukee Grays during the one year the team was part of the National League. In 60 games for the Grays, Goodman had a .246 batting average, 27 RBIs, and in a game on June 25 the distinction of being the first Milwaukee player to hit a home run. Parenthetically, Milwaukee lost the game 11 to 4 to Providence, with the two teams committing a total of 35 errors.[21]

Little is known about Goodman between 1878 and 1882, although he might have played in the minors during this period. He returned to the majors in 1882, playing for the Pittsburgh Alleghenies of the American Association. In his 10 games for Pittsburgh, he had 13 hits in 41 plate appearances for an average of .317. His final game in the majors was May 20, 1882.[22]

In 1890, Goodman suffered a stroke while at his father's home in Reading, and died of paralysis on March 9, 1890, at the age of 37.[23]

Ike Samuels

Earl Samuel (Ike) Samuels was born on February 20, 1874, in Quincy, Illinois, and made his debut in the majors on August 3, 1895, for the St. Louis Brown Stockings. His career lasted just until the end of September that year. During his 24 games at both third base and shortstop, Samuels had 17 hits in 74 at bats for an average of .230. He died in New York City on February 22, 1964, two days after his ninetieth birthday.[24]

Leo Fishel

Born May 3, 1877, Leo Fishel was the first Jewish major league pitcher, although he, too, appeared in just one game. On May 3, 1899, pitching for the New York Giants, he started, completed, and lost his only game, allowing seven runs, nine hits, and six walks.[25]

Following his abbreviated professional career, Fishel earned his law degree from Columbia University and coached varsity baseball there. Thirty years later attorney Fishel appeared before the New York State Supreme Court to argue a case. As Fishel stepped forward, he recognized Supreme Court Justice James A. Dunne as his former catcher on the Richfield Springs Baseball Club where they both had played during summer vacation from college. Fishel identified himself and after the two had reminisced for a few minutes, the case proceeded. After the hearing, Justice Dunne told Fishel, "I'm up here now catching your evidence as I used to catch your speed balls." Fishel replied, "It will be all right so long as you don't make a wild throw and toss it out."[26]

Leo Fishel died May 19, 1960, in Hempstead, New York.[27]

There is no record that any of these six Jewish players had to contend with anti–Semitism in the game, an issue that would become far more pervasive in later decades. In addition, the places where they grew up demonstrate that Jews in baseball in the nineteenth century were living primarily in cities and towns outside the stereotypical ghetto.

3. The Cincinnati Connection

Many of the German-speaking Jews who migrated to the United States between 1850 and 1880 remained permanently in New York City; however, a large number settled in towns throughout the eastern half of the country. Cincinnati, which looked down the Ohio River both to the West and to the entire middle South, became a major commercial center and a popular destination for thousands of these German Jews. Cincinnati's Jewish population increased rapidly, from about 1,000 in 1840 to anywhere from 7,500 to 10,000 by 1860. Many of these Jews were tradesmen who did business with merchants in the smaller towns, moving up from pushcarts to small stores and manufacturing businesses as they became successful.[1]

At least one of the new Cincinnati residents during the mid-nineteenth century was not a merchant. Rabbi Isaac Mayer Wise, a Bohemian Jew, came to Cincinnati with his family and became the leader of the Reform Jewish movement in the United States. Wise established the Union of American Hebrew Congregations, an association of Reform congregations in the United States and, two years later, opened the Hebrew Union College in his Cincinnati temple. By the mid–1870s Cincinnati was not only the headquarters for Reform Judaism in America, it could also be considered the religious center of American Jewry.[2]

Not surprisingly, during the nineteenth century, Cincinnati also produced the earliest Jewish entrepreneurs and executives in professional baseball. They were convinced that baseball would not only afford them a good living, but would also give them an entrée into the social world of the non–Jew, help demonstrate how civic-minded they were, and enable them to assimilate into American culture.[3]

Philip Goldsmith

One of the earliest of the Jewish entrepreneurs who became involved with the business side of baseball was Philip Goldsmith, an Austrian immigrant whose family epitomizes the economic evolution of the German-speaking Jews during the nineteenth century.[4] Born in 1844, Goldsmith came to the United States in 1861 with only a few cents in his pockets and a letter of introduction to a gentleman in New York from whom he borrowed $100. With this stake, he traveled west and settled in Milwaukee where he began peddling notions. By 1865, just four years later, he had accumulated $1,500 and married Sophie Heller. They first moved to Chicago, but Goldsmith's auctioneering business there failed and in 1869, he moved his household to Covington, Kentucky, just across the Ohio River from Cincinnati. In Covington, he opened the city's first 25-cent store.[5]

While Philip Goldsmith was tending his shop, another resident, Wolf Fletcher, was running a retail toy shop and repairing dolls in the rear of his store. Sometime in the early 1870s, Goldsmith became Fletcher's partner and the two began a small doll manufacturing business that soon began to grow, expanding to include the manufacture of stuffed animals. To get through the slow season after Christmas and utilize surplus material from the dolls and toys, Goldsmith and his partner started to manufacture baseballs. In 1875, he and Fletcher began to market the first handmade balls. At that time, baseballs were composed of a core of rubber, a layer of string, and a leather cover. Goldsmith invented and patented a specialized machine to wind the string. Workers then stitched on the leather covers by hand and the ball was inspected for weight, size, roundness and perfection of seams.[6]

In 1878 Fletcher sold out to Goldsmith. By 1882, Goldsmith's firm, now called Covington Industries, was the largest doll company in the United States, turning out one hundred dozen dolls and also fifty gross of balls daily.[7] Soon, Covington Industries was also making other kinds of sports equipment and by 1885 Goldsmith had a national market for all his products.[8]

In July 1894, just one year after Philip's sons, Oscar and Alfred Goldsmith, became partners in the business, Philip Goldsmith drowned while on an outing with his family. The *Kentucky Post* praised him for his quiet yet numerous acts of charity, including the donation of large quantities of dolls to poor children of both Cincinnati and Covington.[9]

Oscar and Alfred reorganized the business, eliminating toys and dolls and concentrating instead on the manufacture of baseballs and sporting goods. In 1900 Alfred Goldsmith sold his interest in the firm to a younger brother, Edgar, and in 1906 Hugo Goldsmith, another son, joined the partnership. The firm's name was changed to P. Goldsmith's Sons.[10] It continued to prosper well into the twentieth century until Macgregor Sporting Goods bought it out.[11]

Jewish Baseball Owners

The Goldsmiths found their niche in baseball indirectly by manufacturing sporting equipment. Five other German Jews in Cincinnati took a direct approach: they became owners and executives of Cincinnati's professional team at various times during the last half of the nineteenth century.

Nathan Menderson

Very little is known about the first of these Jewish owners, Nathan Menderson, who was president of the team from July 6 to September 13, 1880. He was born in Germany in 1820, and died March 31, 1904.[12]

Aaron Stern

Born in 1853 and working as a clothier before entering baseball, in 1882 Aaron Stern became the next Jewish owner of the Cincinnati Red Stockings. A year earlier, the Red

Stockings had been expelled from the National League in a dispute over liquor sales at the ballpark. Under Stern, one of the founders of the more liberal American Association, Cincinnati joined the rival league along with teams from Philadelphia, Baltimore, Cincinnati, Louisville, and Pittsburgh.[13] In 1882, the Red Stockings won the first American Association pennant.[14]

From 1883 through 1885, the Red Stockings' front office was in a constant state of turmoil, as ownership of the team passed from Stern to others and finally back to Stern.[15] In late 1886, Stern bought the Red Stockings from John Hauck, who was active in the German National Bank and who feared that pressure to stage Sunday games in Cincinnati would damage his business.[16]

The Sporting News applauded Stern's repurchasing of the Red Stockings, praised him as a popular member of the American Association and noted, "The Cincinnati Club never thrived as it did when A. S. Stern was at the head of its affairs. He will be there the coming season and matters have already begun to assume a businesslike form under his management."[17]

Stern's management was demonstrated in a number of ways. Stern helped popularize Ladies Day, and was among the earliest owners to sell seat cushions and candy. In 1884 Stern built a new ballpark on the site of an abandoned brickyard. The team would play at that site for 87 major league seasons—until they moved to Riverfront Stadium in 1970.[18] He also staged one of the first opening day promotions in 1889, which drew more than 10,000 fans.[19]

However, cost consciousness was the most unmistakable aspect of Stern's management. All of Stern's contemporary owners could be accused of being mercenary at times, but few documented it as well as Stern. In letters to the team's treasurer, he wrote that he intended to spend "as little money as possible in running the Cincinnati club" and to "shut off the free list and see that every dollar that is in the grounds remains there."[20]

Before the traveling world championship series of 1887 came to Cincinnati, President Stern wrote: "In the game between Chicago and St. Louis use no turnstiles—if they ask for our turnstiles, say they are out of order." Stern also strongly suggested that nothing be said about money collected at a downtown ticket agency so that the Red Stockings could keep the full amount rather than their rightful 20 percent share.[21]

On another occasion, Cincinnati's manager, Gus Schmelz, asked Stern for permission to take the players south for spring training, with the costs split between players and the club. Stern agreed when he realized that the unpaid trip would likely weed out some of his veteran players, resulting in lower average salaries for the upcoming season.[22]

On the other hand, Stern could be very generous to his players. According to the *Brooklyn Eagle*, he made it a practice never to lay off a player without pay, even if the player deserved the action. *The New York Sun* alluded to Stern's generosity when it noted that Stern occasionally gave a player a $10 gold piece if he hit safely at a crucial time.[23]

By November 1889, Aaron Stern was disillusioned with political shenanigans in the American Association. Learning that he had not been invited to a conference held by representatives of five other American Association teams, Stern was indignant and determined to pull his team out of the league.[24] He had two choices. He could affiliate with the newly formed Players' League, or he could return to the National League, which had softened its beer rule.[25] In 1890, Stern's Cincinnati Red Stockings, along with Charles Byrne's Brooklyn Bridegrooms, left the American Association and rejoined the National League.[26]

Stern took with him ten of the players from the American Association Red Stockings of 1889, purchased the contracts of eight additional men, and hired as manager former player

Tom Loftus.[27] The Red Stockings finished the 1890 season in fourth place, 10½ games behind the Bridegrooms.[28]

Cincinnati drew more than 130,000 fans in 1890, a reasonable amount for that time, but at the end of the season, Aaron Stern announced that he was leaving baseball for good, stating bluntly, "There is no money in the games, salaries being too high."[29]

On October 9, he sold his team for $40,000 to a group of investors led by Albert L. Johnson of Cleveland.[30]

Johnson moved the Red Stockings to the Players League for the 1891 season, and when that league folded after only one year, Johnson affiliated again with the American Association. Johnson then very quickly sold the Red Stockings to John Brush, who moved it back to the National League permanently.[31]

After 1890, Stern was never again connected with baseball, returning instead to his clothing business. He died August 4, 1920, at age 67.[32]

Louis Kramer

Louis Kramer was also one of the founders of the American Association and a minor owner of the Red Stockings in 1882. Born in 1848 and a graduate of Cincinnati College, Kramer was admitted to the bar in 1870. He married Emily Stern, but there are no records indicating whether she was related to Aaron Stern. Kramer left the team sometime after 1882, but when Stern bought the Red Stockings again in 1886, he brought Kramer back as a part owner.[33]

On February 17, 1891, when the American Association was in need of strong leadership, Kramer was named to the consolidated office of president, treasurer, and secretary of the league.[34] Six months later, he resigned because he felt that he had been unable to deal with the feud between the Association and the National League.[35] *The Sporting News*, however, praised his work, stating, "No man has ever occupied a position of trust and responsibility in the baseball world and has discharged his duties with better effect or more substantial results than Louis Kramer."[36]

Louis Kramer died at his summer home in Charlevoix, Michigan, on August 19, 1922. He was 78 years old.[37]

Max and Julius Fleischmann

John Brush, who bought the Red Stockings from Al Johnson, owned the team for almost 10 years. It was a mediocre club at best, ending as high as third place only twice and finishing as low as tenth in 1894.[38] After the 1902 season, Brush sold the franchise to a syndicate made up of George B. Cox, a well-known Cincinnati political boss; August "Garry" Herrmann, who was named president of the new organization; and the fourth and fifth Jewish owners, the mayor of Cincinnati, Julius Fleischmann, and his brother, Max Fleischmann.[39]

Julius and Max Fleischmann's father, Charles Fleischmann, was a native of Austria-Hungary who had immigrated to the United States around 1870 and made his fortune by inventing a method to produce compressed yeast, a product which revolutionized the baking industry. In addition to being one of the city's most prominent and successful businessmen,

Charles Fleischmann was also one of Cincinnati's most generous philanthropists. He died December 10, 1898.[40]

Julius Fleischmann, the elder of the two brothers, was born in Cincinnati on June 8, 1872, and educated in the public schools. Instead of attending college, he entered his father's business at the age of eighteen as a clerk and a few years later married Lillian Ackerland; they had two sons and one daughter. Julius was soon in charge of the entire Fleischmann Company, one of the largest unincorporated business enterprises in the country, and also continued his father's philanthropies.[41]

Like his father, Julius Fleischmann was active in the Republican Party.[42] He was a colonel on the staff of Governor William McKinley from 1892 to 1896 and maintained close relations with Mark Hanna, the head of the Ohio Republican Party. At Hanna's request, Julius Fleischmann entered Cincinnati's mayoral race in 1900, defeating his Democratic opponent, a man named Cohen, by an 8,500 plurality.[43] The 1900 mayoral election marked the first time in Cincinnati's history that both candidates were Jewish.[44] Three years later,

Julius Fleischmann easily won a second term, this time by a majority of 17,000 votes, over M. E. Ingalls, president of the Big Four Railroads.[45]

Julius was serving his first term as mayor and was the head of the Fleischmann yeast and milling businesses when he and his brother, Max, bought the Red Stockings in 1902.[46]

Max Fleischmann was five years younger than Julius, born February 26, 1877. He attended the Ohio Military Institute and as a first-lieutenant, commanded a cavalry troop during the Spanish-American War. After the war, Max supervised the manufacturing department of the Fleischmann Company. When the firm was incorporated in 1908, he was promoted to vice president.[47]

Unlike most owners of the time, the wealthy Fleischmann brothers bought the team not as a moneymaking venture but because they loved baseball and the Red Stockings, and they hoped their money could improve the team's performance.[48] Although they were knowledgeable about baseball, they delegated the team's day-to-day affairs to minority stockholder Herrmann, but they maintained close interest in the Red Stockings and participated actively in league affairs.

Julius Fleischmann, heir to a yeast fortune, was one of the earliest Jews to own a baseball team when he and his brother Max purchased the Cincinnati Reds in 1902. In addition to baseball, Fleischmann was active in politics, serving two terms as mayor of Cincinnati and participating in Republican politics at the national and state levels as well. He left baseball in 1915, and died 10 years later while playing polo (courtesy Jacob Rader Marcus Center of the American Jewish Archives).

The Fleischmanns entered baseball at the peak of the baseball wars between the new American and the National Leagues when rowdyism at games was the norm. Julius not only supported a resolution to fine or suspend any player or manager who disrupted the game, but also introduced an amendment forbidding the clubs from paying these fines or continuing to pay a suspended violator.[49] Julius Fleischmann also favored a waiver rule, which removed some of the barriers for weaker clubs to bid for players.[50]

After the 1912 baseball season, the other magnates selected Julius Fleischmann to preside at the hearing between the National League and Philadelphia Phillies owner Horace Fogel, who was charged with defaming the league, calling umpires crooked, and claiming that the pennant race had been "fixed." Fogel was found guilty of five of the seven charges and was forever barred from the National League.[51]

Max Fleischmann was a member of the National Rules Committee in 1903, and often served as the spokesman for the governing body of baseball at that time, the National Commission, which was headed by Cincinnati president Garry Hermann.[52] Max was also lauded for his role in the National League's unanimous adoption of a postseason championship series with the American League. According to the *Cincinnati Enquirer*, "Max Fleischmann is solely responsible for the signing of a working agreement between the American and National Baseball Leagues which resulted in the World Series."[53] Many also credit Max Fleischmann with the agreement between the leagues that eliminated player raids and conflicting schedules.[54]

There were rumors in 1912 that Max Fleischmann was interested in purchasing the Chicago Cubs, but they were never substantiated.

In fact, just three years later, on December 14, 1915, Max and Julius Fleischmann both resigned from the Red Stockings board of directors. According to President Herrmann, there was no friction between him and the brothers, nor was the club for sale. Julius had been absent from the city quite often and Max claimed that he had lost interest.[55]

Under the Fleischmanns, the Cincinnati Red Stockings were the same second-rate team they had been under Brush. Their best season was 1904, when they finished the season in third place, 18 games behind the New York Giants. From 1903 through 1915, the Red Stockings ended in fourth place four times, fifth and sixth three times each, seventh place twice, and in the cellar in 1914.[56]

On February 5, 1925, Julius Fleischmann died in Miami while playing polo. The cause of his death was either a heart attack or apoplexy brought about by the strenuousness and excitement of the match. He was buried in the Fleischmann family mausoleum at Spring Grove Cemetery in Cincinnati.[57]

After Julius died in 1925, Max became chairman of the board of the Fleischmann Company. Four years later he sold the business to the J. P. Morgan firm for approximately $20 million of stock in Standard Brands. On October 16, 1951, Max Fleischmann shot and killed himself at the home of his wife near Santa Barbara, having been diagnosed a short time earlier as suffering from an incurable illness. He was 74 years old.[58]

The deaths of Julius and Max Fleischmann marked the end of an era of German-Jewish owners of the Cincinnati Red Stockings during the late nineteenth and early twentieth centuries. But there were and would be more German-Jewish major league baseball owners; several would have significant impact on the game.

4. Baseball's Most Detested Owner

In 1902, the Fleischmann brothers were able to buy the Cincinnati Reds from owner John Brush because Brush needed money to purchase the New York Giants. Acquiring the Giants meant not only that Brush now owned the team he had always wanted, but also that the most hated owner in baseball, Andrew Freedman, was officially out of the game.

Andrew Freedman, a German Jew, owned the Giants for seven years beginning in 1895, at a time when most Americans found expressions of anti–Semitism quite acceptable. This was especially true in baseball, where racial slurs and unseemly behavior were considered part of the game. And no other Jewish owner in baseball was the target for so much public controversy and so much overt anti–Semitism as Andrew Freedman.

Freedman was born September 1, 1860, in New York City, to grocer Joseph Freedman and his wife, Elizabeth (Davies) Freedman. He graduated from City College of New York with a law degree and entered the real estate business. At the age of 21, Freedman became part of the powerful Tammany Hall organization and a close associate of Richard Coker, a future Tammany boss. His membership on Tammany's finance committee and his tenure as treasurer of the national Democratic Party in 1897 gave him tremendous political power, which he freely exercised to make choice real estate deals. His most important project was providing the bonding for the construction of the New York City subway.[1]

Freedman first got involved in the baseball business as the receiver of Manhattan Field, the ballpark the Giants abandoned when they moved to the first Polo Grounds. In 1895, Giants owner John Day put the bankrupt team up for sale, and Freedman bought the controlling interest for $48,000. It was rumored that he had received help on the purchase from his close friend, Albert G. Spalding, a manufacturer of sports equipment, who was supposedly trying to insure his monopoly in providing baseball supplies to the major leagues.[2] In a very few years, Spalding would come to regret his action.

From the first, Freedman created enemies. Despite a successful performance and a close second-place finish in the 1894 season, the Giants franchise was in serious financial trouble. In an effort to increase revenues, Freedman ended the custom of awarding former players and friends of the ball club complimentary passes, a practice he considered "freeloaders cutting into the team's profits."[3]

It didn't take long before Freedman was also involved in a number of major conflicts with the press. When Sam Crane, a writer for the *New York Commercial Advertiser* and a former major league infielder, accused Freedman of trying to destroy the Giants, Freedman voided Crane's press credentials and refused to admit him to the ballpark even if he bought his own ticket. He went so far as to distribute Crane's picture to his ticket sellers to make sure. On another occasion, Freedman barred two other New York reporters and three Cincinnati writers because they wrote disparagingly about Freedman and his team. Then Freedman banned all reporters at Joseph Pulitzer's *New York Sun* from the Polo Grounds. By 1900, Freedman had filed an estimated 22 libel suits against the *Sun*.[4] On one occasion, Freedman punched a young *New York Times* reporter assigned to cover the Giants when he criticized the team's play.[5] Freedman even wrote a nasty letter to 72-year-old Henry Chadwick, a noted former sportswriter, when he was awarded a $600 pension from the National League. Freedman accused Chadwick of being critical of an owner who helped support his pension. Chadwick retaliated by boycotting all games at the Polo Grounds and urging all Giants fans to do the same.[6]

Freedman went after the press for two reasons. First, he felt they were not giving him enough credit for trying to improve the team. He had bought star outfielder Tommy Burns from Brooklyn and had his scouts constantly looking for new talent to turn the Giants into a pennant winner. Unfortunately, the club performed poorly most years under Freedman, disappointing both the fans and the press and causing sportswriters to generate sarcastic and disapproving accounts of both Freedman and the Giants.

And this was Freedman's second reason for his war with the press. As a product of Tammany Hall, Freedman expected journalists to be loyal and treat him the way he treated his political bosses. The constant criticism was a personal affront to his sense of respectability and his belief that he could run the team as he wished without any public scrutiny. In reality, each club owner at the time felt much the same; the difference between Andrew Freedman and other magnates was only a matter of degree.[7]

In addition to his forays with the press, Freedman took on other owners and the league itself. When Freedman first bought the team, many of the owners had assumed that the stock had actually been purchased for James A. Bailey, the circus magnate. They were shocked to discover that the "plum" New York Giants were actually owned by a wealthy, politically well-connected, but most unpleasant young man. His religion only intensified their dislike.[8]

Described as handsome and dapper, 34-year-old Freedman was also arrogant, opinionated, and tactless. He accused National League President Nick Young of favoritism in arranging the playing schedules.[9] Freedman made wild offers to purchase established stars and when owners refused to sell them to him, he insulted them. He angered the president of the Baltimore Orioles by publicly claiming that the Orioles' championship season was merely a "fluke."[10]

He also suggested that Brooklyn drop out of the League so there would be only one team in the New York area—his Giants.[11] When Brooklyn owner Charles Byrne scorned his suggestion, Freedman's close friends at city hall made sure that none of the new subway lines went anywhere near Brooklyn's ball field, Washington Park.[12]

Freedman's desire to monopolize the New York area also made him a major obstacle to the establishment of an American League team in New York in 1901. Through his links with Tammany Hall, Freedman was able to control most suitable baseball sites and he also persuaded the Interborough Rapid Transit Company, which was considering subsidizing a ballpark near one of its stations, to drop its plans.[13]

If Freedman's relationships with the press and the league were dreadful, his relationships with his managers were worse. During the eight years he owned the Giants, Freedman employed 12 different managers—two of them twice—and often fired them for no justifiable reason.[14] The first casualty was John Montgomery Ward, the successful 1894 manager not rehired for the 1895 season. Some of the managers Freedman then chose were bona fide baseball men such as Giants third baseman George Davis, former Giants player Jack Doyle and veteran player "Scrappy" Bill Joyce. Freedman also tried experienced managers. The twenty-one-year veteran Chicago infielder and manager, Adrian "Cap" Anson, came out of retirement to take over the Giants; he lasted 22 games.[15] In 1900, Freedman hired former Cincinnati pilot Buck Ewing; he stayed only half the season.[16]

The list of Giants managers also included Harvey Watkins, an actor who was working as an office boy when Freedman hired him; Fred Hoey, one of Freedman's Tammany Hall flunkies; and two more incompetents—Horace Fogel (who would later be thrown out of the league) and Heinie Smith.[17] The most pathetic hire was former owner John B. Day. In dire financial straits in 1899, Day took over the managerial post for the man who had bought the team from him. He was gone by early July.

Not even the debut in 1900 of a young Christy Mathewson, one of baseball's all-time stars, could revive the Giants.[18] During the years from 1895 to 1902, the club finished higher than seventh only once—in 1897, when Bill Joyce brought them in third.[19]

Andrew Freedman owned the New York Giants from 1895 to 1902, and was considered by many the most "detestable owner in the history of baseball." He was the victim of religious slurs and almost thoroughly abhorred, yet some baseball people thought Freedman was a farsighted baseball man who clearly saw baseball for what it was—a business (courtesy Transcendental Graphics).

And, of course, Freeman had runins with players. Two long drawn-out disputes greatly increased the number of his enemies. The first collision was with Giant star pitcher Amos Rusie, who in 1894 had won 36 games for the second-place Giants. It was his fourth consecutive year of 30 or more victories.[20] In 1895, the first year of Freedman's ownership, Rusie won only 23 games and Freedman blamed him for the Giants' ninth-place finish. Announcing that his pitcher was being fined $200 for "indifferent work in the final game and breaking training rules," he withheld the money from Rusie's last check.[21] Rusie considered the $200 held back not a fine but a pay cut and refused to report to the Giants in 1896 until Freedman repaid the money. But as Freedman told the *Washington Post*, "The club's position as to Rusie is unchanged. The $200 fine will not be remitted."[22] Freedman claimed that he was simply trying to maintain discipline and deal with "disorganizers."[23] Not impressed with Freedman's logic, *The Sporting News* editorialized, "Every independent fair-thinking man is with Rusie in his stand against the New York Club."[24]

Rusie's popularity in New York went beyond his ability as a pitcher. A handsome man, he could be seen often out late at night, and there was some truth to Freedman's charges that his star pitcher was a carouser.[25] With Freedman refusing to budge, Rusie sat out the entire 1896 season. Attendance dropped as many Giants fans boycotted games in protest of Freedman's action.[26] Other league owners were also anxious to see Rusie come back to help increase their revenues when they played the Giants. Because of this, they chipped in to give Rusie $5,000 for his lost season, pay his fine, and reimburse him for legal expenses.[27] Rusie became one of the few players in baseball history ever to hold out for a full season.[28]

Rusie's return in 1897 marked the only year in Freedman's tenure that home attendance topped the 300,000 mark.[29] Although Rusie won 28 games that year, he never returned to his former greatness. He won 20 games in 1898, his last year with the Giants, then dropped out of the majors for two years, and ended his career in 1901, where he was 0–1 with Cincinnati.[30]

Anti-Semitism, not money, was at the core of Freedman's other player clash. Before the 1898 season, Cincinnati owner John Brush wrote a "Purification Plan" to rid baseball of "obscene, indecent, or vulgar language by players" during the game. Umpires were ordered to report such incidents to the National League Board of Discipline, which could either fine or suspend offending players.[31]

At an 1898 Giants home game against the Baltimore Orioles, former Giant outfielder James (Ducky) Holmes, struck out with the bases loaded. As he was walking back to the Oriole bench, a fan taunted him, yelling, "Hey, Ducky, you're a lobster and that's why you don't play for New York anymore." The ex–Giant shouted back, "Well, I'm glad I'm not working for a sheeny anymore."[32] Freedman charged down the aisle and demanded an apology; Holmes spat at him. Freedman then turned to the game's single umpire, Thomas Lynch, insisting that Lynch remove Holmes from the game under the new league rule against vulgar language. "Holmes should be suspended for the rest of the season for his insulting language at the Polo Grounds to the Jewish race and the Hebrew patrons of the game," declared Freedman.[33] The umpire claimed that he hadn't heard Holmes' comment and that if Freedman didn't leave the field, the Giants would forfeit the game. When Freedman stood his ground, Lynch ordered a forfeit.[34]

Ironically, it was Freedman who was censured first. By interfering with play and intentionally forfeiting a game, Freedman had violated two of the very few National League rules in those days. The league's board of directors ruled that the forfeit would remain, and fined Freedman $1,000 for causing it. As a sop to Freedman, and in awareness of his connections with Tammany, the board also suspended Holmes for the remainder of the season.[35]

This ruling nearly triggered an all-out revolt on behalf of Holmes. Among the protests was a petition signed by all the Boston players, denouncing Freedman for his "spirit of impatience, intolerance, arrogance and prejudice toward players, a spirit inimical to the best interests of the game and the public."[36] Even fellow owners Arthur Soden, Frank Robison, and John Brush, who wrote the new code of conduct, sided against Freedman, an action some believe was based on personal dislike tinged by anti–Semitism.[37]

Although in later years this overt display of anti–Semitism, the first documented in organized baseball, would be clearly unacceptable, ethnic and religious slurs were common during the Gilded Age and not viewed as being particularly reprehensible or offensive. *Sporting Life* reflected these feelings when it wrote that punishing a player for "such a trifling offense as insulting the Hebrew race was a perversion of justice."[38] Besides, Freedman was so personally unpopular that many were delighted to see him embarrassed.

Holmes was reinstated after only ten days due to constant pressure from the press. Freedman protested every game in which Holmes played for the remainder of the year.[39] Gradually the Holmes issue died down, but Freedman never forgot it. He accepted the humiliation imposed by the other magnates, but he reasoned that eventually it would be his turn and he began his campaign for revenge with the 1899 season.

Before the 1899 season began, Freedman cut players' salaries, arguing that low attendance and the team's poor performance in 1898 made it necessary. His pitching staff was decimated when Amos Rusie left and his ace, Cy Seymour, refused to sign his contract until May 11. With the Giants' record of 60 wins and 90 losses, total attendance dropped from more than 365,000 the year before to a little over 121,000. "Baseball affairs in New York have been going just as I wished and expected them to go," said a completely satisfied Freedman.[40]

Freedman had reason to be satisfied. Outside of baseball, things were going very well for him. Tammany was back in power after a "reform" administration had been ousted. Except for his financial losses in baseball, Freedman was prospering, making enormous sums of money from his real estate and bonding businesses and expecting his subway negotiations to be profitable soon. What pleased him most was that other owners, especially those who owned marginal franchises, were losing money because the Giants were not drawing large crowds. Freedman predicted that eventually the magnates would beg him to take charge of baseball and put it on a paying basis.[41] He was now prepared to obtain a major concession from his fellow magnates—the reduction in the number of teams in the National League.

For the past few years, Freedman had been advocating that major league baseball revert to an eight-club league. At the end of 1899 he stated, "I will not attempt to improve the New York club until the circuit is reduced." Fearing even lower attendance in the future, a committee appointed at the league's December 1899 meeting recommended that the Baltimore, Washington, Cleveland, and Louisville teams be dropped. The league adopted the recommendation, leaving teams from Boston, Brooklyn, New York, and Philadelphia in the East, and Pittsburgh, Chicago, Cincinnati, and St. Louis in the West. This would be the makeup of the National League until 1953, when Boston moved to Milwaukee.[42] The reaction was generally positive. One manager announced, "The reduction of the circuit will mean a revival of the great American game throughout the country."[43]

Reducing the number of teams in the circuit was only the beginning. Freedman felt that he still had a score to settle with his fellow owners and he kept adding demands before he would agree to build up the Giants. He insisted that the league dismiss Nick Young as its president and replace him with a stronger president. Freedman demanded that his $1,000 fine in the Ducky Holmes fiasco be returned. He also refused to pay his share when the circuit was reduced unless he was given the rights to certain players. His colleagues continued to appease him. They not only returned the fine, but also added six percent interest; he was given first choice of the Washington players and was allowed to buy any surplus players on the remaining league's clubs at a reduced cost. Finally, the rule barring the Giants from playing Sunday exhibition games was repealed.[44]

All these concessions did nothing to improve the Giants during 1900 and 1901 and their poor play contributed to lower attendance and declining financial return for all the teams. More importantly, the National League was now facing a new and worrisome competitor. Formed in the fall of 1899, the Western League, the strongest of the minor leagues, had changed its name to the American League and was creating its own teams in National League cities. In addition, the new league was luring National League players by offering higher salaries and refusing to recognize the National League's reserve rule. The American League, led by president Ban Johnson, enticed 111 National League players to join his American

League, including stars like Willie Keeler and Cy Young. National League owners were terrified that if they didn't reach some agreement with Johnson's league the number of defectors would increase, and those who remained would demand higher salaries.

Andrew Freedman watched these proceedings, not with alarm, but with great interest. Perhaps the only independently wealthy owner of his time, he alone had the money to fight the rival league indefinitely, and the political clout to keep an American League team out of New York. Realizing his position, Freedman concluded that now was the time he could get the other magnates to accept his leadership to save the National League. His plan was to reorganize the league into a syndicate by eliminating separate ownerships of the eight clubs and pooling all the players, who would be reassigned to teams each season. The league, in effect, would become one gigantic trust and, of course, it would be essentially under Freedman's control. His proposal called for his Giants to hold 30 percent of the stock; Boston, St. Louis and Cincinnati 12 percent each; Philadelphia and Chicago 10 percent each; Pittsburgh eight percent; and Brooklyn a mere six percent.[45] If things went according to Freedman's plan, the American League would collapse and the National League would control a baseball monopoly.[46]

The syndicate, to be known simply as the National League Baseball Trust, was actually just an extension of the interlocking ownerships that already existed in the league.[47] Nor was the idea of a trust anything new. The Baseball Trust would simply emulate those run by the railroad, oil, banking, and steel magnates of the day. Freedman's critics called him a robber baron, but he kept reminding them that baseball was a profit-making business and should be run that way.[48] He even convinced his former detractors, owners John Brush of Cincinnati, Frank Robison of St. Louis, and Arthur Soden of Boston, to support the Baseball Trust.

Freedman's trust was leaked to the public by the *New York Sun*, his long-time adversary, in time for the owners who opposed him to plan their own strategy for the National League's annual meeting in December 1901. The major issue centered on the presidency of the league. In contrast to his earlier stand, Freedman and his forces lined up behind the current president, Nick Young. The anti–Freedman, anti-syndicate owners, Barney Dreyfuss of Pittsburgh, Charles Ebbets of Brooklyn, Alfred J. Reach of Philadelphia, and John Hart of Chicago, came up with the only name in baseball that could possibly defeat Young—Albert Spalding.[49]

This was the same man who, in 1895, helped Freedman buy the Giants, calling Freedman "a clever businessman" and wishing him much success. Four years later, when Spalding's brother resigned from the Giants board of directors; Spalding referred to Freedman then only as an "amusing cuss." By 1901, however, when Spalding accepted the offer to run for president of the National League, he had changed his assessment of Freedman entirely, declaring that, "Andrew Freedman must get out of baseball, absolutely and entirely.... I charge Andrew Freedman with being a traitor ... who has done more to ruin baseball than any other four forces that ever existed in the history of the game."[50] Spalding also called the Giants owner "the incarnation of selfishness supreme."[51]

Freedman was quick to point out the hypocrisy in Spalding's criticism of trusts and monopolies, especially in sports. Not only had Spalding been part of a bicycle trust when the sport of cycling became popular, but he also had a monopoly to supply the league's official baseballs in addition to a license to publish its official guide.[52]

At the league meeting, 25 ballots were taken for president of the National League; 25 times Freedman, Brush, Soden, and Robison voted for Young, and Ebbets, Dreyfuss, Reach and Hart cast their votes for Spalding. Late in the evening, the Freedman faction left the room, leaving the anti-syndicate group behind. The four Spalding supporters then illegally called a quorum and elected Spalding league president 4–0. Before dawn, Spalding went to Nick Young's room, physically took the trunk with the league records, and declared himself president of the National League.[53] Freedman pronounced Spalding's actions illegal and for once the *New York Clipper* agreed with him, calling the bogus election "not only farcical but the crudest thing that was ever attempted at a baseball meeting."[54]

Freedman obtained an injunction barring Spalding from taking over the league, but Spalding left the state and tried to run league affairs through the mail. The presidential deadlock continued until a compromise was reached in the spring of 1902.[55]

Under the agreement, Henry Clay Pulliam, a friend of Barney Dreyfus and formerly an official of the Pittsburgh Pirates, became president of the National League and Andrew Freedman agreed to sell his club to John Brush, who took over formal control of the team in 1903.[56] He told the press, "On account of my many business interests I have found that I have been unable to devote the necessary amount of time to the club."[57] Freedman's sale of the club to Brush seemed to please everyone, especially the Giants' fans.[58]

As a parting gesture before he turned over control of the team, Freedman took one more shot at American League President Ban Johnson. He and Brush bought a controlling interest in the AL's Baltimore club. They then transferred four of the Oriole's star players to the Giants, including Freedman's thirteenth manager, the legendary John McGraw.[59] "I want you as manager," Freedman told McGraw. "You'll have absolute control."[60] McGraw, well aware of Freedman's previous experience with managers, reassured the press, "I know the troubles some other managers have had in New York, but I think that I will have no difficulty in getting along. I will have a contract that will secure me, and do not see that I have reason to fear."[61] On July 2, 1902, McGraw took over the helm of the Giants; he would remain as manager of the Giants for a good portion of the next 30 years.

At the end of September 1902 Freedman formally announced his resignation as president of the New York Giants in favor of Brush. He was then off to Europe for an extended stay. His influence in New York was on the decline, as Tammany Hall's candidate for mayor lost the election to reformer Seth Low. When he returned from Europe, Freedman moved to his home in Red Bank, New Jersey.[62]

Freedman's political power might have been on the decline, but he did have some influence left. The year following Freedman's departure from baseball, 1903, the American League was recognized as a major league and Ban Johnson was allowed to place an American League team in New York. Brush, thoroughly aghast at the idea, turned for help to Freedman, who used his Tammany connections to saddle the American League club with an inferior park location. Freedman forced Johnson to accept some of his cronies as investors in the new team to be called the New York Highlanders.[63] This move did not surprise Ban Johnson, who once said of Andrew Freedman, "In his personal relations he might have been pleasant enough, but as a baseball magnate he seemed to feel that his money and his political pull authorized him to indulge every whim and mood."[64]

On December 4, 1915, Andrew Freedman died of apoplexy; he was 45 years old. A bachelor, Freedman left a small legacy to his brother, sister, and mother, and the remainder of his estate, estimated at $7 million, to establish a home for indigent old people "regardless of race, sex, or creed." In his will, Freedman wrote that he especially wanted to care for old couples who might otherwise be forced to live apart.[65]

In contrast to the usual laudatory remarks in most obituaries, *The Sporting News* wrote of Freedman, "He had an arbitrary disposition, a violent temper, and an ungovernable tongue in anger which was easily provoked and he was disposed to be arbitrary to the point of tyranny with subordinates."[66] Others characterized his years in baseball as the "reign of terror" and Freedman as the "Talleyrand of Baseball." For years, the term "Freedmanism," coined by his enemies, Spalding and Chadwick, was used to represent the "destructive element of our national pastime."[67]

Although it was often overlooked, Freedman did make one important contribution to the Giants when he hired John McGraw as manager. One baseball historian noted that McGraw's arrival finally brought the Giants into the twentieth century, two years after the rest of the world.[68] Under McGraw, the Giants would become the National League's most successful franchise and New York fans finally had the kind of baseball they felt they deserved.[69]

There were also those who consider Freedman a man with farsighted ideas. His concept of a baseball trust was based on an assumption, contrary to the beliefs of many contemporaries and most fans, that baseball was strictly a business venture. To be profitable, Freedman insisted, his fellow owners had to maintain tight control over player salaries, the distribution of player talent, and the minor leagues.[70]

Unfortunately, Freedman lived during America's "age of reform," when the public took a very dim view of trusts in general. In addition, the Baseball Trust was not control of some commodity but rather of what most Americans considered America's greatest competitive sport. Perhaps its biggest handicap was that it was proposed by Andrew Freedman, "the most thoroughly detested magnate in the game."[71]

5. Reshaping the Game

In contrast to Andrew Freedman, his contemporary, Barney Dreyfuss, was one of the most respected owners in baseball. Throughout his three decades as owner of the Pittsburgh Pirates, Dreyfuss's integrity and his love and knowledge of the game earned him the esteem not only of his fellow owners but also of his team, the press, and the fans. Recognized for many positive changes he helped bring about in baseball, Dreyfuss is probably best known as the "Father of the World Series."

Albert Lasker was another influential Jewish owner during some of the most critical years in baseball. Although renowned more for his accomplishments outside the game, Lasker is credited with initiating the plan that established the way baseball has been governed since 1921.

Together, they represent two very different versions of German-American Jews who achieved personal and financial success in the United States but who had in common the love of baseball.

Bernhardt Dreyfuss was born in Freiburg, Germany, on February 23, 1865, to Samuel and Fanny Goldsmith Dreyfuss.[1] After completing his schooling at the age of fifteen, Dreyfuss took a job as a bookkeeper with a bank in Germany and worked there for a year before immigrating to the United States in 1881. Dreyfuss settled in Paducah, Kentucky, to work in the wholesale liquor firm founded by his relatives, the Bernheims. His bookkeeping experience enabled him to succeed in his new job in Paducah. In 1890, Dreyfuss was given a working interest in the business.[2]

Unfortunately, after working nine hours a day and then studying English until midnight, Dreyfuss began to suffer from headaches, poor digestion, and a generally run-down condition. Small and never robust, Dreyfuss, at his relatives' urging, saw a doctor who advised him to spend more time outdoors and suggested that he play baseball, a game that was completely unknown to the young man.[3]

In the 1880s, baseball was quite popular throughout the country, especially in the South. Once he discovered it, the game fascinated Dreyfuss. He tried numerous positions, but liked playing second base best. Eventually, he founded a semipro team, which he owned from 1884 to 1888.[4]

In 1888 the family distillery moved to Louisville and it was there that Dreyfuss met his future wife, who fortunately shared his interest in baseball.[5] Barney Dreyfuss and Florence Wolf married on October 16, 1894; the marriage produced two children—Samuel, born November 9, 1896, and Eleanor, born April 30, 1898.[6]

In Louisville, Dreyfuss became part of organized baseball. Dreyfuss had enjoyed owning his team in Paducah, and as his passion for the game and his finances increased, he considered buying a major league team. Louisville had been one of the original teams in the National League, but in 1882 the team affiliated with the American Association as the Louisville Cyclones. Ten years later, the American Association disbanded and Louisville rejoined the National League as the Louisville Colonels.

Around 1895, Dreyfuss began to invest increasing amounts of money in the Colonels even though the team was among the worst in the League, both on the field and at the box office.[7] He was elected president of the Colonels in 1899. Aware of Andrew Freedman's mission to eliminate weaker teams from the National League, Dreyfuss also bought an interest in the National League's Pittsburgh Pirates. As expected, the Colonels were dropped from the National League in 1900, but the Pirates remained. By that time, Dreyfuss owned half of the Pirates stock and had been elected president of the Pittsburgh team. Although he was paid only $10,000 for the Louisville franchise, he received the right to sell his players on the open market. Instead, he simply consolidated the best players from the two teams, putting together Louisville's Honus Wagner, Tommy Leach, Fred Clarke, Deacon Phillipe, and Rube Waddell, with Pittsburgh's Jack Chesboro, Jesse Tanehill, Ginger Beaumont, Jimmy Williams, and Fred Ely. In this merger, the Pirates received four future Hall of Famers, a number of 20-game winners and batting champions, and, in Leach, a home run leader.[8] Dreyfuss now had a powerhouse team that would capture three consecutive pennants from 1901 to 1903.[9]

One of the keys to Dreyfuss's success was his outstanding ability to find talented players. For many years he served as his own scout, carrying with him a little black book filled with the names and statistics of minor league players he considered prospects for his Pirates. He received the ultimate compliment when other baseball men termed Dreyfuss one of the best judges of baseball talent at that time.[10]

Of course, he wasn't perfect, and missed at least two great prospects. He refused to pay travel expenses to bring a young pitcher to Pittsburgh because he thought the person promoting him was too eager. The pitcher was future Hall of Famer Walter Johnson.[11] Dreyfuss lost another future member of the Hall of Fame because of his aversion to smoking. Dreyfuss was interested in a prospect reputed to be a great batter until he learned that the player was also a cigarette smoker. He passed on the player whose name was Tris Speaker.[12]

Although he was rather autocratic, Dreyfuss was a benevolent despot, and had positive relations with his players as well as his managers. He treated his players fairly and often sent and received contracts with no set amount of money stipulated, as players believed Dreyfuss would pay them what they were worth. He offered to establish bank accounts for players with wives and families and volunteered to invest some of the players' salaries with the understanding that he would guarantee the principal if the investments lost money. One of the star players on the Pirates, Honus Wagner, often allowed his paychecks to accrue, trusting that Dreyfuss possessed a much keener business sense to invest the funds.[13] Dreyfuss was generous to players who were loyal to him and met his standards, but he could also be stern if they didn't.[14]

He had an interesting relationship with his managers. Under Dreyfuss's ownership, managers came and went, but Dreyfuss insisted that he never fired any, allowing them instead to "resign." Some returned as either coaches or scouts. Dreyfuss consistently sided with his managers in all disputes with the players, although some of these managers didn't remain long with the team afterwards.[15]

Dreyfuss also earned the respect of most of the other National League owners, as he quickly became involved in a number of problems unrelated to activity on the field. The first issue was the attempt by New York Giants owner Andrew Freedman to reorganize the National League as a trust, pool its resources, and divide the profits of all the teams. Dreyfuss was a key member of the opposition, and was instrumental in making his friend, Harry Pulliam, the compromise choice for National League president.[16] The more far-reaching part of the settlement with Freedman was the establishment of a three-person executive board to run league affairs. Known as the National Commission, this board would eventually consist of the presidents of the National and American leagues, and a third member selected by the two league presidents.[17] The National Commission would prove to be a pivotal part of the baseball story of Barney Dreyfuss.

Some historians consider 1901, the year the American League became a reality,

Barney Dreyfuss, owner of the Pittsburgh Pirates from 1899 to 1932, was known for his high personal integrity and passion for the game. He began the tradition of the World Series between the National and American leagues, and was instrumental in creating the office of Baseball Commissioner (courtesy National Baseball Hall of Fame Library, Cooperstown, N.Y.).

the beginning of baseball's "modern era." While they were still wrangling with Freedman in 1901, the National League owners now had to deal with the end of their monopoly of the game.[18] Like other National League owners, Dreyfuss watched as Ban Johnson, a founder and later president of the American League, begin to recruit players for his league from the National League. Thanks to his excellent relationship with his players, Dreyfuss did not lose as many players as other National League owners, but he had deep concerns about the rival league based on rumors that Johnson wanted to place an AL club in Pittsburgh. To make sure that Johnson stayed out of Pittsburgh, Dreyfuss outmaneuvered him by leasing all the suitable sites in and around the city where any competing ballpark could be built.[19]

But bullying tactics were not really Dreyfuss's forte; he preferred cooperation. Chosen by his peers as one of the chief negotiators for the National League, Dreyfuss helped work out an agreement between the leagues at the 1903 peace meetings. The final version included a commitment by Johnson to stay out of Pittsburgh, permission for the American League to retain the New York team with all of its players, and promises by both leagues to observe the reserve clause and honor each other's contracts.[20]

Dreyfuss went even further. More than any other owner, Dreyfuss realized that the American League was here to stay and was determined to legitimize the new league. He endorsed a plan for the pennant-winning team in the National League to play the pennant-winning team in the new circuit in what would be baseball's first World Series.[21] This series would not only show that the years of acrimony, which had disillusioned many fans, were over, but also that the two leagues were now equals.[22] From a business standpoint, Dreyfuss also sensed that fans would pay to see a championship series between the two leagues.[23]

When it appeared certain that the Pirates would win their third consecutive National League pennant in 1903, and the Boston Pilgrims would take the American League flag, Dreyfuss wrote Boston owner Henry Killilea proposing the postseason series: "[It would] ... create great interest in baseball, in our leagues, and in our players. I also believe it would be a financial success."[24]

With the approval of the American League, Killilea accepted the challenge and the two owners then worked out a number of rules for this first World Series, some still in practice today. First, the series was to be played in the home parks of the two teams, not on a neutral field. Second, any player not on the team's roster prior to September 1 could not participate in the contest. Finally, it would be a best five-of-nine series that year.[25]

Dreyfuss was confident that no team could defeat his Pirates, but in a surprising upset, partially due to a decimated Pittsburgh pitching staff, Boston won the series five games to three. Nevertheless, because of Dreyfuss's generosity, the Pirate players came out of the series with more money than their winning rivals. Dreyfuss added part of his club's own receipts to each player's share, making the total for each Pirate $1,316, compared with the Boston pay of $1,182 per man.[26] This was Dreyfuss's way of thanking his players for the loyalty they had shown during the interleague war.[27]

The first World Series introduced an issue that Jewish participants in the game deal with even today. The first game, which was played in Boston, fell on the most holy day on the Jewish calendar, Yom Kippur, the Day of Atonement, when many German and Russian Jews, Boston's newest immigrant group, would not attend. Barney Dreyfuss was not there either.

Dreyfuss did, however, attend the second game, along with two invited guests, Rabbi Charles Fleischer, the patriarch of Boston's oldest Jewish congregation, and Dreyfuss's Pittsburgh rabbi, who made the trip east to see the game.[28]

In 1904 the Boston Pilgrims again won the pennant in the American League and the New York Giants were National League champs. There was no World Series that year, as Giants owner John Brush and Giants manager John McGraw refused to play, probably because both still hated Ban Johnson and the American League.[29] Dreyfuss was so committed to the World Series idea that he and his fourth-place Pirates challenged the AL's fourth-place Cleveland Indians to a postseason series.[30] The World Series was only one of many issues which divided McGraw and Dreyfuss.

Barney Dreyfuss had been at odds with John McGraw ever since he had become Giants manager in 1902. In 1905 the tough-talking, belligerent McGraw noticed Dreyfuss sitting behind his team's dugout before a game against the Giants and loudly challenged him to a $10,000 bet on the game's outcome. "Hey, Barney," yelled McGraw numerous times.[31] Dreyfuss chose to ignore McGraw's taunts and McGraw withdrew the offer, but insisted on having the last word, noting sarcastically that Dreyfuss never paid his bets, anyway. Dreyfuss, outraged by McGraw's accusation and the assault on his dignity and integrity, insisted that National League President Harry Pulliam suspend McGraw. Pulliam not only suspended McGraw, he also fined him $150.

Pulliam was trying to carry out his duties under the code written by McGraw's boss, John Brush, which required the league president to fine any suspended player $10 for every day the player was out. In reality, the league president's authority rested on the owners' approval, and they often gave only lip service to their own rules.[32] McGraw refused to pay the fine or accept the suspension. The partisan *New York Evening Journal* took up McGraw's cause and collected 12,000 signatures from New York baseball fans, calling on the National League to dismiss all charges against McGraw.[33] To Dreyfuss's amazement, the National League owners not only absolved McGraw of any wrongdoing, but also scolded Dreyfuss for engaging in a public spat with a manager.[34] The McGraw incident incensed him for years as he suffered the embarrassment of having the crowd chant "Hey, Barney!" in any opposition park in which he appeared.[35]

In 1909 Barney Dreyfuss built Forbes Field, the first of the modern triple-tier baseball stadiums. When it was dedicated on June 30, 1909, Dreyfuss addressed the packed house. "This is indeed the happiest day of my life,"[36] he told them. He would constantly brag about his new ballpark, once boasting, "Why, they told me that the Giants don't have that large a park with all New York to draw from."[37]

To preserve Forbes Field's pastoral setting, Dreyfuss did not allow advertising on the fences. He did, however, permit ads for war stamps during World War I and war bonds during World War II. Forbes Field was the home of the Pittsburgh Pirates until 1970.[38]

Dreyfuss rewarded the fans of Pittsburgh in 1909 by not only building them a new ballpark but also by winning the National League pennant for the fourth time. The Pirates went on to defeat the Detroit Tigers four games to three in the World Series.[39] Dreyfuss predicted that his Pirates would maintain their supremacy for many years to come. He was wrong, as Pittsburgh would not win another pennant until 1925.

From 1913 through 1916, Dreyfuss not only had to get his team back on track, but he and the other major league owners had to contend with another new rival. At the conclusion of the 1913 season, the newly formed Federal League mounted an aggressive campaign to establish itself as a major league by constructing ballparks and signing current big league players. In 1914, the Feds invaded Dreyfuss's turf with the Pittsburgh Rebels and tried to sign his star player, Honus Wagner. Wagner wasn't tempted. "The Feds know there's no use in talking to me," said Wagner.[40]

Repeating his tactics from the American League war, Dreyfuss actively signed his own players, so that by the beginning of the 1914 season, only two Pirate players jumped to the Federal League, catcher Mike Simon, who signed with Chicago, and pitcher Claude Hendrix, who joined the Feds in St. Louis.[41]

Early in January 1915, the Federal League sued organized baseball, claiming the Major Leagues violated the Sherman Antitrust Act. The case was presided over by Judge Kenesaw Mountain Landis, an ardent baseball fan who delayed rendering a verdict, hoping that the leagues would reach an agreement on their own. Landis's plan worked. The Federal League fell apart and the suit was dropped.[42]

Although the Pirates came through the Federal League conflict better than teams in many other cities, Dreyfuss was happy to see that league dissolve after the 1915 season. He blamed the Federal League for the Pirates' second-division finish, claiming that talk of raiding players distracted his team from competing on the field.[43]

Barney Dreyfuss was called on to act as mediator in the concluding negotiations with the Federal League because his good relations with both the American and National Leagues gave him a unique standing. The final settlement included Dreyfuss's plan to return players to the American and National Leagues by allowing teams to choose them in reverse order to their 1915 standings.[44] As evidence of his integrity, Dreyfuss stated that he would not purchase any of the former Federal Leaguers.[45]

The National Commission, baseball's governing body which Dreyfuss had helped create, seemed ineffectual in dealing with the Federal League. In fact, it wasn't long after it was established in 1902 that Dreyfuss began to question its role in baseball. In 1909 Dreyfuss called the commission a "joke," claiming that its members did too much drinking and didn't use sound business practices.[46]

In addition, by 1912 the commission had ruled against Dreyfuss on at least two player issues. Dreyfuss had grudgingly accepted the commission's rulings until 1916, when he totally lost patience with the board over the George Sisler affair. The situation had begun in 1910, when Sisler, while still in high school, signed a minor league contract that was sold to the Pittsburgh Pirates. The National Commission had approved the sale. Instead of playing ball right after graduation, Sisler attended the University of Michigan, where his baseball coach, Branch Rickey, who was also an attorney, told Sisler the contract with the Pirates was invalid because of his age at the time he signed. Dreyfuss wrote the National Commission for a clarification of Sisler's status. Reversing their earlier approval, the commission nullified the Pirates' contract with Sisler, and declared him a free agent.[47]

Sisler then solicited offers from various major league teams, including the Pirates, and in 1915 announced that he had signed with the St. Louis Browns for an annual salary of $7,400. By no coincidence, Sisler's former college coach, Branch Rickey, was now manager of the St. Louis Browns.[48]

Dreyfuss immediately filed a complaint with the National Commission against the Browns, claiming "interference and tampering" by Rickey. With each league president supporting his own team, the decision was ultimately left to Commission Chairman Gary Herrmann, owner of the National League's Cincinnati Reds. On June 10, 1916, Herrmann rejected Dreyfuss's complaint and declared Sisler the property of the St. Louis Browns.[49] Dreyfuss was livid and the sight of Sisler developing into one of baseball's premium first basemen galled him even more.

Dreyfuss was now determined to change the way that baseball was run, launching a campaign against the National Commission. He was willing to retain the three-member body if a neutral chairman replaced Hermann but his ultimate goal was to disband the commission entirely and replace it with a single commissioner. "I have advocated a one man commission for the last four years," Dreyfuss pointed out. "This one-man commission is bound to come—if not this year, surely next year. Just mark what I say."[50]

Slowly but surely Dreyfuss began picking up the support of other owners, including Albert Lasker, one of the new owners of the Chicago Cubs. It would be Lasker, the master of persuasive writing, who would draft the plan that served as the blueprint for the commissioner form of baseball governance.

Albert D. Lasker, known even today as "The Father of Modern Advertising," is credited with transforming advertising into an active marketing force.[51] Lasker was born May 1, 1880, to German-Americans Morris Lasker, a merchant and banker, and Nettie Heidenheimer Davis.[52] He was raised in Galveston, where he became a baseball fan at an early age by watching the Chicago Cubs spring training camp there.[53]

In 1898, Lasker became an office clerk
at the Chicago advertising agency, Lord &
Thomas.[54] Using his sales and copy writing
skills, he succeeded quickly and by 1910 was
the sole owner of the firm.[55] He built Lord
& Thomas, which later became known as
Foote, Cone & Belding, into one of the
country's preeminent advertising agencies
and in the process became a very rich man.[56]

After his advertising business was well
established, Lasker also became active in
politics and baseball. A Cubs fan since his
days in Galveston, Albert Lasker became the
major stockholder when he bought controlling interest in the team in 1916.[57] One of
the others who bought into the Cubs at that
time was chewing gum magnate William
Wrigley, who claimed that he really didn't
know or care anything about the game. Nevertheless, Lasker made it appear that
Wrigley was the lead owner, even changing
the ballpark's name from Cub Park to
Wrigley Field. Wrigley agreed because
Lasker persuaded him that "This will do
your chewing-gum business a lot of good."
Years later Lasker explained that he kept a
low profile because, "You never heard of a
respectable citizen being owner of a baseball team, did you?"[58]

Not only was Albert David Lasker known as "the
father of modern advertising," but it was also
his plan which helped set up the system under
which baseball has been governed since 1921.
He and Barney Dreyfuss are given major credit
for establishing the office of Baseball Commissioner (courtesy Foote, Cone, & Belding).

As owner of the Cubs, Lasker demonstrated the same kind of integrity associated with
Barney Dreyfuss. Shortly after Lasker took control, his president, Bill Veeck, Sr., told him
that a player the Cubs had recently purchased from the Reds had accepted bribes to throw
games. The Reds knew of his dishonesty, and dealt with it by selling him to the Cubs. When
Lasker ordered Veeck to fire the player immediately, the player filed a breach of contract
suit. Other owners advised Lasker to keep the suit quiet and settle. But Lasker defended his
action in open court and won; the player was banned from baseball. "I went into that thing
because my innocence had been abused," Lasker commented. "It is a good thing for a man
to be naïve."[59]

Lasker became a baseball owner just when Dreyfuss was intensifying his campaign against
the National Commission and he soon came to agree with Dreyfuss's thinking and to champion his ideas. The Black Sox scandal, the greatest disgrace in baseball history, hastened the
restructuring of baseball and convinced more owners that a transition was badly needed. In
1919 the American League pennant winners, the Chicago White Sox, considered one of the
best teams in baseball history, lost the World Series five games to three to the National
League's Cincinnati Reds.[60] During the following winter, news slowly began to leak out that
professional gamblers had bribed several White Sox players to "throw" the Series, earning
the Chicago team the infamous name "Black Sox," and greatly disillusioning baseball fans

nationwide. Albert Lasker felt compelled to help baseball regain the public's faith. "I believe in the principle," maintained Lasker, "that the game of baseball belongs to the public and must be governed by the public—not by the owners."[61]

In 1918, the year before the scandal, Lasker had proposed a plan that the commission be turned over completely to non-baseball men.[62] Lasker's proposal, which came to be known as the Lasker Plan, stipulated that three men who were not involved in baseball in any way should have absolute authority to run the game.[63] Many believe that the seeds for the Lasker Plan were sown during discussions with Dreyfuss. The Lasker Plan had been opposed by the American League president and commission member, Ban Johnson, and five AL club owners whose votes Johnson seemed to control—Washington, St. Louis, Detroit, Philadelphia, and Cleveland.[64] The other owners had laughed at the proposal, but after the scandal broke, they began to give the plan more serious attention.

Discussions were held constantly throughout the remainder of 1919 and into 1920 among Lasker, Wrigley, and Dreyfuss. The Lasker Plan had the backing of all the National League owners as well as the three American League owners who did not support Johnson: Charles Comiskey of the White Sox, Jacob Ruppert of the Yankees, and Harry Frazee of the Red Sox. These eleven owners threatened to add another team and form a new National League if the five holdout American League clubs did not accept the plan.[65] Following through on the threat, the backers of the Lasker Plan brought in Detroit as a twelfth club, formed the new league, and approved the plan.[66]

The next task was electing the three commissioners to run the game. Many prominent names had been suggested for the main commissioner post, but Barney Dreyfuss stood firmly behind Judge Kenesaw Mountain Landis, whose settlement of the Federal League case in 1915 had won Dreyfuss's respect.[67] Judge Landis easily won the post of high commissioner. No other board members were ever selected, as everyone soon agreed that the game needed only one commissioner with complete authority to run baseball.[68]

With this move, four of the five pro–Johnson clubs, who really did not relish a new all-out baseball war with the National League, accepted the Lasker Plan. At an owners' meeting on November 12, 1920, the last one, Phil Ball of the St. Louis Browns, capitulated, too. Landis was now officially elected to the post of high commissioner by unanimous vote of the 16 clubs.[69] In January 1921 Judge Landis signed a seven-year contract to take charge of baseball.[70] He served as commissioner for the next 25 years.[71]

Lasker considered the effort to reorganize baseball the "bitterest, most complex and most fatiguing struggle" he ever fought.[72] Once Landis was firmly in charge, Albert Lasker began to tire of the game, and in 1925 he sold his control in the Chicago Cubs to William Wrigley. Lasker's son, Edward, recalled that after selling his shares, "He never went to more than a couple of World Series games the rest of his life."[73]

It is possible that part of the reason Albert Lasker dropped out of the game after the battle over the commissioner were vicious anti–Semitic charges from respected American entrepreneur Henry Ford. Auto magnate Ford had bought an unprofitable newspaper, the *Dearborn Independent*, in 1918, publishing it from 1919 through 1927. The paper soon became notorious for its sensational content and its many anti–Semitic references.[74]

Two of Ford's most virulent attacks against Jews in baseball were aimed at Barney Dreyfuss and Albert Lasker. On September 3, 1921, in an article titled "Jewish Gamblers Corrupt American Baseball," Ford labeled Lasker's and Dreyfuss's proposal to abolish the National Commission a plot by Jews to control baseball.[75] The following week, Ford's scurrilous article was titled "Jewish Degradation of American Baseball." Again, he referred to

Dreyfuss and Lasker, stating, "Anything wrong about baseball can be traced to the Jewish influence on the game."[76] In contrast, Dreyfuss evidently relished both the fight and his victory in establishing a commissioner of baseball. When it was over, he could take satisfaction in having made another major contribution to the game and get back to concentrating on his team.[77]

From 1916, when the Sisler matter had been resolved, through 1920, when Landis was elected commissioner, the Pirates were at best a mediocre team. They ended in fourth place three times, sixth place once, and in 1917, for the first and only time under Dreyfuss's ownership, the Pirates finished in the cellar.[78]

It was not until 1925 that the Pirates won the pennant again, and they went on to defeat the Washington Senators in the World Series. Pittsburgh won the last pennant for Barney Dreyfuss in 1927, barely edging out both the St. Louis Cardinals and the New York Giants. The 1927 season also saw the only other documented instance of baseball anti–Semitism against Dreyfuss. The *New York Sun* related that star outfielder Hazen "Kiki" Cuyler entered the Pirates office on a payday during the season and discovered that Dreyfuss had fined him $50 for failing to slide into second base. Supposedly Cuyler turned on Dreyfuss's son, Sam, who was alone with him in the office, and called him "vile names which reflected on his religion." When Barney heard about the incident, he ordered his manager to bench Cuyler until he apologized. Cuyler not only refused to apologize, but he continued the abusive language. Kiki Cuyler did not play in another game the remainder of the regular season nor did Dreyfuss allow him to play in the World Series.[79] It probably didn't matter. The Yankees team, known for its "Murderers' Row," and considered by many the greatest team of all time, won the World Series in four games.

Barney Dreyfuss began to think seriously of retiring. He resigned as chairman of the National League's scheduling committee, a position he had held throughout most of his tenure as Pirates owner. In tribute to his years of compiling the annual schedule, Dreyfuss was lauded for his expertise, his evenhandedness, and the integrity he exhibited as committee chairman.[80] According to some students of the game, his schedules were models of compactness not equaled since his death.[81]

Dreyfuss looked forward to turning the team over to his son, Samuel, who had been the heir-apparent since graduating from Princeton. As vice president, treasurer, and business manager of the Pirates, Sam Dreyfuss was taking on more responsibility for the team and he and his father enjoyed a close relationship. Early in 1931, Sam became ill, but was diagnosed with simply a bad case of the flu. His condition worsened, however, and on February 19, 1931, Samuel Dreyfuss died of pneumonia, only four days before his father's sixty-fifth birthday.[82]

After Samuel's death, the grief-stricken Dreyfuss called on his son-in-law, Bill Benswanger, to handle the day-to-day operation of the Pirates. Less than a year later, on February 5, 1932, Barney Dreyfuss died. In the 32 years he owned the Pirates, the team had finished third or better 26 times, won six National League pennants, and two World Series.[83]

Tributes began pouring in. John Heydler, president of the National League, stated, "I cannot tell how deeply I feel the loss of Barney Dreyfuss. Dreyfuss discovered more players than any other man in the game. ... his abiding faith in the future of the game continued to the end."[84]

The Sporting News, in an editorial, commented, "Barney Dreyfuss was the last of the generation of history makers, and in his passing the National Game has lost an outstanding figure whose place it will be difficult to fill."[85] The Dreyfuss obituary in the 1932

Spalding Official Base Ball Guide included the following paragraph: "There was no club owner in either major league superior to Dreyfuss in practical baseball information, probably none who was his equal. He knew the percentage ratings of young and old players by heart; he could direct the executive affairs of one of the most important teams in organized baseball; he could draft a playing schedule which few do successfully; he was one of the most open-hearted owners of his league in matters of great importance."[86]

The tribute to Barney Dreyfuss which he would probably have most appreciated, came from his hometown newspaper. "Dreyfuss was a man of the highest integrity. His private life was little short of a splendid example. To have succeeded in an honorable business; to have established a prominent part in giving the American people the game closest to its heart; and to have left behind a reputation unsullied constitute the end and aim of all philosophy; the good life which leads to a happy and serene death. All these things Barney accomplished."[87]

Albert Lasker died in New York City on May 30, 1952.[88] After he left baseball in 1925, Lasker returned to the advertising business until 1942, when he sold his firm.[89] Flora, his wife of 33 years, had passed away in 1936. He had remarried in 1940, and with his second wife, Mary, he entered into a new life of public affairs and Jewish causes, in both the U.S. and Israel.

Lasker became more cognizant of being Jewish in his daily life. He chose to live in Glencoe, Illinois, rather than a more "upscale" Chicago suburb because of its proximity to a Jewish country club, and he made it a rule never to set foot in any club which barred Jews.[90] Lasker spent his last years in New York City, funding medical research for a number of diseases, including cancer, which was the cause of his death.[91]

Albert Lasker remains best known as the master of advertising, but he also holds an honored place for his contribution to baseball, the Lasker Plan, that in many ways was more long-lasting and more basic to the game's structure than any slogan he ever devised.

Certainly, neither Dreyfuss nor Lasker made any secret of their Jewish heritage. Both men were committed if not observant Jews. Still, except for Henry Ford, and in Dreyfuss's case, the isolated Cuyler incident, there seems to be no evidence of any overt anti–Semitism directed against either of them, particularly as compared with Andrew Freedman. In fact, both men are remembered for their accomplishments, the integrity with which they conducted their professional lives, their love of baseball, and their efforts to make it worthy of being called the National Pastime.

6. Baseball and Eastern European Jews

The years from the late 1880s through 1914 marked the largest immigration of Jews to the United States. During that period more than 2 million Jews arrived in America from Russia and other Eastern European countries, compared with the 150,000 mostly German Jews who had immigrated before 1880.[1] German-American Jews would play the most prominent roles in baseball during these years, but by sheer weight of numbers it would be the Eastern European Jews whose culture would shape the American Jewish community, the perception of the American Jew to his non–Jewish countrymen, and his relationship to baseball.

This great mass of Jews fled to the United States after 1880 because of a number of problems in Eastern Europe, including harsh economic conditions in Russia and Galicia, mandatory conscription into the Russian army, political oppression in Romania, and murderous anti–Semitic pogroms in Russia.[2]

In many respects, the Eastern European Jews were similar to their German counterparts. They had left their homelands with few resources, hoping for a better life for their children. Many began by peddling, but both wanted to be successful in a business or profession.

There were, however, striking differences. These "new" Jews had come from a premodern world; they looked and dressed strangely—the men with long black coats and untamed beards—and they insisted on speaking Yiddish. More Orthodox in their religious practices, they spent more time studying and going to the synagogue. German Jews came to America confident that the gentiles living here would accept them; Eastern European Jews (commonly called "Russian Jews") were not so optimistic and tended to band together more closely. Unlike the German Jews, who were geographically dispersed, most of the Russian Jews settled in Eastern cities, primarily New York City, in self-created ghettoes.[3] They and their children had a more difficult time finding their way into mainstream America.[4]

The German Jews were uncomfortable with the hundreds of thousands of destitute and oddly garbed Orthodox Russian Jews. Feeling obligated to aid them in adjusting to life in urban America, German Jews established numerous agencies and social institutions, such as the settlement houses that became models for helping Americanize the newcomers.[5]

Ironically, Russian Jews who left Europe to escape religious persecution often encountered discrimination here. These easily identifiable Jews made up close to 10 percent of all immigrants from 1881 to 1914, and as they competed for jobs gentile Americans began to portray them as the personifications of the greedy Shylock stereotype. A New York working-man vowed that "the people of this country will not be starved and driven to the wall by Jews who are guilty of all the crimes, tricks and wiles that have hitherto been unknown and unthought of by civilized humanity."[6] In the face of this anti–Semitism, the Jews struggled to achieve the vision that had brought them to America—a decent job so they could afford a good education for their children who, they dreamed, would enter a profession and earn a steady income.

Despite efforts by the settlement houses, the part of the American culture that was completely unknown to these immigrant parents was sports. Instinctively, they felt that sports, especially baseball, posed a perilous distraction to their children's studies and preparation for a career.[7] Unlike their parents, however, second-generation Russian Jews loved baseball. It was fun and it gave them an opportunity to show that they were "real Americans."

Unfortunately, not many of these younger Jews were able to play the game as it should be played. During the late nineteenth and early twentieth centuries, they used the streets as their baseball diamonds and improvised with sticks and makeshift balls, adapting their rules to conform to their playing sites. There were few, if any, baseball fields on New York's Lower East Side. Since the immigrants had neither time nor money to travel to large suburban parks, few of the second-generation, inner-city children developed the skills and experience needed to excel at the sport.[8]

Time was another factor that made it difficult for second-generation Jewish boys to play baseball. Instead of learning the intricacies of the game by playing on interscholastic teams after school, most of them had to attend afternoon Hebrew School or they had to work. Some boys could not even attend a public school, but had to find employment to supplement the family income. Jewish sportswriter Shirley Povich once wrote, "At the age when Tom, Dick and Harry are out on the corner lot playing one-old-cat and breaking in their new gloves, the young Jew is working in Papa's store, or otherwise occupied in gainful pursuit in an attempt to keep down overhead."

Parental objection also had a major effect on why so few young Russian Jews were playing baseball. Immigrant parents, especially Eastern European Jews, considered baseball a "silly sport played by men in short pants," a waste of time, and a threat to their children's future and Jewish identity. The late comedian Eddie Cantor always remembered that the worst thing a parent or grandparent could call a child was "you baseball player, you."[9]

In 1903 a Jewish father wrote to the *Forward*, a prominent Yiddish newspaper, complaining that "It makes sense to teach a child to play dominoes or chess ... but not baseball.... I want my boy to grow up to be a *mensch*, not a wild American runner."[10] The parent was surprised when he received a reply that was very similar to the advice given Barney Dreyfuss by his doctor. "Let your boys play baseball and play it well, as long as it does not interfere with their education or get them into bad company. Chess is good, but ... Baseball develops the arms, legs, and eyesight. It is played in the fresh air."[11]

Few parents were convinced by this argument. In 1919 manager Connie Mack offered a young Jew a chance to play for the Athletics. "Son," responded his father, "ballplayers are bums. If you want to play ball go ahead, but you'll have to move out of the house."[12]

Although lack of space, time, and parental support kept many Jews out of the player ranks, lack of physical ability was certainly not a factor.[13] Sportswriter Barry McCormick noted in the *St. Louis Republic* in 1903 that "He [the Jew] is athletic enough and the great number of Jewish boxers show that he is adept at one kind of sport at least."[14]

Perhaps Russian Jewish parents could limit their sons' playing baseball, but they could do little to keep them from becoming fans of the game. Second-generation Eastern European Jews could rarely afford to attend baseball games, but they avidly followed the game through the papers and by word of mouth. Baseball became a major topic of conversation for these Jewish young men, as they not only enjoyed recounting the plays and statistics, but also recognized that knowledge of the game would help them become Americanized. They idealized baseball as a democratic institution that brought to those who excelled in the sport not only credit and status among their peers, but also personal acceptance and respect for themselves and their ethnic group.[15]

For a long time these immigrant fans had almost no Jewish ballplayers to idolize, but little by little, during the first two decades of the twentieth century, more Jews began appearing on the rosters of major league teams. With a few exceptions, they came from areas such as Arkansas, Missouri, and Georgia, which were far removed from the influence of the Jewish ghetto. In these places they had been able to play the game in a proper setting and assimilate more into the mainstream of American life and culture. Here they were not criticized as men in short pants playing a child's game.[16]

These major league Jewish ballplayers of the first decades of the twentieth century quickly learned that baseball was far from the democratic ideal envisioned by the Jewish fan. Rather, the game was dominated by relatively uneducated players and managers who could be quite hostile, especially in the more rural minor leagues. Anti-Jewish epithets from opposing players and fans were common and, as in the case of Andrew Freedman, considered trivial by the press. In addition to ingrained prejudice, old-timers resented the competition from these second-generation Jewish, Slavic and Italian immigrants, fearful that they would take away their jobs, force down salaries, and reduce the status of baseball.[17]

The Jews who became players during the first two decades of the twentieth century, when anti–Semitism was prevalent, developed ways to ward off bigotry. Some ignored it, some fought back, and some changed their surnames to hide their ethnicity and avoid discrimination.

7. A Cohen by Any Other Name

During the twentieth century the number of Jews playing in the major leagues increased. Prior to 1900 only six Jews had made it to the majors, and only Lipman Pike had been an outstanding player. Between 1900 and 1930, an average of four Jewish ball players reached the majors each year.[1] During the first two decades of the twentieth century, a small number were good, and some achieved success in the minor leagues, but few had long major league careers.[2]

For the players during this period, anti–Semitism from fans and other players, even their own teammates on occasion, was virtually a daily fact of life even in the big leagues, and especially in small and often rural minor league towns. Although few admitted it, some Jews reacted to this prejudice by assuming non–Jewish surnames. Ford Frick wrote in 1925, "During the early days of this century the Jewish boys had tough sledding in the majors and many of them changed their names."[3] Baseball historians speculated that in some cases they did so at the urging of owners who feared fans would stereotype them as "temperamentally" and physically unfit for the game.[4]

Five of the eleven players profiled during this time period changed their names. Three of the five were originally named Cohen.

Harry "Klondike" Kane

The earliest player to change his name was Harry Kane, who was born Harry Cohen in Hamburg, Arkansas, on July 27, 1883, and somewhere along the line acquired the nickname "Klondike." A good left-handed pitcher, Kane set a number of pitching records in the minor leagues, but he never really made it big in the majors.

The Philadelphia Phillies signed Kane in 1900 and assigned him to their farm team in Denver. Because of a salary dispute, he left Denver and over the next three seasons played for teams in Friar's Point, Mississippi, San Francisco (before the Pacific Coast League was organized), Los Angeles; and finally Springfield in the Missouri Valley League. While pitching for San Francisco, Kane defeated future Hall of Famer Rube Waddell twice in one day, in two eleven-inning contests.[5] With Springfield, he compiled a record of 20 wins and only one loss. Three of his victories were one-hitters, including one that lasted 20 innings.[6]

Kane made his major league debut with the St. Louis Browns on August 8, 1902. Approximately two weeks before, a story about Kane in *The Sporting News* noted, "His name is Cohen and he assumed that of Kane, when he became a semi-professional, because he fancied that there was a popular and professional prejudice against Hebrews as ball players."[7]

Kane pitched in only four games for St. Louis in 1902, including one complete game. He lost his only decision and finished the season with an earned run average of 5.48.[8]

The following year Kane was back in the minor leagues with Springfield once more, and he pitched three no-hitters. He also pitched a doubleheader, shutting out the opponent in both games.[9] His statistics in the minor leagues earned him another promotion to the majors with the Detroit Tigers late in 1903. Two of his three appearances were complete games, but he lost them both.[10]

For the next two years, Kane was again outstanding with several minor league teams, at one point hurling 52 consecutive scoreless innings for Clarksdale in the Delta League. At the tail end of the 1905 season, the Phillies brought Kane to the parent team, where he finally won his first major league game and only shutout, defeating the St. Louis Cardinals 6–0 in their home park. He finished the season with a record of 1–1.[11]

Harry Kane's last year as a player in the major leagues was 1906. Despite high expectations, in the six games he pitched for the Phillies he won one and lost three with a 3.86 earned run average, and in mid-season returned to Savannah, one of his former minor league teams. Although the Cleveland Indians bought his contract, Kane chose to stay with Savannah until the end of the season and never returned to the major leagues.[12]

When illness forced him to abandon baseball, Kane moved to Arizona, where he made a complete recovery and then became an umpire in the Texas League, He established a record of never missing an assignment in nine years.[13] By 1931 Kane had worked his way up to the Pacific Coast League and as a former San Francisco player he quickly became one of the most popular umpires in that league. One local newspaper described Kane "as just what the Pacific Coast needs. A guy with some action but who doesn't try to steal the limelight from the players."[14]

On September 13, 1932, Kane was umpiring a game in Portland when he suddenly collapsed on the field. He had suffered a heart attack

Harry "Klondike" Kane was born Harry Cohen in 1883, and toiled for four clubs in the first decade of the twentieth century. After pitching for a number of teams in the minor leagues, he became an esteemed minor league umpire (courtesy National Baseball Hall of Fame Library, Cooperstown, N.Y.).

and a physician recommended he remain in bed. Two days later his fellow umpires stopped by his hotel room to check on his condition. They found him dead, the victim of another heart attack. Kane was 49 years old.[15]

As far as anyone knew, Kane was survived by no immediate family. His memorial services were conducted by a Catholic priest and, with his fellow umpires as his six pallbearers, Kane was buried in a Catholic cemetery.[16]

In addition to Harry Kane, four other players during the period 1900 to 1920—Phil Cooney, Henry Bostick, Ed Corey, and Jesse Baker—also changed their names. Their tenures in the majors were even shorter than Kane's.

Phil Cooney

Phil Cooney was not only the second major leaguer born Cohen to change his name, he was one of the few from New York City. Philip Clarence Cohen was born on September 14, 1882, to Philip and Julia Cohen. Officially five feet eight inches tall and weighing 155 pounds, with a pair of legs that looked like pipe stems, Cooney was described as one of the smallest men to make it to the major leagues.[17] He appeared in only one major league game. Late in September 1905, playing third base for the New York Highlanders, Cooney went 0 for 3 and after that single game returned to the minor leagues. His minor league career was notable for two events.

In 1909 Cooney was playing for Portland when the Medford, Oregon, fans made him the target of frequent profanity. After ignoring them for most of the game, Cooney answered back. Several fans jumped on the field, and began to fight with Cooney. Medford's mayor held Cooney responsible, insisting that he be arrested and also fined $15 for using abusive language.[18] The incident was widely covered in the newspapers, but no evidence of anti–Semitism was ever mentioned.

The high spot of Cooney's career was likely the game where he became the first Western Leaguer to execute an unassisted triple play. On July 7, 1917, Cooney was playing second base for the Omaha Rourkes against the Denver Bears. In the sixth inning, with players on at first and second, Cooney caught a line drive, tagged the base runner who had started from first, and then ran to second base to tag the other runner before he could return to the bag.[19]

Cooney, who had a long minor league career, married in 1919 and moved to Paterson, New Jersey. He died in New York City on October 6, 1957; in 1967, he was elected to the Paterson Sports Hall of Fame.[20]

Henry Bostick

Henry Bostick's birth name was not Cohen but he was another player of this era who changed his name when he played in the majors. Henry Landers Lipschitz was born on January 12, 1895, in Boston. According to his official baseball record, which is all that remains of his career, Bostick played two games at third base for the Philadelphia Athletics in 1915. He had no hits in his seven times at bat although he did drive in two runs. There is no evidence of his playing with any other major or minor league team before or after the 1915 season. Bostick died in Denver, Colorado, September 16, 1968.[21]

Ed Corey

Another Cohen who assumed a new name when he entered baseball, Edward Norman Corey changed not only his surname but both given names as well. Born Abraham Simon Cohen in Chicago on July 13, 1899, Ed Corey was among the few to admit he altered his name early in his career because of ethnic slurs from "unintelligent" fans. Ten years after his death, Corey's wife told a Hall of Fame researcher that Corey and his two brothers all agreed to the name change to help them advance in their chosen professions—baseball, medicine, and business, respectively. They derived their new name, Corey, by replacing the *H* in Cohen with an *R* and the *N* with a *Y*.[22]

Chicago White Sox scouts spotted the six-foot, 170-pound right-hander while he was pitching for semipro teams in the Chicago area. They particularly liked Corey's spitball, which was a legal pitch at the time.[23] White Sox manager Clarence Rowland was also impressed by Corey's semipro record in 1917 of striking out 241 batters in 26 games and defeating the usually victorious traveling Negro team, the American Giants, twice by the score of 2 to 1.[24]

An accident during spring training in 1918 cut short Corey's major league career. In an exhibition game in Mineral Wells, Texas, Corey broke the small bones in his right ankle when his spikes caught home plate as he was attempting to slide. Manager Rowland was optimistic, saying, "As soon as he can work out again I want him to start getting into condition. We all believe that he is a comer and will develop into a high class pitcher."[25] *The Sporting News*, however, wasn't so certain: "The injury to Ed Corey was a hard blow, as he was a sure qualifier. If this young spitball pitcher's fractured ankle mends in six weeks, he'll be lucky."[26]

The newspaper's prediction proved accurate. Corey's only major league appearance occurred on July 2, 1918. He pitched two innings, allowing two hits and one run and compiling an earned run average of 4.50.[27]

PHILA. INQUIRER
MAR 24, 1915

HENRY BOSTICK

Henry Bostick was born Henry Lipschitz in 1895 and was one of the players to change his name when he entered baseball. He appeared in two games for the Philadelphia Athletics in 1915 (courtesy Marc Okkonen).

In 1919 the White Sox assigned the hurler to Louisville of the American Association. In 1922 he joined the outlaw Racine Belles, not as a pitcher but as an outfielder. One of Corey's final appearances in baseball was in 1932 in the Wisconsin-Illinois Baseball League for the Milwaukee Red Sox.[28]

Ed Corey died August 17, 1970, in Kenosha, Wisconsin; he was survived by his wife, two sons, a daughter and three grandchildren.[29]

Jesse Baker

The diminutive Jesse Baker was born Michael Myron Silverman in Cleveland, on March 4, 1895. He left his parents' clothing business to pursue his dream of playing professional baseball. Like Ed Corey, Baker's major league career was ended by an injury. On September 14, 1919, Baker made his only appearance in the majors, playing shortstop for the Washington Senators in a game against the Detroit Tigers. While covering second base, Baker was spiked by Tiger star Ty Cobb, forcing him to leave the game before he could be credited with an official at bat. Baker did, however, get credit for a run batted in.[30]

Baker, who also used the first name Mike, played in the minor leagues in 1925 and 1926. In 1925 he hit .299 for the London Tecumsehs of the Michigan-Ontario League and as their "peppery little manager" and shortstop led the team to the playoffs, where they lost the final game to Hamilton. The league dissolved the following year, and Baker played for three other teams in 1926.[31]

Eventually Baker moved to Los Angeles, where he became a regular fixture at racetracks and prizefights, and a friend of Damon Runyon, Walter Winchell, and the Marx brothers. He died July 29, 1976, in Los Angeles.[32]

Other Jewish ballplayers from this era did not change their names. They all were of German-Jewish background, and from the Midwest or South. Two actually had impressive major league careers.

Barney Pelty

Barney Pelty was one of the first Jewish players in the American League and one of the best Jewish players of this era. A record-setting right-handed pitcher, he not only did not change his name but proudly bore the nickname the "Yiddish curver." Although his won-loss record was below .500, Pelty was considered one of the best American League pitchers of his day. He played for the St. Louis Browns from 1903 to 1912 and for the Washington Senators in 1912, appearing in 281 games with a 92–117 record.[33]

Pelty was born on September 10, 1880, in Farmington, Missouri, a small town approximately 60 miles south of St. Louis. He was the youngest of five children born to Samuel and Helena (Haas) Pelty. His father immigrated to the United States from Prussia at the age of 17 to avoid military duty in the Prussian army. He became a cigar maker in St. Louis and eventually moved to Farmington, where he opened a cigar store. Pelty's mother was a more observant Jew than her husband and most likely was the parent who taught the children about Judaism. The Peltys were the only Jewish family in Farmington, a town without a synagogue. Although the Peltys were unable to practice their religion in Farmington, they never denied that they were Jews.[34]

According to Pelty's parents, Barney was a born pitcher who began to play ball while in grammar school. He received a scholarship to Carleton College in Farmington, where he pitched for the varsity team. He also met his future wife, Eva Warsing, at Carleton. In 1902 Pelty signed with Nashville of the Southern League but, because of an injury to his pitching arm, quit the team and returned to Farmington. After his arm healed, he finished the season with a semipro team in Cairo, Illinois.

Pelty began the 1903 season with the Cedar Rapids club in the Three I League, but soon scouts from both the Boston Red Sox and the St. Louis Browns went to Cedar Rapids to check out the young hurler. In August Pelty joined the Browns. He made his major league debut in relief against the New York Giants on August 20, 1903, retiring the last two batters and saving the game for Brownie starter Wee Willie Sudhoff.[35] Two days later, Barney Pelty made his first start for the Browns in a game against Boston at Sportsman's Park. He won the game 2–1, defeating veteran pitcher Bill Dinneen, a future

Barney Pelty, who proudly bore the nickname "The Yiddish Curver," ended his 10-year major league career with a 92–117 record, but many considered him one of the finest American League pitchers of his day. His lifetime earned-run average was an excellent 2.63, and in two years was below two runs per game (courtesy National Baseball Hall of Fame Library, Cooperstown, N.Y.).

American League umpire. Pelty finished his rookie season in 1903 with a record of 3–3, all complete games.[36] Complete games were Pelty's trademark; during his career, he would finish 175 of the 217 games he started.[37] At the end of the 1903 season the *Washington* Post noted, "St. Louis fans are delighted with the showing their new pitcher Pelty has made."[38]

Pelty's most impressive pitch was his curve ball. Newspapers, noting that opposing batters were often unable to solve his curve even in games he lost, soon dubbed him the "Yiddish curver." Pelty was also recognized for his excellent control and his ability to deftly field bunts and turn a double play.[39]

In 1906 Pelty had his best season with the Browns, posting a record of 16 and 11 and the lowest earned run average of his career, 1.59.[40] Pelty also came close to pitching a no-hitter on July 4 that year, only to give up a hit in the ninth when fill-in Brownie shortstop Ben Koehler bobbled a hard shot. Ironically, it was Koehler's only game at short. He had come in from the outfield to replace the regular shortstop, Bobby Wallace, who was injured earlier in the game.[41]

Pelty's record dropped to 30 and 36 over the next three seasons as Browns manager, Jimmy McAleer, began to overuse his pitcher. From 1907 to 1909, Pelty made 67 starts and completed 53 games. It was evident that his arm was tiring from overuse, yet during this three-year period, Pelty's highest earned run average was only 2.57.[42]

In 1910 the St. Louis Browns finished the season in last place, losing 107 games. It was also Pelty's worst full season with St. Louis. For the first time, he finished with an ERA above three and his won-lost record was 5–11. In addition, it marked the first time he had two consecutive seasons in which he walked more batters than he struck out.[43] The brightest spot for Pelty in the 1910 season was his shutout victory over the Chicago White Sox and their ace pitcher, Ed Walsh, on July 1, in the first game ever played at White Sox Park II, later known as Comiskey Park.[44]

Despite rumors he would be released, Pelty stayed with the Browns in 1911 as the team once again lost 107 games. This year, Pelty posted a respectable earned run average of 2.97, the best on the team, even though his record was 7–15.[45]

After he lost five of his first six starts in 1912, the Browns sold Pelty to the Washington Senators for $2,500. Pelty would be the first of a number of Jews to play for Washington. The *Washington Post* praised Senators manager Clark Griffith for the purchase, noting that Pelty never had much chance with the Browns but that "He is a careful, crafty right-hander, an exceptionally good fielder of his position, and a willing worker."[46] *Post* columnist Joe S. Jackson called him "one of the wisest pitchers in the game."[47] For his part, Pelty was excited to join what he considered Griffith's hustling team. "I am mighty glad of the switch which has made me one of the Washington club, and I expect to finish the year with an average on the right side of the .500 mark."[48]

Unfortunately, Pelty's expectations for 1912 were higher than his accomplishments. He won only one game and lost four, and in August the Senators sold Pelty to the Baltimore Orioles of the International League. He never regained his skill, and after moving from the Orioles to the Minneapolis Millers of the Northern League, and back to the Orioles, Pelty stopped playing professional baseball. During his ten years in the major leagues, almost all of them with one of the worst teams in baseball, Pelty had won 92 games, lost 117 and had an enviable earned run average of 2.63.[49] If he encountered anti–Semitism as a player, it was never made public.

Pelty returned to Farmington after his retirement and ran the notions and bookstore founded by his parents. After the Senators released him, Pelty had written Reds president Garry Herrmann, offering to scout for Cincinnati.[50] In addition to a little scouting, Pelty coached several semipro baseball teams, including the Farmington Blues. He also coached the Farmington High School baseball team and was active in state and local politics.

Pelty pitched his last game in 1937—losing an exhibition game to Hall of Famer Grover Cleveland Alexander.[51] Pelty died in Farmington May 24, 1939, from a cerebral hemorrhage. After his death, Barney Pelty was honored by his community as one of only six people considered significant in the town's history.[52]

Erskine Mayer

Erskine Mayer, the other impressive Jewish player of ability during the early twentieth century, was also a right-handed pitcher. He made his major league debut in 1912, Barney Pelty's last year in the majors. Unlike Pelty, Mayer pitched for winners, which enabled him to become the most successful Jewish pitcher of his era, achieving a number of records both as a pitcher and as a Jewish pitcher. He was the first Jewish hurler to win more than 20 games, and the last Jewish 20-game winner until 1963, when Sandy Koufax won 25 games.[53]

James Erskine Mayer was born January 16, 1889, in Atlanta, the second of three sons. His maternal grandmother, who traced her ancestry back to the Mayflower, was a converted Jew; his paternal grandparents were musicians who had emigrated from Germany. His father,

Isaac Mayer, was a concert pianist and music teacher who spent his spare time playing baseball with his three sons. Mayer studied engineering for three years at Georgia Tech until, in 1910, the Georgia Crackers, impressed with his pitching talent, offered him a contract. He dropped out of college and was assigned to Fayetteville of the East Carolina League, where he appeared in 20 games that year with a won-lost record of 15–2.[54] For the next two years, Mayer pitched for Atlanta, Albany, and Portsmouth. Before the Phillies called him to the majors in 1912, he compiled an amazing record for Portsmouth of 26–9 with 226 strikeouts and a stretch of 17 successive wins.[55]

With the Phillies, the 6-foot, 168-pound Mayer developed an underhand and sidearm curve ball delivery that was so slick that Brooklyn Dodger manager Wilbert Robinson nicknamed Mayer "Eelskin." Robinson had great respect for Mayer, but he wasn't loath to further the Philadelphia-Brooklyn rivalry at Mayer's expense. The Atlanta-born Mayer resented any ribbing about the South, so Robinson and his team would whistle "Marching Through Georgia," and according to Robinson, "that would always get a rise out of Mayer."[56]

Mayer's first two seasons with the Phillies were unimpressive as he compiled a record of 9 wins and 10 losses.[57] Mayer established himself, however, as one of the National League's leading pitchers in 1914. Although the Phillies finished the season in sixth place with only 74 victories, Mayer won 21 of those games. Teammate and future Hall of Fame pitcher Grover Cleveland Alexander won 27. "Every time I pitched well," remarked Mayer, "Alexander topped me."[58] (As an interesting side note to the 1914 season, that year Honus Wagner became the second player in the history of baseball to collect 3,000 hits with a double off Mayer.[59])

Erskine Mayer was the first Jewish pitcher to win more than 20 games in a single season, winning 21 games in both 1914 and 1915. He also was one of three pitchers (the other two were Grover Cleveland Alexander and Steve Carlton) to start two games in a World Series for the Philadelphia Phillies (courtesy George Grantham Bain Collection; Library of Congress).

In 1915 the Phillies won the first National League pennant in their history, due to the pitching of Mayer and Alexander. For the second consecutive year, Erskine Mayer won 21 games, compiling an earned run average of only 2.36. Alexander surpassed him once more with 31 games. Mayer could brag that he could at least hit better than Alexander, with 21 hits, including two doubles, one triple and a home run, for a .239 batting average. He almost equaled the team average, as the 1915 Phillies batting mark was a mere .247, a record that would stand until the Mets won the 1969 pennant with a team batting average of .242.[60]

That year was a highlight for Mayer in several other ways. Mayer married on July 4, during the 1915 season.[61] He was also the starting pitcher in the first World Series game attended by a President. Woodrow Wilson, a great baseball fan, attended the second game of the series, watching Mayer, who had allowed ten hits through the first eight innings, go into the ninth with the game tied 1–1.[62] In that inning, the Red Sox pushed across the winning run, giving Mayer the loss, 2–1.

Alexander was scheduled to start the fifth game of the series, but came down with an arm injury. At the last moment Phillies manager Pat Moran rushed Mayer into the game. Unrested and unprepared, Mayer was bombarded and lasted only two and a third innings before leaving the game. The Phillies lost the game and the series four games to one, although Mayer was not the losing pitcher.[63] Nonetheless, that game made him, along with Grover Cleveland Alexander and Steve Carlton, one of only three Philadelphia Phillies pitchers to start two World Series games.

Erskine Mayer's most productive years definitely were 1914 and 1915, when he won 42 games. A teammate later stated that, after his marriage, "...he had trouble finishing games."[64] Whether or not that was the cause, Mayer would win only 40 games the last four years he pitched in the majors. He was a .500 pitcher in 1916, finishing the season with a record of 7–7. The Phillies ended in second place that year, two and a half games behind the Brooklyn Dodgers, and many fans felt that Mayer's mediocre season cost his team the pennant.[65] Mayer improved in 1917, compiling a record of 11–6 with an earned run average of 2.76 in 28 games.

In June 1918, Pittsburgh traded pitcher Elmer Jacobs to the Phillies for Erskine Mayer.[66] That year Mayer participated in one of the most remarkable games in major league history. Starting for the Pirates against the Boston Braves, Mayer pitched 16 consecutive scoreless innings before Wilbur Cooper relieved him. Pittsburgh eventually won the game in the twenty-first inning, 2–0.[67] Mayer's record in 1918 was 16–7, with both the Phillies and the Pirates, and his combined earned run average was a low 2.65.[68]

Mayer began the 1919 season with the Pittsburgh Pirates, winning five games and losing three, before being traded in midseason to the Chicago White Sox, who were driving to win the American League pennant and needed a pitcher with Mayer's experience.

Erskine Mayer made one appearance in the 1919 World Series. Pitching in relief of Lefty Williams, he worked one inning and gave up one walk and one unearned run.[69] That one appearance, however, made Erskine Mayer the first and only Jewish pitcher, and one of only a few major league pitchers, to pitch in a World Series in both the American and National Leagues.[70]

This, of course, was the year of the infamous Black Sox scandal, when several of Mayer's teammates took bribes to lose the 1919 World Series to the Cincinnati Reds. Mayer had been completely ignorant of the "fix" and was never accused of any involvement in the conspiracy. Considering the anti–Semitism in the country and in baseball in the early 1920s, Mayer was indeed fortunate.[71]

Mayer was heartbroken when he learned that the charges against his teammates were true. He left the majors and returned to Atlanta, where he pitched and won one game for the Crackers in 1920, and then retired permanently from baseball.[72] Some claim that Mayer quit because he was physically worn out. More than 40 years later Mayer's wife set the record straight. "Erk loved baseball for the true sport it afforded and he felt if a game had been thrown he was through with baseball."[73]

Mayer retired to California, where he became a successful sales manager. He died March 10, 1957. Mayer's career statistics are very impressive. His won-lost record for eight seasons was 91–70 with a career earned run average of 2.96. He issued 345 walks while striking out 482 and completed 93 of the 164 games he started.[74] Mayer might have been better known had his Phillies roommate, Grover Cleveland Alexander, not overshadowed him.

Sam Mayer

Sam Mayer, younger brother of Erskine Mayer, made his major league debut with the Washington Senators in 1915. Although Sam played only eleven games in the big leagues, he and Erskine became the second set of Jewish brothers in the majors.

The youngest of three boys, Sam was born February 28, 1893, in Atlanta to Isaac Mayer and his wife. Like Erskine, he loved baseball. Ineligible for some unknown reason to play at Georgia Tech, he left school and turned pro, beginning his minor league career in the Northeastern Arkansas League. Mayer was then transferred to Fulton, Kentucky, of the Kitty League, where he batted .400 and helped the club win the pennant. Sam kept advancing through the minors, including stints in Kansas City in the American Association and Topeka in the Western League. Although not considered a heavy hitter, his lifetime average for all minor leagues was around .300.[75]

While he was with Kansas City in 1915, several teams became interested in Mayer, including Brooklyn of the Federal League and the New York Giants, whose manager, John McGraw, was always looking for a Jewish player to attract large crowds to the Polo Grounds. The Chicago Cubs actually made Mayer an offer, but Sam decided to go with Clark Griffith of the Washington Senators.[76]

Mayer entered the majors as a right fielder for the Senators on September 4, 1915, going 0 for 4 at the plate, but his talents as a defensive player were more notable than his hitting. Two days later, Mayer played in both games of a double header against the Philadelphia Athletics. Mayer got his first major league hit in the first game and in the second, hit his only homerun. The Senators won both games. In the eleven games Mayer played, he drove in four runs and got a total of seven hits in 29 official at bats for a .241 batting average.[77]

At the conclusion of the 1915 season, Mayer was sent back to Atlanta, where he was a defensive star from 1916 to 1922. Playing in center field, Mayer patrolled the outfield so well that fans said of him, "He played all fields."[78]

In 1918 Sam Mayer bought part interest in the Crackers and was not only the team's captain but also its business manager. In 1920 Sam was reunited with his brother for Erskine's very last professional game.[79] During these years, Mayer also scouted for his old boss, Clark Griffith, and throughout World War I devoted much of his time to teaching baseball in training camps.[80]

Sam Mayer continued playing minor league ball during the 1920s for a number of teams, including Little Rock, Louisville, and San Antonio. Sam retired from playing in 1929 and became a real estate salesman, but he never completely got away from baseball. In 1958, Mayer managed a team for the *Atlanta Journal's* high-school All Star tournament. Although his team lost, he felt like a winner. "We had forty boys," said Mayer, "and they were from different environments. We never had a minute's trouble."[81]

Mayer, who suffered from diabetes late in life, died of a heart attack on July 1, 1962. He was 69 years old. Earl Mann, the Atlanta Crackers batboy during Sam's playing days, said what many people thought. "I'm sorry to hear it. He was a great fellow, as well as a great outfielder."[82]

Jake Pitler

When Erskine Mayer was traded to the Pittsburgh Pirates in 1918, he became a team-mate of Jake Pitler. Mayer and Pitler were the only Jewish players who played for Barney Dreyfuss, the Jewish owner of the Pirates.[83] Pitler turned out to have a longer and more important career in major league baseball after his playing days ended.

Jacob Albert Pitler was born April 22, 1894, in New York City, one of seven children (three boys and four girls). The family soon moved to Pittsburgh, where Jake grew up. Two of Pitler's brothers were active in sports. Harry became a good lightweight who fought as Johnny Ray; he later managed prominent boxer Billy Conn. Jake's brother Dave became a varsity football player at the University of Pittsburgh in 1918.

To help the family, all three of the Pitler boys sold peanuts, soda, and newspapers at Pittsburgh's Forbes Field.[84] Many of the Pirate players befriended Jake, and he even occasionally worked out with them in their pregame practice. Jake soon became a star in the semipro leagues of Pittsburgh.[85]

Pitler began his professional baseball career in Connelsville, Pennsylvania, in 1912. The next year, for Jackson, Michigan, he played both shortstop and second base. "I fielded pretty good," Pitler admitted, "but I didn't hit too well."[86] Pitler joined the Chattanooga Look-outs at the tail end of the 1915 season and remained with Chattanooga until 1917.[87]

Pitler's major league debut at second base for the Pirates occurred on May 30, 1917. His first game was promising; he singled, stole a base, and scored a run. Jake had trouble with major league pitching even though he managed to hit two triples off Grover Cleveland Alexander. Pitler's average over 109 games in 1917 was a meager .233 with no home runs and 23 runs batted in.[88]

Pitler played in only three games in 1918. In one game he stole two bases in one inning to tie a major-league record. When he was farmed out to Jersey City, Pitler refused to go to a lower classification club, jumping his contract to play "outlaw" baseball in Pennsylvania. Baseball banned him from playing in any major league farm system for nine years, but ultimately lifted the ban.[89]

From 1929 to 1939, Pitler managed a number of minor league teams, including Hazelton, Scranton, Springfield, Portsmouth, and Elmira. In 1939 Pitler got his "big break" when the Brooklyn Dodgers asked him to manage Olean, New York, one of their farm clubs in the newly organized Pony League in Class D baseball.[90] He remained a coach for various teams in the Brooklyn Dodgers organization until he became the first-base coach of the Dodgers, a position he held until 1957. He coached the Dodgers under four managers and befriended a generation of Dodger players.

When Walter O'Malley moved the Dodgers to Los Angeles in 1958, Pitler refused to leave Brooklyn, but he did accept a nominal position as Dodgers scout in the New York area, although he never again coached.

Pitler never hid the fact that he was Jewish. Historian Michael H. Ebner recalled years later that Jake Pitler always made him proud because he never coached on the two most holy Jewish holidays, Rosh Hashanah and Yom Kippur.[91] Nevertheless, Pitler said that he encountered little anti–Semitism. "There was an occasional wise guy, but for the most part I received wonderful treatment."[92]

Brooklyn fans gave Coach Pitler two "nights" at Ebbets Field. Pitler turned over all gifts from one of these celebrations to a leading nonsectarian institution, the Beth El Hospital in Brooklyn, for the establishment of a special Jake Pitler Therapy Room for disabled children. In response, leading New York rabbi Joseph L. Wise praised Pitler for his sportsmanship, his devotion to humanitarian causes, and his faith in observing the High Holy Days.[93]

Jake Pitler died February 3, 1968, in Binghamton, New York, at the age of 73. Burt Shotton, one of the four Dodger managers for whom Pitler worked, once said of his coach, "He's one of the hardest workers I've ever seen. He lives baseball, and he was a wonderful influence on young players."[94]

Jake Pitler played two years for the Pittsburgh Pirates and he and Erskine Mayer were the only two Jewish players on the Pirates roster during the years when Barney Dreyfuss owned the team. Pitler is best remembered for the years he coached first base for both the Brooklyn Dodger farm clubs and the parent club. When the Dodgers moved to Los Angeles, Pitler stayed in his native New York to scout for the Dodgers (courtesy National Baseball Hall of Fame Library, Cooperstown, N.Y.).

Moxie Manuel

Moxie Manuel is still another Jewish pitcher of this era; his claim to fame was his purported ability to pitch with either hand. Mark Garfield "Moxie" Manuel was the son of a German-Jewish immigrant, although his mother was a native of Illinois. Moxie was born in Metropolis, Illinois, on October 16, 1881, and began his baseball career in Vicksburg in the Cotton States League in 1903. Pitching for Vicksburg, he appeared in 34 games and ended the season with a record of 21–11. Manuel spent parts of the 1904 season with Baton Rouge and New Orleans and was brought to the majors by the Washington Senators. He appeared in three games for the Senators, all in relief, but had no record.[95]

Manuel pitched for New Orleans in both 1906 and 1907, appearing in a total of 66 games, with 37 wins and 26 losses during those two years. According to his son, the 5-foot, 11-inch, 170-pound pitcher was one of the principal attractions for the Ladies Day games there.[96]

Moxie was a right-handed batter, but he told a reporter in 1907, "Sure, I can slam over with one hand as good as with another. When a right-handed batter is at the plate, I serve 'em with my right hand. When a left-handed batter is at the plate, I become a southpaw. That keeps 'em all guessing."[97] Moxie's son, John, in a letter to the National Baseball Library at Cooperstown, wrote that he had clippings which confirmed that his father was ambidextrous and that in the minors he would often pitch doubleheaders—one right-handed and one left-handed—sometimes posting shut-out victories in both games.[98]

Although records don't indicate how he pitched, while with New Orleans in June 1907 Manuel did shutout the Birmingham Barons in both halves of a doubleheader with identical scores of 1–0.[99] Manuel issued no walks and allowed a total of only eight hits in the two games. He also compiled a string of 58 consecutive shutout innings, a new Southern Association record.[100]

Chicago White Sox scouts brought Moxie to the attention of the White Sox owner, Charlie Comiskey, and Manuel returned to the majors in 1908. He pitched 18 games for Chicago that year, finishing with a record of 3–4 and a respectable earned run average of 3.28.[101]

One of Manuel's three victories in 1908 set a precedent. On June 14 the Yankees were leading the White Sox 4–2 when Manuel relieved the Chisox starter, Frank Smith, in the fifth inning and held the Yankees scoreless through the top of the eighth. Ed Hahn pinch-hit for Manuel in the bottom of the inning, and the White Sox scored three runs to go on top 5–4. The official scorer gave the victory to the White Sox pitcher who completed the game in the top of the ninth, but American League President Ban Johnson overruled that decision and gave Moxie Manuel the victory. According to baseball historian Eugene C. Murdock, "The American League adopted the 'Manuel Rule' for giving victories to the pitcher whose team went ahead during the inning for which he was pinch-hit."[102]

Statistics don't show if Manuel ever used his ability to pitch from either side in the majors, but his son, John, did confirm that his father was the pitcher in an old baseball story. Philadelphia's Connie Mack once told Hall of Fame pitcher Rube Waddell to keep an eye on Manuel because "he's ambidextrous." Supposedly, Rube replied, "You're telling me. He would just as soon kill you as look at you."[103]

Unfortunately, the White Sox had a number of pitchers better than Manuel. Doc White and Nick Altrock had earned run averages of 2.55 and 2.71, respectively, and While Sox ace Ed Walsh had won 40 games with an ERA of 1.42.[104] Manuel returned to the minors in 1909 and pitched for various teams—Birmingham, Mobile, Great Falls, Missoula, Kewanee, Bloomington and Henderson—until he retired from baseball after the 1913 season.[105]

After leaving baseball, Manuel took a job as a clerk. On April 26, 1924, he died in Memphis, Tennessee, of peritonitis at the age of 43.[106]

Guy Zinn

Guy Zinn has the unique distinction of being the only Jewish player in the short-lived Federal League and the only Jew to play in three major leagues: the National League, the American League and the Federal League.

Zinn was born in Hollbrook, West Virginia, on February 13, 1887, one of five children.[107] He began his professional baseball career with Grafton of the Pennsylvania-West Virginia

League in 1909 as an outfielder, compiling a batting average of .294 in 88 games. The following year he played for three teams, Memphis and Toledo of the American Association, and Macon of the South Atlantic League. In August 1910 Zinn was with Altoona when he was sold to the New York Highlanders, later known as the Yankees, for $1,000.[108]

He appeared in only nine games in 1911, but in 1912 he hit .262 in 106 games and tied the existing club record of six home runs, earning him the nickname "The Gunner."[109] He also tied a Major League record by stealing home twice in one game, a record he still shares.[110]

At the end of the 1912 season, the Yankees sold Zinn to Rochester of the International League.[111] Late the following season, Zinn returned to the majors with the Boston Braves, where he played 36 games and finished the year with a .297 batting average. Despite his hitting, the Braves sold him to Louisville. Zinn never reported there, opting instead to try out for Balti-

more in the newly founded Federal League, which was building its rosters by "raiding" the established leagues for players. In January 1914 Guy Zinn became one of the first players to leave the National League and sign with the Federal League.[112]

Guy Zinn scored the first run in Baltimore's Terrapin Park in 1915.[113] In 61 games in 1914 Zinn hit .280, driving in 25 runs and hitting three home runs.[114] The Terrapins considered Zinn one of the best players on the club, but his season was cut short when his foot caught on the third-base bag and he snapped a bone in his left ankle.[115] He recovered from his injury and returned to the Terrapins in 1915, hitting .269 in 102 games, and recording five home runs and 43 runs batted in.[116]

The Federal League collapsed after the 1915 season. From 1916 to 1922 Zinn played for a number of minor league teams and then retired from the game.[117]

Guy Zinn holds the distinction of being the only Jewish baseball player to play for the American League, the National League and the defunct Federal League, all in a span of five years. After the Federal League folded, Zinn played for a number of minor league teams before retiring in 1922 (courtesy Steve Steinberg).

Guy Zinn died October 6, 1949, at the home of his brother, in Clarksburg, West Virginia. He was 62 years old.[118]

During the next decades, there would be more Jewish involvement in baseball, and many participants would continue to experience anti–Semitism. Some would still react by adopting less Jewish-sounding names, but that practice would become less common as time went on.

8. Keepers of the Stats

Statistics have been an integral part of baseball since Henry Chadwick insisted on a complete record of the games. A variety of baseball statistical associations have been established to document not only records of each game but also of each player from college through the majors, various pitching, hitting, fielding and pitching reports, and the fascinating "firsts" and "lasts" that exist in virtually every imaginable circumstance. Although they were hardly the first to keep statistics, during the first two decades of the twentieth century three Jews founded leading statistical organizations producing data that is still relied upon today.

Louis Heilbroner and the Baseball Blue Book

The *Baseball Bluebook*, published annually since 1909, is probably best known today for records of every college, semipro, and professional player in the game, and is considered the official administrative manual of the major and minor leagues. Founded by a diminutive German-American Jew, Louis Heilbroner, it was only one of his contributions to the game.

Louis Heilbroner was born in Fort Wayne, Indiana, on July 4, 1861. He was one of four children, but the only son of Samuel and Amelia Mayer Heilbroner, Prussian immigrants who had come to the United States the previous year.[1] Louis's father was one of Fort Wayne's most highly respected citizens. A retired merchant, he had helped found Fort Wayne's Jewish temple and, at the time of his death, Samuel Heilbroner was the oldest Jewish resident of Allen County.[2]

Louis Heilbroner was involved in several business activities in Fort Wayne before 1896. That year he began working for brothers Frank and Stanley Robison, who owned Fort Wayne's street car company, as well as a park outside the city that featured band pavilions, riverboats, roller coasters, and eventually a movie theater. Because of his experience managing a motion picture show, the Robisons hired Louis Heilbroner to plan activities at Robison Park and to help run the street railway system.[3]

In addition to their other businesses, the Robisons owned the National League team in Cleveland, the Spiders. In 1899 the Robisons also bought the National League's St. Louis Browns (later to be called the Cardinals) from owner Chris Von der Ahe, who had become discouraged by the poor showing and bleak finances of his team. Frank and Stanley brought Louis Heilbroner to St. Louis to serve as chief of concessions and business manager of the team.

At the time, the rules of syndicate baseball allowed magnates who owned two clubs to transfer players from one to the other. Believing that St. Louis was a better baseball town than Cleveland, the Robisons switched virtually the entire two rosters before the 1899 season. All the good Cleveland players, including three future members of the Hall of Fame— Cy Young, Jesse Burkett, and Bobby Wallace—were transferred to St. Louis. Meanwhile, the old Browns players, now in Cleveland, established the worst record in baseball history—20 wins and 134 losses.[4]

Despite the influx of talent the year before, the Cardinals were mired in seventh place by August 1900. The Robisons decided to fire manager Patsy Tebeau and replace him with rookie player John McGraw. McGraw, however, warned the owners that he was leaving at the end of the season to join the new American League so the Robisons named Louis Heilbroner manager for the remainder of the 1900 season.[5]

Heilbroner's two months as manager of the Cardinals were full of problems. Heilbroner stood less than five feet tall, weighed barely 100 pounds, and had a thin, piping voice. The players, generally described as a bunch of roughnecks, had no respect for him and usually refused to follow his orders.[6] One player threatened to lock Heilbroner in the team safe. On another occasion, Heilbroner fined outfielder Mike Donlin for hitting into a double play when he had been ordered to bunt. In retaliation, Donlin picked Heilbroner up by his feet and dunked him headfirst into a rain barrel.[7]

As if Heilbroner's troubles with his players were not enough, he also had difficulties as the business manager. A long and bitter streetcar strike in St. Louis forced fans to walk to the ballpark and attendance dropped dramatically. The Cardinals went into the red in 1900.[8]

Despite all these problems, the pint-sized Cardinal manager moved his club up two places in the standings, with the team finishing in a fifth-place tie. He even brought them to within one game of .500, as the Cardinals won 23 and lost 25 for a .479 average under his leadership, compared with .457 under Tebeau.[9]

After Heilbroner completed his time as manager, he remained with the team as business manager. He also served as a scout for the Cardinals as well as for other teams, especially the Cincinnati Reds. His scouting advice was well received and he was respected as a baseball man.

After a few years, Heilbroner returned to Fort Wayne and, using the knowledge he had

Louis Heilbroner never played a single game in the major leagues, but he had a long association with professional baseball, serving as manager, scout and President of the Central League. He is best known as the founder of the Heilbroner Sports Bureau, which annually published *Baseball's Blue-Book*, a publication considered invaluable for professional scouts and coaches (courtesy Don F. Graham).

gleaned as a scout, in 1909 established the Heilbroner Sports Bureau, the first baseball statistical organization. This service maintained records of all current and prospective players and issued daily reports to management. To package this data, that same year he began publishing annual volumes of *Baseball Bluebook*.[10] Baseball insiders and fans quickly realized the value of Heilbroner's book, which expanded to include full statistical records of every baseball player in the United States, directories of all leagues, all clubs and all league cities, and the directory of colleges. Heilbroner's *Bluebook* also contained the national agreement board rules, major league purchasing and drafting rules, as well as waiver rules of all leagues.[11] The book became the leading source of information for the National Association of Professional Baseball Leagues, the governing body of the minor leagues.[12]

In addition to establishing a virtual handbook for baseball, Heilbroner was also instrumental in bringing a baseball team to his native city. In 1907 the Central League had assured him that Fort Wayne would receive a franchise and, according to a local newspaper, Heilbroner was already eyeing potential players.[13] Not only did Fort Wayne get a team, in 1913 Heilbroner served as President of the Central League. He helped reorganize the league into six teams and the organization prospered during his term in office.[14]

Louis Heilbroner suffered a heart attack while at a tailor shop and passed away December 21, 1933. Local rabbi Samuel H. Markowitz officiated at his funeral.[15] In tribute, baseball commissioner Kenesaw Mountain Landis called Heilbroner the greatest authority in the world on major and minor league baseball players and their records and American League president Will Harridge stated, "Baseball has lost one of its great statisticians."[16]

Al and Walter Elias

Although the *Baseball Bluebook* is a mainstay for baseball professionals, most fans are far more familiar with—and find more interesting—statistics on the longest hitting streak or the most strikeouts or even obscure details such as how many hitters connected for home runs in their first at bat. These are examples of the data provided by the Elias Sports Bureau, the official statistician of Major League Baseball as well as professional football, basketball and hockey. The bureau is the brainchild of two Jewish brothers, Walter and Al Munro Elias, who turned their passion for baseball into a livelihood that benefited both themselves and the game.

The Elias brothers were born in Charleston, South Carolina, Al in 1872 and Walter around 1877. Their father, Lewis, owned a shoe store. Neither brother played baseball, but both were avid fans of Charleston, one of the earliest teams in the Southern League. Walter told how his brother would argue with other fans even then, adding that, if the dispute dealt with baseball facts or figures, Al's challengers "usually came off on the wrong end."[17]

Shortly after the turn of the twentieth century, both brothers went north to New York City. Al worked in a department store and supplemented his income at night as a dance instructor, eventually becoming a salesman of salad oil. Walter found a job selling shoes and shirts, working out of New York as a traveling salesman in the South and Southwest.

They brought with them their love of baseball, transferring their allegiance to the New York Giants. Walter later recalled, "We would get in the bleacher line early in the morning, each armed with a milk bottle and a lunch box which our sister packed for us. Naturally Mathewson was our hero."[18]

In addition to milk and lunch, the Elias brothers would bring a third item—a scorebook in which they would carefully record the goings-on of their beloved Giants and their opponents.

After getting home from the ballpark, the Elias brothers, using the backs of old envelopes, would figure batting averages for their favorite players, how each Giant had fared against which particular opposing pitcher, or how the teams played against a certain Giant pitcher. Albert and Walter were passionate about statistics, believing that imperfect records would weaken the entire structure of baseball.[19]

Around 1914 a stomach ailment left Al Elias too weak to lift his sales case of salad oil bottles. He was still in his forties and he decided to try to make a living by selling his baseball statistics. Al talked Walter into joining him and within a few days they were pestering newspapers to buy their statistics. The brothers were politely but firmly thrown out of every editor's office.

A different approach was needed. Using a spare room in their sister's house as an office, the brothers printed baseball statistics on the backs of index cards and sold them to billiard parlor and bar operators, who would resell them to the fans who gathered there. They also sold "Food for Fans"—pocket folders of statistics—to bowling alleys and restaurants, pitching them as excellent ways to begin a baseball discussion.[20] To make their business more credible, the brothers began setting up a statistical agency, which they dubbed the Al Munro Elias Bureau.[21]

The Elias brothers got their first break in 1917 when the *New York Evening Telegram* bought some of their statistical tidbits. This seemed to break the logjam for, soon afterward, editor Bill Farnsworth of the *New York American* followed suit. Then Walter Elias's power of observation paid further dividends. While riding in a subway he read a story comparing the current batting averages of the three American League top hitters, Ty Cobb, Joe Jackson, and Tris Speaker. Aware that newspapers generally ran statistics only of the hometown team because the feats of other stars were too hard to get, Elias suggested to Farnsworth that his bureau supply the *American* statistics of the top three batters in both leagues on a daily basis.[22] "Make it the top five leading hitters," Farnsworth replied, "and I'll buy it."[23] The daily box of league leaders had come into existence.[24]

Walter's top five list became so popular that it was sold to newspapers throughout the United States and Canada. Soon the Elias brothers not only featured league leaders in hitting but also in home runs, stolen bases, runs scored, and runs batted in, as well as pitchers' won-lost records, and earned run averages. Al and Walter set the highest standard in statistics reporting. They would get the box scores from the latest editions of local newspapers so that their lists would be as current as possible, but they never sacrificed timeliness for accuracy. Al Elias often said, "There are two kinds of statistics—accurate and worthless. You might go a step further and say that inaccurate statistics are worse than worthless for people depend upon them and are misled by them."[25]

Fans and players would sometimes write to take issue with the accuracy of their records, to question the unofficial averages, and even to criticize official scorers. But the Elias brothers stood behind their data. "We go over [everything] with a fine-toothed comb, looking for errors.... And only when we have looked and looked and can't find anymore, are we reasonably satisfied with our work."[26]

Success followed success. The National League recognized the skill and accuracy of the Elias brothers and in 1922 hired the Elias Bureau as their official statistician.[27] The Associated Press signed on to wire Elias statistics to more than 250 papers. Finally reassured that they could make a living from their statistics, the brothers gave up their sales careers for

Left: Al Elias was a salad oil salesman who was forced to quit his job because a stomach ailment left him too weak to lift his suitcase. He turned his hobby of keeping baseball statistics
into a full-time job when he sold his statistics to various newspapers; thus the Elias Sports
Bureau was founded (courtesy National Baseball Hall of Fame Library, Cooperstown, N.Y.).
Right: Walter Elias, Al's brother and cofounder of the Elias Sports Bureau, came up with the
top-five baseball list, which newspapers eagerly sought and which became the first big success
for the brothers (courtesy National Baseball Hall of Fame Library, Cooperstown, N.Y.).

good. The Elias Bureau eventually became the official statistician for both of baseball's major
leagues and six minor leagues, as well as the other three professional leagues. In addition
to statistical services, the Elias Bureau also published the *Green Book*, the National League's
official annual summary, and the *Book of Baseball Records*, the current name for Charley
White's *Little Red Book*, which the Elias Bureau acquired in 1938.[28]

Although Walter and his brother Al both contributed greatly to making their bureau
number one in the industry, Al Elias was its driving force. His enthusiasm for his work knew
no bounds. A friend once commented that there were only two ways to deal with Elias when
he talked baseball: "One was to listen to what he had to say. The other was to kill him."[29]
In 1923 *Baseball Magazine* wrote, "Al Munro Elias has done more to popularize and improve
stats than anyone before him."[30] Eighty years later, baseball historian and statistician Alan
Schwarz noted that "Al Munro foresaw the widespread appeal of baseball statistics more
keenly than anyone in the first half of the twentieth century, sensing what newspaper readers wanted before the editors themselves." He also points out there was some luck involved,
noting that the Eliases began their business at the same time as Babe Ruth began making
baseball statistics part of the national language.[31]

In 1928 Al Elias's right leg was amputated after he was hit by an automobile. He never fully recovered and in 1934 he dropped out of active management of the Elias Bureau. On August 1, 1939, Al Munro Elias died in New York City of a cerebral hemorrhage at the age of 67. He was survived by his widow and two brothers, Walter and Lawrence.[32]

Nine years later, on May 19, 1948, Walter Elias died at the Medical Arts Center in New York following a heart attack. Walter had carried on as president of the Elias Sports Bureau following the death of his brother in 1939. Neither Al nor Walter Elias had children. After Walter's death, his nephew, Lester Goodman, announced that he would continue the bureau.[33]

Louis Heilbroner and the Elias brothers were pioneers in the area of baseball statistics, and although all three passed away years ago their records are still used constantly, and continue making important contributions to baseball.

9. Baseball's National Anthem

Not as vital to the game as statistics, but almost as universal, is baseball's unofficial national anthem "Take Me Out to the Ball Game." Almost every fan knows the tune which is played during the seventh-inning stretch in virtually every professional baseball park. Very few, however, know that it was written by Albert Von Tilzer, a Jewish composer, who supposedly had never seen a baseball game before he wrote the music.

Von Tilzer was born Albert Gumm, one of six sons of Jacob and Sarah (Tilzer) Gumbinsky, on March 29, 1878. His father ran a shoe store in Goshen, Indiana, before moving to Indianapolis. The family was quite musical; his older brother, Harry, became a successful songwriter, and three other brothers were Tin Pan Alley music publishers.

Albert dropped out of high school to work in his father's shoe store, but his real love was music and he was a self-taught but accomplished pianist. After working as a musical director for a vaudeville troupe, Albert was hired in 1899 as a staff pianist for the Chicago branch of the noted music publishing house Shapiro and Bernstein, where his older brother, Harry, also worked. It was in Chicago that Albert Gumm changed to the same last name that four of his five brothers had previously adopted, not because of anti–Semitism, but for theatrical purposes. Tilzer was his mother's maiden name, and older brother Harry, who wanted to be a songwriter, had added Von because it had an elegant sound.[1]

Like Harry, Albert also hoped to compose music and in 1900 moved to New York, the center of the music publishing industry. To make a living, Albert again worked as a shoe salesman, this time in a Brooklyn department store. Harry joined Albert in New York, where he opened his own music publishing house, the Harry Von Tilzer Music Company. In 1903 Harry's company published Albert's first song "That's What the Daisy Said," with lyrics by their brother Wilbur. That same year Albert, with another brother, Jack, formed the York Music Company, which was to publish all the rest of Albert's songs.[2]

Between 1905 and 1908, Albert Von Tilzer was recognized as a very talented composer whose writing and publishing contributed to the growth of the music industry. Some of his more popular songs included "Put Your Arms around Me, Honey," "I'm the Lonesomest Gal in Town," "Oh, by Jingo," and "I'll Be with You in Apple Blossom Time."[3]

Most of Von Tilzer's songs were written for individual vaudeville acts in collaboration with lyricist Jack Norworth, who was best known for "Shine On Harvest Moon." Despite all the tunes the duo wrote for vaudeville, one 1908 song far surpassed any other piece. "Take Me Out to the Ball Game" not only captured the heart of the nation, it established Von Tilzer as a superstar of popular music and became the unofficial anthem of baseball.[4]

Inspired by a sign on the subway that proclaimed, "Baseball Today—Polo Grounds,"

Norworth wrote the lyrics, and Von Tilzer set them to music. The part of the song sung at the ballparks is actually the chorus. In the verse, which is seldom heard, a "baseball mad" girl named Katie Casey (changed in 1927 to Nelly Kelly) rejects her boyfriend's attempts to take her to a show, responding instead with the refrain "Take me out to the ball game."[5] Norworth's wife and vaudeville star, Nora Bayes, introduced the number, which was soon popularized by various vaudeville acts. The song was such a success that Von Tilzer was given a contract to tour the Orpheum vaudeville circuit to publicize it.[6]

Baseball's national anthem, "Take Me Out to the Ball Game," is one of the three most often sung songs in America. (The other two are the National Anthem and "Happy Birthday.") It was written by a German Jew and one of Tin Pan Alley's most prominent composers, Albert Von Tilzer. The song was written in 1908, allegedly twenty years before its composer ever saw a game played. Today the song is a firmly established part of baseball (courtesy Indiana Historical Society).

Supposedly neither man had ever seen a baseball game at the time they wrote the song and Von Tilzer would not see his first game until 20 years later.[7] Amazingly, though, the song nonetheless captured the essence of a baseball game quite well. Years later, former Dodger pitcher Carl Erskine argued that the song, with its "one, two, three strikes, you're out" lyric, had to be written for pitchers. In fact those words might have been the basic phrase of the song. Von Tilzer once said, "It had sock." Students of music pointed out that, although Von Tilzer did not realize it, the quarter-rest pause between "take" and "me" in the first measure of the chorus was the perfect spot for the "thwack" sound of ball hitting bat.[8]

In 1910 Von Tilzer attempted to capitalize on the popularity of "Take Me Out to the Ball Game," teaming up with Harry Breen to publish "Back to the Bleachers for Mine." Like many sequels, it missed the mark and has long since been forgotten.[9]

By the 1920s Von Tilzer was no longer writing for vaudeville but almost exclusively composing full scores for Broadway. His music became less popular near the end of the decade but talking pictures helped him launch a new career. He moved to Hollywood in 1930 to write songs for motion pictures and retired there in the late 1930s.[10]

Two highlights of Von Tilzer's long career related directly to his most famous song. On June 27, 1940, the Brooklyn Dodgers had a special day for Von Tilzer at Ebbets Field, and in 1949 MGM released the musical *Take Me Out to the Ball Game*, starring Frank Sinatra, Gene Kelly and Esther Williams. Frank Sinatra sang the title song, which by that time was already a part of American folklore.[11]

On the eve of the 1956 World Series, Albert Von Tilzer, a sickly 78-year-old, lay in his Beverly Hills apartment watching television. The Brooklyn Dodgers and the New York Yankees were playing a "subway series," and Ed Sullivan, on his weekly TV show, was introducing some of baseball's greatest luminaries, such as Hank Aaron, Yogi Berra, and Sal Maglie. In honor of the impending World Series, the band played the tune the man in bed had composed 48 years earlier, "Take Me Out to the Ball Game." After the show, Von Tilzer's nurse turned off the television set and tucked the songwriter in for the evening. Sometime before morning, October 1, 1956, Von Tilzer died in his sleep.[12]

Albert Von Tilzer was in show business for half a century and was a charter member of the Association of Songwriters, Composers, Authors and Publishers (ASCAP) and the Songwriters' Hall of Fame. Twenty-four of his songs sold more than one million copies, but he is best remembered for one song—"Take Me Out to the Ball Game." There is no doubt that this song is the most well-known and most beloved composition in all of sports.

10. From the Press Box

Singing about going to baseball games was fun, but for the serious fan, reading about the game was the next best thing to being there. It wasn't long after baseball began regular travel schedules that newspapers recognized the need for a writer who would travel with a team and report every pitch and play of both home and away games. And it wasn't long before Jews entered the field of baseball writing and made outstanding contributions to both the game and to journalism.

Jacob Morse

Jacob Morse was the first noted Jewish sportswriter, the founder of *Baseball Magazine*, and the author of one of the earliest histories of the game, *Sphere and Ash: A History of Baseball*.[1] Morse was born in Concord, New Hampshire, on June 7, 1860, the son of Charles and Sarah (Straus) Morse, both German Jews. In 1866 the family moved to Boston. Jake was educated at the Boston Latin School, where he excelled in sports, and then he enrolled at Harvard. He received his undergraduate degree in 1881, one of only four Jews in his graduating class.[2]

At Harvard, Morse, always a baseball fan, began writing about college baseball for a Boston newspaper. He eventually covered Harvard's baseball games for the *Boston Herald*, and served as Boston sports correspondent for the *New York Clipper*, a position he held for eight years.[3]

After Harvard, Morse enrolled in Boston University Law School, earning a law degree in 1884. Even though he was admitted to the bar the following year, Morse accepted a permanent position on the *Boston Herald* staff, where he had been writing since 1881. He also wrote for other Boston papers, including the *Globe*, *Post*, *Advertiser*, and *Courier*.[4]

When Morse began covering the Boston Braves for the *Herald*, his stories of the games written while traveling with the team were very popular in New England because of their accuracy and completeness.[5] In addition, his writing displayed a remarkable enthusiasm for the game and was unique, using adjectives freely in what many felt was a style 25 years before its time.[6]

Morse did more than cover games for Boston's National League baseball team. He invented the modern style of scorecards, although he never benefited from it financially. He also came up with a type of scoring shorthand that is still used by every baseball writer covering the sport today. Until Morse originated this scoring system, writers had to consume considerable sheets of paper and make voluminous notes to keep track of the progress of the game.[7]

By 1889, and throughout his years with the *Herald*, Jake Morse was one of four men who controlled the destiny of baseball in Boston. He and one of the other four, *Boston Globe* baseball writer Tim Murnane, founded the New England League. For 15 years, Murnane served as president and Morse as secretary. The league, soon dubbed the "Me and Jake League," supplied a number of good players to the National League and eventually the American League. Two of Morse's protégés from this league were Tommy Connolly, who became supervisor of American League umpires, and Hugh Duffy, whose .440 batting average for Boston has never been equaled.[8]

Nineteen hundred was a turbulent year for major league baseball, as the National League pared its teams down to eight and the move to establish a second league major league became more intense. Boston kept the Braves, but the American League was working hard to place a rival team in the city and enlisted the aid of Duffy, Connolly, and Morse. Hugh Duffy found a site for a ballpark and helped sign many of the players for the new team, while Connolly joined the umpiring staff. Morse used his influence as a sportswriter to persuade the public of the advantages of another major league team in Boston. Together, they became known as the Three Musketeers of the American League in Boston.[9]

In 1903, when the new Boston American League team, the Pilgrims, won the pennant and met the Pittsburgh Pirates in baseball's first World Series, it was only natural that Morse should be one of the sportswriters covering the games. Writing in the *Pittsburgh Press*, Morse stated that he was amazed by the huge turnout. "A crowd listed at 18,801, but perhaps larger, swarmed onto the field before the start of the game and surrounded the infield. Someone even swiped second base."[10]

Jacob Morse had as wide a circle of friends as any man in Boston and was on his way to becoming the dean of baseball writers. But he quit the *Herald* in 1907, after 23 years with the paper, citing differences with new management. As he explained years later, "I naturally expected to die in the harness in that institution, but ... changes in management bring about changes in personnel."[11]

Morse might have left the newspaper for other reasons, namely financial. In 1893 Morse had married Josephine Gans, and the couple had two sons, Charles and Reginald. Morse had never made much money as a sportswriter.[12]

Even though Morse had left the *Herald*, he still retained his interest in baseball. The same year, he established baseball's first magazine, called, simply, *Baseball Magazine*. Morse was proud that his magazine was an independent and impartial journal.[13] With the inscription "For Red-Blooded Americans" in flowing red script above the title, it also carried the message that baseball was part of the American culture.[14] Morse was publisher and editor of *Baseball Magazine* from 1907 until 1910 when he sold it to E. C. Lane. At that time, Morse's reputation was so strong that Al Spink, cofounder of *The Sporting News*, wrote, "Mr. Morse's name is known wherever the big game is read or spoken."[15]

After he sold *Baseball Magazine*, Morse tried many jobs unrelated to baseball, including the brokerage business and automobile sales. Finally, in May 1920, he became an agent for Equitable Life Assurance and built a financially successful career.[16]

Morse was truly a Renaissance man. Besides baseball and business, he always had an interest in politics. Unlike most German-Jews, who were staunchly Republican, Jacob Morse was a lifelong Democrat who had come from a family of Democrats. His uncle, Leopold Morse, even served as a Democratic U.S. Congressman for four terms, from 1877 to 1885.[17]

Jake Morse won the Democratic primary for state auditor in 1915. Although he lost the election, he received support not only from his political friends but also from his friends from sports. Hugh Jennings, manager of the Detroit Tigers, congratulated him on the nomination: "I do not think a better man could be found for the office ... and on account of your long connection with the National game, and the fact that you have made and kept friends during those years, ought to insure you the solid baseball vote."[18]

Morse never lost his ability to make new friends. He remained active in numerous fraternal and Jewish organizations, including Temple Israel, where his father and uncle had been presidents. Morse, a long-time resident of the Boston suburb of Brookline, also served on the city's board of aldermen. "For years," noted Morse, "I was the only Jewish member of the committee of thirty."[19]

Regardless of his other careers, Morse was still considered one of the preeminent baseball writers in Boston. When the *Herald* merged with the *Traveler*, Morse was officially kept on as a member of the sports staff until the time of his death. In addition to sports, Morse contributed articles about observances of the Jewish holidays of Rosh Hashanah, Yom Kippur, and Passover.[20]

On April 12, 1937, believing he had recovered from an illness suffered six weeks earlier, Morse returned to his desk at the *Traveler*. Shortly before five o'clock, however, Jacob C. Morse had a heart attack and died at his home at the age of 77. Rabbi Harry Levin of Temple Israel officiated at a private family service but the cremation was open to friends.[21] People representing all phases of Morse's life and career—baseball, the newspaper, and politics—attended.

In a fitting eulogy to Morse, the *Traveler* wrote, "There will be no sorrowing for him because he would not have wanted that. He was kinder to the world than the world was to him, but he never felt that way. He enjoyed every day of his life and he died as so many newspapermen wish—with typewriter ribbon ink virtually on his finger tips. There will be less and less mention of him. Then, some day a young man listening to group conversation and reminiscences

Jacob Morse was truly a Renaissance man. A graduate of Harvard, he was the first noted Jewish sportswriter and covered the first World Series in 1903. Morse founded *Baseball Magazine* and authored one of baseball's earliest histories. He was also active in local and state politics (courtesy National Baseball Hall of Fame Library, Cooperstown, N.Y.).

will ask: 'Who was Jake Morse?' To which someone whose youthful hair has thinned and grayed will reply: 'Kid, you came just a little too late.'"[22]

Dan Daniel

If Jacob Morse was the first Jewish sportswriter to gain regional recognition in that field, Dan Daniel, born 30 years later, was the first to gain a national reputation as a sportswriter. Shortly after Morse had quit the newspaper industry, Dan Daniel began his career, writing both for local papers and for national publications such as Morse's *Baseball Magazine* and *The Sporting News*. Although not a player, Daniel, too, was forced to change his name because of the fear of anti–Semitism.

Dan Daniel was born Daniel Margowitz in New York City on June 6, 1890, the son of a Russian-Jewish father and a German-Jewish mother. His father, Morris, was a pioneer builder of elevator apartment houses in New York, and Dan, as a young boy, worked during the summers on some of his dad's construction jobs. At the young age of 15, he entered City College of New York, intending to study medicine, but quickly found out that he was too squeamish to pursue that profession. Daniel realized that by not studying medicine he would disappoint his parents. "I broke a line of doctors in the family that went as far back as we could trace."[23] Fortunately, he discovered that he had the writing bug.[24]

In 1907 he applied for a part-time job in the sports department of the *New York Herald*, and after waiting three hours on New Years Eve for the editor to return to his desk, Daniel was hired. Compliments from the managing editor on a story he wrote about a college football game confirmed his vocation. "That was the end of me," said Daniel. "I knew it was the newspaper business from then on."[25]

Daniel covered many sports during his long career, but his first love was baseball. He saw his first major league game in 1902, the year John McGraw debuted as manager of the New York Giants, and he became a fan of both the team and the manager. Daniel considered McGraw the greatest manager in baseball history. "I never met a baseball man," recalled Daniel years later, "who ran everything. He organized the club, signed the ball players, watched the farm system, such as it was in those early days. Nobody was near him as a leader and a manager."[26]

Daniel's first big break as a sportswriter was an assignment in 1909 to cover the Brooklyn Dodgers' spring training in Macon, Georgia. He replaced the usual reporter, who had demanded five dollars a day, a two-dollar raise over the three he had been receiving. Rather than pay the extra money, the sports editor chose to send a cub reporter and he picked Daniel, one of the few who was a high school graduate and who could use a typewriter. For his part, Daniel was ecstatic. "I got $21 a week. I was rich. I was famous. And I was done for insofar as anything but sports writing was concerned."[27]

Daniel's encounter with anti–Semitism coincided with another career breakthrough. In 1910 the *Herald* gave Daniel his first byline and Daniel signed the article Daniel Margowitz. Conscious of the anti–Semitism rampant at that time, the editor refused to publish the column under the name Margowitz, suggesting, instead, that it be signed just "By Daniel." As he became a more popular writer, Daniel's readers began addressing mail to him as "Mr. Daniel." Eventually, Daniel wanted to change his name legally to simplify matters but first he asked his immigrant father if he had any objection. "Not at all," his father replied, "Margowitz isn't your real name anyway."[28] At various times in his more than 60 years as a writer, his work appeared with the bylines "Daniel," "Dan Daniel," and "Daniel M. Daniel." He preferred "Dan Daniel."[29]

In 1913 Daniel became a member of the Baseball Writers Association of America. At the time, he was working for the *New York Press* and its sports editor, Nat Fleischer, who paid him the astonishing sum of $35 a week.[30]

As Daniel became more and more prominent, he began getting "inside information" that often proved correct. Once, near the end of the 1915 season, he received an anonymous telephone tip that the upstart Federal League was about to fold and that the New York Giants were going to purchase a pair of Federal League stars. Daniel wrote the story and, even though few believed him, it turned out to be true.[31] It soon became so common for Daniel to know things before other reporters that there was a standard joke in the press box. Whenever a reporter discovered what he felt was new information, a colleague would tell him, "Daniel had it yesterday."[32]

Daniel covered many sports in addition to baseball. In 1922 he helped *Press* editor Fleischer found *Ring Magazine*, boxing's most prestigious publication. He also wrote columns for the monthly periodical, served as an associate editor, and was president of the Boxing Writers of America.[33]

In 1924, after fighting through a myriad of newspaper mergers, Dan Daniel became sports editor of the *World*, later the *World-Telegram*. In addition to covering baseball and boxing, he added a daily column, "Daniel's Dope." He also wrote a weekly column for *The Sporting News*, often sending thousands of words by telegraph to its publisher, Taylor Spink.[34] Daniel's writing style was now described as "fast and bad; his highest stylistic touch was to turn adjectives into verbs."[35]

A heavyset man with a gruff voice and perpetual scowl that masked a warm heart and quick wit, Daniel also wrote a question-and-answer column called "Ask Daniel" that ran for more than 20 years.[36] Daniel took great pride in this column that attracted letters from all over the United States, chiefly from housewives, farmers, and businessmen. Whenever he needed a filler, he ran the question, "Did anyone ever hit a fair

Dan Daniel was the first Jew to gain a national reputation as a sportswriter. In addition to his columns for numerous New York City newspapers, Daniel contributed a weekly column to *The Sporting News*, "Ask Daniel." He won many honors, including the coveted J.G. Taylor Spinks Award for outstanding contributions to his profession (courtesy Daniel Yates).

ball out of Yankee Stadium?" It was justified, according to Daniel, because it was asked "at least five times a week. And no matter how many times I say no, that question keeps coming."[37] Through all of his writings, he developed a standing as a foremost authority on the game, and was often called "Mr. Baseball."[38]

But if baseball was Daniel's first passion, the New York Yankees were a close second. He began covering the team in 1919, when Frank Munsey, owner of the *New York Press*, merged his paper with the *Sun*, and at the *Telegram* Daniel owned the Yankee beat.[39]

The longer Dan Daniel covered the Yankees, the more he became personally involved with them. Daniel boasted that he was responsible for ending Babe Ruth's holdout for a higher salary in 1930, by reminding him that the country was in the midst of a Great Depression, something that Ruth admitted he had not realized. Daniel stated over and over again that he had intervened for only one reason: "Without the Babe there wasn't an awful lot to write about."[40]

Some felt his affection for the Yankees, and for Joe DiMaggio in particular, went far beyond the limits of objective journalism. When DiMaggio made his spring training debut for New York in 1936, Daniel immediately began writing about him as "the replacement for Babe Ruth." Author Roger Kahn called Daniel's prose "promotional copy" and fellow sportswriter Fred Lieb described Daniel's bias towards the Yankees as "riding the bandwagon."[41]

One of the low points in Daniel's career involved allegations over DiMaggio's famed hitting streak. As DiMaggio became a regular, Daniel wrote numerous stories building the outfielder's image—his humble Italian-American origins, his innocence and his unsurpassed baseball skills.[42]

In 1941, when DiMaggio was in the midst of his 56-game consecutive hitting streak, Dan Daniel was the primary scorer at Yankee Stadium and also covered all the Yankee games for the *World-Telegram*. In those years, teams paid travel expenses for their baseball writers, making the writers somewhat beholden to them. And if the writers were the official scorers, the general feeling was that they were inclined to rule in favor of the home team. C. David Stephan, a baseball historian specializing in hitting streaks, questioned Daniel's impartiality as official scorer, claiming that Daniel was one of DiMaggio's staunchest supporters and that borderline calls, plays that could have been errors, were ruled hits for DiMaggio. "Dan Daniel made many questionable calls in DiMaggio's favor," said Stephan. "The writers and players played cards together on the trains. It was very incestuous."[43]

Daniel defended his actions in a letter to *The Sporting News*, claiming that he had never cheated in favor of DiMaggio.[44] On another occasion, Daniel stated, "Joe will tell you that ... there wasn't a hit he wasn't entitled to. I never favored him one iota and made him get his hits as I saw them."[45]

Prior to World War II, Daniel, like most sportswriters, often referred to the ethnic background of a player. By 1940 such references were rare and Dan Daniel, writing for the *Sporting News*, explained why. "I never heard of a fan who held back his cheer for a homer to see if it was walloped by a member of his church. In the spirit of American consensus and unity in the face of world war, fans were concerned with ability and production, not one's religious affiliation."[46]

Daniel was one of the most ardent advocates for racial integration in organized baseball. After Jackie Robinson made his debut for the Brooklyn Dodgers in an exhibition game, Daniel noted that "No buildings collapsed either from the reverberations caused by the epochal event or from the power of Robinson's hitting."[47]

Daniel's beloved Yankees were one of the last major league teams to add an African American to its roster. As the years passed with no blacks on the Yankees, even Daniel had to admit, "If the Yankees weren't guilty as charged, they were certainly going out of their way looking for trouble."[48] Daniel concluded that black ball players like Sam Jethroe, Larry Doby and Jackie Robinson were the fastest men in baseball; they not only excelled, but also added an element of speed to the game.[49]

Daniel received many awards during his long, successful career, but two stand out as being the most meaningful. On February 1, 1959, Daniel received the William J. Slocum Memorial Award for outstanding services to baseball over a long period of years. The only other writer to receive this award was the man for whom it was named, William Slocum. Daniel was honored because of his influence on baseball, his unbending insistence on morality in front offices as well as on the field and his generous assistance to rookies and other youngsters.[50]

The second award of note occurred in 1972. Daniel, along with Frederick G. Lieb and J. Roy Stockton, received the J.G. Taylor Spink Award for contributions to his profession. His name was permanently inscribed on the award's perpetual plaque at the baseball Hall of Fame in Cooperstown, New York.[51]

Dan Daniel died in Florida on July 1, 1981, at the age of 91. A newspaperman to the end, he wrote his own obituary to be used "in the event of my death, which is scheduled within the next 15 years." Daniel was survived by his twin daughters, Roberta Yates and Naomi Stein. His wife, the former Mollie Schrown, had died earlier. Sportswriter Bob Broeg, now deceased, succinctly gave his appraisal of Dan Daniel: "He was a sportswriter always in the pursuit of accuracy."[52]

Shirley Povich

Like Dan Daniel, Shirley Povich was one of the most influential baseball writers of the twentieth century. He gained national renown through his columns in *The Sporting News* and through the sheer power of his words. Povich began his career approximately 15 years after Daniel and reflected in many ways the changes in the Jewish community.

Shirley Lewis Povich was born on July 15, 1905, into the only Orthodox Jewish family in the resort town of Bar Harbor, Maine. His father and grandfather had left Lithuania to escape anti–Semitism, moving to Maine, where the climate was similar to the Baltic region. Like many Eastern European Jews, the Povichs became peddlers, selling their wares from a horse and wagon through the Maine countryside. Eventually, Povich's father established a furniture store in Bar Harbor, and most of his customers were wealthy summer residents. The Povichs and their nine children lived above the store.[53]

Povich always had to explain his name, Shirley, which today is considered a girl's name. "Well," said Povich, "in Maine where I grew up, it was such a boy's name that I went to school with three or four boys named Shirley, but I was named after my grandmother, Sarah. My parents wanted something close to Sarah, and they took the Yiddish transliteration of Sarah, Sorella, and said, "Gee, that's close enough to Shirley."[54]

During his youth, there were at most four Jewish families in the Bar Harbor area and no formal Jewish worship or education. "My father brought in circuit riding teachers who taught us Hebrew. They came in from Boston, year after year. With five boys in the house there was always one preparing for a Bar Mitzvah," recalled Povich.

Like the sons of many Eastern European Jews, Shirley Povich became fascinated by baseball, often waiting for the boat from Boston to bring in the big city newspapers. Povich once said, "Going from reading baseball stories to writing about them was an accident, kind of a fairy tale."[55]

Povich and most of the other high school boys in Bar Harbor caddied for the rich and sometimes famous summer guests. Two of his steadiest customers were prominent newspapermen, Joseph Pulitzer and Edward B. "Ned" McLean. Impressed by the 17-year-old, in 1922 McLean offered to pay Povich's tuition at McLean's alma mater and to let him work on his newspaper while attending school. "I later learned," said Povich, "that his college was Georgetown University and his newspaper was the *Washington Post*."[56]

Povich eagerly accepted the tuition and job, but had to turn down a ride to Washington on McLean's private train, which was scheduled to leave on the Jewish holiday, Rosh Hashanah. Povich explained to McLean that on Rosh Hashanah and Yom Kippur, "We go to synagogue ... and the last thing we do is ride trains."[57]

Povich's action was consistent with his religious attitudes for the remainder of his life. He followed the Jewish custom of postponing his marriage for a year to mourn the death of his father and whenever he was in Washington on Friday nights, Sabbath dinners were mandatory at the Povich household. As one baseball historian stated, "Povich kept his faith and retained his Jewish identity to the end."[58]

Evidently, Povich's refusal to ride with McLean was not a problem for his new boss, for after the Jewish High Holidays, Povich set out for Washington on his own. On the way, he stopped off in New York City, and climbed Coogan's Bluff overlooking the Polo Grounds to see the Giants defeat the Yankees during one game of the 1922 World Series. It was Povich's first major league game and one that Povich called almost half a century later "the real miracle of Coogan's Bluff. Bobby Thomson's historic homer in 1951 was distinctly a second-place event."[59]

Povich worked for the *Washington Post* while he attended Georgetown University, going from the copy desk to the city room, where he became a police

Shirley Povich was one of the most influential and beloved baseball writers of the twentieth century. He gained national renown through his columns in both *The Sporting News* and his "This Morning with Shirley Povich" column in the *Washington Post* (courtesy *The Washington Post*).

reporter and a rewrite man. In 1924 he finally got a chance to work in the sports department, and as an extra bonus he made $5 dollars more a week. Povich remembers well when his editor, Norman Baxter, gave him his first byline. "Wow, was I excited. I didn't wait for the proofs to show up from the composing room. I went down there to see for myself, to actually see with my fingers the type that said 'By Shirley Povich.' Reading it, right to left as metal type must be read was no problem. Those Hebrew lessons paid off."[60]

Two years later, at the age of twenty-one, he became sports editor of the *Washington Post*, the youngest sports editor at any metropolitan newspaper in America. That same year, 1926, Povich began his daily column, "This Morning with Shirley Povich." He remained editor until 1933 and continued writing his column until 1974.[61]

Povich's favorite sport always remained baseball. Throughout his career, the small man, always dapperly dressed in necktie and fedora, covered the Senators. Even though he traveled with the team on the road, Povich took care to maintain his professionalism by distancing himself from the players.[62] He did have favorites, such as the future Hall of Fame pitcher Walter Johnson, but Povich tried to maintain an air of neutrality in his writings while Johnson was an active player. After Johnson retired, however, Povich would visit the former pitcher in nearby Bethesda, Maryland. Said Povich of Johnson, "When I became a sportswriter one of my rewards was watching this great pitcher and respecting the great man all the rest of his years." During the 1930s, Povich also grew close to the Washington Senators' owner, Clark Griffith, a former major league pitcher. He eventually wrote a ten-part series on Griffith and "by the time I was through," said Povich, "I knew more about him than he knew about himself."[63]

His love of baseball was so deep that he thought it odd that anyone would not fall in love with the game. For those who considered baseball "too dull," he had a ready answer, "Only the people who think that way are dull." He constantly touted the appeal of the sport, writing about the ballet-like beauty of the double play or the motions of the pitcher on the mound.[64]

His fellow sportswriters recognized Povich's skill as a journalist. His friend and protégé, Bob Considine, once wrote that Povich "had an absolute command of the most formidable of foes—the declarative sentence."[65] His columns included glorious descriptions of some of the greatest events in sports during the twentieth century. In 1956, when Don Larsen pitched a perfect game, Povich wrote, "The million-to-one shot came in. Hell froze over." In 1939 Povich brought to life Lou Gehrig Day at Yankee Stadium. "I saw strong men weep this afternoon, expressionless umpires swallow hard, and emotion pump the hearts and glaze the eyes of 61,000 baseball fans in Yankee Stadium. Yes, and hard-boiled news photographers clicked their shutters with fingers that trembled a bit."[66] Bob Broeg of the *St. Louis Post-Dispatch* recalled, "He certainly knew how to put one word after another."[67]

There were many who felt that Povich almost single-handedly kept the *Post* alive in the 1920s and 1930s through his column, which they likened to cereal in the morning, warm and inviting. To them he was the warm-hearted guy who said, "Welcome to the day."[68] Ben Bradlee, retired executive editor of the *Post*, candidly stated, "You got the *Post* for Shirley and the sports section. He was the sports section. For a lot of years he carried the paper, and that's no exaggeration."[69]

His only sabbatical from the newspaper was during World War II, when he begged his editors to let him go to Europe as a correspondent. Povich finally got his wish in 1944 when he was assigned to the Pacific Theater. He covered the bloody battles at Okinawa and Iwo Jima, going in on the first plane to land on Iwo Jima.[70] After recovering from two broken vertebrae suffered in Okinawa, he returned to the *Post*.[71]

Like his contemporary, Dan Daniel, Shirley Povich was one of the most outspoken critics of the color line in professional baseball and other sports. Part of this opposition to discrimination no doubt arose as a result of what he had learned as a child about the persecution of Jews in Russia.[72]

As early as 1941 Povich wrote that by keeping out African Americans, the big leagues were "missing out on a couple million dollars worth of talent."[73] In 1946, when the Brooklyn Dodgers signed Jackie Robinson, Povich noted, "Four hundred and fifty-five years after Columbus eagerly discovered America, major league baseball reluctantly discovered the American Negro."[74] Povich even brought long overdue recognition to an early black player in a column titled "No More Shutouts," which discussed the 1884 career of Moses Fleetwood Walker. Walker had caught for Toledo in the American Association, which at that time was a major league.[75]

Even after the major leagues were integrated, Povich continued to urge baseball to accelerate the pace of desegregation. He wrote a 15-part feature for the *Washington Post* in 1953 on the African American contribution to baseball, which generated considerable hate mail, and he continued to prod Clark Griffith to integrate the Senators: "Mr. Griffith would give Washington fans dark players from other lands, but never an American Negro."[76]

Povich also censured George Preston Marshall, owner of the Washington Redskins, for not integrating his team in the 1960s when most other teams were finally signing African Americans. According to Povich, "The Redskin colors are burgundy, gold and Caucasian." After football star Jim Brown helped lead his Cleveland Browns to victory over the Redskins, Povich began his column with, "Jim Brown, born ineligible to play for the Redskins, integrated their end zone three times yesterday."[77]

While Povich penned numerous columns about the plight and accomplishments of the African-American athlete, his column was seldom devoted to Jewish-American athletes. Povich did note that baseball star Hank Greenberg was often the target of both subtle and blatant anti–Semitism, but he did not even write an obituary for him when Greenberg died in 1986.[78]

Many reasons have been given as to why Povich neglected Jewish related subjects. Some felt that Povich, who always tried to write a fair and balanced column, could not be objective about his own ethnic group. Baseball historian Peter Levine argued that, as Jews became more acculturated within American society, writers found it less important to emphasize their ethnic and cultural identity.[79]

Povich received many awards during his long career. In 1964 he received the Grantland Rice Award for "outstanding sports writing." This annual award was named for the late Grantland Rice, a columnist who achieved one of the largest followings in the history of sports journalism.[80]

In 1975, like Daniel, Povich received the J.G. Taylor Spink Award and his name, too, was added to the plaque in Baseball's Hall of Fame. In 1987 he became a member of the Hall of Fame's Veterans Committee, which selects old-time players, executives, and officials passed over by the baseball writers.[81] Probably the honor he would have liked most is a small ballpark with only 606 seats located in the nation's capital. It is named Shirley Povich Field.[82]

Shirley Povich died June 4, 1999, of a heart attack at the age of 92. Even though Povich had officially given up a daily column 25 years earlier, he had continued to write for the *Post*, turning in his last column just one day prior to his death.[83] He was survived by his widow, Ethyl Friedman Povich, two sons, David, a lawyer in Washington, D.C., and Maury, the television talk show host, and a daughter, Lynn, a managing editor at MSNBC. According to his wishes, he was buried with a traditional Jewish service. Many eulogies were given, but George Solomon, Assistant Managing Editor for Sports at the *Post*, may have said it best, "He was a giant in his field, one of the greatest sports journalists who ever lived. There will never be another one like him. We loved him at this newspaper."[84]

Morse, Daniel, and Povich differed in many ways. They were alike, however, in one important respect—all three esteemed Jewish journalists were able to clearly express their unshakable love for baseball.

11. The Last of the Pseudonyms

The decade of the 1920s was a time of two somewhat conflicting trends for American Jews—increased anti–Semitism and a growing love for baseball.

The anti–Semitism grew out of a number of factors. Following World War I and the Bolshevist Revolution, Jews who came to the United States as part of the mass deportations of radicals from Southern and Eastern Europe were accused of being subversives.[1] The notorious *Protocols of the Elders of Zion*, a Russian forgery that purported to be a Jewish plot for conquering the world, was widely circulated.[2] And the Ku Klux Klan reemerged, this time targeting not only African Americans, but Jews and Catholics as well.[3] In general, this anti–Semitism meant discrimination and quotas for Jews—in immigration, in their chosen professions, and in the colleges they could attend.[4]

Anti-Semitism also affected Jews in baseball. Small towns and rural America contained not only most of baseball's minor league teams, but also the strongest fears of Jews corrupting Christian values.[5] The Black Sox scandal, which involved a number of Jewish gamblers, added to feelings of distrust.[6] Henry Ford, whose *Dearborn Independent* blamed Jews for almost every evil in society, specifically condemned Jews for demeaning America's National Pastime.[7] Even *The Sporting News*, which advocated equality of all players (as long as they were white) was quick to emphasize the ethnic identity of Jewish players.[8]

Despite these obstacles, the second trend affecting Jews and baseball in the twenties was a growing obsession with the game. Acculturated second-generation Eastern Europeans followed baseball almost religiously, attended more games, and often dreamed of being major leaguers, some with their parents' blessing.[9] Because of anti–Semitism, some Jews were still forced to change their names when they entered the professional ranks, but as teams recognized the potential of a Jewish fan base, that pressure subsided. Except for French-born Duke Markell (Harry Duquesene Makowsky), who appeared in five games for the St. Louis Browns in 1951, the 1920s would mark the entry of the last of the players who adopted different names for baseball. Most of these players had short tenures but some had very credible careers.[10]

Reuben Ewing

Reuben Ewing was born Reuben Cohen in Odessa, in Ukraine, on November 30, 1899, to Simon and Bessy Cohen. After immigrating to the United States, the Cohens settled in Hartford, where Reuben's father was a dry goods dealer. Reuben graduated from Hartford High School and in 1920 entered Lebanon Valley College.

He was still in college when he made his major league debut, appearing in three games for the St. Louis Cardinals in 1921 under the name Reuben Ewing. As a pinch hitter in his first game, the five-foot, four-inch, 145-pound Ewing struck out. In his second appearance, he was a late-inning defensive replacement, and in his third and last game in the majors, he was a pinch runner. He had one at bat.

After his time with the Cardinals, Ewing reverted to his birth name Cohen, and reentered Lebanon Valley in 1922. He remained in Hartford and passed away September 17, 1962.[11]

For more than 70 years, until Victor Cole became a pitcher for the Pittsburgh Pirates in 1992, Reuben Ewing had the distinction of being the last major leaguer born in Russia.[12]

Joseph R. Bennett

Joe Bennett appeared in one major league game, playing third base for the Philadelphia Phillies at home against the St. Louis Cardinals on July 5, 1923. Bennett had one assist in the field but never came to the plate.

Bennett was born July 2, 1900, in New York City. He attended both New York University and the University of Missouri but never received a degree. In 1923, Bennett was playing for Lancaster before being called up by the Phillies. After his one game in the big leagues, he formed a semipro team in Red Bank, New Jersey, where he also ran a sporting goods store. Bennett also had a long military career, serving in both World II and the Korean War. After he retired from active duty in 1955, he managed the officers club at Fort Monmouth, New Jersey.[13]

Reuben Ewing was born Reuben Cohen and appeared in three games in 1921 for the St. Louis Cardinals. Until Philadelphia Phillies hurler Victor Cole made his major league debut in 1992, Ewing was the last Russian-born player to reach the major leagues (courtesy Marc Okkonen).

Bennett died in California, July 11, 1987, survived by two daughters, six grandchildren, and two great grandchildren.[14]

In 1964, more than 40 years after he left the majors, it was confirmed that Bennett was Jewish. He used the name Joseph Rosenblum Bennett, but it seems likely that he was born Joseph Rosenblum and changed his name when he began playing ball.[15]

Sam Bohne

The last Cohen to change his name for major league baseball, Sam Bohne was one of the most successful Jewish players during the 1920s. Bohne was born Samuel Arthur Cohen on October 22, 1896, in San Francisco. Nine-year-old Sam learned about baseball in a youth group, playing for the group until he was 18.[16]

Bohne began his professional baseball career in 1916 with Tacoma in the Northwestern League. A good hitter and an excellent fielder, he was promoted to the Cardinals that same year, appearing in a major league uniform for the first time on September 9, 1916, against the Cincinnati Reds. Entering the game as a pinch hitter, he remained to play shortstop in the tenth inning when the Reds scored three runs to defeat the Cardinals 6–3.[17] He played a total of 14 games with St. Louis.

Bohne's real major league career did not begin until 1921. In 1917 he played for both St. Paul and Milwaukee of the American Association, spent 1918 in the service, and in 1919 and 1920 played in the Pacific Coast League. His best record in the minors was with the Seattle Rainiers in 1920, where he hit .333 with 20 home runs.[18]

In the fall of 1920 the Cincinnati Reds purchased Bohne's contract. *The Sporting News* was not surprised that the likeable, medium-built infielder would return to the majors in 1921. "It was a cinch he would be up again, unless all the scouts were blind to his merits. Captain Sam is ... the best prospect in the league for a berth on a major club."[19]

Bohne's first season with Cincinnati, 1921, was the best of his career. He was the league's number one second baseman with a fielding percentage of .973 and led the National League in the number of games played. He was also among the top ten in number of at bats, runs scored, triples, and stolen bases. Bohne finished the season with a batting average of .285 with 28 doubles and 44 runs batted in.[20]

Although he batted .274 in 1922, he did not equal his previous season and his stats dropped still further in 1923. However, Bohne was recognized for three attention-getting feats that year. During spring training he had five hits in one game—four home runs and a single. "It was a Texas exhibitioner," recalled Bohne, "but it made headlines everywhere."[21]

The second event took place on June 17, 1923, in a game with the Brooklyn Dodgers. Not only were the Reds being shut out, but Dodger hurler Dazzy Vance had retired 26 consecutive Red hitters, just one out shy of a perfect game. With the Dodgers ahead 9–0, all that stood between Vance and immortality was Sam Bohne. More than 40 years later, Bohne still vividly remembered that game. "I hit the third pitch through the pitcher's box that almost knocked Vance's cap off." Bohne was thankful that the game had been played in Cincinnati and not in Brooklyn: "...in Ebbets Field, the rabid Brooklyn fans might have mobbed me for cheating their idol out of pitching immortality." Fortunately, Vance and Bohne were good friends. After the game, over a pitcher of beer, Vance told Sammy, "I'd be the last man in the world ever to ask another ballplayer to ease up and make me a present of a no-hitter, no matter how badly I wanted it. I forgive you, but I won't forget it. Never take a toehold on me at the plate again."[22]

Sam Bohne, born Samuel Arthur Cohen, played with the Cardinals, Reds and Dodgers during his successful seven-year career in the major leagues. In 1921, while with Cincinnati, he led the major leagues in games played, with 153 (courtesy George Grantham Bain Collection, Library of Congress).

His third achievement was winning the fielding crown again for the best second baseman of the 1923 season.[23] (An interesting side note: in both 1922 and 1923, all four Reds infielders—Bohne, Ralph "Babe" Pinelli, Lew Fonseca, and Jimmy "Ike" Caveny—were from the San Francisco area.)[24]

After the 1923 season, it was rumored that Bohne would be traded to the New York Giants. Obviously, Bohne's name change had not masked his Jewish identity, for one of the reasons *The Sporting News* gave for the alleged trade was that the Giants longed to have a "Hebrew player" on their roster.[25] No trade was made and Bohne remained with the Reds.

In 1924, the award-winning second baseman played nearly half his games at short. *The Sporting News* congratulated him on the way he mastered the new position and the number of dazzling plays he made there.[26]

Bohne played only 73 games for the Reds in 1925 and, after 25 games in 1926, he was traded to the Dodgers. Earlier that year, the respected journal *Baseball Magazine* had noted the lack of Jewish players, pointing out that Sam Bohne was "the only Jewish ball player who has become a sensational regular since the days of Erskine Mayer." The magazine called him "a brilliant fielder ... and also a good hitter."[27] Bohne agreed that there ought to be more Jews in baseball. "Baseball is a hard profession, to be sure," claimed Bohne, "but I believe that Jews ... have keen and active minds and that is what counts decisively in baseball."[28]

Bohne played the last games of his major league career with the Dodgers in 1926. Over a span of 663 games in the big leagues Bohne's lifetime batting average was .261.[29]

After he retired from baseball, Bohne returned to San Francisco where he worked in the garment industry and later the real estate business. He died in San Francisco on March 23, 1977.[30]

Perhaps Bohne's most important baseball legacy was found in an article written in the *American Hebrew* at the request of Reds owner Garry Herrmann. There is no record of the name Bohne used before Cincinnati bought his contract, but it is clear that when the Reds acquired him in 1921, they convinced him that anyone named Cohen would not be popular with the majority of fans. Bohne, the Reds argued, sounded "more Italian, or perhaps might be mistaken for either Norse or Scottish."

The article stated that if Cincinnati management could do things over, "it is doubtful that the name of Cohen would be changed at all." Admitting that it was too late to change Bohne's name back to Cohen, the Reds doubted that any Jewish player in the future would be asked to change his name before entering the big leagues.[31]

Jimmie Reese

The prediction was almost right. Jimmie Reese was actually the last Jewish player to enter the major leagues in the first half of the twentieth century to change his name, but it was his choice. Knowing that people with Jewish names had it rough in baseball, he adopted a name from his Irish mother's side of the family.[32]

James Herman ("Hymie") Solomon, better known as Jimmie Reese, was born October 1, 1904, in Los Angeles. He became part of baseball at an early age as the mascot and batboy of the minor league Los Angeles team from 1917 to 1923.[33]

Reese, a second baseman like Bohne, broke in with the Oakland Oaks of the Pacific Coast League in 1924 and remained with the team for six complete seasons. He and Lyn

Jimmie Reese, born James Herman Solomon, was a utility player for the New York Yankees from 1930 to 1931, where one of his major responsibilities was to see that his roommate, Babe Ruth, made it to games. Reese also played for the St. Louis Cardinals in 1932. He spent many years as fungo coach for the San Diego Padres until his death in 1994 at the age of 93 (courtesy Jacob Rader Marcus Center of the American Jewish Archives).

Lary were both sold to the New York Yankees in 1927 but were told not to report until 1929. Unfortunately, Reese had a bad year in 1928 and remained with Oakland, but he turned things around in 1929, hitting .337 and leading all Pacific Coast League second basemen in total chances accepted.[34]

Reese spent 1930 and 1931 with the Yankees, primarily as a second baseman, although he could also play shortstop. His first year in the majors Reese hit a respectable .346, but his average slipped to .241 in 1931. "The curve ball got me," he explained. "The first year I was hitting second in front of Babe. They didn't want to walk me, so I was always getting fastballs. Then later on, they moved me in the order and I started getting breaking balls."[35] Reese's teammate, Lefty Gomez, felt that Reese was too hard on himself: "It wasn't the curve ball that got Jimmie. No, no—he had a tough guy to beat out at second—Tony Lazzeri." Gomez added that as a utility player on a glamorous team, "[Reese's] anonymity obscured his talent."[36]

Despite his Irish name, many knew that Reese was Jewish and he felt that he was on the Yankees partly for his promotional value in the New York area. Reese stated that being Jewish was not as universal a problem as hitting a curve ball, but it was real enough in 1930. "There was probably racism, there always is," he downplayed it years later, "but I never had it the way Jackie Robinson did. You're a human being, that's it."[37]

During his two years with the Yankees, Miller Huggins, the Yankee manager, assigned Reese as a roommate for Babe Ruth, in the hope that Reese's sober lifestyle might rub off on the Babe. One day, while Ruth was "entertaining friends" in their hotel room, Reese, standing in the hallway, pleaded with Ruth to hurry up. When they both arrived in the dugout only minutes before game time, Huggins immediately yelled, "Reese, where the hell have you been?"[38] Jimmie never minded the times Ruth got him in trouble. He always insisted that the Yankee slugger treated Reese like a son, and he called Ruth the finest man he ever knew.[39] His favorite saying was, "I didn't room with Babe, I watched Babe's bags." He verified that Ruth could gamble and drink all night, eat five plates of steak and eggs in the morning and then go to the ballpark and hit home runs.[40] Even after the trials of living with Ruth, Reese still idolized him: "He did more for baseball, I think, particularly after the Black Sox scandal, than any individual in baseball."[41]

The Yankees sent Reese to the minors in 1932, but late in the season he was elated to learn that the St. Louis Cardinals had purchased his contract.[42] In 90 games for the Cardinals in 1933, Reese hit .265.[43] That was the end of his career as a major league player, but hardly the end of his career in baseball.

He played again in the minors from 1933 to 1939 and for the next three decades was a coach, manager, and scout for various minor league teams. In 1972 he returned to the major leagues when the Los Angeles Angels hired him as one of their coaches, and he soon became one of the most prolific and accurate fungo hitters in baseball.[44]

Sometime during his years on the West Coast, Reese played in a celebrity game where he batted against Jewish songwriter Harry Ruby. Ruby's catcher was former major leaguer Ike Danning, who was also Jewish. Rather than use signals, Danning decided to call the pitches to Ruby in Yiddish, sure that none of the opposing batters would understand. Jimmie Reese got four hits that day and Harry Ruby, dumbfounded, told Reese, "I didn't know you were that good of a hitter, Jimmie." To which Reese replied, "You also didn't know that my name used to be Hymie Solomon."[45]

Reese remained an Angel coach until his death on July 13, 1994, at the age of 92. He had spent 78 of those years in the game. Gene Autry, owner of the Angels in '72, spoke for all of those who knew Reese, "He is a tremendous loss to the game of baseball. He loved the game for its purity, its honesty, and for the joy it brought to the millions of children throughout the United States and around the world."[46]

The fact that Jewish players would no longer be forced to change their names did not indicate that anti–Semitism was no longer an issue. But it did reflect a higher comfort level with being a Jew in America and, in some cases, a Jewish name was actually of value to a major league player.

12. McGraw's Mission

The Sporting News described the 1923 New York Giants as "the most powerful baseball team ever put together," and Giant manager John McGraw heartily agreed. Unfortunately, Giant fans were not as enamored of the team as were *The Sporting News* and McGraw. Attendance at the Polo Grounds had dipped from 920,000 in 1922 to 820,000 in 1923 and McGraw knew why. Giant fans were crossing the East River to the Bronx to watch Babe Ruth hit home runs in the newly constructed Yankee Stadium. As both manager and part owner of the Giants, this frustrated McGraw, who charged his scouts to find him a Babe Ruth. Realizing that upper Manhattan and the Bronx were both heavily populated by Jews, he added, "Find me a Jewish one."[1]

During baseball's early days, the majority of professional players were Irish, German, or Scandinavian. Beginning in the 1920s and continuing into the 1930s, however, the Jewish and Italian base of fans in several major league cities grew large enough that club owners had to give them serious consideration. In 1920 Jews made up more than a quarter of New York's population and were an untapped market among sports teams. McGraw assured the New York press that the Giants were trying to sign a Jewish prospect. As he told the *New York Tribune*, "A home run hitter with a Jewish name in New York would be worth a million."[2]

Mose Solomon

In September 1923, New York Giant scout Dick Kinsella exulted that he had found the Jewish star McGraw was seeking. His name was Mose Solomon and he was a native New Yorker to boot. Kinsella predicted that Solomon would be as popular at the Polo Grounds as Babe Ruth was in the Bronx.

At the time, Solomon was playing first base for Hutchinson, Kansas, although he could also play the outfield. But it was Solomon's hitting that excited Kinsella. When the Giants signed him, Solomon was hitting .421, and in 134 games, he had 49 homeruns.[3] What was more, he could take care of himself. He had been involved in numerous fistfights because of remarks about his being a Jew. "In every case," reported Kinsella, "Solomon has won the fight without extending himself and the players of other nationalities in this league have learned to respect him to the limit."[4] *The Sporting News* reported, "In Moses (sic), the Giants have just the sort of hero McGraw has wished for."[5]

Solomon was born December 8, 1900, in New York City, on Hester Street, the center of Jewish activity on the Lower East Side. He was the son of Benjamin Solomon, a Russian Jew, and his wife Anna, an Austrian Jew. Both parents were observant, although this piety did not rub off on Mose.[6] The name on his birth certificate was Morris, but Mose—not Moses—is what he called himself, and what his family called him. Benjamin Solomon was a peddler. He moved his family to Columbus, Ohio, where he became a junk dealer but the family remained very poor.

Mose eventually became proficient in both baseball and football. He was playing football for the Carlisle Indian School when Ohio State University offered him free tuition to play on its football team, but he could not afford to be a full-time student.[7] His father was pleased that Mose would continue contributing to the family income, particularly since he felt that neither baseball nor football was acceptable for a young Jew. Ironically, boxing was. Mose's brother, Harry, was a champion boxer who fought under the name Henry Sully. When people asked the parents what Harry was doing for a living, Benjamin Solomon would not hesitate to reply, "Boxing." But if they asked about Mose, his parents would only say, "He's out West working."[8]

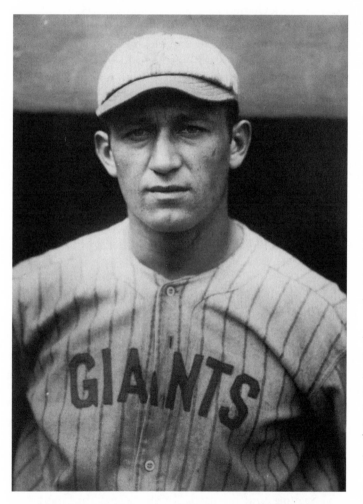

After Mose Solomon hit 49 home runs for Hutchinson, Kansas, he was hailed as the "Rabbi of Swat" and the "Jewish Babe Ruth." John McGraw immediately signed him to a major league contract, believing he would be the player who would draw Jewish fans into the Polo Grounds. Unfortunately, Solomon appeared in only two games for the Giants that year, his only two appearances in a major league uniform (courtesy Jacob Rader Marcus Center of the American Jewish Archives).

According to Mose Solomon's son, Joseph, his father began his baseball career as a pitcher like Babe Ruth, but was converted to an everyday player because of his hitting prowess.[9] He turned pro in 1921 with Vancouver of the Pacific Coast International League, playing both first base and the outfield and batting .313 in 115 games the first year. The following year he played for Vancouver and then Tacoma.[10]

Although Mose Solomon was not an observant Jew, he was fully aware of his ethnic background and while he was in the minor leagues he would not tolerate religious slurs or insults, enforcing respect with his fists. Word soon spread that, "You better lay off the big Jew."[11]

In 1923 Solomon moved to the Hutchinson Wheat Shockers in the Class C Southwestern League. Also known as "Hickory Mose," Solomon began to attract attention. His 49 homers broke the old minor league record of 45, set in 1895, and his .421 average led the league. He was also at the top of the league in runs, hits, and doubles. The press dubbed Solomon the "Jewish Babe Ruth" and the "Rabbi of Swat."[12]

Hutchinson intended to sell Solomon to a Class A or AA team when the 1923 season ended. The team, along with other scouts who reported to McGraw, felt Solomon was not even close to major league status, primarily because his fielding was so bad. He made 31 errors in 131 games playing first base at Hutchinson. When the Wheat Shockers converted the hitting star into an outfielder, his fielding average in right field was a pathetic .862. McGraw tended to agree with the scouting report, but he went ahead and signed Solomon to a major league contract.[13]

As soon as he was signed, Solomon became the most talked-about member of the New York Giants. He was swamped with invitations to various socials and dinners. Prominent Jews arranged to have the rookie escort their daughters around the city. Solomon's son agrees that his father might have been slightly overwhelmed with his reception by the Jewish community, but he argues that his father was able to ignore it. "He knew he had to prove himself as a ballplayer."[14]

Solomon joined the Giants while they were fighting the Reds for the 1923 National League pennant. Despite his hitting ability, McGraw didn't play Solomon until the Giants had clinched the title, keeping him on the bench along with two future Hall of Famers who were also rookies that year, Hack Wilson and Bill Terry.[15]

Solomon finally made his major league debut at the Polo Grounds on September 30, 1923, the Giants' last regular home game that season.[16] *The New York Tribune* reported that the fans that day had lost patience. "The voices in the stands were calling for and to Mose all afternoon. Wails went up when the Giants' lineup was given out without Solomon's name.... The wailing become so loud that McGraw weakened and sent in Solomon in the second inning in place of star outfielder Ross Young. As the words "Solomon playing right field for New York" resonated from the announcer's megaphone, fans grew jubilant, shouting "Oh, you Mose!" and "We're with you, Solomon."[17]

In the bottom of the tenth, with the game tied 3–3 and Frankie Frisch, the runner, on second, Mose Solomon stepped to the plate. Against Joe Oeschger on the mound for the Braves, Solomon socked the first pitch for a double to drive in Frisch and give the Giants a 4–3 victory. Solomon appeared in one more game for the Giants, finishing his abbreviated season with a .375 batting average.[18] He never played another major league game.

Solomon's statistics seemed to qualify him to return to the club in 1924, but he was released immediately after the '23 season. Ostensibly he was let go because of his weak fielding skills, but most historians think the real reason was McGraw's insistence that Solomon stay with the club through the World Series even though he was not eligible to play and would not be paid. Solomon replied that he had an offer to play professional football in Portsmouth, Ohio, and since his family still needed the money, he could not afford to stay with the Giants. "If you leave," McGraw told Solomon, "you will not return to the Giants." Solomon took the football job anyway, and the Giants released him to Toledo of the American Association.[19] According to Solomon's son, Mose learned of his release from the newspapers. Furious, he never again spoke to his former manager, John McGraw.[20]

Mose Solomon played in the minors from 1924 through 1928.[21] Although he was never as good as he had been in 1923, he did hit over .300 with several teams.[22]

After he retired from baseball, Solomon and his wife, the former Gertrude Nachmanovitz, moved to Miami, where Solomon became a successful building contractor. He died there of heart failure on June 26, 1966.[23] An article in *Sports Illustrated* evaluated

Solomon's baseball career both succinctly and correctly when it stated, "He was a designated hitter, born 73 years too soon."[24]

Andy Cohen

John McGraw was disappointed that Mose Solomon did not become the Jewish star he sought to increase attendance at the Polo Grounds. Three years later, in May 1926, McGraw thought his quest was finally over when the Giants promoted their Waco, Texas, shortstop, Andy Cohen, to the parent club. Advertised as "The Great Jewish Hope," Andy would become the first Cohen to play under his real name.[25]

Andrew Howard Cohen was born in Baltimore, on October 24, 1904. Both his father, Manus, and his mother, Lena, were born in Eastern Europe, but came to the United States to escape the pogroms. His father became an avid baseball fan and a skilled player who even got a tryout with the old Baltimore Orioles. He taught Andy the mechanics of the game. Andy's parents separated before he was seven. Because of respiratory problems, his mother moved Andy, his five-year-old brother, Sydney, and his baby sister, Eva, to El Paso.[26]

In El Paso, Lena maintained an observant Jewish home for Andy and his siblings, keeping the dietary laws and saying daily prayers.[27] Unlike many Eastern European Jews, Andy's mother did not discourage him from participating in sports, an area in which her son did very well, saying that if he was content, she was satisfied.[28]

After graduating from El Paso High School, where he excelled in baseball, football, and basketball, Andy was offered a baseball contract with Galveston in the Texas League. Unsure about his future, however, Andy instead accepted a scholarship to the University of Alabama. The Galveston team felt he was worth waiting for and told Cohen that when he completed his education, "You can report to us."[29]

At Alabama, Cohen again competed in three sports, pledged a Jewish fraternity, and in the spring of 1925, at the end of his junior year, was elected captain of the baseball team. He was the first Jew ever to be chosen a sports captain at Alabama. But Cohen left the university that summer to play professional baseball.[30]

Cohen did not go back to Galveston in 1925, but reported to Waco, which had purchased the Galveston franchise while he was in college. Many friends advised him to change his name when he began his baseball career in the Texas League, but he refused, replying that he did not want to try to hide the fact that he was a Jew, and he also did not want to hurt his mother by assuming another name. Since he had done pretty well up to then as Andrew Howard Cohen, he reasoned, he would keep that name.[31] And he continued to do "pretty well," hitting .321 in 126 games for Waco that year.[32]

He made his first appearance for the Giants in June 1926, when McGraw sent him in to pinch-hit for Frankie Frisch. The *American Hebrew* described him as a "pleasant faced youth with rugged features of an unmistakably Jewish cast." Andy singled off Phillies pitcher Ray Pierce and the *Hebrew* proclaimed this hit with a fervor typical of the way his future achievements would be reported in the Jewish community: "Cohen's clear single on the first [pitch] started Andy off on a career which is very likely to make his name a household fixture."[33]

When he came back to the dugout, McGraw told the 1-for-1 rookie, "Young man, congratulations. Today you are leading the National League in hitting."[34] Cohen appeared

Although manager John McGraw hoped he would be the Jewish superstar who would attract
Jewish fans to the Polo Grounds, Andy Cohen had only a three-year major league career with
the New York Giants. After his retirement in 1930 due to an injury, Cohen spent many years
as a minor league coach and manager (courtesy Jacob Rader Marcus Center of the American
Jewish Archives).

in only 32 games for the Giants in 1926, and finished the year with a batting average of .257.[35]

One of the games which Cohen played in 1926 was against the Cincinnati Reds and their Jewish shortstop, Sam Bohne. Before the start of the game, Bohne, whose real name was also Cohen, sent Andy a note, "Welcome to the big leagues, kid. Good luck." Cohen never forgot Bohne's kindness during what was to be Bohne's last year in the majors.[36]

McGraw felt Cohen needed more seasoning and sent him to Buffalo of the International League for the 1927 season. Andy had a spectacular year, hitting .353 with 14 home runs and 118 runs batted in and playing on the International League All-Star Team.[37] *The New York Times*, which followed Cohen's minor-league career, predicted in the summer of 1927, "the chances are that Handy Andy will be back for a real trial in the big league either this season or next. He has earned it."[38]

Buffalo's Jewish population embraced Cohen as their hero, as did Jewish communities in all the International League cities where Cohen played. He was given a "special day" by Syracuse, and everywhere he went he had a following among both Jewish fans and the Jewish populace in general.[39]

In 1928 New York fans were flabbergasted when McGraw traded Giant superstar second baseman Rogers Hornsby to the Boston Braves for Shanty Hogan and Jimmy Welsh. Some historians insist Hornsby was traded because he was unpopular with his teammates and because he had a gambling problem.[40] Others maintain that John McGraw, unwavering in his belief that New York City needed a good Jewish baseball player, had to open up second base for Andy Cohen. After competing with Babe Ruth and his "Murderer's Row" in 1927, McGraw felt the time was right to bring Cohen back to New York for the 1928 season. Insisting that "Cohen will draw like Ruth or Gehrig," McGraw fervently hoped that Andy would attract a huge turnout of Jewish fans to the Polo Grounds.[41]

Having learned his lesson with Mose Solomon, McGraw immediately put Cohen into the Giant lineup in 1928. On opening day, against the Boston Braves, 30,000 fans saw second baseman Andy Cohen lead his team to a 5–2 victory. He scored two runs, drove in two runs and got three hits in four trips to the plate. Even the non–Jewish press got into the act, reporting, "Andy Cohen took New York by storm. He captured the hearts of 30,000 fans as only a Ruth or Walter Johnson could grip them."[42]

Cohen vividly remembered that day. "Thousands of Jewish fans rushed the field, lifted me on their shoulders as they would a new Jewish bridegroom and literally carried me around the Polo Grounds. I was finally rescued by my teammates, who escorted me to the steps of the center-field clubhouse."[43]

McGraw's reaction to Cohen's exploits was simple. After the game he put his arm around his second baseman and told him, "Young man, now you only got 153 to go. Don't get too cocky. It's just one ball game."[44]

Others also took a less positive view of Cohen's feats. Arch-conservative Westbrook Pegler, who could never be called friendly to Jews, told his Chicago readers, "If Cohen succeeds at second base the Giant firm could do business in the Jewish trade alone. If Mr. Cohen will stand up, the Giants will have the offset of Jake Ruppert's Babe Ruth, who will have to hit home runs against Cohen's singles."[45]

As Cohen continued his hot hitting, the adulation and passion continued unabated. His high batting average at the beginning of the season caused many newspapers to foolishly compare his average with that of his predecessor, Hornsby. Cohen became the toast of New York. Sportswriters referred to him as "the young Semite," "Moses," and "the young Jewish player," and his picture appeared on the cover of *Time* magazine. The *Jewish Daily Forward* began to print Giant box scores on the front page of its newspaper. Polo Grounds vendors sold ice cream Cohens, and some Jewish fans, having no knowledge of baseball, asked for seats right behind second base so they could be close to Andy. The Giants had to hire additional secretaries to keep up with his fan mail. It was even suggested that Coogan's Bluff above the Polo Grounds be renamed Cohen's Bluff—quite a contrast to all the Cohens who were renamed for baseball.[46]

While the New York Jewish community welcomed Andy Cohen with open arms, and while most of his teammates readily accepted him, a number of Jew baiters were not so kind. He received a large number of unsigned letters addressing Cohen as "you stupid Hebe," "you showy sheenie," and "you cockie kike." Many periodicals, including *Baseball Magazine* used such terms as "Hebrew nose," "black beady eyes," and "thick eyebrows" to describe Cohen. One cartoon depicted the Giant second baseman's supporters with beards and long coats and spouting Yiddish dialogue, deliberately ignoring the fact that most of Cohen's fans were actually second-generation, assimilated Jews.[47]

The team which rankled Cohen the most during the 1928 season was the Chicago Cubs. The Cubs' abuse became so vitriolic that umpire Beans Reardon threatened to throw out the next player who uttered an anti–Semitic remark. Everything was quiet when Cohen came to bat, until Cohen yelled toward the Cub bench, "'What's the matter with you guys over there, losing your guts?' They began to let me have it then and Reardon turned to me and said, 'Well, kid, you asked for it'.... They all accepted me after that. What a swell guy Reardon was."[48]

Through May, Cohen was hitting a phenomenal .350, but by the end of the season his batting average fell to .274 in 129 games. His good fielding, with only 24 errors in 126 games, helped the Giants finish in second place, only two games behind the pennant-winning St. Louis Cardinals. Ironically, Rogers Hornsby, the player traded to make room for Andy Cohen, won his seventh and final batting title in 1928 with an average of .387.[49] Many consider Cohen's 1928 stats quite acceptable for a ball player with limited power and defensive range.[50] More importantly, it seems that Cohen fulfilled McGraw's hope of improved attendance, as the Giants increased their 1928 total to more than 916,000 fans, compared with the 858,000 attendees they drew the previous year.[51]

After the 1928 season, Cohen continued in his role as Jewish folk hero. He was invited to many store openings, where he would give customers an autographed league ball for every suit or topcoat purchased.[52] Cohen also teamed up with the 265-pound catcher, Shanty Hogan, in a vaudeville act. Calling themselves "Cohen and Hogan" (except in Boston where they changed to "Hogan and Cohen" in deference to Boston's large Irish population) the two players told stories and sang parodies, receiving the then-huge sum of $1,800 per week.[53]

In 1929 Cohen improved his batting average to a respectable .294 and made only 20 errors in 101 games at second base.[54] During the season, in a game against the Cincinnati Reds, Cohen suddenly slowed down going to first even though he had hit a clean single to center. When that happened, McGraw said, "Well, it looks like young Cohen has got football legs, slowing up."[55] Cohen's release to the minors came as a surprise to *The Sporting News* reporter, who fully expected Cohen to be back with the Giants in 1930. The paper commented, "McGraw, the master baseball man, is sweet on Andy [who] can hit, field and run. He has dash and courage. He is aggressive and ambitious."[56]

Nonetheless, Andy Cohen was sold to the Newark Bears of the International League in 1930, where he played for two seasons. Toward the end of the 1931 season, after Cohen had set the International League record for consecutive chances without an error, McGraw sent one of his scouts to Newark to see if Andy was ready to come back to the majors. Unfortunately, Cohen heard something pop when he threw to first base after fielding a grounder, and he had to be carried off the field. This ended any opportunity to return to the Giants.[57]

Cohen never blamed others for his demotion to the minors but he did agree that being a Jewish player in the majors made him stand out. "I thought I was somebody important that they pointed their fingers at because of my nationality. I guess I tried too hard to live up to my reputation, which led to some bad moments on the field."[58]

Through the end of the 1938 season, Cohen played with the Newark Bears and the Minneapolis Millers.[59]

Because of his experience as a long-time player, in 1939 Larry MacPhail hired Cohen as a player-manager for the Brooklyn Dodger organization. For the next two years, Cohen managed Class C teams, moving up to the Class A Elmira, New York, team in 1941 and 1942.[60]

Cohen joined the Army in 1942, taking part in the invasion of North Africa and serving in Italy. During the war, he married a woman he had met in Elmira. She was not Jewish, but Cohen's mother accepted and grew to love her new daughter-in-law.[61]

After his military discharge, Cohen returned to El Paso as player-manager and part owner of the El Paso Texans in the Mexican National League. This was followed by various managerial positions in the minor leagues, including Denver, New Orleans, and Indianapolis.[62]

In 1960, after an absence of 31 years, Cohen returned to the major leagues as coach of the Philadelphia Phillies. Right after the season opener, Phillie manager Eddie Sawyer suddenly resigned. Gene Mauch was hired as his replacement, but since Mauch was unable to join the team in time for the next game, Cohen was named Phillies manager for that one game. Andy Cohen was elated. "I've been waiting for 30 years for a chance to manage in the big leagues," Cohen said. "Now I'm hired and fired all in one day."[63]

The Phillies, with Don Cardwell pitching, defeated the Milwaukee Braves at Connie Mack Stadium 5–4. Cohen would later boast that no manager in baseball history ever had a better winning percentage: "I was the only Phillies manager never to lose a game."[64]

After he left the Phillies, Cohen returned to El Paso again where he served as the baseball coach at the University of Texas-El Paso. At the same time he continued to coach for the local minor league team, the El Paso Sun Kings, a Los Angeles affiliate.[65] Although Andy was not an observant Jew, he always tried to attend services on the Jewish High Holidays.[66]

Cohen received many honors during these years. The new El Paso baseball park was named for him and his brother Sydney.[67] He was selected a member of the College Baseball Coaches Hall of Fame and was the first person ever elected to the El Paso Athletic Hall of Fame.[68]

Andy Cohen died October 29, 1988, of complications from a stroke. He was 84 years old. Years after he retired from baseball, Cohen remarked how pleased he was that young Jews still read about him in a book depicting the lives of Jewish athletes and still looked to him as a role model. "I get a lot of letters from kids telling me that they read the book and that they are real proud of what's in the book. I feel proud of it too."[69]

In assessing Andy Cohen's influence on baseball as a Jewish player, one baseball historian stated that, while hero worship from the Jewish community did not help nor hurt his baseball career, his brief stay in baseball definitely encouraged other Jews to try to play in the major leagues. His achievements in baseball also helped lessen stereotypes about Jewish weakness and showed immigrants and their children that they could feel very comfortable as both Jews and Americans.[70]

Harry Rosenberg

Neither Mose Solomon nor Andy Cohen became the Jewish attraction that John McGraw had hoped for, but in 1930 McGraw thought he had at last found the Jewish star he had been seeking. His name was Harry Rosenberg.

Harry Rosenberg was born in San Francisco, on June 22, 1909. He had ten siblings, including Louis, who played three games in the majors for the White Sox in 1923.[71] When Harry Rosenberg also made it to the majors seven years later, the Rosenbergs became the third set of Jewish brothers who were major league players.

In 1930, while working as a shovel operator for a San Francisco construction company, Harry tried out for the San Francisco Missions of the Pacific Coast League. A right-handed hitting outfielder, Harry won the position but refused to give up his construction job, driving his truck in the morning and playing the outfield for the Missions in the afternoon. He was signed to a full-time contract in June 1930.[72]

Going into July, Rosenberg was hitting .368, with 88 hits and 53 runs batted in for the Missions. McGraw heard about the prowess of the young outfielder from his scouts and the newspapers which described Rosenberg as an inexperienced San Francisco outfielder who "covered centerfield like a master fly hawk," and who could become immensely popular with Jewish fans if brought up to the Giants.[73]

McGraw opted to do just that, buying his contract from San Francisco for between $35,000 and $50,000. Rosenberg felt he was entitled to a percentage of the purchase price, approximately $5,000, and refused to report unless he received his bonus.[74]

He also received a great deal of publicity when he finally reported to the Giants, making his major league debut on July 15, 1930. He walked in his only time at bat that game. Rosenberg appeared in just nine games for the Giants, primarily as a pinch hitter or pinch runner. After going hitless in just five at bats, Rosenberg was sent to Newark of the International Association, ending his major league career.[75] For John McGraw, not even the third time was the charm as he again—and for the last time—failed to find his quintessential Jewish baseball star.

From 1931 to 1941 Rosenberg played for a number of teams in the American Association and Pacific Coast League.[76] In 1941, when Rosenberg was playing for the Hollywood Stars in a game against the Los Angeles Angels, a local columnist noted, "Now that the Angels have Phil Weintraub, both local clubs have a Jewish player who can wallop the agate. Harry Rosenberg already has a big following of Hollywood fans with his hustle, heavy hitting and fine throwing."[77]

John McGraw hoped that Harry Rosenberg would be the Jewish star he had long sought when he signed him to a major league contract in 1930. Unfortunately, Rosenberg played only nine games for the Giants that year, and never returned to the major leagues. He and his brother Lou, who played three games for the Chicago White Sox in 1923, are one of the six sets of Jewish brothers to make it to the major leagues (courtesy National Baseball Hall of Fame Library, Cooperstown, N.Y.).

Rosenberg did not play in 1942. He was lured out of retirement in 1943 by the San Francisco Seals in an attempt to bolster a very weak batting attack.[78] Rosenberg turned down a Seals contract in 1944 to work full time in the construction industry.[79] He also served in the United States Army from 1944 to 1945. After the war, Rosenberg returned to San Francisco, where he died on April 13, 1997, at the age of 88.[80]

There are two ironies to McGraw's quest. First, McGraw missed several good Jewish players during the 1920s and early 1930s who went on to have great success with other teams. Even sadder, the Giants would ultimately have very good Jewish players, but they would not join the team until after McGraw was gone.

13. The Unsung Star

At the same time that John McGraw was searching for a good Jewish player with staying power, the Washington Senators owner, Clark Griffith, signed Buddy Myer, an excellent Jewish infielder, whose career was to last 17 years and whose achievements were so outstanding that many believe he should be in the Baseball Hall of Fame.

And yet, despite his longevity and his considerable skills, Myer never attracted the attention and adulation given to Andy Cohen or even Mose Solomon. The reason is simple. Myer played most of his career for Clark Griffith in Washington, where the Jewish population was a fraction of New York's and where a player's ethnic background was inconsequential.[1] Griffith signed Myer only because he thought Myer was a good player.

Like Andy Cohen and most other Jewish players of his time, Charles Solomon "Buddy" Myer did not come from New York City. He was born on March 16, 1904, in Ellisville, Mississippi. His father, Charles Myer, was a German-Jewish merchant and cotton buyer, and his mother, Maud, was not Jewish.[2] Little is known about Myer's religious upbringing or how Myer felt about being Jewish but Myer identified himself as a Jew throughout his baseball career.[3]

After he graduated from high school, Myer enrolled at Mississippi Agriculture and Mechanical College in 1921, where he excelled at basketball, football, and baseball. In 1923 the Cleveland Indians offered Myer a baseball contract. Buddy accepted but told the Indians he would first have to complete college, which he did in 1925. After he graduated the Indians claimed him and attempted to send him to Dallas in the Texas League for more seasoning. Myer did not like the terms Cleveland offered him and he refused to report. Because he never signed a contract with Dallas, Myer was free to play elsewhere and negotiated a higher salary with New Orleans in the Southern League. His statistics at the plate there were dazzling: in 99 games, he batted .336, hitting 21 doubles, eight triples and three homeruns. He also had speed on the base paths, scoring 76 runs and stealing nine bases. But he did not move well in the field and his fielding average was only .938, although in one errorless game against Little Rock, Myer had nine putouts, nine assists, and was involved in six double plays.[4]

In August the Washington Senators bought Myer's contract for $25,000 and he debuted in a Senators uniform on September 26, 1925. He played the final four games of the regular season at shortstop, getting two hits in eight at bats.[5] The Senators had won the pennant in 1925 and were to face Pittsburgh in the World Series. Under World Series rules, Myer would not have been eligible to play, but the Senators' regular third baseman, Ossie Bluege, was beaned by Pirate hurler Vic Aldridge during game two and Myer replaced Bluege at third. Myer singled his first time at bat, and got an additional hit later, but the Pirates won the series in five games.[6]

In 1926, the five-foot, 10-inch, 163-pound Buddy Myer replaced the Senators' regular shortstop, Roger Peckinpaugh, playing in 132 games. He hit .304 that year—the first of nine seasons he would hit above .300—but his fielding still left a lot to be desired. Before the season was even half over, the Senators manager, Bucky Harris, became convinced that the rookie was not yet ready for a major league "berth." "I really feel," stated Harris, "that Myer is at least one year off from being a big leaguer and may be further away than that. He has been given ten times the chances a rookie ordinarily gets, but has failed, and he has forced me to go back to the old combination of Bluege at third and Peck at shortstop."[7]

Harris was right about Myer's play at shortstop. In 1925 the Senators led the American League in double plays with 166. The following year, with Myer replacing the slick-field-ing Peckinpaugh at short, only the St. Louis Browns made fewer double plays than the 129 turned in by the Senators. While Myer is credited for helping the Senators lead the American League in hitting in 1926, some blame his fielding for the team's barely finishing in the first division that year.[8]

Despite his doubts, manager Bucky Harris was willing to try Myer again in 1927, but at third base replacing Bluege, who would move to shortstop. Harris assured the press that Myer's new position would give him more time to make the throw to first, and help him overcome his greatest weakness—balls hit to his right—"by hugging the foul line a little closer."[9]

One month into the 1927 season Myer had appeared in 15 games for the Senators and his greatest asset, his hitting, was a weak .216. In the hope of getting a more dependable fielder, owner Clark Griffith traded Buddy Myer to the Boston

Buddy Myer is one of the most underrated players ever to play in the major leagues. He played 16 of his 17 seasons for Clark Griffith and the Washington Senators. Although not a power hitter, his lifetime batting average was a very respectable .303 and his 2,131 hits are the most of any Jewish ballplayer. Many believe he should be in the Baseball Hall of Fame (courtesy National Baseball Hall of Fame Library, Cooperstown, N.Y.).

Red Sox for Emory "Topper" Rigney even though Rigney was hitting only .111 at the time. But Griffith liked the trade, noting that Rigney was a fast double-play man, who had figured in 87 the previous year, 33 more than Buddy Myer.[10]

Clark Griffith and Bucky Harris may have been pleased with Rigney, but Boston Red Sox manager Bill Carrigan was excited to get Myer. He considered Buddy Myer "a young player and the type I'm looking for. I look for Myer to become one of the game's greatest shortstops. He has all the qualifications that make up a star. I intend to play Myer regularly at short."[11]

Myer had an outstanding year in 1928 with the Red Sox, not only finishing the season with a batting average of .313 in 147 games but also leading the American League in stolen bases with 30. His statistics were good enough to place him ninth in the balloting for Most Valuable Player in 1928.[12] Rigney, on the other hand, lasted 45 games with the Senators before leaving the major leagues for good.[13]

When the 1928 season ended, Clark Griffith finally admitted that sending Myer to the Red Sox was "the dumbest trade I ever made." He became obsessed with getting Myer back, but his obsession came at a heavy price. On December 15, 1928, the Senators sent five players—pitchers Milt Gaston and Hod Lisenbee, infielders Bobby Reeves and Grant Gillis, and outfielder Elliott Bigelo—to the Red Sox in return for the ex–Senator Buddy Myer.[14] A quarter of a century after the Myer deal, Clark Griffith still talked about his mistake in getting rid of Myer in the first place. "When it's time to admit a mistake, the best thing to do is to admit it," said Griffith. "I sold Buddy Myer to Boston for a shortstop named Topper Rigney. ... later I bought Myer back for $120,000 worth of players, and it was one of the best deals I ever made."[15] Why did Griffith trade Myer? Griffith answered that he had listened to manager Harris, who was convinced by their newly acquired star, Tris Speaker, "that if we only could get Rigney from Boston to play shortstop for us, we could win the pennant in '27." And why did he give up so much to get Myer back? Griffith jokingly replied that it was partly "to do something nice" for former Senators' star Walter Johnson, who became the manager in 1929.[16]

Myer would spend the rest of his major league career as a Senator, no longer at shortstop but at second base. As baseball historian Bill James wrote, "Buddy Myer was not a great defensive second baseman, but a solid, consistent second baseman, among the best in the league in his better years."[17] His fielding had improved so much that Myer twice in his years in the majors led the American League in fielding for a second basemen.[18]

After Myer had captured his first fielding crown in 1931, Shirley Povich, the *Washington Post* sportswriter, noted in his daily column that "Myer ... is now Griffith's ideal type of ballplayer, steady in the field with sensational possibilities, a strong hitter and fast on the bases." Povich also commended Myer for his qualities as a leadoff man, "a good batter, a good waiter, able to make use of his speed on the bases."[19]

Nineteen thirty-three was a memorable year for Buddy Myer. On the positive side, Myer hit over .300 for the fifth time in his career, helping the Senators capture the American League pennant again. The year 1933 also marked the second and final time Myer would appear in a World Series. This year, the Senators lost to the New York Giants in five games, but Myer had a very good series, getting six base hits in 20 at bats, for a .300 average. He also scored two runs and batted in two runs.[20]

Nineteen thirty-three also was the year of his fight with Yankee player Ben Chapman, one of the ugliest anti–Semitic incidents during Myer's years in baseball. Myer, on many occasions, had had to fight anti–Semitic opponents and Chapman was known as one of the worst racists and Jew-baiters in baseball.[21] In a game in 1933 between the Yankees and the Senators, Chapman had gone into second base with a hard slide, nearly spiking Myer in the chin. The next game, on April 25, Myer was again guarding second when Chapman, trying to break up a double play, went plowing into him. Although much smaller than Chapman, Myer came up swinging and Chapman went down. A general melee broke out on the field between the two teams. Fans began to leave the stands and head for the field. The umpires eventually restored order, but the fracas was one of the worst in baseball history. Both Myer and Chapman were fined $100 for their parts in the brawl and both were suspended for five games.[22] Shirley Povich made no direct mention of anti–Semitism in his *Washington Post* stories, but he did write that "Chapman cut a swastika with his spikes on Myer's thigh."[23]

The Chapman incident demonstrated that Buddy Myer would never let anyone step all over him. This came as no surprise to his teammates. George Case, who played with Buddy Myer from 1937 to 1941, described him as "one of the nicest, most placid guys in the world off the field, but the moment he put on his baseball uniform his personality changed; he became aggressive and pugnacious. It was the most amazing thing; you wouldn't think it was the same person."[24]

Buddy Myer's top season for the Senators was 1935. One of his achievements was winning the American League batting title, which he did in dramatic fashion. Myer trailed Cleveland Indian outfielder Joe Vosmik by one percentage point entering the final day of the season. Trying to protect his slender lead, Vosmik opted to sit out the first game of Cleveland's doubleheader. He did enter the game as a pinch hitter but failed to get a hit. Myer, however, had four hits in his game and, although Vosmik played the nightcap, one hit in three at bats was not enough to overtake Myer. By going four for five, Myer took the crown by edging out Vosmik .3489 to .3469.[25]

In addition to leading the league in hitting, Myer also scored 100 or more runs for the fourth and final time, and led the American League with 460 put outs and 138 double plays. Hank Greenberg won the American League's Most Valuable Player Award that year, but Buddy Myer came in fourth.[26]

Following the 1935 season, the New York Yankees made an offer to buy Myer's contract. They needed a replacement for their regular second baseman, Tony Lazzeri, who was slowing up, but more importantly, with Babe Ruth off the team, the Yankees desperately needed a player to bring fans to Yankee Stadium. The Yankee owner, Colonel Jacob Ruppert, began to realize what John McGraw knew years earlier. With the large Jewish population in the New York metropolitan area, an outstanding Jewish player would be the answer. Ruppert instructed his general manager, Ed Barrow, to find that Jewish player. The Yankees attempted to sign Hank Greenberg, but with Lou Gehrig a fixture at first base, Greenberg opted to stay with the Detroit Tigers. Then Barrow offered Griffith more than $100,000 for Myer, but Griffith turned Barrow down flat.[27]

Nineteen thirty-six, the year after Myer's outstanding season, was disappointing for both Myer and the Senators. After only 51 games, Myer developed a mysterious stomach illness which put him on the voluntary retired list for the remainder of the season. But in 1937 Myer returned to form and finished the season with a .293 batting mark. Myer appeared in more than 100 games for the last time in 1938. He had a season batting average of .336, the second highest of his career, and for the second time his fielding average led all second basemen in the American League.[28]

Although he hit over .300 for the final time in 1939, Myer played a total of only 202 games over the next three seasons. On October 8, 1941, Buddy Myer was officially released by the Washington Senators. In announcing his departure, the Washington owner, Clark Griffith, briefly stated, "I'm sorry I have to do it, but I have to make room for some of my younger players."[29] The 37-year-old Myer had intended to retire a year earlier, but stayed on at the urging of Griffith, who told him that the condition of the Senator's infield was very unsettled. "Mr. Griffith told me I would be doing the club a favor if I'd play one more season. I told him then it would be my last."[30]

After he left the Senators in 1941 Myer turned down several opportunities to manage big league clubs, although he once toyed with the idea of trying to buy one. He retired to Baton Rouge, where he became a successful mortgage banker, and died there on October 31, 1974, at the age of 70. He was survived by his widow, Minna Williams, and two sons.[31]

In his 17 years in the major leagues, Buddy Myer compiled a lifetime batting average of .303. He had 2,131 hits, more than any other Jew who played in the major leagues and he appeared in more major league games than any other Jewish ball player—1,923. Although he hit only 38 homers, he had 130 triples, 353 doubles, scored 1,174 runs, and had 850 runs batted in.[32]

Buddy Myer is a member of both the International Jewish Hall of Fame and the Mississippi Sports Hall of Fame. He is not, however, a member of Baseball's Hall of Fame at Cooperstown, although many, especially baseball statistician and authority Bill James, feel he merits that honor. James compared the careers of infielder Hall of Famer Billy Herman and Buddy Myer, taking into account such factors as batting average, runs scored, runs batted in, fielding percentage, and double plays executed. James concluded, "How in the world can you put one of those people in the Hall of Fame and leave the other out?"[33]

The only justification for omitting Myer from Cooperstown is his lifetime home run total of only 38. Unfortunately for Myer, he played baseball when hitters such as Babe Ruth were knocking the ball out of the park with regularity. Myer also had the misfortune to play for a team that often ended the season in the second division, where national media attention was rare.[34]

Nevertheless, Myer is definitely on a par with many players who have been selected to enter Cooperstown. There is no question that, next to Hank Greenberg, Buddy Myer was the outstanding Jew to play in the major leagues prior to 1948.

14. The Clown and the Spy

Two Jewish players—one a pitcher, the other a catcher—began their major league careers around 1920. While both were relatively good players, today they are remembered not for their playing abilities, but rather for their feats as non-players.

Al Schacht

The San Diego Chicken, the Philly Phanatic, and the Cardinal's Fredbird have become almost as much a part of their teams as the players themselves. Today, nearly every major league baseball team has a mascot whose sole job is to entertain the fans. The forerunner of these costumed creatures was a former major league pitcher and coach, Al Schacht, the original "Clown Prince of Baseball."[1]

He was born Alexander Schacht on November 11, 1892, in a two-room tenement apartment on New York's Lower East Side. His Orthodox Jewish parents, Samuel and Ida, were both born in Russia. Samuel Schacht was a locksmith and talented ironworker; Ida, the daughter of the town rabbi, came from an aristocratic family. Like many Russian Jews, Samuel had taken his family and fled to avoid conscription in the Czar's Army.[2]

Al Schacht first discovered baseball when the family moved from the overcrowded Lower East Side across the East River to the Bronx, where Yankee Stadium sits today. When the Schachts moved there, however, the Bronx had vast areas of open space where the children played. "My love of baseball began here," Schacht recalled.[3] Al played baseball wherever he could, in schoolyards, in vacant lots, or in the city streets.[4]

He also discovered anti–Semitism while still a youngster. Because one day he forgot to bring his books to his first-grade class, his teacher screamed at him, "You damn kike." "When I heard that, I kicked her in the shin," recalled Schacht. He was expelled for his behavior.[5] When he was a little older, he was frequently pummeled by Irish and Italian gangs who lived in his Bronx neighborhood and roamed the streets picking on Jewish kids. After a number of beatings, Schacht tried to avoid their wrath by recruiting a few of his tormentors for jobs lighting the stoves of Orthodox Jews on the Sabbath. "I'm not sure that the Irish kids accepted me in their crowd," said Schacht, "but they did tolerate me."[6]

As he grew up, Al Schacht kept his burning passion to play baseball, much to the displeasure of his mother, who wanted him to become a rabbi. Informed of his ambition, she reacted in the classic manner of many first-generation Eastern European Jews. "You will grow up to be a bum or a loafer."[7]

Although Schacht lived in the Bronx, he used to walk from his home to the Polo Grounds, stand on Coogan's Bluff and watch the Giants play. By the time he was 15, he was running errands for the Giant players, especially for Giant star pitcher Christy Mathewson. In a few years Mathewson would repay the favor by teaching Schacht how to throw a screwball or fade away pitch.[8] According to Schacht, "There is nobody I would say I was indebted to for my success, except Mathewson."[9]

Schacht enrolled at Commerce High School in 1908 and immediately informed his baseball coach that he wanted to pitch for the team. At only 125 pounds, Schacht seemed too skinny to pitch, but he persevered and ended up pitching for what some consider the greatest high school team ever assembled.[10]

To earn money during the summers, Schacht pitched for a semipro team that toured the "Borscht Belt" in the Catskill Mountains. After he turned the money he had been paid over to his mother, she never again said much about his playing ball.[11]

For a while, Schacht pitched for his high school and played semipro baseball in the Catskills. But at the end of the 1910 high-school season, when Schacht's school was to play for the city championship, the board of education disqualified Schacht from playing anymore sports at Commerce because of his paid status. Schacht dropped out of school, never to return.[12]

From 1911 to 1912, on the weekends, Al Schacht played semiprofessional baseball for teams in New York, Pennsylvania, and Ohio. Despite his small stature, he had winning records for many of them.[13]

Schacht was with the Walton, New York, team when he first began clowning, an activity which would have a profound effect on his future in baseball. Before some games, he would impersonate well-known actors, or mimic a pitcher who was getting "roughed up" by opposing batters but would not go to the showers. The more the fans showed their approval of Schacht's clowning, the more he would do.[14] Early in his clowning career, a young sportswriter for the *Buffalo Courier*, Jack Yellen, gave Al Schacht the nickname which would remain with him for the rest of his life—"The Clown Prince of Baseball."[15] (Jack Yellen went on to become a Tin Pan Alley writer of many hit songs, including "Happy Days Are Here Again.")[16]

Although he was becoming known for his clowning, Schacht was also pitching well, winning 16 consecutive games for Walton.[17] One day, he learned that Cincinnati scout Mike Kehoe was going to watch him pitch. Always concerned that he looked too thin, Schacht donned extra socks, two sweatshirts, sliding pads and anything else that would make him look heavier. The weather was unusually hot that day, and with the extra equipment Schacht struggled on the mound. Although he pitched a relatively good game, he lost 2–0. The scout never spoke with Schacht.

Suddenly, a few weeks later, the depressed pitcher received a wire inviting him to see Clark Griffith, who was then manager of the Cincinnati Reds. Griffith, astounded by the appearance of the 132-pound Schacht instead of the 160-pound pitcher Kehoe had described, nonetheless offered Schacht a farm-team contract, but Al declined, saying he could make more money in semipro ball.[18]

From 1913 to 1916, Schacht spent most of his time in the International League.[19] Certain he would be drafted to fight in World War I, Schacht dropped out of the minors and spent part of 1917 with the Bethlehem Steel Company team. He was not drafted until 1918 and spent his entire army stint playing ball at Fort Slocum, New York.

After his release in 1919, Schacht had the best year of his career, playing for the lowly

An arm injury forced Washington Senator pitcher Al Schacht to retire as an active player after only three years in the major leagues, although he had a successful coaching career with the Senators. Schacht is best known for entertaining his teammates and the fans with his clowning antics, earning the nickname "The Clown Prince of Baseball." He also entertained the troops during World War II and later opened a restaurant in New York City (courtesy National Baseball Hall of Fame Library, Cooperstown, N.Y.).

Jersey City Skeeters of the International League. The Skeeters won only 45 games the entire season, but Schacht won 20 of them, including 10 shutouts.[20]

While Schacht was pitching for Jersey City, he read in *The Sporting News* that former Reds manager Clark Griffith, who was now owner of the Washington Senators, sorely needed pitchers. Soon Griffith began receiving newspaper clippings every time Schacht won a game for the Skeeters, each accompanied by a brief note, signed "Just a Fan." A typical note would read, "Enclosed you will find clipping of Al Schacht's work. He is without doubt the best pitcher in the International League.... Why don't you get wise to yourself and get this fellow? Yours truly, Just a Fan." Needless to say, Al Schacht was "Just a Fan."[21]

Griffith finally decided to go to Jersey City to scout Schacht for himself. After watching him hurl his tenth shutout of the season, Griffith bought Schacht's contract that evening and brought him to Washington, D.C.[22] Schacht made his major league debut September 18, 1919, and he defeated the St. Louis Browns in the first game of a doubleheader, 12 to 3.[23] He ended the 1919 season with a record of 2 wins and no losses, and an earned run average of 2.40.[24]

Schacht returned the following year as a regular member of the Senators' starting pitching rotation, and by the end of June 1920 had a 5–2 record. In 1920 Walter Johnson was the pitching star of the Senators. The Big Train had hurt his arm throwing a no-hitter against the Boston Red Sox the day after Schacht lost his second game of the year. Johnson was scheduled to pitch when the club came home from Boston, and a large crowd had shown up eager to see Johnson throw another gem. But Johnson was unable to pitch that day and Griffith, in a panic, asked one of his hurlers to volunteer to replace him. Schacht raised his hand. Gratefully, Griffith told him, "If you win this game today, Al, as long as I have anything to say about this ball club you will have a job with me. I mean it. I don't care if you never win another game this season—you've got to win this one."[25]

When Schacht took the mound, the disappointed fans began throwing soda bottles and seat cushions on the field, as well as giving Al Schacht catcalls for replacing Johnson. But Schacht ignored the crowd, and defeated the Yankees 4–1. Unfortunately, this was Schacht's last win in 1920. In a later game as a reliever he got on base, but when the next batter attempted to bunt Schacht to second, Tiger shortstop Donie Bush leaped to take the throw and came down on Schacht's pitching arm, injuring Schacht's shoulder. He appeared in only 22 games the entire season, ending with a record of 6–4, and an earned run average of 4.44.[26]

Before the start of the 1921 season, *Baseball Magazine* featured Al Schacht as "a player you ought to get to know." The journal predicted that the Senators should do even better in 1921 with Schacht pitching for the team.[27] Schacht did come back to pitch in 1921 after his season-ending injury the previous year, but he finished the 1921 campaign with a record of six wins and six losses, appearing in only 29 games. The 1921 season was Schacht's last in the majors as an active player. His lifetime record was 14–10, with an earned run average of 4.48, and a total of 53 games.[28]

For the next two years Schacht was a player and coach for several minor league teams. In 1924 he returned to the Senators as assistant to Bucky Harris, the new manager of the Senators. True to his earlier pledge, Griffith gave Schacht the $300 necessary to purchase his release from his minor league contract.[29]

Schacht's more enduring baseball career began in the majors in 1920 while he was still an active player with the Senators. That year, in spring training, he met coach and former Senator player Nick Altrock, who had previously done a routine with Germany Schaefer, baseball's first clown.[30] Altrock and Schacht immediately formed a new team and became baseball's premier clowning duo. Physically, they were perfect for each other. Altrock had a craggy face, a heavy build, and the general look of a losing ex-pugilist. He made an excellent foil for Schacht's wiry, agile body, expressive face, and impertinent wit.

Together the two men held their own mock infield practice after the regular one ended. They also pantomimed a slow motion pitcher (Schacht) and batter (Altrock) and engaged in burlesque fights. Once the game had started, they resumed their regular coaching duties, Schacht at third base and Nick Altrock at first.[31]

The fans loved the two clowns, Altrock and Schacht were happy with what they were doing, and, most of all, Clark Griffith was elated. Not only did his team have two "official" clowns when other teams had none, but the two were extremely capable coaches on the base paths. Senators manager Bucky Harris was also pleased with his assistants: "They were both sound baseball men."[32]

Altrock and Schacht both found "clowning" financially lucrative. Yankee owner Jacob Ruppert hired the duo to entertain at the 1921 World Series, where they received rave reviews from both the fans and the press. Over the next 15 years, they gained national prominence by performing an endless variety of skits and satires at various sporting events, including the World Series, All-Star games, basketball and hockey games, and tennis matches. They went into vaudeville and theater circuits, where Schacht boasted playing on the same bill as Bing Crosby. The team received $350 per week.[33]

Although the two coaches made people laugh with their routines, few, if any realized how much they disliked one another.[34] Luckily their comedy act did not depend on sound, because much of the time while they worked together, they refused to speak to each other.[35] In fact, they stopped talking to one another completely after 1929.[36]

Many reasons have been offered to explain the animosity. Some suggest that the two fought because Altrock was jealous of the younger Schacht. Others claim that the rift occurred because Altrock refused to enter the film business. Altrock's anti–Semitism is another often-repeated reason given for the rift between the two men. Two stories illustrate this theory. In one of their skits, Schacht was supposed to hit Altrock over the head with a glove filled with a foam rubber ball. At the last moment, Schacht switched to a harder ball and knocked Altrock out cold. According to a newspaper article, when Altrock, regained consciousness he muttered, "I'll teach that Jew to pull his punches after this."[37] On another occasion, Altrock, after having imbibed a little too much one evening, called Schacht "a Jew kike bastard" because Al wouldn't go out drinking with him.[38] Schacht never explained the real reason, but the two men would continue working together until 1936.[39]

Nineteen thirty-four was another watershed year in Schacht's life. That year Clark Griffith traded his son-in-law, Joe Cronin, to the Boston Red Sox. Cronin insisted that Schacht be included in the deal and go with him to Boston. "Schacht may be a clown," said Cronin," but I regard him as the best man in the business when it comes to flagging down runners at third base or sending them home."[40] It is interesting to note that, although Schacht coached the Senators during much of Buddy Myer's career, there is no record indicating that the two men were close. In contrast, Moe Berg, Schacht's teammate on the Senators for a few years, and later on the Red Sox, was referred to as Schacht's good friend.[41]

Schacht stayed with the Red Sox until he retired from coaching in 1936. He then struck out on his own, and in his signature top hat and cutaway tails over a baseball uniform, performed solo in minor and major league parks, country fairs, 25 World Series and 18 All-Star Games.[42] His routines included sitting on the base path reading the paper oblivious to the game around him, walking an imaginary tight rope on the ground, or giving the ball to the batboy to give to the first baseman and demanding a receipt; other times he would chase a ball around wearing a huge catcher's mitt; often he would go into the stands to kiss the girls and escort the ladies to their seats.[43]

When the United States entered World II, Schacht entertained thousands of troops in North Africa, Europe, and the South Pacific.[44] He felt that baseball stories helped homesick GIs "over the hump." His stories were a big hit with American troops wherever he went.[45] Schacht also wrote three books, including his 1941 autobiography, *Clowning through Baseball.*[46]

In 1946, 13 years before Dan Daniel, Schacht received the William J. Slocum Award for the highest contribution to baseball over a long period of time.[47] That same year, Schacht got married and opened a restaurant in New York City. His restaurant became the gathering place for athletes and other celebrities, and Schacht became a wealthy man. In January 1952, at the annual dinner of the B'nai B'rith Sports Lodge, Schacht was honored for his efforts in entertaining hospitalized veterans.[48] Al Schacht made his final performance at a baseball game in Hartford at the age of 81, where he claimed that he had performed live for more people than any other entertainer in history.[49]

Schacht died on July 14, 1984, in Waterbury, Connecticut, at the age of 92.[50] Throughout his lifetime at every interview, Schacht would list his religion as Jewish, his politics as impartial, and his first love as baseball.[51]

It is evident from these remarks that Jews were definitely making progress in baseball. Anti-Semitism still existed but Jewish baseball players were openly admitting that they were Jews. Although he said it tongue-in-cheek, Al Schacht proved this point when he once commented: "There is talk that I am Jewish—just because my father was Jewish, my mother is Jewish, I speak Yiddish and once studied to become a rabbi and a cantor. Well, that's how rumors got started. The fact is that I am Jewish, plenty Jewish."[52]

Moe Berg

Al Schacht's renown was as a baseball clown rather than as a successful pitcher and coach. Moe Berg, although he spent 15 years in the major leagues, is far better known for his activities totally outside baseball. Berg, who was a friend and teammate of both Al Schacht and Buddy Myer, was unusual not only for the depth and breadth of his knowledge at a time when most ballplayers were relatively uneducated, but also for his unique personality and peccadilloes. Casey Stengel referred to Berg as "the strangest man ever to play baseball."[53] Yet, at the same time, he was also referred to as "the brainiest guy in baseball."[54]

Morris (Moe) Berg was born March 2, 1902, in a coldwater flat in Manhattan a few blocks from the Polo Grounds. His parents, Bernard Berg, a druggist, and Rose Tashker, were both Russian-Jewish immigrants. Moe was the youngest of three children; his brother, Sam, became a doctor and his sister, Ethel, a schoolteacher. Moe also followed his parent's wishes and became a lawyer.[55]

When Berg was still small, his father moved the family to a middle-class neighborhood in Newark; the Bergs were one of the few Jewish families living there. Although the Bergs were not observant Jews, Moe Berg's Jewishness contributed greatly to his sense of being an outsider in mid-twentieth century America.[56]

When he was three years old, Moe was already displaying an athletic bent. He would often squat down like a catcher, using a manhole cover as home plate, and play catch with the beat patrolman in front of his father's pharmacy. Usually Moe was able to catch anything the officer threw at him.[57] When he was seven, he joined the Roseville Methodist Episcopal Church baseball team. At the urging of his coach, he assumed the less ethnic sounding pseudonym of Runt Wolfe.[58]

In 1918, at the age of 16, Berg graduated from Barringer High School, where he was named the team's "best third baseman." He attended New York University for one year before transferring to Princeton University, a remarkable achievement for a Jewish boy from a middle-class family at a time of quotas for Jews at elite colleges.[59]

While at Princeton, Berg encountered some anti–Semitism. On one occasion, one of his teammates was nominated for membership into one of the prestigious dining clubs considered important to social life at the university. Berg's teammate accepted on the condition that Berg also become a member. The club agreed, but insisted that Berg not bring any more Jews into the club. Not only did Berg fail to accept this condition, the incident so infuriated him that he never returned to Princeton for class reunions.[60]

Berg graduated *magna cum laude* in 1923, twenty-fourth in a class of 211. He was an excellent linguist, studying Latin, Greek, French, Spanish, Italian, German, and Sanskrit.

And, of course, he played baseball—third base, first base, and primarily shortstop, on the Princeton baseball team. The *Princeton Alumni Weekly* wrote, "He was slow and lacked hitting power but had a slingshot arm and an ability to hit in the clutch." In his senior year, he led his team to a record 18 consecutive wins.[61]

On June 26, 1923, Princeton lost to Yale at Yankee Stadium in the Big Three title game, but Berg put on a good show for scouts from the New York Giants and the Brooklyn Robins,[62] who were looking for Jewish players to appeal to the many Jewish fans residing in New York. It was the year Giants manager John McGraw was especially active in his search for a Jewish star, but, unfortunately for Berg, the Giants already had two great shortstops—Dave Bancroft and Travis Jackson. On the other hand, the mediocre Robins needed fresh talent and offered Berg his first professional contract for $5,000 to sign with them.[63]

After graduation, Berg planned to enter law school. He had hoped first to go to Paris to study languages at the Sorbonne, but he lacked the funds. Uncertain whether to sign the Robins' contract, Berg consulted

Moe Berg may not have been the most skilled major leaguer, but he was certainly one of the most scholarly athletes ever to don a major league uniform. A secretive man throughout his life, his exploits as a spy during World War II have been well documented (courtesy National Baseball Hall of Fame Library, Cooperstown, N.Y.).

successful attorney and former Yale pitcher Dutch Carter, who advised, "When I was your age I had a chance to pitch in the National League but my family looked down on professional sports.... I've always been sorry I listened to them, because it made me a frustrated man. Don't you become frustrated. At least give it a try."[64] Berg accepted the $5,000 signing bonus, which he used to attend graduate school at the Sorbonne; he later earned his law degree during three off-seasons.[65]

Berg joined the Robins immediately in a game against the Phillies, and in his first major league at bat he singled to drive in a run. He remained with the Robins the rest of the year, appearing in 49 games—47 at short and two at second base. Berg's fielding was superb but he managed only nine base hits in 129 at bats for an average of .186.[66]

Berg went to spring training with the Robins in 1924, but manager Wilbert Robinson was not impressed with the six-foot, one-inch, 185-pound Berg, and optioned him to the Minneapolis Millers. At first, Berg threatened to quit, but then reluctantly reported to the

Millers where he became their regular third baseman. After a successful first half, Berg's average plummeted and he was benched.[67]

His shortcomings at the plate were responsible for one of the most enduring lines in baseball. The Robins' scout, Mike Gonzalez, had been instructed to follow the progress of Moe Berg. After watching him play, he sent the Robins the curt, but now famous description, "Good field, no hit." This reputation would follow Berg wherever he played.[68]

As if to prove the scout wrong, in 1925 Berg played for the Reading Keys and hit an unbelievable .311, attracting the Chicago White Sox to buy his contract at the tail end of the season.[69] In 1926 White Sox owner Charles Comiskey granted Berg's request and allowed him to miss spring training so he could finish the semester at Columbia University Law School.[70] Berg played 41 games for the White Sox that year and reverted to a more typical batting average of .221.[71]

Comiskey was not so agreeable in 1927 when Berg again asked permission to report late. "The time has come," Comiskey wrote, "when you must decide as to the profession you intend following." There was no question that Berg wanted to play baseball, so instead of completely missing spring training, he got a leave of absence for the remainder of the academic year from his law school dean.[72]

Because he still reported late, Berg spent the first three months of 1927 riding the bench. In August his whole major league career changed. No one knew at the time, but this event would greatly prolong Moe Berg's stay in the big leagues. Ray Schalk, the catcher-manager of the White Sox, broke his hand during the game. Then Chisox backup catcher Buck Crouse split one of his fingers on a foul tip. Unbelievably, third-string catcher Henry McCurdy then fractured a finger. Manager Schalk yelled, "Get me another catcher, quick."[73] Knowing that first baseman Earl Sheely had caught in the minors, Berg told his manager that the team already had another catcher. Schalk misunderstood, thought Berg was volunteering, and sent him in. Berg had never caught before but performed flawlessly.[74]

Although he became a shrewd and accomplished catcher, Berg still left much to be desired as a hitter. One day, as he took his usual walk back to the dugout after another strikeout, fellow catcher Buck Crouse drawled, "Moe, I don't care how many of them college degrees you got, they ain't learned you to hit that curve no better than the rest of us."[75]

Berg's move behind the plate proved to be a fortunate one for him and from 1927 until his retirement as a player in 1939, he was solely a catcher.[76] Berg confessed that becoming a catcher was the best break he ever had in baseball. He knew he lacked speed and that he would never have been able to remain in the lineup long enough to develop as a hitter, but he was wily and quickly learned the weaknesses of the hitters and the strengths of his pitching staff. His strong arm enabled him to throw out the fastest base runners. Casey Stengel, a good judge of baseball talent, compared him favorably with two of baseball's premier catchers, Mickey Cochrane and Bill Dickey.[77]

While many Jewish players who preceded Berg were victims of anti–Semitism during their careers, Moe Berg's personality helped diminish personal ethnic slurs.[78] Even in his early days in baseball, he experienced little prejudice as a Jew, especially at the major league level. "I believe," Berg stated, "that there is a future in this greatest of pastimes for members of my race."[79]

Berg's best year in the majors was 1929. He played in 107 games for the White Sox, and led all catchers defensively, allowing only five stolen bases. Berg batted .287, scored 37 runs, and had 47 runs batted in.[80] He even received two votes for Most Valuable Player.[81]

While playing for the White Sox, Berg completed his law studies at Columbia, receiving his degree in 1930. After the 1930 season, Berg took a job with a well-respected Wall Street law firm, but baseball remained his chief passion.[82] Because of a torn knee ligament suffered in April 1930, Berg played few games for the White Sox that season. Berg was already slow on his feet, and Casey Stengel remarked after hearing of Berg's injury, "A turtle could now beat him to first base."[83] The Cleveland Indians picked him up for the 1931 season when the White Sox put him on waivers, but he could manage only 10 games for the Indians and had one hit in 13 plate appearances the entire year.[84]

Cleveland released Berg in January 1932 and he now signed with the Washington Senators, who already had two Jews on the roster—Buddy Myer and Berg's friend from earlier days, Al Schacht. In his *Washington Post* column, Shirley Povich took note of the new Senator by writing, "The average mental capacity of the Washington Ball Club was hiked several degrees by the acquisition of the eminent Mr. Moe Berg."[85] Berg had recovered enough from his injury to set an American League record with the Senators by catching in 117 consecutive games without an error. This record stood for 12 years. In 1932 he hit only .236 but threw out 35 base runners.[86]

In 1933 Berg played on his only pennant-winning team, although the Senators lost the World Series to the New York Giants. Berg did not appear in the World Series, but he was happy just to be with the team. During the season, he remained effective defensively, but swung his usual weak bat, hitting a mere .185 and eliciting another well-known comment that "Berg can speak 12 languages, but can't hit in any of them."[87]

On July 25, 1934, Clark Griffith released Moe Berg to make way for a new catcher, Cliff Bolton.[88] Griffith regretted getting rid of Berg, stating, "We don't need him to catch particularly, we need him to talk. He's just the man to talk to some of these foreigners. The way things are going now, we sound like a row in the League of Nations."[89] Berg's season was not over, however. On August 1, Cleveland Indian manager Walter Johnson, who had managed Berg at Washington in 1932, offered Berg the reserve catching job to replace the injured Glenn Myatt. Berg caught 29 games that year at Cleveland and hit .258 for the Indians.[90]

Former teammate and Red Sox manager Joe Cronin brought Berg to Boston in 1935, where he again met up with his old pal, Al Schacht. From 1935 through 1939, Berg completed his major league playing career in Boston, although he averaged fewer than 30 games per season. Berg played his final game in the majors on August 30, 1939, hitting his sixth career home run off Detroit Tiger hurler Fred Hutchinson.[91]

Generally a serious person, Berg's sly but gentle sense of humor made him popular with reporters. A favorite story involved Washington outfielder Dave Harris, a genial, slow-moving Southerner with little formal education, who along with his teammates often consulted the erudite Berg about various problems. One day Harris told Berg he was feeling ill, so Berg asked Harris to stick out his tongue. After looking at him carefully, Moe told Harris, "Dave, you are suffering from a bit of intestinal fortitude. Just lay off the heavy food and get some rest today." When Harris came to breakfast the next morning and announced that he was feeling just fine, he credited Berg. "You were right. That little touch of intestinal fortitude I had is all gone."[92]

Casey Stengel said that "Berg had all that knowledge and used them penetrating words, but he never put on too strong. They thought he was like me, you know, a bit eccentric. He was very well liked."[93]

In addition to his knowledge of law and languages, Berg also had an amazingly wide grasp of many disciplines, including science, history, literature, and politics. On one occasion the team bus got lost while returning from an exhibition game in the Deep South. It was pitch dark and the bus driver had no idea where he was. Moe had the driver stop the bus and he got off, studied the constellations for a moment and then told the driver which way he should head. When the driver asked Berg how he knew, Berg told the driver "So say the stars." Moe and the stars were right.[94]

In the late 1930s Moe Berg appeared three times on the popular radio quiz show *Information Please*. He astounded a national radio audience when he correctly answered a number of difficult questions, including identifying all of the Seven Sleepers, the Seven Wise Masters, the Seven Wise Men, the Seven Wonders of the World, and the Seven Stars.[95] The show received so many letters every time Berg appeared that Baseball Commissioner Judge Kenesaw Mountain Landis wrote, "You did more for the image of baseball in half an hour than I have since I became commissioner."[96] Berg was a very private person. He stopped appearing on the show when moderator Clifton Fadiman began to ask what Moe considered too many personal questions.

Sportswriter John Kiernan later remarked, "Moe wasted his time in baseball. He could have been a Supreme Court justice with that rare brain he possessed."[97] Berg retorted, "I'd rather be a ballplayer than a justice on the U.S. Supreme Court."[98]

After he retired as a player, he spent 1940 and 1941 as the bullpen coach for the Red Sox, a role he thoroughly enjoyed. He took pleasure in working with young pitchers and he earned a reputation as a great teacher.[99] He was one of the most popular members on the team. One of his teammates commented that Moe was really something in the bullpen. "We'd all sit around and listen to him discuss the Greeks, Romans, Japanese, anything. Hell, we didn't know what he was talking about, but it sure sounded good."[100]

No baseball man appreciated Moe Berg more than his manager at both Washington and Boston, Joe Cronin. He considered Berg as necessary to his Red Sox as if he were on the field catching every game. Cronin stated that Berg's work in the bullpen with young pitchers was valuable for the team's morale. "When I managed the Washington Senators to their pennant in 1933," said Cronin, "Berg's presence on the team had much to do with the club's victorious drive."[101]

Berg quit baseball in 1941 because, as he told Arthur Daley of the *New York Times*, "All over the continent men and women are dying. Soon, we, too, will be involved. And what I am doing? Sitting in the bullpen telling stories to the relief pitchers."[102] In his 15 years in the major leagues, Berg appeared in 663 games and had a lifetime batting average of .243.[103] There is no doubt that Berg's longevity in the majors was due to his defensive skills and his knowledge of baseball.[104]

Berg announced his retirement the same day his father, Bernard, died in Newark following a long illness.[105] One of Moe's few regrets about his life in baseball was his immigrant father's unchanging attitude toward the game. Like many Eastern-European Jews who came to the United States, Bernard Berg considered baseball a waste of time and he would not attend any of Moe's games.[106] Berg's brother, Samuel, sided with Moe. Once, Samuel and his father were discussing the difficulty in making a living during the Depression when Samuel mentioned that at least Moe was doing well playing ball. "A sport," the father responded, and he turned his head and feigned spitting.[107] As Berg was entering his final season as a player, he confided to friends that it would be his greatest joy to see his father in the stands, but, "No matter how much I entreat the man, my father will not see me play."[108]

During his years with the Senators, the handsome Berg could often be seen at social events where he met influential people in government. It is possible that these connections were the impetus for his work during World War II. Prior to the outbreak of the war, Moe Berg made two trips to Japan. In 1932, when baseball was just catching on there, he went with his close friend, White Sox pitcher Ted Lyons, and Dodger outfielder Lefty O'Doul. The three men gave pitching, hitting, and catching clinics together at six universities. Berg even studied some Japanese prior to the trip and he learned more while in Japan. According to Lyons, "They loved him [Moe] in Japan."[109]

Berg made his second trip to Japan two years later with a group of American All Stars which included Babe Ruth, Lou Gehrig, Earl Averill, Charlie Gehringer, Jimmie Foxx, and Lefty Gomez. Since Berg was far from an All-Star, the story was that he had come along to write travel pieces for the *Boston American*. It soon became obvious that he was in Japan for other reasons. On November 29, 1934, he went to St. Luke's Hospital in Tsukiji, supposedly to visit the daughter of the American ambassador, Joseph Grew. Berg never saw the ambassador's daughter; instead he snuck onto the roof of the hospital, one of the tallest buildings in Tokyo, and filmed the city and the harbor with the new movie camera he had taken with him to Japan. Apparently, the United States government had recruited Berg as a spy, for when General Jimmy Doolittle's bombers raided Tokyo, their targets were plotted by referring to the films taken by Berg eight years earlier.[110]

In February 1942, two months after Japan had bombed Pearl Harbor, Berg made an impassioned plea to the Japanese, in their own language, to resume friendly relations with the United States. Telling the Japanese people that their leaders were betraying them, Berg warned his listeners, "Believe me when I tell you, you cannot win this war."[111] The speech may or may not have had an effect on the Japanese people, but it had a definite effect on the Japanese government. Within a year of Berg's speech, baseball was banned in Japan, the government calling it "a decadent American sport."[112]

In 1943 Berg joined the Office of Strategic Service (forerunner of the CIA) headed by General William Donovan. His specialty was talking to rocket scientists who were thought to be building an atomic bomb for Adolf Hitler. Because of his fluency in German and his depth of knowledge, the United States considered Berg the perfect man to absorb complicated scientific information in German.[113] He was sent to Italy to determine if Italian scientists were also capable of making an atomic bomb. When Berg was selected for the secret work in Italy, a Donovan aide asked the General, "Do you know who they gave us for this mission? A ballplayer named Moe Berg. You ever hear of him?" Donovan answered, "Yes, he's the slowest runner in the American League."[114]

Once, Berg was required to disguise himself as a German army officer, enter a munitions plant in Italy, and see if new weapons were being developed there. As a Jew, he put himself at an especially great risk.[115] When Germany fell in 1945, Berg's information proved quite valuable, enabling the Allies to move scientists to England before the Soviet army could apprehend them.[116]

In 1952, during the Cold War, the United States wanted to present Berg with the Medal of Freedom, but would not allow him to tell people why he won it, since the information was still classified. He refused to accept the medal on those terms. After he passed away, Moe's sister, Ethel, wrote to the government and claimed the award, which is now in the Baseball Hall of Fame in Cooperstown.[117]

From 1945 until his death in 1972 Berg had no real job and lived off his friends, who put up with him because he was so charming. He lived with his brother, Samuel, for seventeen years until Samuel asked him to leave. Moe refused and Samuel had him evicted. Berg then moved in with his sister in Belleview, New Jersey, where he remained until his death.

Berg never wrote about his amazing life. He once nearly consented to one of the many offers he received and agreed to discuss a book with a publishing house representative. When the book rep gushed to Berg that he had seen all of his pictures, Berg asked him, "Who do you think I am?" "Why, aren't you Moe of the Three Stooges?" Berg stood up and walked out.[118]

Even as a young man, Berg had some notable peculiarities. He always carried two suitcases on baseball trips, one for his clothes, one for books, magazines, and newspapers. No one could ever touch the newspaper until Berg had read it. When he put it down and said, "It's dead," you could then read it.[119]

His eccentricities intensified as he grew older. He wore one black suit, always with a white shirt, black tie and black shoes. He liked to take two or three half-hour baths daily. When he arrived in New York after his retirement he could be found taking a bath in his hotel room the minute he checked in.

Berg never lost his love for baseball and often would watch games in New York with his friend, sportswriter Jerome Holtzman. He had a lifetime pass to all Yankee home games.

On May 26, 1972, Moe Berg, in a hurry to get to the bathroom, accidentally fell against the corner of a table and jabbed his midsection. He lay in bed at home until Ethel forced him to go to a hospital. Three days later, on May 29, 1972, Berg died from internal bleeding. Supposedly, his final words to a nurse were, "How did the Mets do today?"[120] His remains were cremated and spread over Mt. Scopus in Israel. His brother and sister survived him.[121]

No doubt Casey Stengel was correct when he described Moe Berg as "strange," but he was deeply loved by his friends. His close friend Ted Lyons said, "He made up for all of the bores in the world and he did it softly, stepping on no one."[122]

Berg knew his limitations as a player, and shortly before his death he commented that even though he was not in the Hall of Fame he was elated that he had had the opportunity to play pro ball and was especially proud of all the contributions he had made to his country: "Perhaps I couldn't hit like Babe Ruth, but I spoke more languages than he did."[123]

Moe Berg was a different kind of hero to Jews who saw that it was possible to be scholarly and also a good athlete. No one knew Moe Berg better than his brother, who once said of him, "I'll never understand why Moe wasted his time in baseball; all it ever did was make him happy."[124]

15. The Revolutionary Umpire

In a number of ways the lives of "Dolly" Stark and Al Schacht run parallel to one another. The two were both born on Manhattan's Lower East Side, the sons of poor Jewish parents. Both loved baseball and hoped to make it their career.[1] Schacht, of course, played for a few years, but made his fame and a very successful life as a coach and clown. Stark would never play in the major leagues, but would become the first Jewish umpire of modern times, and one of the most capable and respected umpires in the history of baseball. Unfortunately, Stark's life would not be a happy one.

Albert "Dolly" Stark was born in New York City on November 4, 1897.[2] His father died when he was a child and, because his mother was unable to care for him, he spent many years in a homeless shelter. Stark attempted to make money as a pushcart peddler. "I used to be up at three in the morning," he said, "no matter what the weather was."[3] He went to school whenever he could, but dropped out before he entered high school. At only 115 pounds, he could not make it as a major league player, although he did try out with the New York Yankees and the Washington Senators. Stark played with both semipro and minor league teams, but for the most part his weak hitting kept him from advancing.[4]

Stark found his true calling one afternoon in 1921. He was attending a college baseball game at Burlington, Vermont, when the coach of the University of Vermont's team, Clyde Engle, approached him. Engle, a former Boston Red Sox outfielder, asked Stark if he could umpire. "I sure can," responded Stark, "and I'll show you some of the best umpiring you ever saw." Stark recalled that he was the only ump on the field and "those collegians sure ran me ragged. But it was good training."[5]

Stark lived up to his promise, for after that day his services as an umpire were in great demand among the Eastern colleges. He was also hired by Dartmouth as its varsity basketball coach during the winter months.

Stark broke into the professional ranks in 1927, when he was asked to relieve Hugh Rorty, the Eastern League's chief umpire, who had broken his arm. One of the spectators at that game was Bob Emslie, famous National League arbitrator and scout. Emslie was so impressed by Stark's work that he immediately recommended him to John Heydler, president of the National League.[6] Stark even impressed New York Giant manager John McGraw, who also sent a complimentary letter to Heydler.[7]

Stark finished out the 1927 season in the Eastern League and, after only one season in the minors, the 30-year-old umpire was hired by the National League for the 1928 season.[8] This was quite an honor since at this time most umpires were former players who were too old to compete on the field and they usually had to spend at least four or five years umpiring in the minor leagues.

Stark was appointed an umpire along with 16-year veteran and former National League player Sherry Magee. The hiring of Magee was, in one respect, a vindication for him because in 1911 he had been suspended for hitting an umpire.[9] *The Sporting News* noted the contrast in the appointments of Stark and Magee and predicted that Stark would be more successful because, "Few men who have gone high as players have made good umpires. Here's hoping both men make good because baseball can stand both types. To maintain its balance it needs both."[10]

Soon after he entered the National League, Stark became the protégé of Hall of Fame umpire Bill Klem, who taught him the finer points of umpiring.[11] And yet Klem, the veteran umpire, always said he learned more from watching Dolly Stark than from anyone else, despite the difference in their ages. Stark's style of umpiring was unique for his time. He was the first umpire actually to move around the bases with the runner, putting him in the right position to call every play. He also had a zest for his work and always wanted to improve himself.[12]

After one game, Klem stopped Stark and asked him who taught him to go from side to side behind the plate and to follow plays on the bases the way he did. Stark thought he had done something wrong but told Klem truthfully that nobody had taught him; he had always done it in order to stay on top of the plays. "You've got it, boy," Klem responded. "You're the first natural I've seen in years."[13]

Nevertheless, Stark was unsure of himself. He quit umpiring after 1928 and sat out most of the 1929 season and the first half of 1930 feeling like a failure because the players gave him such a rough time.[14] With the encouragement of Bill Klem, however, Stark returned to umpiring in July 1930. Fans, players, and owners eagerly welcomed his return, as he was already recognized as one of baseball's most conscientious and highly qualified umpires. Harry Caplan of the *New York Evening Gazette* wrote about how much he had been missed and hoped he would stay this time. His mentor, Bill Klem, dean of the National League umpires, called Dolly, "the best young official that ever came to the majors."[15]

League officials noticed his diligence and hard work. In 1931, Dolly Stark received another honor rare for a young umpire when John Heydler appointed him and Bill Klem the National League umpires for the World Series between the Philadelphia Athletics and the St. Louis Cardinals.[16] Stark remembered that series, not only because it was his first, but because of two incidents. In game two, the Cardinals were leading 2–0 in the top of the ninth. Athletics batter Max Bishop hit a long foul fly to right. As Cardinal first baseman Jim Bottomley dashed after it, Stark ran with him every step of the way. Bottomley climbed up on the Athletics' bullpen bench, leaned over, and caught the ball in the stands. Stark, who was right there, ruled it a legal catch. Stark received many compliments for his hustle, but he shrugged them off, saying it was just his duty to be on top of the play.[17]

The second memorable moment for Stark came in the seventh game of the series. The Cardinals were leading 4–2 in the ninth, but the bases were loaded, two men were out, and the count on the batter—Max Bishop again—was 3 and 2. As the plate umpire, Stark realized that one pitch could radically change the game and the outcome of the series. "I said to myself," recalled Stark, "don't blow this one. Bishop may take it and it may be close. You need a good eye here. Forget the crowd, forget everything but that pitch." Fortunately for Stark, when Cardinal pitcher Bill Hallahan threw the next ball, Bishop flied out to Pepper

Martin in left-center to end the tension—and the series. "I sure thanked Bishop for not taking that ball. I was glad I didn't have to call that last pitch."[18]

In 1934 Stark was selected as one of the National League umpires for that year's All-Star Game, and the following year he not only umpired at the official season opener but also was appointed an umpire for the 1935 World Series. Following both the 1934 and 1935 seasons, Dolly Stark was voted the National League's "Best Umpire," receiving even more votes than Bill Klem, who came in second.[19]

On August 24, 1935, fans at the Polo Grounds witnessed the first and only "Day" held in honor of an umpire. Before the game between the Cubs and Giants, the president of the National League, Ford Frick, presented Dolly Stark with a Packard automobile. According to Frank Slocum, who wrote publicity for the National League and was present at the ceremonies, "There they were, thousands of fans, cheering an umpire."[20]

But even on "Dolly Stark Day," Stark was still the target of verbal abuse. During the game, Stark called a strike on Giants star Mel Ott to even the count 2–2. Ott turned and said something to Dolly, which touched off the home crowd. When Stark called Ott out looking on the next pitch, he talked to Stark again on his way back to the bench, and the Giant faithful showered the umpire with imprecations. Stark later explained what Ott actually said, "He knew they were both strikes. The first time he said 'Dolly, I'd give ten bucks to have that one back.' The second time he said, 'How can I take two beautiful pitches like that in a row?'"[21]

Stark may have been popular with the players, but at one point the players' wives wanted to "kill" this ump. He sent out Christmas cards to many players after receiving his "best umpire" honor in 1935, and with nothing but friendly intentions signed the cards "Dolly." When the wives saw the cards, they immediately confronted their husbands, demanding to know who "Dolly" was. When told that "Dolly" was a National League Umpire, the more suspicious spouses then asked, "Since when does the National League employ women umpires?"[22]

Following his honors in 1935, Stark quit the game again in 1936. This time the issues were money and dissatisfaction with his job. On the salary side, Frick was offering Stark $9,000, which included all transportation expenses, and would have made Stark the second highest-paid

Jewish umpire Albert "Dolly" Stark was one of the most respected and innovative umpires in the major leagues. Few people actually were aware of his loneliness on the field and his unhappiness off the field (courtesy National Baseball Hall of Fame Library, Cooperstown, N.Y.).

umpire in the major leagues. "It's an excellent living," said Frick, "when you stop to consider you work five-and-one-half months and have the rest of the year [off]. On top of that, a man with 15 years' service can retire on a $1,500 pension for life."[23]

But finances were only part of Stark's dissatisfaction. "The thing I dislike most about umpiring is the loneliness. There is no camaraderie—not even with other umps. You stay at different hotels. After a game, a guy would say, 'So long, see you tomorrow, and that was it.'"[24] The hard-bitten, old-time veteran umpires could not understand Stark's sensitivity. They had become immune to the people around them. To them, neither the fans nor the ballplayers existed.[25]

In return, Stark never understood their acceptance of this isolation. "Umpiring is a hard business. You have no friends, you can't talk to and live with the players and the highest praise for an umpire is silence. I don't think I can take the jeering and the booing any more."[26]

Ford Frick refused at first to accept his resignation and hoped that Stark would reconsider for at least one more season. He even told Stark that if he left now but returned the following year he would be welcome.[27]

In February 1936, Ford Frick officially granted Stark a leave of absence so he could try his hand at some other line of work. "If he wants to come back next year," reiterated Frick, "we will have a job for him."[28] A month later the Dartmouth Athletic Council released Stark as basketball coach. Dolly Stark was now completely unemployed.

His unemployment didn't last long. The Philadelphia Phillies hired him to do their play-by-play on the radio for the 1937 season at a salary of $11,500. After hearing Stark announce the Phillies' opening game, Bill Dooly of the *Philadelphia Record* wrote, "Dolly should be able to make the grade as the nation's ace baseball announcer, for he ... has the edge on his rivals in his knowledge of the game."[29] Bob Ray, columnist for the *Los Angeles Times*, also felt that Stark would do well behind the mike, but wondered, "if $11,500 is enough for having to watch the A's and Phillies play all their home games."[30] Stark's tenure in Philadelphia lasted only one year. He had done a good job, but for 1938 the Phillies got a new sponsor who brought in his own announcer.[31]

Stark accepted Frick's offer and returned to umpiring in 1938. In 1940 he was granted another leave of absence to recover from a "nervous condition" after he collapsed on the field and was carried off on a stretcher.[32] Dolly Stark returned to umpiring for the last time in 1942. After announcing his return, Stark received a multitude of letters from friends expressing their good wishes for the upcoming year. He wrote *The Sporting News* to say, "Knowing that everyone in baseball reads your paper as regularly as I do, I would appreciate it very much if, through the columns of your paper, you would thank the many fans and friends who have written or wired me."[33]

Stark left umpiring at the end of the 1942 season. He was a corporate recreational director for a time and in 1945 went into the dress business, where he did well. Retaining his old nickname, his business cards read: "L. Neuberger & Co., featuring Dolly Stark fashions."[34]

Ever restless, a few years later Stark reentered the sports world when he became a radio and television commentator for CBS, with a show titled, *Your Sports Special*. On one of his programs, Stark regretted that television was not available earlier. "The television camera is a great teacher.... Any kid who might want to become an umpire can learn more by watching an ump on the television screen than he can by reading a dozen textbooks on 'The Art of Umpiring.'"[35]

His radio and television career lasted just a few years and although he tried to land a job in baseball he was unsuccessful. The last few years of his life Stark was forced to live on his meager Social Security checks. His personal life was filled with tragedy. He married late, but his marriage ended in divorce. He was forced to spend much of his income caring for his blind mother, who passed away shortly before he did, and his sister, who was sick most of her life and ultimately committed suicide. Four months prior to Stark's death he even had to apply for unemployment compensation. On August 24, 1968, Dolly Stark died at the home of a friend, apparently after suffering a heart attack. He was 71 years old.[36]

Dolly Stark's legacy to baseball is apparent. Every time an umpire runs down the line or shifts his position behind the plate to more accurately call the balls and strikes, he is using the techniques that Dolly Stark introduced during his years in the game.

16. Jewish Owners—The Next Generation

During the 1920s and '30s, three Jewish owners of major league baseball teams each carried on the traditions of earlier owners. Two of them loved the game so passionately that their dream was to own a team. Ironically, they would be the ones to acquire the worst teams and lose them after only a few years. The third owner, although he became involved in baseball only to help his family, would control his team the longest and with the most success.

Emil E. Fuchs

Emil Edmund Fuchs was born in Hamurg, Germany, in 1878, but he grew up on New York's Lower East Side. Fuchs learned about baseball as a 13-year-old catcher for the University Settlement House team, and made the starting team at the College of the City of New York. He even played semipro ball, but an injury ended his playing days. Fuchs received a law degree by attending night school at New York University. He soon began his formal relationship with professional baseball as a lawyer for the New York Giants, owned at that time by Andrew Freedman. Fuchs drew up the agreement for his friend John McGraw and two partners to buy the Giants from Freedman.[1]

Fuchs built a large and prosperous law practice. He also became active in politics, associating with prominent Democrats like Al Smith, Jimmy Walker, and Fiorello LaGuardia. Through his political connections, he was appointed the city's youngest deputy attorney general. He acquired the lifelong title of "Judge" by serving one term as a New York City magistrate from 1915 to 1918, but gave up politics in 1921 to concentrate on baseball.[2]

Judge Emil Fuchs had a boyhood ambition—he wanted to own a major league baseball team. When John McGraw learned that the owner of the Boston Braves was interested in selling his team, he arranged a small dinner party with Fuchs, food concessionaire Harry M. Stevens, and Broadway star and songwriter George M. Cohan to discuss the Braves sale. Neither Stevens nor Cohan were interested, but when McGraw turned to Fuchs and said, "Why don't you buy it?" Fuchs surprised him by replying, "Sure, but on one condition. I want Christy Mathewson to help run the team."[3]

Little did Fuchs know that McGraw had already approached Matty about becoming president of the Braves and the former Giant was excited about the prospect. Except for one game with Cincinnati, Mathewson had spent his entire 17-season baseball career with the Giants and McGraw was aware that his friend was eager to return. Mathewson's severe tuberculosis prevented him from taking a physically active role, but he thought he would be able to help run a major league team, even though his doctors warned him that he would last only two years if he returned to baseball. At their home in Saranac Lake, New York, he discussed the offer with his wife, Jane, who was as opposed as his doctors. Nevertheless, Christy wired Fuchs, "I would rather spend another two or three years in the only vocation I know than to linger many years in Saranac Lake."

On February 21, 1923, the announcement was made that a New York syndicate headed by Fuchs and including Mathewson and New York banker James MacDonough had bought the Braves for approximately $500,000.[4] Unlike most of his predecessors, Fuchs moved his family to Boston after he purchased the Braves, and the short, likeable, deliberate, and polite man went out of his way to win over the hostile New England press.[5]

Fuchs' best friends were members of the press; he liked them and they considered him agreeable, frank and generous. He used to call the baseball writers who covered the Braves "my board of directors," and he never hesitated to consult them.[6]

In the Braves' organization, Mathewson was named president, Fuchs vice president, and Fred Mitchell was retained as manager.[7] Fuchs assured Matty that in no way would he be a figurehead. As things turned out, however, it was actually Fuchs who had to run the team. Mathewson's health continued to be a problem and he had to commute frequently from Boston to Lake Saranac for rest and treatment. Fans who saw him occasionally at the Polo Grounds, where Mathewson would watch his Braves play the Giants, noticed the once robust pitcher was now frail and walking with a cane.[8]

Fuchs (right) is pictured here with his close friend and president of the Boston Braves, Christy Mathewson (center), and baseball commisioner Judge Kenesaw Mountain Landis (courtesy Mrs. Helen Ann Meltzer).

In 1923, the Braves lost 100 games, winning only 54 and finishing in seventh place.[9] At the end of the season, Mathewson fired Mitchell and hired Dave Bancroft, a veteran New York shortstop, to replace him. The Braves had worked out a deal with McGraw to get Bancroft and outfielders Casey Stengel and Bill Cunningham in exchange for journeyman outfielder Billy Southworth, pitcher Joe Oeschger, and cash. McGraw was blunt in assessing the deal: "I wanted to help Matty and at the same time it gives Bancroft his chance at managing, something he's always wanted."[10]

Prior to the 1924 season, Fuchs issued a very optimistic statement, something he would do many more times. "With the added strength just announced, the Braves of 1924 will be fighting it out with the best of them all for the highest honors of the game."[11] Unfortunately, the prediction never materialized, as Bancroft was no more successful than Mitchell. In 1924 the Braves lost 100 games again, and dropped to the bottom of the standings.[12] Tragedy contributed to the Braves' poor showing; the team's hard-hitting third baseman, Tony "Elmer" Boeckel, died in an automobile accident.[13]

In 1925 the Braves improved their record to 70–83 and climbed to fifth place in the standings. They also turned in one of their highest team batting averages, .292, but finished fifth behind the pennant-winning Pirates' average of .307.[14]

Tragedy struck the Braves again in 1925. The prediction of Christy Mathewson's doctors that he would last only two years in baseball came true. On October 7, 1925, the day the World Series was to begin, Mathewson died at the age of 45. Shortly after his death, Fuchs was elected president of the Braves.[15]

Early in the 1926 season, a tablet in memory of Christy Mathewson was unveiled at Braves Field, but it did little to spur the Braves into improving their play. In both 1926 and 1927, under Bancroft, the team continued its losing ways and finished the season in seventh place both years.[16]

The year 1928 was significant for Emil Fuchs and the Braves for several reasons. First, Fuchs was finally successful in bringing Sunday baseball to Boston. The Judge had long urged that the city's "blue law," which prohibited baseball on Sunday, be put to a vote. Using $200,000 from his own pocket, Fuchs helped place placards in every streetcar in Boston urging the passage of the referendum.[17]

The vote went his way but Fuchs ran into legal and political trouble. During a follow-up investigation, more than 75 notables were called in to testify to Fuchs'

Judge Emil Fuchs, who owned the Boston Braves from 1923 to 1935, had always wanted to own a major league team, but never achieved much success. He is better known for being the manager of his own team one year and as the last major league owner for whom Babe Ruth played. Fuchs wisely left baseball after the 1935 season and resumed his law practice in Brookline, Masachusetts (courtesy National Baseball Hall of Fame Library, Cooperstown, N.Y.).

character, including numerous baseball men and his old political friends, former New York governor Al Smith, and New York mayor James J. Walker. The vice president of the Braves, Charles F. Adams, also praised Fuchs: "To me, Judge Fuchs has proven himself a gentleman."[18] On behalf of his team, Emil Fuchs pleaded *nolo contendre* to the charge of spending money to influence the vote and he was fined $1,000 in municipal court costs.

Unfortunately for Fuchs and the Braves, their first Sunday game in Boston, scheduled for April 21, 1929, was rained out and the honor of Boston's first Sunday game went to the Red Sox. They opposed the Athletics at Fenway Park the following Sunday, April 28. Still another week passed before the Braves finally played their first Sunday game at home, losing to the Pirates, 7–2.[19]

The second notable event in 1928 involved the management of the team. After two back-to-back seventh-place finishes, Fuchs axed the Braves manager, Dave Bancroft, and replaced him with former college coach Jack Slattery.[20]

He also resumed trading to try to build up the team. The Giants needed to make room for Andy Cohen, and were willing to give Fuchs star player Rogers Hornsby in exchange for Shanty Hogan and Jimmy Welsh. Early in the season Fuchs also obtained 35-year-old first baseman George Sisler from the Washington Senators.[21]

Slattery lasted 31 games (11 wins and 20 losses) and then resigned.[22] Fuchs hired Hornsby in his place, but even Hornsby could not end the series of losing seasons for the Braves. For the third consecutive year, the Braves finished in seventh place. Fuchs was greatly disappointed. His new players had certainly done well. Sisler hit .340 and Hornsby won the National League batting title with a .387 average, but after losing five of nine consecutive double headers in September, the best the Braves could do was to stay out of the cellar.[23]

In August, Fuchs had announced that Hornsby would remain the Braves' manager for at least six more years and that he would not be traded or sold. Late in the season, however, when the Braves were in Chicago on their last western trip of the year, Hornsby approached Fuchs. "Judge," he said, "what you need is a young club. Now, I have about one year left.... Why don't you let me make a deal for myself with Chicago? It would help everybody concerned."[24] In November 1928 Fuchs sent Rogers Hornsby to Chicago for five players, two from the Cubs' roster and three from one of their minor league farm clubs. More importantly, the Cubs also gave Fuchs $200,000.[25] (To be accurate, Hornsby had slightly more than one year left. He played for eight more seasons in the majors and in 1929 led the National League in games played, runs scored, and slugging percentage.)[26]

Hornsby left Fuchs and the Braves on the friendliest of terms. He called Fuchs one of the grandest men he had ever met in baseball: "He wasn't the smartest baseball man around, but he took second place to nobody in the way he felt about the game."[27]

In the six years Fuchs had owned the Braves they had finished below .500 and in the second division every season. Fuchs concluded that if no professional manager could lead them out of the doldrums, he might as well run the team himself. After the 1928 season, Fuchs announced that for 1929 he would be the Braves manager. "If I don't make good," reasoned Fuchs, "no one will realize it quicker than I, and it will be perfectly simple for me, as club president, to remove myself as manager." National League president John Heydler was not enthusiastic about the idea, but he reluctantly agreed that Fuchs could manage if coach and former player John Evers handled the day-to-day operation of the club.[28]

At first things went well. The Braves won seven of their first nine games under Fuchs, and remained in first place for several weeks. But soon Fuchs learned the same lesson as other owner-managers such as Charles Ebbets and Andrew Freedman had learned in the

past—managing looks easier than it is. As manager, Fuchs found himself turning more and
more to his players for advice during a game, often asking the basic question, "What do we
do now, boys?"[29] By August 19, the Braves had fallen to last place, where they finished the
1929 season with a record of 56–98, 43 games behind the first place Chicago Cubs.[30]

It was during this one-year experiment as manager that Fuchs' reputation as a character became widespread and gave rise to many stories which are now part of baseball folklore. Once Fuchs called back a right-handed batter and replaced him with a left-hander even
though the pitcher was a southpaw. When his coaches criticized this move, he answered
that he hadn't really noticed who was on the mound.[31]

Fuchs loved to tell stories to his players during games. On one occasion, the Braves
were leading by a wide margin, and Fuchs had his players gathered round him in the dugout
while he told a rather lengthy story. At some point, one of the Braves interrupted Fuchs to
tell him that the other team had three men on base with nobody out and suggested that
his manager get another pitcher ready. "Oh, yes," Fuchs said to one of his pitchers. "Run
down to the bullpen and get warmed up. I'll tell you the rest of the story when you get
back."[32]

There are two anecdotes that best illustrate Fuchs' lack of baseball knowledge. During
a tied game, the Braves' leadoff batter tripled to left-center. Fuchs asked his veteran shortstop, Rabbit Maranville, what to do and Maranville suggested that Fuchs call for a squeeze
play. "Not on your life," Fuchs told his shortstop. "Either we win this game fairly and squarely
or we don't win it at all."[33] The other story concerns another time Fuchs was in the dugout
talking to his players when Coach Evers interrupted to remind his boss that the count was
three and one on the batter and to ask Fuchs for instructions. "Tell him to hit a homerun,"
Fuchs responded.[34]

Although Fuchs was good-natured, he would not tolerate outright rudeness. In one
game, Fuchs told Joe Dugan to take the shortstop position. Dugan, who had little respect
for Fuchs, asked his manager where shortstop was on this field. Offended, but under control, Fuchs turned to another player and directed him to "Show Mr. Dugan where the clubhouse is and how to take off his uniform."[35]

One year as manager was enough for Fuchs, who announced the hiring of veteran skip-
per Bill McKechnie for 1930. McKechnie had been only a mediocre player, but he had turned
out to be an excellent manager. He would lead the team the final five years of Fuchs' ownership and for two years after that. A conservative manager who knew how to get the best
from his pitchers, McKechnie always had the respect of his players.[36]

McKechnie brought the Braves up two notches to finish sixth in 1930, the last major
league season for Sisler. In 1931 the Braves dropped to seventh again, but in 1932 the Braves
jumped to fifth place with a record of 77–77, the first time they finished with a .500 percentage since 1921. In both 1933 and 1934 McKechnie's Braves squeaked into the first division with fourth-place finishes each year. Their 83 victories in 1933 were the most for any
Braves team since 1916.

Although Fuchs was not bringing winning teams to Boston, he was always trying to
draw more people to the park. Like many other owners, he tried to attract more women
fans. In 1932 he announced, "In addition to our free Fridays, ladies are admitted half-price
on Mondays, Tuesdays, Wednesdays, and Thursdays." He also put numbers on the uniforms
to help women identify their favorite players.[37]

In addition to Sunday baseball, which Fuchs had helped to bring about, he also favored
twilight games for the 85 percent of Boston's baseball fans who worked until four o'clock

during the summer and could not attend afternoon games.[38] He also signed the first baseball broadcasting contracts for the Braves.[39]

Fuchs was working so hard to increase revenues because most of the money used to operate the Boston Braves came directly from his pocket. Unfortunately, he was not receiving an adequate return for his money, but he had still another plan. Fuchs announced during the winter meetings in 1934 that he intended converting Braves Field into a dog racing track and moving his team to Fenway Park, home of the American League Boston Red Sox. Fuchs, unfortunately, failed to inform the Red Sox owner, Tom Yawkey, or any baseball official of his intentions. Once Yawkey heard of Fuchs' plan, he quickly vetoed it. Similarly, Baseball Commissioner Landis declared that baseball and dog racing could not coexist, and the National League president, Ford Frick, bluntly stated, "Any suggestion that dog racing will be permitted at the Braves' park is 'preposterous.'"[40]

Fuchs had tried to introduce dog racing at Braves Field mainly to pacify team stockholders, who pressured Fuchs to either improve team finances or sell the club. Since the Braves' poor play in the field was hardly a drawing card, Fuchs felt he needed something to help shore up a losing enterprise.[41] In November 1934 Fuchs' friend, Massachusetts governor-elect James Michael Curley, suggested what Fuchs thought might do the trick—he would bring Babe Ruth back to Boston, the town where the Babe began his major league career and where the fans still loved him.[42]

In February 1935 Fuchs called Ruth and offered him a $25,000 contract with the Braves. Ruth assumed he was being hired as a player and assistant manager, with the understanding that he would be named manager of the club in 1936.[43] Despite Ruth's assumptions, Fuchs was very careful not to make any hard promises.[44] By this point in Ruth's career, the Yankees were elated to give him his release. Yankee owner Colonel Jacob Ruppert refused to take any money for him and wished Ruth well in Boston.[45]

On opening day in Boston in 1935 more than 20,000 ecstatic fans welcomed the Babe back to Beantown. It was the largest home opener for the Braves in many years. Ruth responded to the fans' welcome by cracking his first National League home run on a Carl Hubbell fastball.[46] The 40-year-old Ruth was out of shape and could hardly swing a bat or run the bases. His best day in a Braves uniform was on May 25, when he slugged three home runs in a single game against the Pittsburgh Pirates, only the second time in his career that he had a three-home run game. He played in 28 games for the Braves in 1935; they were the last games of his career.[47]

When Ruth realized that he had no chance of becoming the Braves manager, he told Fuchs off and announced his retirement from baseball.[48] Simultaneously, Fuchs issued a statement: "I have given Ruth his unconditional release and he is through with the Braves in every way."[49] In a reversal of traditional roles, manager McKechnie gave owner Fuchs a vote of confidence after he fired Ruth: "Judge Fuchs' action in the elimination of Ruth will help the ball club again function to the full efficiency and regain the standing it has enjoyed for the past several years."[50]

The Ruth fiasco marked the end of the road for Emil Fuchs as a baseball team owner. In 1935, the Braves finished in last place with a winning percentage of .248, the lowest of any team in the major leagues during the twentieth century.[51] Out of funds, Fuchs severed his connection with the Boston Braves and resumed his law practice in Brookline. Charles Adams, Fuchs' vice president and chief creditor, acquired Fuchs' heavily mortgaged stock and control of the team.[52]

Emil Fuchs died on December 5, 1961, in New York City, following a ten-week illness. His widow, Oretta, two sons, and a daughter survived him.

When Fuchs purchased the Braves he was a millionaire, and when he left the team he was bankrupt. It was his misfortune to be, as one of his contemporaries described him, a fan who attempted to be an owner. But his efforts did not go unnoticed. In his honor, the Boston sportswriters whom he had always befriended established a trophy which they still award each year to the city's outstanding athlete.[53]

The Sporting News said of Emil Fuchs, "With his own resources he kept alive a franchise that would have collapsed. He kept it in Boston, where the Braves lasted for almost two more decades before the franchise was moved to Milwaukee. For these efforts, baseball should be grateful to Emil Fuchs."[54]

Sidney Weil

When Sidney Weil purchased the Reds he resumed the line of Jewish owners in Cincinnati, becoming the first in more than ten years since the Fleischmanns had left the organization in 1915.

Weil's ownership overlapped that of Emil Fuchs, but, although there were many similarities, Weil's savvy management earned the respect and support of other owners who gave him credit for the team's later successes.

Sidney Weil was a native Cincinnatian, born December 23, 1891, to Isaac and Minnie Mook Weil, both descendents of German Jews who had come to the United States in the 1850s. The marriage produced three sons—Sidney, the oldest, Gordon, and Burt. Weil's grandfather originally sold vegetables from a pushcart, but soon abandoned the cart for a partnership in horse stables, the chief transportation business of the late nineteenth century.[55]

Sidney Weil and his family were active in a Reform temple in Cincinnati, but unlike most German Jews, the Weils followed many traditional observances. For example, Sidney strictly kept the Jewish dietary laws and he and his family attended Temple every Saturday morning.[56]

Weil quit school at the age of 16 to help his father run the family business. From the beginning, his first love was baseball, which he and his neighborhood friends played in the city streets. "As early as seven," Weil wrote, "I knew that I wanted to own a club. I would draw a score-board for the Cincinnati Reds in chalk on the sidewalk, and I would get the report on the latest inning by peeking under the swinging doors of the saloon."[57]

In 1917 Weil enlisted in the Army. While in Washington, where he hoped to get an officer's commission because of his experience in the horse business, he met Florence Levy, the daughter of Eastern European Jews who was the secretary for a West Virginia Congressman. Sidney and Florence married July 1, 1919. The union of a German and a Russian Jew was unusual at the time, but it was a very successful marriage and produced two daughters and one son.[58]

After the war Sidney Weil quickly realized that automobiles would soon replace his beloved horses and bought into a Ford agency. By the early 1920s, Weil was general agent for Henry Ford in Cincinnati. As soon as the anti–Semitic Ford found out that his Cincinnati general agent was Jewish, he attempted to oust Weil from his position. But Weil fought back, threatening Ford with court action to prove that being a Jew should not preclude him from being a general agent. Ford backed down. As Weil said, "Ford may have been a bigot, but he was no fool in business."[59]

Weil began to invest in other business activities, including a Jewish funeral home operated by his brothers, and a parking garage. Like many others during the decade, he also invested heavily in the stock market, often buying "on margin," but claiming he always paid at least 50 percent.[60]

In 1929 Sidney Weil's boyhood dream came true—he became the new majority owner of the Cincinnati Reds. Taking advantage of a power struggle among the three current holders, Weil simply came in and bought them all out, paying far more than their shares were worth.[61] "When I finally knew I had control, I called a press conference ... and took over as president just before the season ended in September."[62] The day Weil purchased the Reds, he told a reporter, "I feel like a kid on Christmas." His wife Florence had mixed emotions. "He always gets

In 1929 Sidney Weil resumed the history of Jewish ownership of the Cincinnati Reds. Although the team fared poorly during his ownership, other owners greatly admired and respected Weil and credited him for the future successes of the Cincinnati Reds (courtesy Cincinnati Reds).

so upset when [the Reds] lose a game; I fear what his disposition will be when they lose one now that he's the owner." Weil reportedly replied that he did not intend to lose any games.[63]

No one could blame Weil for his enthusiasm; his childhood dream had come true and he looked forward to team ownership as an enjoyable hobby.[64] There were two facts, however, that should have tempered his elation fairly quickly. First, financial disaster was not far off. Just one month after buying the Reds, the stock market crash of October 1929 would usher in the Great Depression, making the investments in his team and his personal portfolio virtually worthless.[65]

The second fact was the team he had just purchased. In 1929 the Cincinnati Reds finished the season in seventh place with a record of 66–88. Only the eighth-place Braves, which Emil Fuchs had managed that year, had a worse record.[66] Weil had a lot of work ahead of him to turn the team around.

After he purchased the Reds, Weil first had to straighten out the front office. He hired his sister-in-law, Frances, as his secretary; she would remain with the team long after Weil left. Dan Howley, who had led the St. Louis Browns to first-division finishes in 1928 and 1929, became the new manager. Weil then raised the salaries of some star players, including Red Lucas, Horace Ford, Hughie Critz, and Ethan Allen, and bought two veteran outfielders from the American League, former Detroit Tiger star Harry Heilmann, and the regular left fielder of the New York Yankees, Bob Meusel.[67]

Despite these good moves, Weil regretted the players he lost because he did not have the money to sign them. Among others, his scouts had recommended Joe DiMaggio, Billy Herman and "Big" Bill Lee, but Weil had had to pass. "I know they could have made my team a lot better than it was," Weil lamented.[68]

Weil's first notable trade took place at the National League winter meeting in December 1929. Leo Durocher, who had played three years with the Yankees, had been released on waivers. Weil claimed him and in exchange sent Clarke (Pinky) Pittenger, a journeyman shortstop to the Yankees. Pittenger never reported.[69] The trade wasn't perfect for Weil and Cincinnati, either. A star shortstop, Durocher was a child about money, and had come to the Reds with a mountain of debt. Weil took him under his wing, virtually becoming a father to him. In fact, had it not been for Weil's mentoring, Durocher might not have lasted very long in baseball.[70] Despite Weil's guidance, Durocher did not change his ways. When he left the Reds early in 1933, he owed more money than ever. [71]

Despite all the roster changes, the 1930 Cincinnati Reds still lacked pitching and ended the season in seventh place again, with an even worse record of 59–95.[72]

The Reds fared still worse in 1931. Although former player Ed Roush came back from a holdout year and hit .271 for the Reds, everything else seemed to go wrong for the team.[73] A promising rookie, Mickey Heath, appeared in seven games before he broke his arm, and rain washed away several of the Reds' lucrative home dates.[74] The 1931 Cincinnati Reds finished in last place with a record of 58–96, 43 games behind the first-place St. Louis Cardinals.[75]

During his ownership of the Reds, Sidney Weil made many friends among his contemporaries, but his closest friend was Branch Rickey, general manager of the Cardinals and later the Brooklyn Dodgers. On the surface they appeared to have little in common. Rickey was a devout fundamentalist, a Southern Baptist, and an experienced baseball man who had built the Cardinals into a winning franchise. Weil was a German Jew who loved baseball, understood business, but had no experience running a team. Each man seemed to respect the other's religious dedication. When Weil began to have financial difficulties, Rickey tried to help whenever he could, often setting up baseball trades between the Reds and the Cardinals. Irwin Weil, Sidney's son said of Rickey, "He was one of the few people, to my knowledge, who played ... the paternal role to Sidney that Sidney played to the rest of the world."[76]

Weil worked hard to make 1932 a better season for the Reds. Weil and Rickey agreed on a trade that sent pitcher Benny Frey, first baseman Harvey Hendrick, and cash to St. Louis for outfielder Chick Hafey, one of the National League's finest players and a future Hall of Famer.[77] Weil also was optimistic about his spring training acquisitions of infielder Wally Gilbert, outfielder Babe Herman, and young catcher Ernie Lombardi from the Brooklyn Dodgers. The Reds had given up catcher Clyde Sukeforth, second baseman Tony Cuccinello, and third baseman Joe Stripp in exchange.[78]

As late as June 1, the Reds were playing .500 ball, but after a ten-game losing streak, the club went downhill. Three of Weil's acquisitions—Hafey, Herman, and Lombardi—had excellent years, all hitting above .300.[79] Despite the Reds' good offense, their pitching simply could not compete, and the team finished in the cellar again in 1932 with a record of 60–94.[80]

The Depression was really starting to take its toll as club owners began to prepare for the 1933 season, all looking for ways to lift their sinking fortunes.[81] In another effort to improve the Reds, Weil replaced Howley as manager with 16-year veteran Donie Bush. Bush, who had been involved in Al Schacht's career-ending accident, had played shortstop for the Tigers and managed the Senators, the Pirates, and the White Sox.[82]

Short of finances to operate the Reds, Weil reluctantly sold Babe Herman to the Chicago Cubs for $80,000 and four players—pitcher Bob Smith, outfielders Johnny Moore and Lance Richbourg, and catcher Rollie Hemsley.[83]

Weil then proceeded to deal with his favorite trading partner—Branch Rickey's St. Louis Cardinals. He obtained veteran first baseman "Sunny" Jim Bottomley in return for Owen Carroll and 11 minor league players. After only 16 games in 1933, Weil and Rickey made a more important trade. The Reds sent Leo Durocher and pitchers Jack Ogden and Dutch Henry to the Cardinals in exchange for pitchers Paul Derringer and Allyn Stout and third baseman Earl (Sparky) Adams.[84]

The trade was a perfect example of a deal which was beneficial to both teams. For St. Louis, Durocher filled a gap at short and he would become an important member of the famous Gas House Gang.[85] For Cincinnati, the key man in the deal was hurler Paul Derringer. Weil would not be associated with the team at the time, but Derringer would help the Reds win two consecutive pennants, one in 1939, when he would win 25 games, and another the following year, when he would win 20 games.[86]

Despite all of Weil's trades, everything went wrong for the team again in 1933. Manager Donie Bush was ill and missed most of the season. The team was crippled by numerous injuries, and lost too many close games. After the Reds had two 10-game losing streaks, one in July and another in August, it was no surprise to anyone when the Cincinnati Reds finished in last place in 1933 for the third consecutive year.[87]

After the season ended, Sidney Weil realized that his career in baseball was over. He had battled in a losing cause for four years. Although the other National League owners tried to help him, the Central Trust Company, which had held Weil's stock for three years, foreclosed and took the team and his personal assets.[88] In November 1933, he stepped aside as president and resigned as a director of the Reds, wishing the team success and thanking everyone for the loyalty and friendship shown him. "I will still be a red-hot fan," he stated.[89]

In 1934 the stock was sold to broadcast entrepreneur Powel Crosley, one of the bank's directors, who immediately renamed the ballpark Crosley Field.[90] A Cincinnati paper implied that the team's new general manager, Lee MacPhail, had actually manipulated the foreclosure. Regardless of the truth of the assertion and despite all the machinations of Crosley and MacPhail, the Cincinnati Reds remained in the cellar in 1934.[91]

The Great Depression had a devastating affect on Sidney Weil. He had lost "my capital, my business and my house—everything except that which counted most—my family, my religion, and my love for baseball."[92] In 1937 a business acquaintance convinced him that with his world of friends, he could do very well in the life insurance business, and, like Jacob Morse many years earlier, Weil became one of the most successful insurance salesmen in the country. For 23 consecutive years, he qualified for the Million Dollar Round Table, the insurance industry's most elite group.[93]

Weil became active in local and national Jewish charities as well as an ardent Zionist. He attended as many Cincinnati Reds games as possible, and was always welcome in the dugout. And he stayed close with his friends in baseball, including Bill Veeck, Jr., son of his old friend Bill Veeck, Sr., who had been president of the Chicago Cubs during Weil's ownership of the Reds. When Bill Sr. died, Weil became a second father to Bill, Jr. Veeck, who at various times, owned the Indians, Browns and White Sox. Veeck always offered to include Weil in his syndicates, but Sidney was no longer interested in owning a baseball team: "I like it better this way. I have all the fun and none of the headaches."[94]

On January 14, 1966, Sidney Weil died in Cincinnati in a traffic accident. He was 75 years old. At the time of his death he was one of Cincinnati's most prominent Jews. His widow, Florence, two daughters and a son survived him.[95]

Devastated by Weil's death, Bill Veeck wrote of him, "Sidney Weil excelled in kindness, piety, thoughtfulness, generosity, humility, intelligence and courage." Bill DeWitt, owner of the Reds in 1966 called Weil "a great sportsman, a fine gentleman, one of the greatest Cincinnati fans we ever had." Sportswriter and radio commentator Bill Stern added, "Sidney Weil was the finest sportsman I've ever known."[96]

Sidney Weil, too, was a fan who had tried to become an owner. Unlike Fuchs, Weil probably had the business acumen to succeed, but his problem was poor timing. He bought a bad baseball team at a time when baseball was a luxury that most people simply could not afford. Weil was acknowledged, however, for having laid some of the groundwork for the successful Reds teams that came after him.

William Benswanger

Even more than his contemporaries, Emil Fuchs and Sidney Weil, William Benswanger followed in the footsteps of previous Jewish owners. Although a baseball fan, Benswanger did not have a lifelong desire to own a baseball team but agreed to run one as a family obligation to his wife's parents, Barney and Florence Dreyfuss. Ironically, he was to retain control of his team, the Pittsburgh Pirates, for 16 years, far longer than either Fuchs or Weil.

William Benswanger was born in New York City, February 22, 1892, to Edward and Kathryn Benswanger. At the age of five, his parents moved to Pittsburgh. As a youngster Bill had a passion for baseball, but his mother, an accomplished pianist, insisted he study the piano rather than waste his time playing baseball. When he got tired of practicing, he would steal away for a while to play baseball, confessing that at that point, "I guess I liked baseball a little better than music." As he grew older, however, music developed into his passion.[97]

After high school, Benswanger entered his father's successful insurance firm in Pittsburgh. His main love was still music, but his summer recreation was baseball. At Central High in Pittsburgh, Benswanger had met the daughter of Pirate owner Barney Dreyfuss, Eleanor, whom he married in 1925 after a lengthy courtship.

In 1931, William Benswanger had a successful career in the insurance business. On February 19 he received a call from his father-in-law telling Bill that Samuel, Barney's only son, had died of pneumonia.[98] Benswanger agreed to help the bereaved father by giving up his own lucrative insurance job and taking over Samuel's work as vice president, treasurer, and business manager of the Pittsburgh Pirates, managing the day-to-day operation of the ball club.[99] Less than a year after Samuel passed away, Barney Dreyfuss died. His widow, Florence, immediately turned to her son-in-law: "Bill, you're the only who is left. I want you to be the new president of the Pirates."[100] At the age of 40, Benswanger became one of the youngest club presidents on record.[101]

Sportswriters who covered the Pirates described the young owner as short, with glasses that gave him a scholarly appearance.[102] Despite some lighthearted moments, when Benswanger would don one of Pirate star Lloyd Waner's old uniforms and work out with his team, and despite his love of the game, Benswanger did not expect running the Pirates to be easy. In fact, he was to comment later, "It was nothing but one headache after another."[103]

Benswanger's first problem was that he assumed control in the midst of the Great Depression, and like most baseball moguls, he had to look for ways to encourage attendance. In direct opposition to his former father-in-law, Benswanger advocated Sunday baseball as his first strategy. In a letter to *Baseball Magazine*, Benswanger backed Sunday baseball in Pittsburgh, arguing that it would improve the moral life of the city by offering an alternative to gambling parties and that it would not only bring people into the ballpark, but also be a boon to hotels and restaurants. "Pennsylvania has finally placed itself where it rightfully belongs—in the front rank with the other liberal and progressive states of the Union."[104]

In 1932, following the death of his son, the Pittsburgh Pirate owner, Barney Dreyfus, asked his son-in-law, William Benswanger, to take over day-to-day operations of the club. Benswanger ran the Pirates for nearly 15 years (courtesy Pittsburgh Pirates).

It took a year, but on April 29, 1934, the Pirates played their first Sunday game, defeating the Cincinnati Reds 9–5 before a shivering crowd of 20,000 fans. Two of Benswanger's star players, brothers Lloyd (Little Poison) and Paul (Big Poison) Waner, both future Hall of Famers, had outstanding games.[105]

Benswanger tried to lure fans into the ballpark in other ways. Like almost all other owners, he started ladies' days and boys' days in 1932 and the following year put numbers on his players' uniforms. When a fan, in 1932, suggested that Benswanger paint the distances from home plate on the various fences so that all fans could see how far a hitter had socked the ball, the club president was happy to comply.[106]

Even as the Depression was coming to a close, Benswanger was still instituting plans to bring fans to the game. In 1940, Forbes Field became the seventh major league park to have lights for night baseball.[107]

If the Depression had any positive effect on the Pirates, it would be the re-affiliation of one of their greatest stars, Honus Wagner. "The Flying Dutchman," one of Benswanger's boyhood idols, had played for Barney Dreyfuss in Louisville and then stayed with Pittsburg until his retirement in 1917. Wagner had been in the sporting goods business since his retirement but now was in serious financial straits. In a visit to Benswanger in 1932, Wagner's wife pleaded for a job for her husband with the Pirates, "specifically one with a uniform." Although Benswanger already had two coaches—former Giants Doc Crandall and Grover Hartley—he created a third coaching position for Wagner, subject to the approval of Pirate manager George Gibson, who agreed to the move without hesitation. Gratefully, Wagner remarked, "It does my heart good to return to the Pirates."[108]

Wagner's job was to travel with the team to spring training, to coach rookies, and to act as a "good-will ambassador for the Pittsburgh Pirates." Benswanger could hardly believe the affection shown the former star shortstop. "I don't know whether Honus is traveling with the Pirates or the Pirates are traveling with Honus, but it's a great feeling to have the Dutchman back in the uniform he loved so well."[109] In addition, Benswanger maintained, "[Wagner] was a real coach, a counselor for the young players and a good-will ambassador. And who should be better able to teach youngsters how to hit?"[110]

During the 15 years that Benswanger ran the Pittsburgh Pirates, he hired only four managers. In 1932, 1933, and part of 1934, George Gibson was the field boss of the Pirates.[111] He led the Pirates to a second-place finish in both 1932 and 1933, and then suddenly resigned after 51 games in 1934. Benswanger had a strict rule that he violated only twice—he never allowed himself to enter the clubhouse regardless of the situation. "The manager gets paid for managing and all the decisions on the field are his. When we're in my office upstairs, then it's a different matter."[112] The first time was in 1934, when he came to the clubhouse to tell his players that Gibson had resigned as manager.[113] Benswanger replaced Gibson with star third baseman Pie Traynor. Traynor was player-manager for three years, then retired as an active player but continued to manage the Pirates for two more seasons.[114]

During the 1930s under Gibson and Traynor, the Pirates finished in the first division eight years out of ten and only two games out of first in 1938.[115] This was Benswanger's most frustrating season during the thirties. In September the Pirates were 10 games ahead, but a dramatic home run by the Cubs' Gabby Hartnett against Pirate pitcher Mace Brown shifted the momentum. It also shifted the position of Pirate owner Bill Benswanger.[116] Some accounts say that Benswanger fainted after Hartnett's clout, but the Pirate president maintained that excitement caused him to fall right out of his seat. Benswanger also claimed that the real reason the Pirates lost in 1938 was a hurricane in the East that rained out games for a week, knocking the Pirates "off stride."[117]

During the early 1940s, the effort to integrate the all-white major and minor baseball leagues intensified. Many baseball people thought that with the armed forces siphoning off a large number of white players, the time might be right to bring African Americans into professional baseball.

For many years it had seemed that Pittsburgh would be the ideal place to break the color barrier in baseball. The city was considered the capital of African-American baseball with two teams—the Crawfords and the Homestead Grays. The *Pittsburgh-Courier*, one of the first black newspapers to publish both locally and nationally, and the most widely circulated black weekly in the nation, supposedly pressured Benswanger on many occasions to hire black players.

Certainly, Benswanger sounded positive about integration: "If it came to an issue, I'd vote for Negro players. There's no reason why they should be denied the same chance that Negro fighters and musicians are given."[118]

According to the *Courier*, Benswanger had offered to purchase the contracts of two premier Homestead sluggers, Josh Gibson and Buck Leonard, but at the last minute, changed his mind.[119] Benswanger had a different view of the incident. He claimed the Gray's owner, Cum Posey, talked him out of it because he feared that the signing of Gibson and Leonard would cause the collapse of the Negro leagues.[120]

In 1943, with still no blacks in the majors, Benswanger gave in to pressure from Nat Low, sports editor of the *Daily Worker*, and agreed to give tryouts to African-American players, second baseman Sam Hughes, pitcher Dave Barnhill, and catcher Roy Campanella. In his biography, Campanella recalled that Benswanger's letter contained so many conditions that he was discouraged even before he had completely read the invitation to a tryout. Campanella accepted, nonetheless, and a tryout was scheduled for August 4. It never took place, because Benswanger cancelled, citing unnamed pressures.[121] Campanella later got another chance, but Hughes and Barnhill did not.[122]

Of course, Branch Rickey was responsible for breaking the color barrier in major league baseball, not William Benswanger, probably because Benswanger was too conservative to back up his words with action.[123]

Frankie Frisch managed the Pittsburgh Pirates during World War II; his teams ended the season in fourth or fifth place every year except 1944, when they finished second, 14½ games behind the first place St. Louis Cardinals.[124]

Players who returned from the military following the war brought with them a new air of determination. They wanted a new relationship with the owners, a review of the detested reserve clause, a regular pension plan, and the end of arbitrary salary cuts. The returning players were in step with the change in the labor climate in the United States, which included many New Deal laws protecting the rights and increasing the power of labor unions. Robert Murphy, an attorney for the Congress of Industrial Organizations, urged baseball to form its own union, the American Baseball Guild.[125]

One of the teams that Murphy approached was the Pittsburgh Pirates, which looked like the kind of team likely to help organize the Guild. Despite the presence of excellent players like Ralph Kiner, Bob Elliott, Ken Heintzelman, Bill Cox, and "Preacher" Roe, the Pirates were not a very good team and many of the players were at the tail ends of their baseball careers. When Murphy approached the Pirates in May 1946, the team was carrying more than the allowed number on their roster, and cuts were imminent. There was an uneasiness in the clubhouse, as the roster had to be cut to 30 by June.[126]

Murphy began recruiting players to support the guild, and he was convinced that by May he had 90 percent of the team signed up.[127] When Benswanger heard that the Pirates were being organized in the new Baseball Guild, Benswanger laughed it off and facetiously replied: "Good! This team has been disorganized for so long I'm glad the boys are finally starting to pull together."[128]

Benswanger found out it was no laughing matter when Murphy announced a meeting with him on June 5 to work out plans to determine if the guild represented a majority of Pirate players.[129] Appalled at the thought of a union in baseball, Benswanger remembered that his father-in-law had always discouraged his players from even discussing the idea. On June 5, Benswanger announced he needed more time. Some Pirates wanted to strike immediately, but Murphy told them a strike would be unfair to the 26,000 fans who had already come to Forbes Field for the game.[130] He did state that if Benswanger did not recognize the guild, "I guarantee that there will be a strike tomorrow night unless the clubs come across."[131]

On June 7, 1946, Benswanger entered the team clubhouse for only the second time during his ownership. Murphy also tried to get in, but security officers would not allow him to enter. Two hours before the game, with the club attorney next to him, Benswanger addressed his players. As he told the press afterwards, "I haven't had any trouble with a ballplayer since I became president 15 years ago, and they cannot refute that statement. I have never hurt a ballplayer. I am leaving it up to them to decide whether to play."[132]

Management had two strong advocates in veteran pitcher Eldon "Rip" Sewell and utility infielder Jimmy Brown. Sewell was so outspoken against the guild that he volunteered to recruit his own team to play that evening against the Giants. "I know I can get nine men to play and I think there are quite a few players on the team who will follow me, too. There are ways of settling grievances besides unions. We can do without a racket run by a man who knows absolutely nothing about baseball."[133]

The vote against playing was 20 to 16, short of the two-thirds majority needed. The guild threat was over and nearly 20 years would pass before Marvin Miller, another man with strong union ties and far greater experience in labor negotiations, would successfully apply collective bargaining principles to major league baseball.[134]

The end of World War II brought not only a change in the attitude of the players, but also a change in the nature of team ownership. Until the 1940s, major league teams were generally owned by individual moguls whose chief source of income was baseball. They were first and foremost fans of the game and were usually active in the operation of their clubs. After World War II, a new generation of owners appeared on the scene. Teams were now being purchased by syndicates and consortiums, or by individual capitalists who viewed baseball as a financial opportunity more than an enjoyable sport.[135]

During the 1946 season Benswanger realized his team was ripe for the selling. By August the Pirates were in the cellar and ended in seventh place, their worst finish since 1917.[136] There were other factors as well. The morale of the Pirates was shaken by Murphy's efforts to unionize the team, and Benswanger had no guarantee there would not be another confrontation with labor unions. Forbes Field was completely rundown, because Benswanger, conservative as always and aware that he was managing the family's assets, pinched pennies on the upkeep of the park.[137]

Several potential buyers bid on the team. In August 1946 the winning group of four partners, Frank McKinney, one of the majority stockholders of the Indianapolis club of the American Association; Thomas P. Johnson, a Pittsburgh lawyer and businessman; Columbus real-estate tycoon John Galbreath; and Hollywood entertainer Bing Crosby, purchased the Pittsburgh Pirates baseball club, Forbes Field, and four minor league properties for $2.25 million.[138] The new owners asked Benswanger to remain for a while in an advisory capacity, but the sale ended the 47-year Dreyfuss family ownership of the Pittsburgh Pirates.[139]

Even after he severed his ties with the Pirates, Benswanger was not physically far from Forbes Field. He continued as director of the Peoples First National Bank and Trust Company, near Forbes Field, which had acted as the financial center for the Pirates through the years.[140]

He also stayed in touch with the Pirate organization in a number of ways. Benswanger maintained an active correspondence with many players from his own years with the team and with some who had played for his father-in-law, including Tommy Leach, Max Carey, and Deacon Phillippe.[141]

In 1959 Benswanger attempted to organize the celebration of the fiftieth anniversary of the construction of Forbes Field, offering to pay the expenses of all the surviving members of the 1909 club to attend. The Pirates decided to concentrate on bringing the All-Star Game to Pittsburgh instead.

He was successful, however, in leading the drive to finance a monument in honor of

Honus Wagner. On April 30, 1955, a magnificent bronze statue of Wagner was unveiled in Schenley Park, near the left field bleachers of Forbes Field. A thousand guests were present when the statue was dedicated. By this time, Wagner was too frail to take his place on the dais; he sat in an open car to witness the proceedings, at which Benswanger presided. The great shortstop died in his sleep eight months later.[142]

Benswanger also served on numerous musical boards, was a leader of the city's civic and charitable activities, and was an outstanding member of Pittsburgh's Jewish community.[143]

William Benswanger died January 15, 1972, after a long illness. He was 79 years old and was survived by his widow, a son, and two grandchildren.[144]

During the 1930s, three Jews, William Benswanger, Sidney Weil, and Emil Fuchs, all ran major league baseball teams, all were active in the Jewish community, and all three made no secret of their religion. There is no indication that any of them suffered any overt anti–Semitism, even though the decade was characterized by both world-wide and domestic hatred of Jews. This anomaly might be attributed to the fact that they were ethical in their baseball dealings and their lives, earning the respect of their peers and the communities where they ran their teams. When Hank Greenberg became an owner just a few years after Benswanger left baseball he would find a different situation.

17. The Golden Age Begins

The 1930s were an exceptionally stressful time for Jews in the United States. The Great Depression caused both Jews and non–Jews to question the validity of the American dream. The emergence of Nazism in Germany, where Jews had been accepted for years, soon occurred in the United States in the form of the German-American Bund.[1] Father Charles Coughlin and anti–Semitic organizations such as the Silver Shirts, the Friends of Democracy, and the National Union for Social Justice seemed to compete for the specific purpose of denigrating Jews. Although there were no pogroms in the United States, there continued to be Jewish quotas in most universities and professions, "exclusive" neighborhoods where Jews were not accepted, and white-collar jobs where "Jews need not apply."[2]

The Jewish community in the United States had also changed by the 1930s. Jewish children were remaining in school longer, families were moving to the suburbs where children could play on lawns and in parks, and American Jews were becoming more assimilated. What was unchanged was the great fascination Jews had for baseball, but these would-be players, with some exceptions, were the children of sports fans who supported their ambitions and were elated if their sons were gainfully employed.[3]

There were more Jews playing professional baseball in the 1930s than ever before. Baseball historians count 24 Jewish major league ball players in the decade with a high water mark of 12 during 1936, the same year Adolf Hitler was barring Jewish athletes from competing in the Olympics.[4] More importantly, more good Jewish players were beginning to reach the major leagues. As expected, many of them faced bitter and often physical anti–Semitism from other players and fans. Even the baseball establishment showed its true feelings when Commissioner Landis fined umpire George Moriarty, who had stopped a game because of anti–Semitic actions against Hank Greenberg.[5] Most importantly, these Jewish players in America's national game physically invalidated the charges of anti–Semites and reassured the Jewish community that Jews would make it through a difficult period.[6]

Hank Greenberg, the greatest Jewish major league baseball player during the first century of organized ball, played eight of his 13 years in the majors during the 1930s. The following six players, like Greenberg, spent all or nearly all of their careers in the American League.

Jonah Goldman

Infielder Jonah Goldman made his debut in the majors in 1928 but played his final two years in the 1930s. Goldman was born August 29, 1906, in New York City. He excelled in both baseball and football in high school and at Syracuse University. In January 1928, while still in college, he was signed by the Cleveland Indians, who sent him to their farm club in the Texas League.[7]

Goldman debuted with the Indians on September 22, 1928, and played seven games that year.[8] He spent the 1929 season with Albany in the Eastern League, hitting well at .293, but was especially noted for his outstanding fielding, as he participated in 127 double plays.[9]

Goldman played the full season at shortstop and third with the Indians in 1930. He appeared in 111 games, hitting .242 for the year, including 78 doubles and his only career home run.[10]

During spring training in 1931, Indian manager Roger Peckinpaugh told the press, "he has demonstrated at daily workouts that he is to be the shortstop this year or to know the reason why."[11] Unfortunately, Goldman did not perform up to expectations and after only 30 games in 1931, the Indians sent him back to the minor leagues.[12] The Indians gave up on Goldman following the '31 season. He continued in the minors until forced to retire from baseball in 1935 because of a serious thumb injury.[13]

After he left baseball, Jonah Goldman became president of Atlas Men's Shops. He died on August 17, 1980, in Palm Springs, California, at the age of 73, survived by his wife, Freda, and a brother and sister.[14]

Jonah Goldman debuted with the Cleveland Indians and played shortstop in 1928, 1930, and 1931. He was forced to retire after the 1931 season due to a thumb injury. He appeared in 148 games for the Indians and had a lifetime batting average of .224 (courtesy Jacob Rader Marcus Center of the American Jewish Archives).

Jim Levey

Like Mose Solomon, Jim Levey played professionally in both football and baseball. From 1930 to 1933 he played baseball for the St. Louis Browns, and from 1934 through 1936 he was a halfback with the Pittsburgh Pirates (now the Steelers).[15] During his baseball career he was a contemporary of both Hank Greenberg and infielder Jonah Goldman.

Levey was born in Pittsburgh on September 13, 1906. As a youngster, he loved baseball, but because he was too small to qualify for his high school baseball team, he became the batboy and mascot for a semipro team in Pittsburgh, the Shady Tree Triangles. After his sophomore year he dropped out of high school and joined the Triangles as an outfielder, working in the iron mills between seasons to build his strength. Discouraged by his lack of success in baseball, in 1923 he joined the Marines where he played both baseball and football at Quantico, Virginia. By now, he had switched from the outfield to shortstop.

In 1928, while on recruiting duty in Boston, Levey met Tom Keady, a coach and baseball scout for the New York Giants, who had seen Levey play. Knowing McGraw was on the lookout for Jewish players, Keady told Levey to go to New York and try out for the team. Levey was in such a hurry to leave that he forgot his baseball gear. At the Polo Grounds, Levey explained to John McGraw's personal assistant, Roger Bresnahan, that he left his gear in Boston but figured he could borrow a glove and shoes from one of the Giants. "You figured wrong," Bresnahan told Levey. "No equipment, no workout. You better beat it."[16]

Fortunately, the Giants were not the only team that had an eye on Levey. A few days later, St. Louis Browns scout John Freeman not only signed Levey, but the vice president of the Browns, with the aid of a United States senator, arranged for his discharge from the Marines.[17]

Levey played in the minors the rest of 1929 and until late in 1930. He made his major league debut on September 17 at Sportsman's Park against the New York Yankees. Levey hit safely twice that day, drove in two runs and scored two. He appeared in eight games for the Browns in 1930 and finished the season with a batting average of .243.[18]

Levey was the Browns' regular shortstop in 1931. He started the season with a bang by being the first Brownie to hit a home run that year.[19] If the Browns thought that was a portent of things to come, they were sadly mistaken. Levey would hit only four more homers that year, and, playing in 139 games, he finished the season with a batting mark of only .209 with a mere 38 runs batted in.[20] Despite Levey's poor showing in 1931, there was one interesting aspect to the season. When the St. Louis Browns played the Cleveland Indians, Harry Glantz, writing for the Los Angeles *B'nai B'rith Messenger*, noted that the shortstops for each team, Jim Levey and Jonah Goldman, were both Jewish, although another sportswriter claimed that Levey was not Jewish. Levey responded, "You tell him and everyone else who cares to know that I am a Jew and mighty proud of it."[21] Levey's comments clearly indicate that by the 1930s Jewish players were playing under their birth names, and were also openly acknowledging their Jewishness. Although his 1931 statistics were hardly overwhelming, *Baseball Magazine* mentioned him as "One of the Players You Ought to Know."[22]

To improve his hitting, in 1932 Levey's manager, Bill Killifer, converted the young infielder to a switch-hitter.[23] Obviously Killifer's move paid off, for Levey had his best year

Jim Levey was unique in that he excelled in both professional baseball and professional football. From 1930 to 1933 he was the starting shortstop for the St. Louis Browns. After his baseball days Levey was also a halfback for Pittsburgh's professional football team, which at that time was nicknamed the Pirates (courtesy National Baseball Hall of Fame Library, Cooperstown, N.Y.).

in 1932. He had a .280 batting average with 30 doubles, eight triples, four home runs, and 63 runs batted in.[24] *Baseball Magazine* attributed Levey's improvement to "an uncommon baseball phenomenon—a turn about hitter."[25] John McGraw was so impressed with Levey's improvement, that following the 1932 season he told a writer, "I'd trade my right arm, left leg and seven ballplayers for that young fellow."[26] Levey even received five votes for Most Valuable Player in the American League in 1932.[27]

Levey had little success in 1933. In 141 games, his batting average was .195. His hitting was inconsistent and his fielding irrational. The new Browns manager, Rogers Hornsby, intimated that he was seeking a new shortstop.[28]

Hornsby did not have to say anything. Levey appeared in the major leagues for the last time in 1933, and concentrated on pro football the next three years for Pittsburg. Back in baseball in 1937, Levey played for a variety of minor league teams, including Hollywood, Tulsa, Dallas and Buffalo and then managed in the minors until he retired from baseball in 1946.[29]

Jim Levey died in Dallas on March 14, 1970 after a lengthy illness. Levey had been the first Jew to play on the St. Louis Browns since Barney Pelty. Although he was nowhere near the quality player Pelty was, Levey delighted the fans of St. Louis with his speed on the bases and his hustle on the field.

Milt Galatzer appeared in 251 games during the 1930s, the "Golden Age" for Jewish baseball players. He wore a Cleveland Indians uniform from 1933 to 1936, and appeared in three games for the Cincinnati Reds in 1939 (courtesy Marc Okkonen).

Milt Galatzer

Two years after Jonah Goldman left the Cleveland Indians another Jewish ballplayer, outfielder Milt Galatzer, debuted with the team. Galatzer was born May 4, 1907, in Chicago. In the late 1920s he played semipro ball in Chicago, and was in the professional ranks with minor league teams in 1927 and 1928. Galatzer returned to professional baseball in 1930 with Frederick, Maryland, in the Blue Ridge League. In 1931 and '32, he played for a variety of minor league teams, always hitting very well. During his entire minor league career, from 1927 to 1933, Galatzer never hit below .300.[30]

Galatzer began the 1933 season at Toledo, but was promoted to the Indians when outfielder Joe Vosmik became ill. He debuted on June 25, 1933, in Cleveland in the first game of a double header and walked four times. Galatzer appeared in 57 games for the Indians in 1933 and hit only .238.[31]

Nineteen thirty-four was a repeat of the previous year. Galatzer began the year with Toledo, and after 111 games there, he returned to Cleveland. That year he appeared in 49 games and finished the 1934 season with the far more respectable average of .270.[32] Commenting on his two partial years with the Indians, *The Sporting News* said: "Hitting success alone will mean much in Milt Galatzer's attempt in 1935 to make the grade with the Indians. Milt has been trying since 1930 to win a regular berth with the Tribe, always showing plenty of defensive ability, but falling shy with the bat."[33]

In 1935 Galatzer played his longest major league season—93 games—and had his best season at the plate, hitting .301.[34] Galatzer's last season in the major leagues was 1936, when he appeared in 49 games for the Indians, hitting only .237 that year. On August 26, 1936, Galatzer pitched his only major league game, the final six innings of a contest against the Washington Senators. Galatzer allowed three runs on seven hits and ended the game with an earned run average of 4.50. He did not get the decision.[35]

In all of 1938 and most of 1939, Galatzer played in the minors. At the tail end of the 1939 season, Galatzer played three games with the Cincinnati Reds. After his brief appearance with the Reds, Galatzer returned to the minors through 1942. He spent 1943 to 1945 in the military service and his last year in professional baseball with Milwaukee in the American Association in 1946.[36]

Galatzer died in San Francisco, at the age of 68, after a long bout with cancer. Jewish funeral services were held for him in Chicago. In 1936, the Indians had brought a rookie pitcher to the big leagues, Bob Feller, who said of Galatzer, "There might have been better ballplayers than Milt Galatzer, but there will never be a better man."[37]

Bill Starr

William "Chick" Starr was one of several Jewish players with the Washington Senators during the 1930s. Bill Starr was born on February 26, 1911, in Brooklyn, to Russian-Jewish parents who had met and married in the United States. His father and uncle were ordained rabbis, but his father did not make his living as a rabbi.

Beginning in 1931 through the middle of the 1935 season, Starr played for a number of minor league teams. A talented catcher, he made his major league debut with the Washington Senators on July 23, 1935, replacing Sammy Holbrook in the tenth inning at Comiskey Park. He finished the year playing in 11 more games for the Senators.

The following year Starr spent most of the season with the San Diego Padres of the Pacific Coast League. Late in the season the Senators again called him to join the team.

Bill Starr, who played 13 games for the Washington Senators, was another Jewish ballplayer signed by Clark Griffith. He later spent a number of seasons in the minors, and eventually bought the minor-league San Diego Padres. As team owner, Starr signed the first African-American player in the Pacific Coast League (courtesy Marc Okkonen).

This year, he appeared in only one game and had no at bats. He left the majors at the end of the 1936 season; his entire career consisted of 13 games and five hits in 24 at bats.[38]

When Starr rejoined the Padres in San Diego in 1937, two of his teammates were Jimmie Reese and Ted Williams. In one game, Starr had to pinch-hit for Williams because the manager wanted a bunt and he was not confident that Williams could execute one. Coming in with one strike on the batter, Starr bunted foul for the second strike before he flied out. Years later Starr would state, "I think I was the only man ever to pinch hit for Ted Williams."[39] Starr completed the 1937 season and played a few games in 1938 before breaking his leg.[40]

In 1944 Starr headed the group that purchased the Padres, his former team. In 1948, as Padres owner, he hired John Richey, the first African-American player in the Pacific Coast League.[41] Starr also created an intricate scouting system for the Padres long before even the major leagues used such a system. One of his finds was Luke Easter, who would become a dominant player with the Indians.[42]

After he left the Padres, Starr became a developer of condominiums, apartment buildings, and shopping centers. In 1989 he wrote a book entitled *Clearing the Bases* in which he criticized the new methods of player training. Starr died on August 12, 1991, in La Jolla, California.[43]

Sydney Cohen

Sydney Cohen, who pitched for the Washington Senators in 1934, and again in 1936 and 1937, was one of five Jewish ball players on the Senators' roster during the 1930s. The younger brother of Andy Cohen, who played for the New York Giants in the 1920s, he and Andy formed another set of Jewish brothers who played ball in the major leagues.

Sydney Harry Cohen was born in Baltimore, May 7, 1908, but moved to El Paso at the age of six. After he graduated from El Paso High School, where he won letters in baseball and basketball, Syd attended Southern Methodist University and then followed his older brother to the University of Alabama, where he played baseball. Even though Sydney Cohen was a pitcher in the major leagues, he played the infield in college.

John McGraw, who was already hoping to turn Andy into a star, sent a scout to watch Syd play college ball and then invited him for a tryout. McGraw was neutral about his chances, "This boy Sydney has some earmarks of being a real ball player. He certainly can field beautifully. As to his hitting, of course, I do not know."[44]

Sydney Cohen left the University of Alabama after two years and signed as a left-handed pitcher with the San Francisco Seals of the Pacific Coast League in 1930.[45] In 1931 Cohen returned to his hometown of El Paso to play for Nogales in the Mexican League. Teams in that league were limited in the number of Americans they could carry on their roster. Nogales was over their limit, but since Cohen spoke fluent Spanish and had a dark olive complexion, he was able to pass himself off as the Mexican Pablo Garcia. The truth came out years later but no one seemed to care. When he returned to Mexico as the manager of the Juarez Indians, the fans recognized him and greeted "Pablo" with cheers and applause.[46]

Cohen left Nogales after two seasons, and in 1933 and 1934 spent time with several minor league teams, including two months with his brother Andy at Minneapolis. During the 1934 season, Cohen began to pitch really well for Chattanooga, becoming one of the top hurlers for the Lookouts. The Senators brought him to the major leagues to close the last two weeks of the season.[47]

Sydney Cohen, a southpaw relief pitcher for the Washington Senators in 1934, 1936 and 1937, had only three major league victories, but was able to contain one of the top sluggers in the American League, Lou Gehrig. Syd and his brother Andy comprised one of six pairs of Jewish brothers who reached the major leagues (courtesy Neal Ross).

In his short time with the Senators in 1934, Sydney Cohen had two distinctions. It was Babe Ruth's final season in the American League and Sydney Cohen was the last pitcher in that league to strike him out. But on September 29, 1934, when Ruth clouted his 708th home run, Cohen also became the last American League pitcher to throw Ruth a home run ball.[48] Cohen had a record of 1–1 in his brief stint with the Senators in 1934, and spent 1935 again pitching for Chattanooga, where he won 16 games.[49]

During the 1936 and 1937 seasons, the Senator southpaw was used primarily in relief and compiled a record of two wins and six losses. During his entire career with Washington, he made 55 appearances and had a 4.54 earned run average.[50]

Despite Cohen's mediocre record, there was one major leaguer who had a difficult time hitting against him. Lou Gehrig, the Yankee slugger, faced Cohen seven times in his career and fanned five. In 1934, 1936, and 1937, Gehrig's average against all pitchers he faced was .385; for those three seasons against Cohen, his batting average was a puny .167.[51]

From 1938 through 1939, Cohen pitched at various times for Baltimore, New Orleans, Dallas, and Fort Worth. He even tried umpiring in 1940, but felt it was a dead-end job. In 1941, Sydney Cohen caught on with Portland, where he remained for five years. His last big year was 1945, when he compiled a 14–8 record to help Portland win the pennant.[52]

After his playing career, Cohen turned to managing and led the Juarez Indians to the Arizona-Texas League championship in 1950. In the 1970s he was the pitching coach with the El Paso Diablos and he and his brother Andy were volunteer coaches for the UTEP baseball program.[53] Sydney and Andy Cohen were greatly loved in El Paso. The new baseball park there was named in their honor and in 1963 Sydney Cohen joined brother Andy once more by being voted into the El Paso Hall of Fame.[54]

Sydney Cohen passed away April 9, 1988, at the age of 81. Services were conducted at Temple Mt. Sinai in El Paso.[55] The owner of the El Paso team Cohen managed in the 1950s, Dick Azar, called Sydney Cohen a competitor but a perfect gentleman: "He was just a great guy, a great example for kids. Any time little kids wanted to play ball, Syd was there to help 'em."[56]

Fred Sington

Fred Sington, still another Washington Senator during the 1930s, could also have played both professional baseball and football, but chose to stick with baseball. Sington was born on February 10, 1910, in Birmingham, Alabama, and like the Cohen brothers attended the University of Alabama. At college, Sington joined Zeta Beta Tau, a Jewish fraternity, and was the star tackle on the football team. He also played on the university's baseball team; first he was a pitcher, and then he switched to the outfield. After he received his AB in 1931, Sington spurned offers to become a professional football player and signed a contract with the Washington Senators in 1932.[57]

Sington played with teams in the mid–Atlantic League, the Southern Association, and the old Southeastern League during the 1932 and 1933 seasons, hitting above .300. In 1934, with Albany of the International League, he had an excellent year, batting .338 and clouting 29 home runs. He drove in 100 runs and was voted the team's most valuable player.[58] The Senators noticed Sington's play and promoted him to the majors, where he made his debut on September 23, 1934, driving in Buddy Myer with the winning run against the Philadelphia Athletics. Sington said of his debut, "I'll always consider that as one of the greatest thrills I've had."[59] He appeared in nine games for the Senators in 1934, hitting .286 with 35 at bats.[60]

Fred Sington spent two years in Brooklyn, and was one of several Jews who played for the Washington Senators. An outfielder, Sington appeared in 181 games and compiled a .271 lifetime batting average (courtesy National Baseball Hall of Fame Library, Cooperstown, N.Y.).

The next two years, 1935 and 1936, were very similar to the year before except that now Sington was with Chattanooga of the Southern Association, where in both years he won the league batting title, and in 1935 was voted MVP. In the majors in 1935, he did manage to play 20 games for the Senators, but his average was only .182, with four singles in 22 plate appearances.[61] In 1936 Sington played 25 games for the Senators and hit his first major league home run against the Detroit Tigers. This year, Sington ended the season with a .319 batting average.[62]

Clark Griffith was elated with Sington. "Sington proved to me," said Griffith, "he is a real prospect. He's a run-driver-in and that's what we need."[63] Manager Bucky Harris was also impressed by Sington's play. "He isn't a polished fielder yet, but he has shown much improvement."[64]

The hype about Sington proved premature. In 1937 Sington had his only full major league season. He appeared in 78 games and batted .237 with three home runs.[65] At the end of the season, Sington was traded to the Brooklyn Dodgers, where he joined another Jewish player, Goody Rosen. The Dodgers expected him to strengthen their outfield, but in two years, 1938 and 1939, Sington played in only 49 games for Brooklyn and, although he had 42 hits in 137 at bats, the Dodgers released him.[66]

After he retired, Sington went back to Birmingham, where he was active in the community and became chief referee and president of the Southeastern Conference Officials Association for many years.[67] In 1955 he was inducted into the College Football Hall of Fame, the only Jewish baseball player to receive that honor. He was also chosen Birmingham's Man of the Year in 1970 and was elected to the Southern Athletic Hall of Fame in 1974.[68]

Even though he was always acknowledged as a Jew, Sington supposedly converted to Christianity at some point in his life.[69] He died on August 20, 1998, at the age of 88. In 1981, he told an interviewer, "Nothing but great things have happened to me. The Lord has looked out for me."[70]

The National League, too, had its share of Jewish players, including the following three who played on the New York Giants during part of their careers. Any of these three could have been the Jewish player John McGraw had long sought.

Harry Danning

For nearly 25 years the New York Giant manager, John McGraw, had been looking for an outstanding Jewish baseball star to attract the vast New York Jewish population to the Polo Grounds. The year after McGraw retired as Giant manager, his successor, Bill Terry, discovered a Jewish star and brought him to the major leagues. His name was Harry Danning.[71]

Harry "The Horse" Danning, one of the most interesting men ever to wear a baseball uniform, was born in Los Angeles on September 6, 1911. He was the son of a Russian father and a Latvian mother, the fourth of six children. One of his older siblings was Ike Danning, who appeared in two games for the St. Louis Browns in 1928, the same year Harry graduated from high school. It was Ike whose example inspired Harry's interest in baseball. When Harry Danning became a major league player, the Dannings became another set of Jewish brothers to accomplish that feat.

After his high school graduation, Danning worked for a wholesale rug house, sweeping the floor and hanging the rugs. "I made 90 bucks a month," he said.[72] But he spent most of his time playing semipro ball, always as a catcher. "We used to play on the sandlots when I was about eleven or twelve and nobody wanted to play catcher, so I told them I was a catcher. I had never caught before in my life but I wanted to play, so that is why I became a catcher,"[73] he added.

In 1931 George Washington Grant, former president of the Boston Braves and a resident of Los Angeles, recommended to Giant owner, Charles A. Stoneham, that he sign Danning for the Giants' organization. Stoneham agreed, and sent him to the Eastern League that year.[74] Danning spent a little over two years in the minors, including a stint in Buffalo. Danning always credited Ray Schalk, a former catcher and Buffalo manager, with really teaching him how to catch.[75]

Danning was called up from Buffalo to the Giants in July 1933. Gus Mancuso was the first-string catcher for New York and Paul Richards was next in line. Danning performed the mechanical duties of a third-string catcher—warming up relievers in the bullpen and catching batting practice. He appeared in only three games that year and went hitless in three times at bat.[76]

Danning continued his role as a backup receiver for the following three years, although he was beginning to see more action. Once in a while he would catch the great Giant star Carl Hubbell, but Mancuso continued to do the bulk of the catching. In 1934, Danning appeared in 53 games and hit .330; in 1935 he appeared in 65 games, but his batting average plunged to .243; and the following year, he appeared in 32 games, hitting a mere .159.[77]

He did manage to play in the 1936 World Series against the New York Yankees as a sub for Mancuso. During the Series, Ted Husing, series broadcaster, referred to Danning as "Harry the Horse," because Harry appeared to work like a horse and—in those days—with about as much grace. The name caught on for another reason—it was the same as a character in the very popular Damon Runyon stories.[78]

Even though Danning was not a starting catcher the first four years as a Giant, he only had positive things to say about his manager, Terry. "It was great playing for the Giants under Terry. He let us play and we learned from that and got better."[79]

In 1937 Mancuso broke his finger during the season and Danning got his chance to move up to first-string catcher; he showed he was more than ready. On June 9, Danning hit a game-winning home run in the bottom of the ninth. On July 13 he hit home runs in both games of a doubleheader. On August 20 he got five hits—four singles and a triple—in one game. And on August 25 he drove in the final winning run of an 11-inning game against the Cubs. Danning's batting average was .288 and his hitting helped the Giants win the pennant again that year.[80] One New York writer stated, "If all the subs were as good as Danning, the Giants would be sitting pretty."[81]

The Giants lost the World Series, but Danning's performance in 1937 earned him the job of starting catcher, and he did not relinquish it until he was drafted into the army following the 1942 season. The *Los Angeles Times* noted that John McGraw had spent a fortune trying to get a Jewish ballplayer who could help offset the drawing power of Babe Ruth of the New York Yankees. "Now," wrote the scribe, "the Giants apparently have a Jewish hero who has been a sparkplug in their drive toward the pennant—and he's a Los Angeles boy."[82]

Danning followed the 1937 season with his three best years. In 1938 he hit 306, playing in 120 games; in 1939 he hit .313, playing in 135 games; and in 1940, he hit .300, playing in 140 games. In all, he played in 890 games over a ten-year period.[83] His lifetime batting average is .285; his fielding average for ten years of catching is an outstanding .985.[84] John Carmichael, in *Who's Who in the Major Leagues*, called Danning "one of the best handlers of pitchers in the league and a master strategist." Carmichael hailed Danning's "deadly

Harry "The Horse" Danning spent his entire 10 years in the major leagues as a catcher for the New York Giants. He was the first-string catcher from 1938 until he entered the armed forces in 1942; he never played on the Jewish High Holy Days (courtesy National Baseball Hall of Fame Library, Cooperstown, N.Y.).

Ike Danning, Harry's older brother, appeared in only two major league games, both for the St. Louis Browns in 1928. The Dannings constituted another of the six sets of Jewish brothers who played major league baseball (courtesy Ben Danning Collection).

throwing accuracy and speed on defense."[85] Danning was selected for the National League All Star game four times—in 1938, 1939, 1940, and 1941.[86]

Throughout his entire playing career, Danning never hid the fact that he was Jewish and on a few occasions he met many forms of anti–Semitism. The press sometimes called Danning the "Jewish catcher," "hawk nose," or "schnozz." It was not uncommon even for the New York newspapers to refer to Danning in such ethnically disparaging terms. "I remember some bench jockeys needling me about my large nose," recalled Danning. "Pitch under his nose. He can't see the ball," the opposing team would yell.[87] "I also had to endure many anti–Semitic comments from the crowd," Danning stated, "but I kept my mouth shut and went out and played."[88] "I'm Jewish so I got called every name in the book and was thrown at a lot. You just accepted it and played. You couldn't let them show that it bothered you or you'd get more of it."[89]

Danning also related that in 1934 the Giants had made a hotel reservation at the Flamingo Hotel in Miami Beach. When the team arrived, the hotel desk clerk informed Danning and his Jewish teammate, Phil Weintraub, that they could not stay at the hotel. Manager Bill Terry was furious. He told the desk clerk that the hotel would take everybody or nobody. According to Danning, the entire team stayed at the Flamingo Hotel.[90]

Danning would not play ball on Yom Kippur, the most holy Jewish holiday. He also observed Rosh Hashanah, the Jewish New Year. "I don't have any trouble whatsoever," stated Danning. "I would tell Terry I don't play. I went to a synagogue in New York on 47th Street. If Christmas was during the baseball season, half of the guys wouldn't have played."[91]

In 1945 Danning returned to civilian life after three years in the Army and retired from baseball. Military doctors and his own physician had advised that if he played baseball his leg would lockup and he would have a stiff leg the rest of his life.[92]

Danning went into the automobile business in Los Angeles and was a newspaper and magazine distributor and an insurance executive until his retirement in 1976. He remained an avid follower of baseball and often expressed his feelings toward the game. For example, he was ardently opposed to the reserve clause and elated when it was repealed, and was also against the designated hitter because he felt it took away strategy from the game.[93]

In August 2004 the Baseball Hall of Fame honored Jewish major leaguers at a ceremony in Cooperstown, but Danning, who had been in a wheelchair for three years by then, could not make the trip. "In the last month, he had been in and out of hospitals quite a bit, but he went home Saturday," said his brother, Ben, of Los Angeles. "That night," Ben Danning said, "my brother returned to the hospital, where he died of pneumonia."

Danning and his wife, Viktoria, had moved to Indiana to be closer to their only child and lived in an apartment above their daughter's home. Danning spent his days watching TV and answering the multitude of fan mail that still came. At the time of his death, Danning was the sole surviving member of the pennant-winning 1937 New York Giants. At the age of 93, he was also the oldest Jewish major leaguer.[94]

Phil Weintraub

Harry Danning debuted for the Giants in 1933, the same year John McGraw died. Both Danning and another player who started that year would have been the answer to his prayer for a Jewish star. The other player was Phil Weintraub.

Philip "Mickey" Weintraub was born on October 12, 1907, in Chicago, the son of Russian-born Jews, and the third of six children. His father owned a small shop that he expected Phil would operate some day. Phil's parents reacted to his ambition to play ball for a living the same way as Al Schacht's parents did, declaring that "All ball players are bums." It was only after Weintraub threatened to run away from home at the age of 17 that they signed his first professional contract.[95]

After Weintraub graduated from Loyola University, he pitched semipro baseball in the Mississippi Valley League from 1926 to 1927, and in the Texas League in 1928. His father's death in 1929 caused him to leave baseball temporarily to take over the family's auction business.[96]

In 1930 Weintraub signed a minor league contract but was out most of the season because of an injury to his throwing arm, which he worried might end his baseball career. It proved, in the long run, to be a good break for him. He returned to the minors in 1931, and for two seasons played not as a pitcher but as a first baseman, hitting well above .300 both years.[97]

In August 1933 Weintraub was with the Southern League when the Giants signed him as a utility outfielder. He debuted with the Giants on September 5 and two days later hit his first major league home run. Weintraub appeared in only eight games that year and hit .200.[98]

Weintraub went to spring training with the Giants in 1934, but they intended that he start the 1934 season at Nashville. Jewish fans inundated the front office with calls, letters, and telegrams protesting the move. For a time, Giant manager Bill Terry was tempted to recall Weintraub, but decided to leave him in Nashville. For his part, Weintraub was determined to return to the majors. At his request, Nashville manager Charlie Dressen moved Weintraub from first base to left field. Weintraub showed his appreciation by leading the league in hitting, with an average of .401, the first time any player in the Southern League had hit over .400 in 30 years.[99] At the end of July, the Giants recalled him and for the parent club in 1934 he played in 31 games and hit .351.[100]

A scribe for the *New York Mirror*, writing in *The Sporting News*, implied that Bill Terry would "get rid of Weintraub in a minute" if he were not afraid of being branded anti–Semitic.[101] But, despite Weintraub's hitting, Terry was not yet convinced that Weintraub was ready for the majors and Weintraub spent most of the next three seasons in the minors. In 1937 Weintraub was sold to the Cincinnati Reds, where he was reunited with his manager from Nashville, Charlie Dressen.[102]

In December 1936 Weintraub had secretly wed Jeanne Holsman before a justice of the peace in Waukegan, a Chicago suburb. After they told their families they were married, Jeanne's mother asked Weintraub what he did. Phil proudly informed her that he was a ballplayer. She replied, "That's nice, but what do you do for a living?"[103] The families insisted on a "proper" ceremony they could witness so, according to Weintraub, the couple repledged their vows at the bride's home "with a rabbi officiating."[104]

The new bridegroom played 49 games with the Reds in 1937, hitting .271. He was popular with his teammates, who nicknamed him "Phil Weintraub, the Jewish fashion plate from Chicago."[105] When the Reds played the Cubs in Chicago, Weintraub usually took a delegation of Cincinnati players to meetings of the Chicago Lawndale B'nai B'rith Lodge where he was a member.[106]

On July 3, 1937, the New York Giants reacquired Weintraub and pitcher Walter Brown from the Reds and sent them to their farm club in Jersey City. Weintraub rejoined the

Phil Weintraub easily could have been the popular Jewish star John McGraw had long sought. Unfortunately, McGraw was no longer Giant manager when Weintraub debuted with the Giants in 1933. Not a superstar, Weintraub had a respectable seven-year career in the major leagues with the Giants, Reds, and Phils, and ended his major league career after the 1945 season with a lifetime batting mark of .295 (courtesy Transcendental Graphics).

Giants once again in September, played in six games, and returned to the minors for the remainder of the season.[107]

In 1938 Weintraub was traded to the Philadelphia Phillies, playing in 100 games and hitting .311. For the Phillies, he got the last hit at the Baker Bowl before the team moved into their new home, Shibe Park.[108] Like his former teammate, Harry Danning, Weintraub did not play baseball on Yom Kippur.[109]

It was back to the minors again for Weintraub in 1939. In 1940, he was selected to play in the American Association All-Star Game.[110] From 1941 through 1944, he was with several minor league teams, including the Los Angeles Angels, where he played against one of McGraw's former protégés, Harry Rosenberg, who was then an outfielder for the Hollywood Stars.[111]

In 1944, the Giants reacquired Weintraub for the third time, and this year's total of 104 games played was the highest during his entire major league career. He accomplished a number of feats that year. On two occasions he scored five runs in a single game, and in another game batted in 11 runs, hitting a home run, a triple, two doubles, and drawing a bases-loaded walk. This was one RBI less than the record set by Jim Bottomley of the Cardinals 20 years earlier. After the game, Babe Ruth told Weintraub, "Kid, that was some performance. You knocked in enough runs for a month. Some guys don't get that many in a season."[112]

Weintraub played his final season in the majors in 1945 for the Giants, appearing in 82 games. In seven seasons in the major leagues on three different teams, Weintraub had a career batting average of .295. He had 407 hits, which included 32 home runs; he scored 215 runs and drove in 207.[113]

After his retirement, Weintraub represented a food company in New York and dabbled in real estate in Palm Springs, California, where he died on June 21, 1987, at the age of 79. When he was once asked why he had such a limited career in the majors, he answered, "I frankly don't know why I was a minor leaguer for so long, but I suppose the final explanation is that it is just baseball. It certainly is a strange game."[114]

Morrie Arnovich

When Phil Weintraub was traded to the Philadelphia Phillies in 1938, he teamed up with Morrie Arnovich, another Jewish ballplayer, who had been with the Phillies for two years.

Morrie Arnovich was born in Superior, Wisconsin, on November 20, 1910, the son of Orthodox Jewish parents. Two of Arnovich's cousins and an uncle were rabbis, and, as a child, Morrie studied Hebrew. He starred in basketball at Superior State Teachers College, playing two consecutive years for the All Wisconsin basketball team.[115]

Dave Bancroft, former Giants shortstop and Boston Braves manager for Emil Fuchs from 1924 to 1927, also lived in Superior. He felt that Arnovich had all the potential to be a big leaguer and, in 1933, Bancroft brought him to Dick Wade, manager of the Superior team in the Northern League.[116] Although Arnovich wanted to play shortstop or third base, Bancroft suggested he play the outfield instead. It was a good move. Arnovich played two years for Superior, hitting above .300 both years.[117]

The Philadelphia Phillies purchased his contract in 1935 and optioned him to the New York-Penn League where he played until late in the 1936 season. That year, Arnovich led the league in total bases and tied for the lead in home runs.[118] The Phillies brought him to

Morris Arnovich was one of the most beloved citizens of Superior, Wisconsin. He spent seven years in the major leagues, more than half of them with the Philadelphia Phillies (courtesy National Baseball Hall of Fame Library, Cooperstown, N.Y.).

the big leagues at the tail end of 1936. He appeared in 13 games, getting 15 hits, including one home run, for a .313 average.[119]

In spring training in 1937 Arnovich clinched a starting job in the Philly outfield. In Boston, on opening day of the 1937 season, Arnovich hit the first of his 22 career homers, in the 13th inning off Brave hurler, Guy Bush, to lead the Phillies to a 2–1 victory.[120] He played regularly all year and in 117 games hit 10 home runs and a very respectable .290.

In September 1938 Eddie Feinberg joined Arnovich and Phil Weintraub, giving the Phillies three Jewish ball players on their roster. Feinberg would play two years with the Phillies and appear in 16 games.[121]

In 1939 Arnovich's religion was causing pressure on the young Philly outfielder, but not in an anti–Semitic fashion. Both the secular and the Anglo-Jewish press began to take note of Jewish participation in the major leagues, constantly referring to Arnovich as "the son of Israel," or the next "Jewish star." Arnovich was not simply a major leaguer but a "Jewish athlete," "the chunky Hebrew lad," or "the little Hebrew."[122] The *American Hebrew* predicted that Arnovich would certainly make "his people proud of him." Sportswriter Dan Daniel indicated that Arnovich, as well as other Jewish ballplayers, may well "give the Chosen People something to talk about in a baseball way."[123]

Even though Arnovich was having an outstanding season in 1939, all these expectations were beginning to affect his play. "All this has finally made him tighten up and go into a tailspin," his manager, Doc Prothro, observed. "He went 29 times with no hits so I decided to let him rest for four or five days. He'll be back in the lineup when we get to St. Louis."[124]

On July 16, 1939, Philadelphia fans celebrated "Morrie Arnovich Day." Attending the game were members of the Jewish War Veterans, the YMHA (Young Men's Hebrew Association), local synagogues, and the B'nai B'rith. Arnovich's father had come for the first time to see his son play in the major leagues.[125]

Arnovich enjoyed his best season in the majors in 1939. At midseason he was leading the league in hitting with .375 and was chosen for the All-Star game. He finished the season with an amazing .324 average for the last-place Phillies, who lost 106 games that year and won only 45.[126]

Despite his great season in 1939, Arnovich got off to a dreadful start in 1940, hitting only .199 after the first 39 games. The Phillies traded Arnovich to the Reds for outfielder Johnny Rizzo. Instead of the cellar dwellers, Arnovich was now with the team that would win the 1940 National League pennant, giving him the chance to participate in his first World Series. He appeared only once—on October 5—and was hitless in his only at bat.[127]

Arnovich continued his role as a utility outfielder with the New York Giants in 1941, where he played 85 games and hit .280.[128] He spent the next four years in the military service, and when he was discharged he played in one more game for the Giants before retiring as an active player.[129] Arnovich then managed several teams in the Chicago Cubs organization.[130]

After he quit managing, he returned to Superior, married Bertha Aserson, and served as president of the Hebrew Brotherhood Congregation in Superior. He also did some scouting for the Phillies, was the co-owner of a sporting goods store and a staunch supporter of athletics in the Superior area.[131]

On July 20, 1959, Morrie Arnovich died in Superior of a coronary occlusion at the age of 49. He was survived by his widow and buried in Hebrew Cemetery.[132]

Despite all the press, Arnovich never set the baseball world on fire, but he was a dependable and timely hitter with a lifetime major league average in the .280s, a popular player, and well respected in his community.[133]

Other Jews who played briefly in the major leagues during the 1930s include Lou Brower of the Tigers; Harry Chozen of the Reds; Izzy Goldstein of the Tigers; and Cy Malis, who played for the Phillies.

18. The Brooklyn Dodgers

During the 1930s and '40s, there were well over a million Jewish residents in Brooklyn, many of whom were dedicated fans of their local baseball team, called the Robins until 1931 when they reacquired the nickname "Dodgers."[1] Surprisingly, only eight Jewish major leaguers played for the Robins/Dodgers before 1948. Moe Berg began his career with the Dodgers in 1923 but played most of his games in the American League. Both Sam Bohne and Fred Sington ended their playing days with the Dodgers, Bohne in 1926 and Sington in 1939.[2] Each of the remaining five players added his own bit of history to the baseball team that diehard Brooklyn fans still venerate.

Alta Cohen

Alta Cohen was the third major league "Cohen" who did not change his name during his career. Cohen, the son of a rabbi, was born on December 25, 1910, in New York City. His teammates gave him the nickname "Schoolboy" because of his youthful good looks. Cohen graduated from South Side High School in 1927 and played the outfield for a number of minor league teams during the next three seasons.[3]

In 1931 the Dodgers' spring training base in Clearwater, Florida, seemed like a miniature League of Nations, as it included Italian Ernie Lombardi, Spanish-American Alfonso Lopez, Val Picinich of Czech descent; French-Canadian Del Bissonette; Babe Herman of Germanic extraction; Irishman Frank O'Doul; and Jewish players Alta Cohen and Max Rosenfeld. *The Sporting* News called the Robins "a Baseball Melting Pot."[4]

Cohen immediately caught the press's attention because his batting style was so similar to Mel Ott's. What worried Cohen was that the Robins already had an excess of outfielders on their roster. "It's like trying to break into a bank with a penknife," commented Cohen on his effort to win a job with the Robins.[5]

But he got his chance on April 15, 1931, in one of the most unusual debuts in major league history. It was the second day of the season and the Robins and Braves were engaged in a high-scoring battle in Boston. Right fielder Babe Herman missed a number of balls which manager Wilbert Robinson thought he should have caught and he let him know it when Herman returned to the dugout. Herman, the unpredictable outfielder, yelled at Robinson, "If you think someone can play the position better, I'm through."

Robinson intended to send in Ike Boone in place of Herman, and let Boone pinch-hit for the pitcher. After the inning ended, Robinson realized that putting in Boone, a slow-footed fielder, had been a poor defensive move. He then told the rookie, Alta Cohen, to take over for Boone in the outfield. As the replacement for Boone, Cohen would be hitting in the pitcher's place in the line-up, not Herman's. But when the Robins came up to bat, the eager Cohen stepped to the plate in the cleanup position, normally Herman's spot, and promptly singled to right. Cohen had hit out of order, but the Braves did not appeal. The Robins kept the inning alive and when Cohen's correct turn in the batting order, ninth, came around, Cohen batted again and got his second hit of the inning.[6] After that game, Cohen was kept on the roster for another three weeks, and then sent to the minors.[7]

Cohen appeared in nine games with the Dodgers the following year and in 1933 was traded to the Phillies, where he played 19 games before being sent to the Toledo Mudhens of the American Association. With Toledo, Cohen became a left-handed pitcher and played from 1933 through the 1935 season. Cohen never did return to the majors.[8]

Following his retirement from the game, Cohen founded his own business in New Jersey. He was inducted into the Dodger Hall of Fame in 1997 and died March 11, 2003. At the time of his death, Alta Cohen was the oldest member of the Brooklyn Dodgers Alumni Association.[9] Two sons, a daughter, five grandchildren and three great-grandchildren survived him.

Max Rosenfeld

When Max Rosenfeld and Alta Cohen joined the Brooklyn Robins in 1931, they were the fourth and fifth Jews to play for the Robins. Rosenfeld, who was born December 23, 1902, was also a native New Yorker, but his family moved later to Birmingham, Alabama. Like Andy and Sydney Cohen and Fred Sington, Rosenfeld attended the University of Alabama, where he played football and baseball.[10]

Rosenfeld began his professional baseball career with Springfield of the Western Association and played with a number of minor league teams until, in 1931,

Alta Cohen, a rabbi's son, was nicknamed "Schoolboy" by his teammates because of his good looks. His debut with the Brooklyn Dodgers in 1931 is considered by many to be one of the most unusual in baseball annals (courtesy National Baseball Hall of Fame Library, Cooperstown, N.Y.).

Max Rosenfeld was a teammate of Alta Cohen for three years when they both played for the Brooklyn Dodgers from 1931 to 1933. Rosenfeld was a utility outfielder who appeared in 42 games (courtesy National Baseball Hall of Fame Library, Cooperstown, N.Y.).

the Robins placed him on the spring training roster.[11] Several prospects were vying for utility roles on the Robins that year, but *The Sporting News* noted that Rosenfeld's chances of making the team seemed good. "Rosenfeld is quite a finished ballplayer, a hustler and gamer. He is a short line drive hitter, rather than a slugger, and adept at hitting the base knocks to any field."[12]

Rosenfeld debuted for the Robins against the Phillies, replacing Johnny Frederick in center field. He failed to hit his first time at bat, but doubled in the ninth inning in a losing effort for the Robins. Rosenfeld batted only seven more times that year and finished with an average of .222.[13]

In 1932 Rosenfeld appeared in 34 games for Brooklyn, hitting his only two major league home runs and batting .359. He played in five games in 1933, his last year in the majors, and finished with a lifetime batting average of .298 in 42 games over a span of three years. Rosenfeld completed 1933 with Jersey City of the International League, where he played both second base and the outfield.[14]

A fan from Miami complained in a letter to *The Sporting News* when Rosenfeld was sent down to the minors: "I have talked to a hundred players in the International League who played with Rosenfeld," claimed the fan, "and none can explain why he was waived.... What has been done to Rosenfeld is a great injustice."[15]

From 1934 to 1939 Rosenfeld played with several minor league teams, including Syracuse, Knoxville, Newark, Tulsa, Oklahoma City, Dallas, Jackson, and Panama City.[16]

During 1940 and 1941, Rosenfeld served as president, business manager, and field manager of the Miami Beach Flamingos of the Florida East Coast League. He gave up managing in 1942, but continued his association with the Flamingos until 1946.[17]

Rosenfeld then devoted his time to the realty business in Miami Beach, but he was still active in a number of organizations, including the Old Timers Professional Baseball Association of Greater Miami. Rosenfeld died in Miami on March 10, 1969, at the age of 67 and was buried at Temple Israel Cemetery. He had one daughter and three grandchildren.[18]

Harry Eisenstat

Harry Eisenstat was the sixth major leaguer to play for the Brooklyn Dodgers prior to 1948. The left-handed pitcher was also a native of Brooklyn.

Harry Eisenstat was born October 10, 1915, and began as a first baseman for his high school team. During one game, the team was suddenly without pitchers, and Eisenstat's coach, Art Wunderlich, asked him to move to the pitcher's mound.[19] Eisenstat protested, but began pitching and struck out five of the six men he faced. His coach started him in the next game, and this time he pitched a no-hitter. According to Wunderlich, "From the start, Harry had the best control and poise I ever saw in a youngster. But I've got to admit that I never thought he'd develop fast enough to make the Dodgers or any other major league club one year after he left me."[20]

His parents were disappointed with their son's choice of baseball as his career, expressing the hope that Harry would "do something more honorable like law or medicine."[21]

But Eisenstat quickly drew the attention of baseball scouts, including Dodger pitching coach Otto Miller. The Dodgers signed Eisenstat and sent him to Dayton in 1934, where he won five games and lost one.[22]

In 1935 Eisenstat went to the Dodgers training camp at Orlando, where he impressed the Dodger brass with two scoreless innings against the Cincinnati Reds, and on the following day threw one inning in relief that gained a victory against the Detroit Tigers. A week later he started against the Tigers, pitched four innings, and received the win. During his four-inning outing, he struck out future teammate Hank Greenberg with two men on base.[23]

His spot on the 1935 Dodger's roster seemed secure until his next appearance, when he allowed the St. Louis Browns to score seven runs. Because he was a "hometown boy," Dodger manager Casey Stengel let him stay in camp until the team left Florida and then Eisenstat returned to Dayton for the second time. He pitched most of the 1935 season in Dayton, winning 18 and losing 8, and came back to the Dodgers near the end of the year but he appeared in only two games.[24]

In his very first game in 1935, he ran into the perennial question faced by Jewish athletes—whether to play on the Jewish High Holy Days. Eisenstat, knowing the issue might arise, had consulted his rabbi, asking specifically about Rosh Hashanah. According to Eisenstat's rabbi, this day—the Jewish New Year—was a day of happiness and celebration. So when Eisenstat was asked to enter the game in relief against the Giants on Rosh Hashanah, he took the mound, positive that it was all right. The first pitch he threw in the major leagues was hit for a grand-slam home run.[25]

In 1936 Eisenstat went to Dayton for the third time, but returned briefly to the Dodgers in September, where his record was one win and two losses. That win was his first major league victory. It was against the Philadelphia Phillies in a game which went only 6½ innings. In 1937 Eisenstat played his last year with the Dodgers, winning three and losing three.[26]

His life was changed in 1938 in two ways: he married Evelyn Rosenberg, a marriage that would survive until his death,[27] and Commissioner Landis issued a ruling that a team lost its rights to a player if they farmed him out three times. Since this exactly described Eisenstat's situation with the Dodgers, he was

Pitcher Harry Eisenstat's eight-year major league career included stints with the Brooklyn Dodgers, Detroit Tigers, and Cleveland Indians. At Detroit, Eisenstat was a teammate and close friend of Hank Greenberg (courtesy Mrs. Evelyn Eisenstadt).

now a free agent who could sign with any team. "I signed with the Tigers," Eisenstat related in an interview, "because I was quite friendly with Hank Greenberg. He was from New York as well and we were quite close. He said they needed left-handed pitching and I would do well with them."[28]

Greenberg not only encouraged Eisenstat to join the Tigers, he also tried to guide the new pitcher. One of the first words of advice he gave Eisenstat was never to use the fact that he was Jewish as an excuse: "It should be more of an incentive to be successful."[29] Greenberg taught him how to dress and how to talk to the press. He also introduced the young man to a number of important Jews in Detroit.[30] He even stood up for him when Eisenstat became the target of anti–Semitism from other players.

Eisenstat had really not experienced much anti–Semitism. He once said that he noticed traces of anti–Semitism in the minor leagues, especially with players who were from the South, younger, or just immature.[31] Eisenstat's chief source of anti–Semitism in the majors came from White Sox first baseman Joe Kuhel. To counter the abuse, Mickey Cochrane, the Tigers' supportive manager, told Eisenstat to throw at Kuhel whenever he was at bat. Those times when Kuhel managed to reach first, Tiger first baseman Hank Greenberg would quietly tell him, "I'll meet you under the stands."[32] Eisenstat once said, "Greenberg, in my opinion, is the greatest ballplayer today."[33]

In 1938, the first year Eisenstat was with the Tigers, he relieved in both games of a doubleheader. In the first game he hurled five shutout innings, and in the second game he pitched four innings without allowing a run. His teammate Greenberg hit three home runs in the two games. After the Tiger sweep, manager Mickey Cochrane jokingly warned Greenberg and Eisenstat, "Fellas, lock yourselves in your rooms tonight because the Jews in Detroit are going crazy."[34]

Eisenstat appeared in 42 games for the Detroit Tigers, eleven as a starter. In 1938 he compiled a record of nine wins and six losses and an earned run average of 3.73. He was the opposing pitcher on October 2, 1938, when Cleveland's Bob Feller set a modern strikeout record with 18.

On June 15, 1939, the Tigers traded Eisenstat to the Cleveland Indians for outfielder Earl Averill. Cleveland manager Oscar Vitt sardonically commented, "Eisenstat can beat only one team in the world and that's the one I'm manager of. He beat us three times last year."[35] Pitching in 19 games for the Indians in 1939, Eisenstat won six games and lost nine.[36]

"When I came to Cleveland," said Eisenstat, "the fans sort of resented the trade for Averill because he was very popular, but after a while I did well and they accepted me. I liked Cleveland very much after my wife and I got acquainted there."[37]

From 1940 to 1942 Eisenstat appeared in 77 games for the Indians, both as a starter and reliever and ended his eight-year major league career following the 1942 season.[38] His career record was 25–27, with an ERA of 3.84.[39]

Following the end of the 1942 season, Eisenstat, like so many other Jewish major leaguers, joined the armed forces; he served as a lieutenant in the Pacific.

Instead of returning to baseball following the war, Eisenstat settled in the Cleveland area and opened a hardware store and also sponsored children's ball teams. According to Eisenstat, "They had a good Jewish population and they accepted us very rapidly."[40] He sold the business in the 1960s and became sales manager and vice president of Curtis Industries. For his achievements in baseball, he was inducted in the Detroit Jewish Hall of Fame.

Eisenstat died March 21, 2003, at the age of 87. Evelyn, his wife of 64 years, their daughter, and four grandchildren survived him.[41]

Goody Rosen

Goodwin George "Goody" Rosen was the seventh Jewish player on the Brooklyn Dodgers prior to 1948, and the only Jewish member of the Canadian Baseball Hall of Fame.

Rosen was born August 28, 1912, in Toronto, the fifth of eight children. His parents were Russian-born Jews, Samuel and Rebecca Rosen, who had come to Canada from Minsk to escape the pogroms of czarist Russia. While some Jewish major leaguers had attempted to hide their Jewish heritage, Goody was just the opposite: "I always had a lot of trouble convincing people I was a Jew because of my pug nose. I banged it up during a football game in high school. There was a strong rumor when I was with the Dodgers that I was only pretending to be a Jew so I'd be popular in Brooklyn."[42]

Goody knew he wanted to play baseball from early on. He played in a Canadian youth league, and at fourteen was part of the team that won the Canadian Amateur Baseball Championship.[43] He then joined a semipro team, where he batted against the great African-American pitcher, Satchel Paige. "During one at bat," Rosen remembered, "Satchel struck me out before I had the bat off my shoulder."[44]

By shagging balls at the practice sessions of the minor league Rochester Red Wings, who had come to Toronto to play the Maple Leafs, Rosen got the opportunity to go to Rochester for a tryout with the team. Warren Giles, then business manager of the Red Wings, and later president of the National League, was the first to tell the skinny Rosen what he would hear from many managers and owners. "Son," said Giles, "you've got a lot of ability, but you'll never be a ballplayer. You're too small."[45]

A year and a half later, Rosen got a tryout with the Louisville Colonels and made the team. When the 20-year-old Rosen entered the clubhouse, the trainer thought he was a batboy. Rosen explained that he was not a batboy but a member of the team. The trainer gave Rosen a disgusted look and asked, "Then exactly where the hell do you think I'm going to get a uniform to fit you?" Rosen had to wear a uniform bunched up at the knees.[46]

Rosen spent five seasons at Louisville and hit over .300 each season. He did not hit many home runs, but he made his presence felt in a ball game. When the Louisville *Courier-Journal* picked the Colonels' all-star team, the newspaper not only selected Rosen but also named him "the greatest outfielder we ever had."[47] As for anti–Semitism during this time, Rosen stated that when he and other Jewish players experienced it on or off the field, "We took care of ourselves, we gave as good as we got and we emerged stronger than ever."[48]

Near the end of the 1937 season, the Dodgers called Rosen to the big leagues. He had hit .312 at Louisville, and in 22 games with the Dodgers in 1937, Rosen finished the season with the exact same average.[49] Because Rosen showed so much promise in 1937, management decided to give him a chance to be one of their regular outfielders in 1938. Brooklyn's general manager, Larry MacPhail, had another reason for wanting to have Goody Rosen on the Dodgers. Like McGraw years earlier, he felt his team needed a Jewish player because of the large number of Jewish residents in Brooklyn.[50]

MacPhail was absolutely correct when he predicted the impact of a Jewish player on his roster. Goody Rosen became a Jewish hero when he played for the Dodgers. In return, he helped the community. At one fundraiser for a Brooklyn orphanage, Rosen was so moved by their efforts to raise funds to purchase sports equipment, he offered, "If someone will donate $100, I'll tell a story in Jewish." Goody's Yiddish tale received thunderous applause, and Rosen announced he would make an additional donation.[51]

Rosen played in 138 games in 1938, hitting .281 with four home runs and 51 runs batted in. On two occasions he broke up no-hitters, one by Hal Schumacher and the other by Bill McGee. He also led the National League in fielding, with a .989 percentage, and in assists with 19.[52]

At first, Rosen was popular with his management team. Burleigh Grimes, who had come from Louisville the same year Rosen entered the majors, managed the Dodgers during Rosen's first two years with the team. The two men got along splendidly. Babe Ruth, the Dodgers' first base coach, took a liking to Rosen, even giving him tips in batting practice and kidding him good-naturedly. But when Leo Durocher took over the managerial post in 1939, the future looked dark for Rosen. He and Durocher simply did not get along and Durocher left Rosen out of the starting lineup for the season.[53]

Durocher finally gave Rosen a chance to play, and Rosen did so well that he was leading the league in hitting. Unfortunately, he injured his left ankle and the doctor advised that he not play for a few weeks. Ignoring the doctor, Durocher insisted that Rosen stay in the lineup "because the team needed him." Goody continued to play, but his average dropped. The feud between the two intensified when Durocher used Rosen's performance as an excuse to ship him to Montreal.[54] Rosen returned to the Dodgers in August and finished the 1939 season with an average of .251 in 54 games.[55]

The general manager, Larry MacPhail, had also changed his attitude toward Rosen because he had returned his first 1939 contract unsigned. Despite Rosen's popularity in Brooklyn, in 1940 MacPhail sold Rosen's contract to Columbus of the American Association.[56] When Rosen went to Columbus, manager Burt Shotton warned Rosen, "I'm going to cure you—you're a rebel and I'm

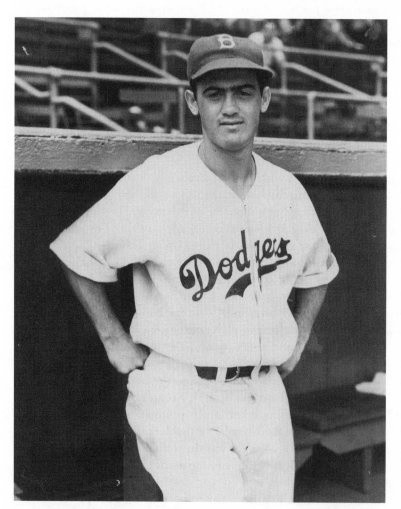

George Goodwin "Goody" Rosen was one of the eight Jews to play for the Brooklyn Dodgers prior to 1947 and the only Jewish member of the Canadian Baseball Hall of Fame. He had a solid .291 lifetime batting average and completed his major league career by playing 100 games for the New York Giants (courtesy National Baseball Hall of Fame Library, Cooperstown, N.Y.).

going to put you in your place."[57] The relationship between Shotton and Rosen only worsened, and Rosen packed his bags and went home.

A few days later, MacPhail sent Rosen to Syracuse, not far from Rosen's home in Toronto. Rosen was made team captain and remained with Syracuse for four years, leading the club to the Little World Series. Rosen never reached the .300 mark in hitting, but was one of the team's most popular players.[58]

In May 1944 the Dodgers reacquired Goody Rosen.[59] In 89 games as a reserve outfielder with the Dodgers that year, Rosen hit .261.[60]

Rosen credits Dodger third-base coach Charlie Dressen for helping make the next year, 1945, Rosen's best season in the majors. Rosen was down on himself early in the season, but Dressen kept urging him to "just keep hanging in there."[61] Dressen's advice worked. For most of the year, Rosen led the league in hitting and finished third with an average of .325. He had 197 hits, including 12 home runs, and 75 runs batted in. With 126 runs, Rosen was second only to teammate Eddie Stanky, who scored 128. Rosen played 145 games, the most in his six-year major league career. There was no All-Star game in 1945 because of the war, but sportswriters picked a team of All-Stars anyway. It included Goody Rosen, the first Jewish player from the National League to receive that honor.[62]

After Rosen made the starting lineup that year, he sat on the bench only once the remainder of the year, at his own request. Monday, September 17, 1945, was Yom Kippur, the Day of Atonement, and he informed his manager, "There will be no game for Goody this day."[63]

Soon after his excellent 1945 season, Rosen began to negotiate his 1946 salary with new Dodger general manager, Branch Rickey, who had replaced MacPhail. Rosen asked for three times his 1945 salary and Rickey agreed, but warned Rosen that he would attempt to trade him if he could. Sure enough, Rosen played only three games for the Dodgers in 1946 when he read in a newspaper that Rickey had traded him to the New York Giants for two players and $50,000.[64]

In his first game in his new uniform, Rosen and the Giants faced the Brooklyn Dodgers in a doubleheader. Rosen started in center field for the Giants. In the two games, Rosen was on base ten times out of eleven at bats; he had five hits, scored four runs, and hit a three-run homer to win the second game. The Giants beat the Dodgers in both games.[65]

That deal between the Giants and Dodgers unnerved the Dodger front office and they stopped trading with the Giants. Even a decade later, Dodger road secretary Lee Scott recalled the deal with a shudder. "Rosen murdered us," Scott said. "I guess everybody with the Dodgers thought a long time after that before making another deal with the Giants."[66]

Unfortunately, shortly after the doubleheader, Rosen ran into a brick wall while chasing a fly ball in Pittsburgh, and this time he seriously injured himself. He spent 12 weeks with his arm in a cast and, although he managed to finish the year with the Giants, he told management he was finished as a major leaguer. His lifetime batting average in the majors was a respectable .291.[67] The year after his injury he gave in to pressure and played briefly for the Maple Leafs. After 1947 he retired for good and became an executive at Biltrite Rubber in Toronto.[68]

When Rosen reminisced about his years playing for the Dodgers, he always talked about how much he disliked Leo Durocher, saying that he "was not much of a person." Durocher felt the same about Rosen, yet Duke Snider once told Rosen that Durocher wrote in his book about Rosen: "Rosen couldn't run, couldn't hit, couldn't throw, couldn't field, but if I had nine guys like him, I'd win the pennant every year." On the other hand, Rosen had the deepest admiration for Branch Rickey, the man who traded him to the Giants. "Branch Rickey was always fair with me," Rosen said.[69]

Years after Rosen retired from baseball, he spoke of his pride in his Jewish heritage. His mother was an Orthodox Jew who kept a kosher home, but because he was so preoccupied with selling newspapers to make ends meet and playing all sorts of sports he had very little formal religious training. He regretted that he was not Bar Mitzvahed. Yet he maintained that he was always aware of his Jewishness: "I've always, since I was a small kid, walked proudly that I was a Jew, and never took any crap, pardon the word, from anyone."[70]

Goody Rosen's wife died after 59 years of marriage, and Rosen never recovered from her death. He died from pneumonia in Toronto, on April 6, 1994, at the age of 81. A son, two sisters, a brother, four grandchildren, and two great-grandchildren survived him.[71]

Sam Nahem

Sam Nahem was the last of the eight Jewish major league ballplayers with the Brooklyn Dodgers while Hank Greenberg was still an active major league player. He was also one of only a few Jewish major leaguers whose backgrounds were Sephardic (i.e., from Southern Europe, the Middle East and the Mediterranean region).[72]

Nahem was born on October 19, 1915, in New York City. His family was from Syria, and settled on Manhattan's East Side before moving to Brooklyn. Nahem spent his early years in a Syrian Jewish neighborhood where his first language was Arabic.[73]

Sam loved baseball and played a great deal of sandlot ball. He was first a catcher on the sandlots, but turned to pitching when he began wearing glasses and could not get a catcher's mask over them. Unable to make the team at New Utrecht High School in Brooklyn, he qualified for the Brooklyn College baseball team. In 1935, Nahem went to Ebbets Field, where Casey Stengel was managing the Brooklyn Dodgers. "Casey must have liked me," said Nahem, "because when I was pitching batting practice he grabbed a bat and got up there to hit against me. He found out he couldn't get the ball out of the infield."[74]

Nahem was farmed out to Allentown in the summer of 1935 and did some relief pitching there. The following winter he studied law at St. John's Law School and dreamed of baseball. In the spring of 1936 the Dodgers sent him to Jeanerette. "I never heard of the place," said Nahem. "It was a town in the Evangeline League, Class D in Louisiana."[75]

When Nahem told his mother he was going to play ball she was confused: "You're grown up already, why are you going to play ball?" He then told her that he was going to be paid $150 a week. She replied, "Go play."[76]

For the next two years, he continued studying law in the winter and playing ball in the spring and summer. In 1937 he had 15 wins and five losses for Clinton, Iowa; in 1938 in the Eastern League, his record was 9–7.[77] While in the minor leagues, Nahem was generally the only New Yorker and the only Jew his teammates had ever met. He was nicknamed "Subway Sam," a sobriquet that he would retain for the remainder of his life.[78]

The Dodgers promoted Nahem to the big leagues toward the end of the 1938 season, and he debuted on October 2, 1938, where he won his first major league game, going the distance and defeating the Phillies 7 to 3. In addition to winning the game, Nahem got two hits and drove in one run. It was his only game with the Dodgers.[79]

In 1939 Nahem divided his season between Montreal of the International League and Nashville of the Southern Association. At spring training with the Dodgers in 1940 he was belted for 13 runs in one inning and relegated to pitching batting practice by Dodger manager Leo Durocher. When a sportswriter asked Nahem, "What good are you doing the team?" Nahem answered, "I am now in the egregiously anonymous position of pitching batting practice to the batting practice pitchers."[80]

The Dodgers were never really enthusiastic about Nahem. They heard reports about him—not about his curve or control—but how he liked to curl up with a volume of Shakespeare, or talk torts or evidence. He read constantly, which was the major reason he had to wear glasses. However, his reading paid off, because he passed the very difficult New York State bar exam the first time he took it.[81] In many ways, Sam Nahem was very similar to another lawyer-baseball player. Nahem once met Berg at the wedding of a Boston Red Sox player in the late 1930s. "Berg was a very smart, very nice man, very intelligent, considerate," said Nahem.[82]

He began the 1940 season with Louisville of the American Association, but was acquired by the St. Louis Cardinals later that year and sent to their farm club in Houston. Eddie Dyer, a man known for developing pitchers, managed Houston, and under his tutelage Nahem worked in 15 games, winning eight and losing six. He finished the 1940 season with an outstanding 1.65 earned run average. In spring training camp in 1941 Nahem so impressed Cardinals manager Billy Southworth that he stayed with the club as a reliever.[83] Southworth was not disappointed. Nahem appeared in 26 games for the Cardinals, 18 in relief, and had a won-loss record of 5–2, with an earned run average of 2.98.[84]

Nahem's next stop was with the Phillies, who acquired him in a trade following the 1941 season.[85] The 1942 Phillies were considered one of the worst teams of the twentieth century, winning only 43 games all season while losing 109 and getting a tie in one.[86] Nahem was used primarily in relief; he appeared in 35 games, made two starts, and had a record of one win and three losses.[87]

After the 1942 season, the Phillies sent Nahem to the minor leagues, but he was drafted a short time later, and did not come back to the Phillies until 1948. Nahem pitched in 28 games that year and had a 3–3 record. At the end of that season he retired from baseball. In his four years in the major leagues, Sam Nahem won ten games, lost eight, and saved one game. His earned run average was 4.69.[88]

Sam Nahem worked for Standard Oil in California and became an active trade unionist, a passion for political activism he had developed in the 1930s. He headed

"Subway Sam" Nahem was the last of the eight Jewish ballplayers to enter the major leagues while Hank Greenberg was still an active player. One of the few Jewish major leaguers with a Sephardic rather than an Ashkenazi background, he pitched for three teams in the four years he played (courtesy National Baseball Hall of Fame Library, Cooperstown, N.Y.).

his local chapter of the Oil, Chemical, and Atomic Workers Union before his retirement in 1980.

In addition to being a Jew, Nahem differed from most of his teammates in believing that baseball should be integrated. "I was in a strange position," he once said. "The majority of my fellow players were very much against black ballplayers. The reason was economic. They knew these guys had the ability to be up there, so they felt their jobs were threatened directly, and they did all sorts of things to discourage black ballplayers."[89]

Nahem died April 18, 2004, in Berkeley, California, at the age of 88. Two sons, a daughter, and three grandchildren survived him.

In the years since Sam Nahem played for the Dodgers in 1938, the Dodgers had only five additional Jews on their roster through the end of the twentieth century. Cal Abrams played in Brooklyn from 1949 to 1956; Sandy Koufax was the only Jewish Dodger to play in both Brooklyn (1955–1957) and Los Angeles (1958–1966); Larry Sherry played in Los Angeles from 1958 to 1968; and his brother, Norman, played in Los Angeles from 1959 to 1963. The Sherrys were the sixth and last pair of Jewish brothers in major league baseball.[90]

19. The War Years

World War II did more to diminish the outward expressions of anti–Semitism and discrimination in the United States than almost any other force. Nazi atrocities outraged Americans, and as these atrocities intensified so did the desire of Jews in this country to join together as Americans to defeat Germany. The result was a united America with one goal in mind—preserve democracy and freedom in the world.[1]

Anti-Semitism still existed, but it was repressed for the most part during the War, only to reemerge when World War II was over. For a number of reasons Jews were better able to contend with it then.

In baseball, not only Jewish sportswriters like Dan Daniel and Shirley Povich but also the press in general dropped ethnic identifications and tended to look at individuals as baseball players first, and specific minority groups second. For these years at least, baseball truly illustrated the melting pot theory with regard to ethnicity in America.[2] And on the occasions when Jewish players did encounter anti–Semitism, more tended to react forcefully to counter it.

In terms of the number of Jewish players during this decade, the golden age had continued. A number of Jewish players who began their careers in the 1930s played into the early 1940s before retiring. At least eight other Jewish major leaguers debuted before 1948, although they had short, fairly undistinguished careers. Four Jewish players who entered the major leagues during the 1940s were notable for various reasons, and one, in fact, was one of the better Jewish players in the game.

Murray Franklin

Murray Asher "Moe" Franklin was born in Chicago on April 1, 1914. While in high school he played baseball, basketball and football. He turned down a scholarship from Northwestern University to attend the University of Illinois, where he played second base on the university's baseball team. Tiger scout Wish Egan had seen Franklin play a college game and the team offered him a contract after he graduated. Franklin agreed to sign with the Tigers against advice from his Illinois teammate, third baseman Lou Boudreau, who signed with the Cleveland Indians.

In 1938 Franklin was assigned to Beckley, West Virginia, in the Mountain State League, where he hit .439, the highest batting average in all of organized baseball that year. For this feat, baseball awarded Franklin the Louisville Slugger Award as the Batter of the Year. In addition to his phenomenal average, Franklin also set a league record of ten consecutive hits, led the league with 26 home runs, and tied for the league lead in triples with 13.[3]

During 1939 and 1940 Franklin played for Beaumont of the Texas League. In 1939, just three weeks into the season, he broke his right leg sliding into home. When he returned to the lineup in July, Moe moved to third base, but batted only .228 for the season. The next year, Franklin, playing third base again, hit .290.

At the end of the 1940 season, the Tigers brought him to Detroit, but he did not debut in the majors until August 12, 1941. Franklin had his first major league hit two days later against White Sox hurler Thornton Lee. A few days after that, Franklin, who by now was hitting .333, reinjured his right leg reaching for a fly ball. He was out of the lineup for the remainder of the year.[4]

A year later, in July 1942, Tiger manager Del Baker decided to shake up his lineup. His team was in a slump, having lost 15 of its last 18 games. Franklin, who had been hitting the

Murray "Moe" Franklin played shortstop for the Tigers in 1941 and 1942 and then joined the navy. After the war, he learned he was no longer on the Detroit roster and played for Mexico and Cuba in 1947 and 1948 (courtesy National Baseball Hall of Fame Library, Cooperstown, N.Y.).

ball well, but was having a rough time defensively, was returned to the lineup replacing Billy Hitchcock. He finished the season with a batting average of .262.[5]

Franklin joined the navy after the 1942 season, serving until 1945. It was understood that teams would reserve places for their returning veterans, but Franklin discovered that the Tigers had removed him from their roster. Rather than shop around the rest of the majors looking for a spot, Franklin took an unusual option. During the winter of 1945, Jorge Pasquel, a multimillionaire Mexican liquor distributor who controlled the Mexican League, decided to entice major leaguers with what he considered generous salaries and benefits. He visualized that his Mexican League would become a bona fide rival of the major leagues.

In all, 18 major leaguers responded to Pasquel's offer, including Franklin and another Jewish major leaguer, Harry Feldman. The sportswriters referred to players who went South as "Mexican jumping beans." In May 1946 baseball commissioner A. B. Chandler declared that major leaguers who were now playing in Mexico would be "ineligible" to play with teams in organized baseball for five years. Regardless of this ruling, Franklin played in Mexico and Cuba in 1947 and 1948, but became disenchanted with life in Mexico and returned home. Franklin was not unhappy with his move to the Mexican League. "I found that Senor Pasquel more than lived up to his promises," he said. "I made more money by my move than I figured I could earn through baseball in the United States in five years."[6]

By 1949 four players who "jumped" to Mexico had brought two antitrust suits against major league baseball. Always spooked by the thought of antitrust action, the owners capitulated and instructed Chandler to lift the blacklist and settle with the plaintiffs out of court.[7]

As soon as organized baseball gave amnesty to the "jumpers" in 1949, Franklin joined the minor league Hollywood Stars as an infielder and with his .317 average helped his team win the pennant. He played with Hollywood until 1952, when he joined the San Diego Padres of the Pacific Coast League where Jimmie Reese was a coach.[8]

Moe Franklin died on March 16, 1978, in Harbor City, California. He was 63 years old.

Harry Feldman

Harry Feldman, the other "Mexican jumping bean," was born in the Bronx on September 10, 1919, the son of a Romanian-Jewish father and a Polish-Jewish mother. His parents named him Harold, but he changed it to Harry.[9] Feldman credits an older brother not only for interesting him in baseball but also for teaching him everything he knew about the game.

Harry pitched for both his junior and senior high baseball teams, once pitching two successive no-hit games at a park located across the street from Yankee Stadium. He always dreamed of pitching for the New York Yankees and his diamond hero was Babe Ruth. "I guess that was natural, though," said Feldman, "as the Yankees played in the Bronx. After we played our school games we used to scale a fence and climb into the center field bleachers. I never did get to see Ruth play, but one day we ... saw Lou Gehrig hit a home run."[10]

Even though he was a Yankee fan, his first tryout was a very brief one at the Polo Grounds. A Giant fan bombarded the Giants with so many letters touting Feldman's pitching prowess that he was invited back for another trial. This time it was Feldman's persistence that brought success. Taking time out from his job working at a shirt factory, Feldman pitched batting practice for three days and badgered the Giant manager, Bill Terry, to just tell him if he had the ability to pitch in organized ball. Terry finally gave Feldman a closer look, liked what he saw, and signed Feldman on the spot to a contract for 1938.[11]

The Giants sent Feldman to Blytheville, Arkansas, where he won 13 of his first 14 starts, and then promoted Feldman to Fort Smith. Although his record was only 7–7 his first year in Fort Smith, it was there that Feldman met his future wife, Laureate Matt, and where he moved in 1941. "New York is a good place for playing ball," said Feldman, "but not for raising children. I ought to know; my dad was a painter in the Bronx and I was the [youngest] of 16 children. New York is too crowded, and a kid has to knock somebody down to get along. Now, in Arkansas, there's really a chance for a growing young generation."[12]

After pitching for almost two years at Fort Smith, Feldman was again promoted, this time to Jersey City of the International League. In 1940 and 1941 Feldman compiled a record of 19 wins and 29 losses. Since 18 of his 29 losses were by one run, Feldman earned the nickname "Hard Luck Harry."[13]

Despite his record, Feldman impressed the Giants. He joined the parent club in August

Harry Feldman, a native New Yorker, combined with Harry Danning to comprise the first all-Jewish battery in the major leagues. After he lost his first two games in 1946, Feldman was one of many major leaguers to "jump" to the Mexican League, and although Baseball Commissioner Happy Chandler pardoned him, he never again appeared in a major league uniform (courtesy National Baseball Hall of Fame Library, Cooperstown, N.Y.).

1941, and made his major league debut on September 10 against the Pittsburgh Pirates at Forbes Field. In a losing effort, Harry pitched the first seven innings before being relieved.[14]

A week later, Feldman started and won against the Boston Braves. With Harry Danning as his catcher, Feldman and Danning formed the first Jewish battery in the major leagues.[15] Two other Jewish players on the Giants played prominent roles in Feldman's victory—Morrie Arnovich and Sid Gordon had key hits for the Giants.[16] Feldman finished the 1941 season with a record of one win and one loss, and an earned run average of 4.05.[17]

The following year, 1942, under the new manager, Mel Ott, Feldman won seven games and suffered only one loss.[18] He had an earned run average of 3.16, and on May 1 Feldman even clouted his first major league home run.[19]

Feldman's 1943 record was four wins and five losses. He had been called up by the military but in September the Army rejected him because of a lung condition. Feldman continued pitching for the Giants in 1944 and 1945, with a combined record of 23 wins and 26 losses. In 1945 he was one of four Giant pitchers in double figure wins.[20] On September 8, 1945, Harry Feldman defeated the Chicago Cubs at Wrigley Field, 3–0, for his sixth shutout and 35th and final victory for the Giants.[21] Harry Feldman had a major league career of 35 wins and 35 losses for the Giants during six seasons. His career earned run average was a respectable 3.80.[22]

On April 27, 1946, Feldman and his teammate, Ace Adams, accepted offers to pitch in the Mexican League. Feldman told the Giants that he was leaving because he needed money to pay off the mortgage on his home. According to newspaper reports, he and the Giants parted amicably. Both Adams and Feldman were aware that once their names appeared in the lineup in the Mexican League, they were barred for five years from organized baseball.[23]

Feldman and Adams announced that they both would be pitching for the Vera Cruz Blues. During his first workout, Feldman announced, "I got plenty tired running, but I'll try my curve later and see how it works at this altitude." In September, less than six months after he left the Giants for the Mexican League, Feldman announced that he had quit.[24]

During the time he was banned from professional baseball in the United States, Feldman played in the independent Quebec Provincial Baseball League.[25] Even after the Mexican Leaguers were reinstated, he did not return to the majors, but pitched for the San Francisco Seals in the Pacific Coast League during the 1949 and 1950 seasons. He had two losing seasons, six and nine in 1949 and 11 and 16 in 1950, before he retired from baseball in 1951.[26]

Feldman opened a record store in Fort Smith, where he and his wife now had five children, one son and four daughters. Allegedly, some time after his marriage, Feldman converted to Christianity. In March 1962, Feldman had a seizure during a fishing trip. Rushed to a hospital, he suffered a fatal heart attack, and died at the age of 42 on March 16, 1962.[27]

Cy Block

World War II ended during the summer of 1945, and major leaguers began returning from the military to their respective clubs. Hank Greenberg returned in July and helped spark the Detroit Tigers to a slim first-place finish in the American League, one and one-half games ahead of the Washington Senators.

Their opponents in the World Series were the Chicago Cubs. While Greenberg's .423 batting average in the series helped his Tigers defeat the Cubs four games to three, another

Jewish player, also returning from the service, made one brief appearance in the series as a pinch runner for the losing team.[28] His name was Cy Block.

Seymour "Cy" Block was born on May 4, 1919, in Brooklyn. As a child he lived in the shadows of Ebbets Field and he and his friends, ardent Dodger fans, would often attempt to sneak into the Dodgers games. He loved baseball and played outfield constantly as a child, but when he tried out for his high school baseball team, his coach told him he had no baseball skills. Block could not stay out of baseball, and organized all of the neighborhoods into a league. He was captain of his team, "The Falcons."[29] Block's parents, both Eastern European Jews, never could understand why their son, "a nice Jewish boy," wanted to go into baseball. They did not think it was a good idea.[30]

In 1937 Block suffered another blow to his baseball career. In a tryout for his beloved Brooklyn Dodgers, he made the final cut and reported to Elmira, but officials told him that he was not needed and to go back home.[31]

The following year he went to Orlando to a baseball school run by former Cub great Joe Tinker, who became Block's mentor. Block was small in stature, but with Tinker's encouragement and special attention, Block excelled at Tinker's school, and was given an opportunity to try out with the Memphis Chicks of the American Association. The Chicks sent Block to their class–D club in Paragould, Arkansas, as an infielder. "I still remember my debut," recalled Block. "It was on April 28, 1938, and we beat Jonesboro ten to seven. I went up to bat five times and got two hits, both doubles."[32] He had a good year at Paragould, hitting .322, with 74 runs batted in. Near the end of the season, he was sent to Memphis where he entered a few games as a pinch hitter and started one game.[33]

Block spent the next three seasons in the minors. In 1939 he hit .320 and drove in 67 runs. He led the South Atlantic League with a batting mark of .357 in 1941 and was voted the league's most valuable player.[34]

Years later, Block would speak of his days in the minors, especially in the South. He insisted that every Jewish player he knew was "the butt of anti–Semitic jibes, remarks and

In 1945 Cy Block was the last Jew to play for the Chicago Cubs in a World Series game. He appeared in only 17 games during his major league career, and went on to success as an insurance salesman and author (courtesy National Baseball Hall of Fame Library, Cooperstown, N.Y.).

obscenities." He recalled headlines in the newspapers in Jonesboro, Arkansas, which encouraged the locals to "Come See the Jewish Second Baseman," and he noted the numerous times opponents would spike him. Block also stated that he would retaliate and on one occasion he put a tag on an offensive player who attempted to steal second. "I got the ball and planted it squarely in his mouth, knocking out six teeth. He wasn't in too much of a position to call me a Jew bastard," Block recalled.[35]

Cy Block's widow, Harriet, attested to the anti–Semitism her husband had to withstand. Cy would often tell her of the reception he received in the minor leagues. "They thought he had horns," she stated.[36]

In 1942 Block was promoted to Tulsa of the Texas League and from there, late in the season, finally reached the majors with the Chicago Cubs, where he appeared in nine games, getting 12 hits in 33 at bats. At the end of the season, Block joined the United States Coast Guard and, while in the service, he wed Harriet Spektor.[37]

Block served three years in the coast guard and then rejoined the Cubs on September 13, 1945, shortly after his release; he appeared in two games at the end of the season. Commissioner Chandler decreed that all returning servicemen released prior to September 27—such as Block—were eligible for the World Series.[38] He was in only game six, when he pinch ran for Heinz Becker.[39]

Evidently other members of the team were not pleased by Block's return. The Cubs voted to give Block $250 from the World Series pot; they voted to give their batboy $982.50. This treatment of Block, plus the fact that manager Charlie Grimm had used him only once in the World Series, convinced many that Grimm was biased against Jewish ballplayers.[40]

Block was not with the Cubs at the start of the 1946 season; he had been sent to the Cubs' farm team in the Pacific Coast League. He injured his leg after playing 40 games that season, and was sent down to Nashville when the doctor suggested a warmer climate might help heal his leg. After hitting .351 with Nashville, Block joined the Cubs near the end of the season and managed to play in six games, but did not hit well.[41]

Block played his last major league game in 1946. He had always thought that he would replace the aging Stan Hack, who was the Cubs' mainstay at third base, but it never happened. Block returned to Nashville in 1947, and spent the next three years at Buffalo, retiring after the 1950 season. When he got his outright release from Buffalo, he sat in his hotel room and reflected on his 14 years in organized baseball, with a total of only 17 games played in the majors: "I had learned my lesson. It was time to get to work and stop dreaming." But, he added, "If I had to do it all over again, I would do the same thing, except this time I would work twice as hard to reach the major leagues."[42]

After baseball, Block went into the insurance business. Mentored by Sidney Weil, former Cincinnati Reds owner, he was very successful, founding CB Planning, a pension sales firm with $100 million in annual sales.[43] "All the dreams I had for baseball came true in business," Block stated. "It's funny how it turns out."[44] He was also active in many philanthropic organizations, including B'nai B'rith.

Throughout his career, Block had been an outspoken advocate of players' rights and was one of the few baseball players in those days to challenge management. He testified before Congress about the "infamous" reserve clause, and in the 1980s he became involved with Major League Baseball in his efforts to reform the players' pension fund, especially for those who played before 1947.[45]

Block died September 29, 2002, at the age of 85. His wife of 61 years, three daughters, seven grandchildren, and two great-grandchildren survived him.[46]

Sid Gordon

The Giants' player who came closest to John McGraw's vision of the ideal Jewish ballplayer was probably Sid Gordon. A native of Brooklyn, Gordon was one of New York's most popular players while with the Giants in the 1940s.

Gordon was born in the Brownsville section of Brooklyn on August 13, 1918, the son of Morris Gordon, a Russian-born Jew, and Rose Myerson Gordon. "It was a tough neighborhood," Gordon would say, "but no worse than lots of others where kids are forced to grow up in crowded quarters, with no living space, and no money. You had to fight for everything you got."[47]

Gordon starred in both high school baseball and basketball. In 1936 his high school baseball coach, Joe Solomon, arranged a tryout for Gordon with Casey Stengel, then Brooklyn Dodger manager. Stengel liked Gordon but was fired by the Dodgers before he could find a spot for him.[48]

Sid Gordon was one of the greatest Jewish ballplayers of all time. In his 13-year career with the Giants, Braves, and Pirates, Gordon hit 202 home runs and compiled a .283 lifetime batting average. He would certainly have qualified as the "outstanding Jewish star" that John McGraw had been seeking for more than 30 years (courtesy National Baseball Hall of Fame Library, Cooperstown, N.Y.).

In 1938 George Mack, a scout for the New York Giants, noticed Gordon playing sandlot ball and offered him a tryout with the Giant farm club in Milford, Delaware, if Gordon would pay his own way. According to Mack, he would be reimbursed if he made the team. Gordon's father died before Gordon could leave for Milford, and Sid felt it was his duty to run his father's coal business. "I didn't want to leave mom and my two young sisters alone, and decided to forget baseball. But mom insisted. If I'm in baseball today, it's because of mom," said Gordon.[49] His mother urged her son to follow his dream; she would run the business. She even gave him the $32 for the trip.[50]

Gordon reported to Milford, and within three days was named the team's third baseman, with a salary of $17.32 a week. Gordon won the 1938 Eastern Shore League batting title with a .352 average in 112 games. He hit 25 home runs, led the league with 145 total bases, and was one of three players in the league to score a hundred or more runs.[51]

Gordon spent the next three years in the minors, and continued his solid hitting. He batted .327 and hit 24 triples in the Three-I League in 1939 and by 1940 was playing at the AAA level with the Jersey City Giants, hitting over .300 in both 1940 and 1941.[52]

At the end of the 1941 season, the Giants brought Gordon to the parent team; he appeared in nine games, getting eight hits in 31 at bats.[53] In those games, he was one of four Jewish players on the roster: he and Morrie Arnovich in the field, Harry Feldman on the mound, and Harry Danning behind the plate.[54]

Gordon was switched to the outfield and played six games with the Giants at the start of the 1942 season. For the last time in his career, he went back to the minors, where he hit .300 for the rest of the year with Jersey City.

In 1943, Gordon's first full season in the major leagues, he hit only .251, but struck out only 32 times and drew 43 walks, demonstrating discipline at the plate.[55] The Giants did very poorly in 1943, winning only 55 games while losing 98, and finishing in last place, 49½ games behind the first-place St. Louis Cardinals.[56]

Many major leaguers were in the service in 1943, but two years earlier Gordon had married his high school sweetheart, Mary Goldberg, and as a father, Gordon was classified 3-A and deferred as long as possible.[57] That changed very quickly as the war intensified, and in September 1943 the Coast Guard drafted Sid Gordon. He spent 1944 and 1945 in the service, becoming a civilian again in December 1945.[58]

The 1946 Giants were as bad as the 1943 club. Although Gordon hit .293 that year, his team finished in last place with a record of 61 wins and 93 losses.[59]

Things were different in 1947. This year Mel Ott's New York Giants improved to 81 wins and 73 losses, good for a fourth-place finish, but 13 behind their arch-rivals, the pennant-winning Dodgers.[60] The Giants' improvement was due, in large part, to their team's home run barrage. They led the National League in home runs with 221, a major-league record at that time. Johnny Mize, Walker Cooper, Willard Marshall, and Bobby Thomson each hit more than 29 homers, and Sid Gordon hit 13, his highest number since he joined the Giants.[61]

During his three seasons with the Giants, Gordon had played more than 100 games each year, but he had no set position. When the Giants went to spring training in Phoenix in 1948, new manager Leo Durocher told the press, "We'll play Sid where we need him in the infield or the outfield, but we'll play him every day."[62]

As good a hitter as Gordon had been, the advice Giant coach Red Kress gave him during spring training that year made him even better. Kress had decided that with Gordon's powerful build, he should be more of a power hitter. "I want you to turn around a bit at the plate, face left field, and pull the ball. Get a little closer, too, so you can cover the spot left open by facing left."[63] After Kress turned him into a pull hitter, Gordon hit between 25 and 30 home runs each of the following five years. In 1948 Gordon hit his major league high of 30 home runs, drove in 107 runs, and compiled a .299 average.[64]

Even though Gordon played for Brooklyn's "enemy," the Giants, the people of Brooklyn, especially his Jewish admirers and neighbors, never forgot that Sid was a native son and in 1948 gave their hero a "day" at Ebbets Field. On "Sid Gordon Day," the fans presented Gordon a number of gifts, including an automobile. Gordon hit two home runs before his Brooklyn fans that day.[65]

Gordon received two other honors in 1948. He was selected to play in the annual All Star Game, and he received a plaque as "the outstanding New York athlete of 1948" from the Men's Club of Temple Israel at the Grand Street Boys Association clubhouse.[66]

Gordon played his final full season for the Giants in 1949, in the outfield, at third base and at first base, hitting .284 with 26 home runs. He also tied a league record by hitting two home runs in one inning. For the second consecutive year, Sid Gordon was selected for the All Star Game.[67]

In June 1949, Gordon was the victim of an alleged case of anti–Semitism. The reaction to it by the press and other players illustrates how much had changed in the public's acceptance of such abuse. The incident stemmed from a game in St. Louis, when the Cardinals' bench was "all over" Gordon, supposedly yelling anti–Semitic remarks. The New York papers assailed the Cardinals for their "personal comments on Gordon's religion." One New York writer noted that the Giants had been subjected to this kind of jockeying for some time.

The Cardinal manager, Eddie Dyer, claimed that Gordon, a friend of his, had not been attacked because he was Jewish, but simply because he was a good player. According to Dyer, "Good players always receive the attention of the bench jockeys." *St. Louis Post-Dispatch* sportswriter J. Roy Stockton said, "The rank and file Cardinals admire Gordon as a player and like him personally."[68] Gordon never said anything publicly about the incident.

Following the 1949 season, Sid Gordon, Willard Marshall, Sam Webb, and Buddy Kerr were shipped to the Boston Braves in return for infielders Eddie Stanky and Alvin Dark. Fans in both cities loudly booed the trade.[69] The Giant manager, Leo Durocher, simply stated, "I desperately needed a double play combination. The only man I regretted losing was Sid."[70]

Durocher was not the only Giant sorry to see Gordon leave the team. After he traded Gordon, the Giants owner, Horace Stoneham, told Sid, "It broke my heart to let you go. There are certain guys I like to have around and you're one of them."[71] The Braves manager, Billy Southworth, called Gordon to tell him how happy he was to have Sid on his team.[72]

Gordon played for the Braves from 1950 through 1953, moving with them from Boston to Milwaukee. In 1950, Gordon hit .304 with 27 home runs and tied a major league record when he hit four grand slam home runs in a single season. "I had at least twenty chances to break the record by getting a fifth," he recalled. "Once I socked the ball on a line to the fence. It bounced on the top rail and then fell inside the park. That would have been something."[73]

In 1951 Gordon hit .257 for the Braves and in 1952, although the Braves finished in seventh place, Gordon hit a respectable .289. The following year, the 35-year-old Gordon, now with the Milwaukee Braves, hit .274, driving in 75 runs and hitting 19 home runs.[74]

In 1954 the Braves traded Gordon to the Pittsburgh Pirates, where he hit .306. Early in the 1955 season Gordon went back to his original team, the New York Giants, where he ended his 13-year major league career. During his tenure in the majors, Gordon had a lifetime average of .283, hitting 202 home runs, and batting in 805 runs; he also drew 731 walks compared with only 356 strikeouts.[75]

Sid Gordon is not considered one of the superstars of major league baseball, but he was highly regarded and respected. When Walter O'Malley was eagerly seeking a Jewish player for Brooklyn and found Sandy Koufax, he told a reporter that he hoped that Koufax would be as good as Hank Greenberg and Sid Gordon.[76]

In 1956 Gordon appeared as a player-coach with the Miami Marlins of the International League. He then went into business in New York as an insurance underwriter. As a private citizen, Gordon made sure his children received a Jewish education and he helped the Jewish Education Committee and other Jewish groups whenever he could, often lending his name to their projects.[77]

Although throughout Gordon's career many fans and sportswriters brought up McGraw's search for a Jewish star, Gordon always downplayed the comparison. "The fans come out to see a ball game," he asserted. "If a fellow can play good enough to help the home club, the fans are for him regardless of race or religion. They wouldn't care if he were an Eskimo."[78]

On June 17, 1975, Gordon was playing softball in New York's Central Park when he suddenly collapsed with a heart attack. He was rushed to Lenox Hill Hospital, where he died shortly afterwards. His wife of 35 years and their two sons survived him.[79]

Five Jewish players spent only one year in the major leagues during the 1940s: Eddie Turchin with the Cleveland Indians in 1943; Herb Karpel with the New York Yankees in 1946; Mickey Rutner with the Philadelphia Athletics in 1947; Hal Schacker with the Boston Braves in 1945; and Bud Swartz with the St. Louis Browns in 1947. Three others managed slightly longer careers during this decade: Dick Conger, a pitcher with Detroit, Pittsburgh, and the Phillies from 1940 to 1943; Mike Schemer, a first baseman with the Giants who played 31 games in 1945 and one game in 1946; and Harry Shuman, a pitcher with the Pirates and the Phillies from 1942 to 1944.[80]

Four others—Al Rosen, Marv Rotblatt, Joe Ginsberg, and Saul Rogovin—entered the majors late in the 1940s and played all or almost all of their major league years after 1948.

There would be more Jewish players in the years to come, but never as many as during the decades of the 1930s and the 1940s.

20. The First Jewish Superstar

Almost three-quarters of a century went by from the time Lipman Pike became the first professional Jewish player until Hank Greenberg, the first unquestioned Jewish superstar, entered the major leagues. Greenberg set baseball records throughout his career, establishing his right to be considered not only one of the best Jewish players of all time but one of baseball's all-time best. Notwithstanding all of Greenberg's abilities, nothing was made easy for him—not even getting into professional baseball in the first place.

Henry Benjamin Greenberg was born January 1, 1911, in New York City, the son of Romanian-Jewish immigrants David Greenberg, who owned a cloth-shrinking business, and Sarah Schwartz. When the family moved to the Bronx, Greenberg became an outstanding high-school athlete and was named All-City in soccer and basketball, but his favorite sport was baseball.[1] His high school coach often stated that the six-foot, four-inch, 215-pound Greenberg was so big for his age and so awkward that he became self-conscious. "The fear of being made to look foolish drove him to practice constantly, and, as a result, to overcome his handicaps."[2]

The Yankees offered Greenberg a major league contract in 1929 when he was still a senior in high school. At a tryout at Yankee Stadium, Yankee scout Paul Krichell tried to sign Greenberg by telling him that Lou Gehrig was "all washed up" but Greenberg knew better.[3] "The Yankees had Lou Gehrig on first base and I didn't see how I would have much chance of playing regularly there," he said.[4] "I felt that by signing with the Yankees, my major league career would be indefinitely postponed."[5]

John McGraw, manager of the New York Giants, had long sought a Jewish star who would bring throngs of Jews to the Polo Grounds. The Giants gave Hank Greenberg a tryout, but club secretary Jim Tierney informed Greenberg that he would never succeed in baseball because he was too clumsy. Another version of the story comes from Steve Greenberg, Hank's son. In 1928 his father asked the Giants if he could shag fly balls during batting practice at the Polo Grounds. Allegedly, McGraw replied through an intermediary, "Henry Greenberg has already been scouted by the Giants, and he will never make a ballplayer." McGraw never saw Greenberg work out with the team.[6]

Washington was the third club that showed some interest in Greenberg. The Senators offered him $12,000 to sign with their team, but they had Joe Judge entrenched at first, and Greenberg declined again.[7]

After high school in 1929, Greenberg attended New York University for one semester on an athletic scholarship, and then dropped out of college and signed with the Detroit Tigers.[8] Greenberg trained with the major league club in Florida, but except for one at bat at the tail end of the 1930 season, which marked his official major league debut, he spent 1930 through 1932 in the minors.[9]

"In many of the small southern towns where I played," recalled Greenberg, "I think I was the first Jew they'd seen. They seemed surprised I didn't have horns and a long beard. I encountered some hostility, but I'd say much more curiosity than hostility."[10] Unlike most other Jewish players, he would encounter a lot more hostility in the majors.

His most productive year in the minors was 1932, when he hit 39 home runs and drove in 131 runs with Beaumont in the Texas League. "After we won the Texas League pennant, and I was voted the league's Most Valuable Player, they called me up to the major leagues."[11] Except for his military service in the 1940s, Greenberg would remain in the major leagues until his retirement following the 1947 season.[12]

After Greenberg sat on the bench for a few weeks in 1933, Tiger manager Bucky Harris gave him an opportunity to play, and, once in the lineup, he remained the Tigers' regular first baseman the remainder of the year. From the beginning, Greenberg was the object of a great amount of vicious anti–Semitic bench jockeying. First base in Detroit was only forty feet from the visitors' dugout, the source of constantly shouted epithets from the opposing team. Obviously not the only Jewish ball player of his day, Greenberg was the most outstanding. He was also a very aggressive, tough player. The more the opposition got on him, the tougher he became.[13] Despite the pressure, Greenberg hit .301 his first year in the majors and, although he clouted only 12 homers, he drove in 87 runs.[14]

The Tigers finished in fifth place in 1933 and, for 1934, owner Frank Navin dismissed Harris and brought in Mickey Cochrane from Philadelphia as playing manager. He also acquired Goose Goslin from the Washington Senators. A much better ball club that year, the Tigers won the American League pennant, their first since 1909.[15] In 1934 Greenberg, showing great line drive power, led the American League in doubles with 63, batted .339 with 26 homers and drove in 139 runs. The Gas House Gang St. Louis Cardinals defeated the Tigers in seven games. Although Greenberg hit .321 in the series, he fanned nine times.[16]

During the pennant drive in 1934, Greenberg had to confront the Jewish player's dilemma—whether to play on the Jewish High Holy Days. The Tigers faced the Boston Red Sox in a key game scheduled for September 10, the same date as Rosh Hashanah, the Jewish New Year, and the first of the High Holy Days in 1934. "The team was fighting for first place," Greenberg said, "and I probably was the only batter in the lineup who was not in a slump. But the Jewish religion has a tradition that one observes the holiday solemnly, with prayer.... I wasn't sure what to do."[17]

Greenberg sought the opinions of local rabbis. Rabbi Leo M. Franklin, prominent Detroit rabbi, basically said, "Mr. Greenberg must decide for himself whether he ought to play or not. In the last analysis, no rabbi is authorized to give or withhold permission for him to do so."[18] Another Detroit rabbi cited Talmudic evidence that seemed to imply that Greenberg could play ball. Greenberg chose to follow this counsel.[19] After Greenberg had made his decision, the newspapers ran the headline "Talmud Clears Greenberg For Holiday Play."

Greenberg was still agitating about what he would do when he arrived at the ballpark. Marv Owen, the Tiger third baseman, reassured Greenberg, telling him "to do what he had to do." When batting practice was over, Greenberg announced that he intended to play.[20] He hit two home runs to lead the Tigers to a 2 to 1 victory.[21] The next day, the headline on the *Detroit Free Press* wished Greenberg a happy new year—in Hebrew. This was the first time the secular press had mentioned a Jewish holiday.[22]

Greenberg did not play on Yom Kippur, the most solemn Jewish Holy Day, in 1934.

Hank Greenberg was without a doubt the first Jewish superstar and one of the greatest players ever to wear a major league uniform. The first of two Jews to be inducted in baseball's Hall of Fame in Cooperstown, Greenberg played 12 of his 13 seasons for the Detroit Tigers, even though both the New York Yankees and the Washington Senators courted him. In 1938 Greenberg came within two home runs of tying Ruth's single season record of 60 home runs (courtesy National Baseball Hall of Fame Library, Cooperstown, N.Y.).

He was not particularly devout, but there are several reasons why Greenberg may have observed the Day of Atonement. One was a response to more than a thousand letters and telegrams chastising him for playing on the Jewish New Year, and urging him not to play on Yom Kippur.[23] Another explanation was that his father, unhappy that his son had played on Rosh Hashanah, put his foot down about Yom Kippur.[24] Finally, the Tigers had all but clinched the pennant by then. When Greenberg arrived at the synagogue that day, services stopped, and the congregants gave him a rousing round of applause.

In 1935 the Tigers won the pennant again, finishing three games ahead of the New York Yankees. The Tiger infield, with Greenberg at first, Charlie Gehringer at second, Billy Rogell at short, and Marv Owen at third, was superb both in the field and at the plate. Greenberg had the most spectacular year. He was the American League home run champ with 36 four-baggers, and led the league with 170 runs batted in. As a team, the Tigers drove in more than 400 runs for the second consecutive year. For his achievements in 1935 Greenberg was named the Most Valuable Player in the American League, the first Jew to receive that honor.[25]

In the World Series in 1935 the Tigers defeated the Cubs in six games. Unfortunately for Greenberg, he had to sit out most of the series as he broke his wrist in the second game and was forced to watch the series from the sidelines. He managed to bat six times, but got only one hit.[26] Even in his limited role, Greenberg recalled that the Chicago Cubs "rode" him mercilessly during the series, calling him "Jew this and Jew that."

In 1936 Greenberg started the season on a high note with 16 RBIs in 12 games. Those would be the only games Greenberg would play in 1936, for he broke the same wrist in a collision at first base with Jake Powell and missed the rest of the year.[27] Even without Greenberg, the Tigers finished the season in second place, but 19½ games behind the first-place Yankees. There was speculation that Greenberg's career might be over.

That speculation was misplaced. Greenberg had the finest season of his career in 1937. That year, playing in 154 games, Greenberg hit .337, with 40 home runs and 49 doubles. As far as Greenberg was concerned, however, his most important achievement was leading the American League in runs batted in with 183. Greenberg felt that runs batted in meant more than either batting average or home runs. He always claimed that his biggest disappointment was in failing to break Gehrig's American League record of 184.[28] "That's what wins ball games," he would constantly say, "driving runs across the plate."[29]

In 1938 Greenberg came very close to breaking what at that time was the major league record for home runs in a single season—60—set by Babe Ruth in 1927. Greenberg made a determined assault on that record by hitting 58, which tied him with Jimmy Foxx for the most home runs in a single season by a right-handed batter.[30] Although he reached 58 with five games left in the season, Greenberg was unable to break Ruth's record. He did set a record, however, for most multi-homer games in a single season, with eleven.[31]

Some people claim that Greenberg's religion was the reason he did not break Ruth's record, since opposing teams did everything they could to stop him. Greenberg did not believe that for a moment; he never blamed his failure on his religion. "I failed to break Ruth's record," said Greenberg, "because I ran out of gas; it had nothing to do with my being Jewish. In fact, most players were rooting for me. In one game with the Yankees, their catcher, Bill Dickey, was even telling me what was coming up."[32]

That's hardly to say that Greenberg was not still dealing with anti–Semitism—and dealing it with fairly successfully. Eldon Auker, Greenberg's teammate during the 1930s, recalled an incident with the Chicago White Sox: "... Hank walked to the door of their cramped clubhouse and said, 'I want that guy who called me a yellow Jew bastard to get on his feet.' Nobody confessed, so he walked around the room and stared into the face of every man in there. Nobody blinked—that guy with the big mouth was the luckiest guy in the world, in my opinion, because if he had stood up, there's no telling what Hank might have done."[33]

In 1939 the Tigers slipped to fifth place despite Greenberg's 33 home runs, 112 runs batted in, and .312 batting average. Part of the Tigers' problem was Greenberg's teammate, Rudy York. York was an excellent hitter but a terrible fielder. The Tigers tried him at third base, in the outfield, and behind the plate, but at each position he lost as many games with his glove as he won with his bat. Unfortunately for both the Tigers and Greenberg, the only position York could play was first base. The only solution was to play York at first base and move Greenberg to left field.

In 1940, by accepting the change to left field, Greenberg proved he was not only a great individual player but also a great team player. Greenberg had a number of legitimate concerns about playing left field. Using a first baseman's mitt for so many years, Greenberg was unaccustomed to using the finger mitt worn by outfielders. He had to struggle with sunglasses, which he had not worn at first base. He had to unlearn the sidearm throw that he used in the infield. Playing in left field, Greenberg was forced to play the opposite side of the field, and he was often bothered by the different angle at which the ball left the bat. He was quite concerned that he would look ridiculous on fly balls.[34]

The move paid off, however, for both Greenberg and the Tigers. In 1940 Greenberg hit .340, and led the American League in home runs (41), doubles (50) and runs batted in (150). Greenberg received his second Most Valuable Player Award, this time as a left fielder, becoming the first major league player to win the award at two different positions.[35]

The Sporting News praised the choice of Greenberg for the award. It noted the fine seasons of both Bob Feller and Joe DiMaggio, Greenberg's closest competitors, but praised him for his willingness to play a new position in 1940. Concluded the The Sporting News, "Considering all the elements which help to make a player the most valuable to his team, the baseball writers making up the committee did a fine job in naming Greenberg, who deserved the honor bestowed upon him in 1940 even more richly than in 1935, when he won a similar accolade."[36] The Tigers also won the pennant in 1940, their first since 1935.[37]

The Tigers met the Cincinnati Reds in the 1940 World Series, losing to the National League champs in seven games, even though Detroit out-pitched and out-slugged the Reds. Bobo Newsom won two of the three games for the Tigers, but he lost the seventh game to Paul Derringer by a score of 2–1. Greenberg played all seven games in the outfield, and hit safely 10 times in 28 at bats for an average of .357.[38]

When World War II broke out, Greenberg was a bachelor and the first major leaguer to volunteer for the service. He was inducted into the Air Force on May 7, 1941, at age 30, after playing only 19 games for the Tigers in 1941. Greenberg, who attained the rank of captain, spent most of his time serving in India and China, where one of his assignments was with a B-29 bomber unit in the China-Burma-India theatre.[39] He would not return to baseball until July 1945.

In 1945 Greenberg appeared in 78 games for the Tigers. He considered two of these games the most memorable of the season. In his first outing since 1941 Greenberg hit a home run to help win the game. The other unforgettable game was the season finale in which Greenberg hit a grand slam home run in the ninth inning to win the pennant for the Tigers. This time, the Tigers won the World Series, defeating the Chicago Cubs in seven games. Greenberg hit .304 in the series, including two home runs, and had seven runs batted in.[40]

In 1946 Hank Greenberg played his first complete season since 1940. He led the league with 44 home runs and 127 runs batted in, but his batting average dropped to .277, the only time he ever hit below .300 while playing a full season for the Tigers. The 1946 season was also Greenberg's final season in a Tiger uniform. Greenberg heard over the radio that, rather than raise his salary, the Tigers had waived him out of the American League to the Pittsburgh Pirates. After 12 years in the American League, Greenberg was thinking about retiring rather than moving. "I was so shocked and hurt I quit baseball. Simply quit. I told the press I was retiring and that was that."[41]

But three of the Pirates' new owners, John Galbreath, Frank McKinney, and Bing Crosby, were anxious to showcase Greenberg on their team, and tried to accommodate him in a number of ways. They increased his salary to $100,000, making him the first player in the majors to earn a six-figure salary. (Eleven years later, Stan Musial would be the second).[42]

In Detroit, the left field fence was 340 feet from home plate but in Pittsburgh, Barney Dreyfuss, who hated "cheap" home runs, had had left field extended in 1918.[43] For Greenberg, the Pirates built a bullpen in front of the distant left field wall, which the fans quickly labeled "Greenberg's Gardens."[44]

As his final condition, Greenberg informed the Pirate ownership that he would retire at the end of the 1947 season.[45] Although Greenberg hit a disappointing .249 in 1947, he did hit 25 home runs. He also served as a hitting instructor and helped advise his protégé, Ralph Kiner. At the end of the 1947 season, the Pirates kept their word and gave Greenberg his release. When Greenberg retired after the 1947 season, the left-field bullpen became known as "Kiner's Korner."[46]

Hank Greenberg was one of the most awesome power hitters in major league baseball. His statistics are all the more impressive when one remembers that he lost more than four years of his playing career while serving his country during World War II. He helped the Tigers win four pennants (1934, 1935, 1940, 1945); on four occasions he led or tied the American League in home runs; and he also led both leagues in runs batted in four times. Greenberg was selected to the American League All-Star team four times, and in 1935 and 1940 was voted the Most Valuable Player in the American League. He ended his career with an amazing .605 slugging percentage, one of the highest in the major leagues. He ranks third in the major leagues and second in the American League in the most runs batted in for a single season. His lifetime batting average is .313 and in 5,293 times at bat he clouted 331 home runs, in addition to batting in 1,276 runs.[47]

All of Greenberg's hard work and his amazing statistics earned him a place in Cooperstown, as he was elected to the Baseball Hall of Fame in 1956. "This beats everything," said Greenberg when he was informed he had been elected to the Hall. "I feel more thrilled about this than when I won the MVP twice. This is a climax to an ambition every player has, but never figures to reach."[48] Greenberg's election marked the first time in major league history that a Jew had been selected for the Hall of Fame.[49]

After Greenberg retired as a player, he embarked on a second career in baseball management, remaining a team executive for 14 years, despite finding discrimination here, too, although in much subtler forms. Bill Veeck, whom Greenberg met at the 1947 World Series, had recently purchased the Cleveland Indians. Veeck and Greenberg developed a deep admiration for one another. Veeck once said that Greenberg would make a wonderful commissioner of baseball.[50] Greenberg joined him in the Cleveland front office in 1948, serving as farm director, treasurer, general manager, and part owner of the Indians.[51]

Veeck sold his share of the Indians after the 1949 World Series, but Greenberg stayed on as general manager.[52] Greenberg experienced a good deal of anti–Semitism in the job. The Cleveland press criticized him for placing too many blacks on the Indians, more than any other team in the American League. Greenberg also desegregated the Texas League in 1952, when he signed an African-American player to Dallas, a Cleveland farm club. He was determined to promote desegregation while he was an executive, no doubt, because of his own experience with intolerance in baseball.

The Cleveland sportswriters, who were prejudiced against both African Americans and Jews, condemned Greenberg for replacing "nice Catholic boys" Bob Kennedy and Ken Keltner with Harry Simpson, a black, and Al Rosen, a Jew. Even though the new players were better than the men they replaced, the fans "rode Greenberg terribly." "In 1954, the year I brought Art Houtteman and Hal Newhouser over to shore up our pitching staff," said Greenberg, "we also acquired a catcher by the name of Joe Ginsberg and, of course, that was all the press talked about, adding another Jewish ballplayer to the team."[53] He added, "Even as an executive, I had problems staying in some of the fancy hotels in Phoenix, and even in Cleveland, I refused to have a board of directors meeting at the Union Club because ... no Jews were allowed there."[54] In an effort to protect his players from this kind of discrimination, he instructed the Indians' traveling secretary to inform hotels that "... they would either take all of the players, or none at all."[55]

The board of directors dismissed him in 1957.[56]

Greenberg married Caral Gimbel, the department store heiress in 1946; they had three children before they divorced in 1959.[57] That same year, 1959, Bill Veeck bought the Chicago White Sox, and again sought out Greenberg to purchase some of the team stock and serve as general manager and vice president. The White Sox won the pennant in 1959, the first since the Black Sox Scandal of 1919. In 1961 Veeck became ill and had to sell the team. When Veeck passed away many years later, Greenberg commented, "They think the only thing he ever did was bring a midget to bat."[58]

After Veeck left the White Sox, Greenberg gave some thought to acquiring a majority interest in the club, but decided to pass because of all the prejudice against him from the other owners: "I reached the conclusion that if I ever needed any help, I sure wouldn't get it from my fellow owners. It would be closed ranks against me." Greenberg admitted that it was the first time he felt anti–Semitism actually affected him unfavorably.[59] It may have also been among the few times when he knew that direct confrontation would not help.

After selling his shares in the White Sox for a tidy profit, Greenberg moved to Beverly Hills and in 1966 married actress Mary Jo Tarola. Hank Greenberg died at his home in Beverly Hills on September 4, 1986, after suffering from cancer for 13 months. His wife, three children, a sister, and eight grandchildren survived him.[60]

Ever since Lipman Pike became the first Jew to play in the major leagues, most Jewish baseball players admitted that they were forced to endure anti–Semitic insults and abuse from opposing players and fans, and even, on some occasions, from their own teammates. These players usually rationalized that all ethnic groups were targeted and that the remarks were not necessarily aimed at their Judaism. There is much evidence to contradict this assumption, and nowhere is this more evident than in the case of Hank Greenberg. Probably no player put up with more abuse than Hank Greenberg, because he was, without a doubt, the greatest Jewish baseball player during the first century of baseball.

Greenberg could not have chosen a more difficult time to debut in baseball. His first full season, 1933, corresponded with the rise of Adolf Hitler in Germany, which gave impetus to neo–Nazi organizations in every large American city.[61] In addition, Greenberg did not sign with a New York team, where he would have had a supportive home crowd, but in Detroit, a city that was a hotbed of anti–Semitism, where it was difficult for a Jewish player to succeed. Not only was Detroit the home of the powerful anti–Semite, auto magnate Henry Ford, but it was also home to a radio priest, Father Charles Coughlin, who was spewing out anti–Semitic propaganda against the "international banker conspirator Jew."[62]

Greenberg noted in his autobiography, "How the hell could you get up to home plate every day and have some son of a bitch call you a Jew bastard and a kike and a sheenie ... without feeling the pressure? If the ballplayers weren't doing it, the fans were."[63] Another favorite term for Greenberg and other Jewish players was "Christ-killer."[64] Birdie Tebbetts, one of Greenberg's teammates, said, "Hank consistently took more abuse from bench jockeys than anybody I'd ever known. And not only from the opposing team. ... out in the stands ... you'd hear 'Jew bastard' or 'kike son of a bitch.' Nobody else could have ever withstood the foul invectives that were directed toward Greenberg, and he had to eat them. Or else he would be out of every game he ever played."[65]

But even Greenberg realized that no one escaped the bench jockeys. As he once put it, "Everybody got it. Italians were wops. Germans were krauts, and the Polish players were dumb polacks. Me, I was a kike or a sheeny or a mockey. They reserved a little extra for me."[66]

One of Hank Greenberg's major contributions was in helping change the way the press viewed ethnicity and baseball. During the 1930s the press seldom if ever acknowledged any anti–Semitism in baseball. Newspapers during the decade printed numerous articles about anti–Semitism elsewhere in America, but almost no paper admitted that it existed in baseball. To do so, most historians reason, would have ruined the "unspoiled image of America's national pastime" and, by reflection, the melting pot theory of American society at large.[67]

And yet, from almost the time that Jews first appeared in professional baseball, they were identified in the press by their religion. This became even more apparent during John McGraw's much-discussed search for a Jewish superstar. Whenever the press mentioned major leaguers such as Mose Solomon, Andy Cohen, Jim Levey, Phil Weintraub, or Sid Gordon, their names carried an added appellation such as "The Jewish Babe Ruth," "The Next Jewish Superstar," or "The Hebrew Slugger." In most cases, there was no anti–Semitism intended, merely an emphasis on ethnic background. To be fair, Jews were not the only ethnic group identified; at one time or another, nearly every nationality was singled out.

The de-emphasis of ethnic identity in sports did not disappear overnight. Throughout the 1930s, when there was "no anti–Semitism," the press continued to emphasize Greenberg's ethnic identity. But during the war years media references to Greenberg as a Jewish standard bearer declined. Greenberg was the first major league player to enlist in the armed services after the outbreak of World War II. Although he was discharged December 5, 1941, he reenlisted immediately after Pearl Harbor. The press, without referring to Greenberg's religion, noted that, unlike many baseball players who served as "athletic directors" during the war, Greenberg volunteered for combat. Soon, comments about Greenberg's ethnicity became almost nonexistent. He was now the "big slugger" in the press instead of "the Jewish slugger." During the 1930s the press called Greenberg the "Jewish first baseman"; now he received the title "Captain Henry," a name used by writers constantly during Greenberg's postwar career.[68]

The best example of how the press no longer cared about a player's ethnicity is the story by Whitney Martin of the Associated Press about Greenberg's release from the air corps.

Martin wrote that all other ball players in the service who were afraid that their absence from the game might harm their effectiveness and ability to earn a living should observe Greenberg. Nowhere in Martin's story did the journalist call Greenberg "a symbol of hope," or even a Jew, but simply a returning serviceman who was praised for his patriotism.[69] Fortunately, the need for a Jewish standard bearer greatly diminished as most Jews assimilated into the secular community. Today's press so seldom includes any sort of ethnic identity that not many baseball fans—not even the Jewish ones—know which present major league baseball players are Jewish.

Although Greenberg was personally not very religious, he was a very important symbol to Jews. Years later Greenberg stated that he used to resent being singled out as a Jewish ballplayer. He wasn't sure why or when he changed, but he began to recognize that he wished to be remembered not only as a great ballplayer but even more so as a great Jewish ballplayer.[70]

Once Greenberg acknowledged that he was a Jewish baseball player, he quickly understood that he had become a role model to a new generation of Jewish kids who were growing up in the 1930s, and he admitted that he did not wish to do anything which would reflect badly on his heritage or disappoint his fans.[71]

Not only did he set an example for young American Jews, Greenberg also proved for the older generations that a Jewish ballplayer could be a respectable citizen. Baseball historians agree that Greenberg might not have been an "observant Jew," and that religion might not have played a major role in his life, but being Jewish did.

Greenberg also had an influence on the way non–Jewish fans perceived Jews. After Greenberg died in 1986, a non–Jewish Detroiter named Rosemary LeBoeuf wrote a letter about Greenberg to the *New York Times*, "He was becoming a hero to *goyim*, too. I grew up in Catholic Detroit. To my classmates' recital of Jewish faults, I had always the last word: 'Yeah? What about Hank Greenberg?'"[72]

As Greenberg changed the way he looked at himself, other Jews began to change their own outlooks. Just as Hank Greenberg challenged the stereotype of Jews as weak, other Jews, with Greenberg as an example, were inspired to use their athletic abilities to try to achieve their dreams. Even nonathletic Jews began to believe that they, too, could succeed in life if they used whatever abilities they had.[73] Greenberg was virtually every Jew's champion. The late actor Walter Matthau said that Greenberg was "part of my dreams." He recalled joining the Beverly Hills Tennis Club in the hopes of meeting Greenberg, who was a member there. "I didn't even know how to play tennis," Matthau admitted. It is no wonder that noted attorney and author Alan Dershowitz went so far as to declare that Greenberg was "the most important American Jew of the 1930s."[74] Greenberg set a living example for Jews and non–Jews of how to be successful in a purely American enterprise without sacrificing traditions or integrity.

When professional baseball first originated during the second half of the nineteenth century, only half a dozen players were Jewish and there were few Jewish fans of the sport. By the beginning of the twentieth century, more Jews were participating in baseball, as the sport attracted the wave of Eastern European Jewish immigrants who loved the game for itself and viewed baseball as a means of becoming acculturated. Although this process was slow, it was steady, and by 1948, baseball had truly become a national pastime. Things certainly had changed from Pike to Greenberg.

Epilogue

After 1948, Jewish participation in baseball would continue and, in some cases, expand. On the management level, there would be more Jewish owners such as Jerry Hoffberger of Baltimore, Jerry Reinsdorf of the Chicago White Sox, Walter Haas of the Oakland Athletics and Bob Lurie of the San Francisco Giants. Jewish owner Bud Selig of the Milwaukee Brewers would become commissioner of baseball. Under the leadership of Marvin Miller and, later, Don Fehr, the players would finally get the reserve clause repealed and become what some call the most powerful union in the United States.[1]

Jewish sportswriters such as Jerome Holtzman, Dick Young, and Leonard Koppett would become the Daniels and Povichs of the next generation. With the expansion of broadcast media would come Jewish play-by-play announcers like the great Mel Allen, and color commentators such as Howard Cossell and Chris Berman.

A new field of baseball fiction would also emerge in the 1950s, led by Jewish writers Bernard Malamud, Philip Roth, Mark Harris, Eric Rolfe Greenberg, Peter Levine, and Eliot Asinof.[2]

Beginning in the 1950s, the number of Jewish major league players began to drop from the highs of the 1930s and '40s. One reason the game saw fewer Jews can be attributed to the changing suburban American culture that limited children's free time for the sandlot games where young players often developed into future stars. More significantly, however, opening baseball's doors to African Americans, Latinos, and Asians, which most Jews strongly supported, greatly increased the competition for coveted positions with major league teams.[3]

Despite this increased competition, there would be good to excellent Jewish players in the game after 1948. Sandy Koufax of the Dodgers became the second Jew in Baseball's Hall of Fame; Cleveland's Al Rosen was an American League MVP; Ken Holtzman pitched for several teams and, with 174 victories, has the most wins of any Jewish pitcher. The Sherry brothers, baseball's sixth pair of Jewish brothers, Ron Blomberg, Richie Sheinblum, Mike Epstein, and Steve Stone, just to name a few, were all noted players.[4]

Anti-Semitism among the players also decreased as time went on. Al Rosen, who began his career at the end of the 1940s, credited Greenberg with making things easier for him and his contemporaries.[5] Even in the 1960s, Ken Holtzman said he experienced some anti–Semitism, but nothing like what Greenberg endured.[6] In contrast, by the time Ross Baumgarten played in the late 1970s and early 1980s he was able to report that he "never had one instance of anti–Semitism" in major league baseball.[7]

Most of all, despite competition from other sports, many Jewish fans remain true to their first love—baseball. They fill the stands, they follow every play and listen to every commentator on TV, and they even buy satellite radios so as not to miss a single pitch of any major league game. And right after the last out of the last game of the World Series, they begin counting the weeks until pitchers and catchers report to spring training and strains of "Take Me Out to the Ball Game" resound again.

Notes

Chapter 1

1. David Block, *Baseball Before We Knew It: A Search for the Roots of the Game* (Lincoln: University of Nebraska Press, 2005) 22–31.

2. John Thorn, "Four Fathers of Baseball," Thorn Pricks, http://thornpricks.blogspot.com/2005/07/four-fathers-of-baseball.html (accessed April 21, 2006). Block, *Baseball Before We Knew It*, 67–93.

3. Melvin Adelman, *A Sporting Time: New York City and the Rise of Modern Athletics, 1820–1870* (Urbana: University of Illinois Press, 1986), 122.

4. Sean Lahman, *A Brief History of Baseball Part I*, December, 1996, 1, found on www.baseball.com.

5. Ford C. Frick, *Games, Asteriks and People: Memoirs of as Lucky Fan* (New York: Crown, 1973), 11; Lahman, *A Brief History of Baseball Part I*, 1; John Thorn, Phil Birnbaum, and Bill Deane, *Total Baseball: The Ultimate Baseball Encyclopedia* (Wilmington, DE: Sports Media Publishing, Inc, 2004), 31.

6. Adelman, *A Sporting Time*, 179.

7. Lahman, *A Brief History of Baseball*, 1.

8. David Voight, *Base Ball History—A Quick Synopsis* on-line extracted from his book *Baseball, An Illustrated History*.

9. Thorn et al., *Total Baseball*, 36; Lahman, *A Brief History of Baseball*, 1.

10. *Ibid.*

11. Thorn et al., *Total Baseball*, 39–40; Lahman, *A Brief History of Baseball*, 1.

12. Howard M. Sachar, *A History of Jews in America* (New York: Alfred A. Knopf, 1992), 38–39.

13. Isidore Singer (ed.), *Jewish Encyclopedia 1964* (New York: Funk and Wagnall's, 1964), 370.

14. Arthur Hertzberg, *The Jews In America: Four Centuries of an Uneasy Encounter* (New York: Simon & Schuster, 1989), 103–104.

15. *Ibid.*, 104; Ronald Sanders, *The Downtown Jews: Portraits of an Immigrant Generation* (New York: Harper & Row, 1945), 47–48.

16. Stanley Feldstein, *The Land That I Show You*, (Garden City, NY: Doubleday, 1978), 64.

17. Hertzberg, *The Jews in America*, 107–108.

18. Sachar, *A History of Jews in America*, 99.

19. John Higham, *Strangers in the Land: Patterns of American Nativism 1860–1925* (New York: Atheneum, 1966), 26–27.

20. Hertzberg, *The Jews in America*, 108.

Chapter 2

1. Charles C. Alexander, *Our Game: An American Baseball History* (New York: Henry Holt & Company, 1991), 26; Robert Smith, *Baseball in the Afternoon* (New York: Simon & Schuster, 1993), 80; Bernard Postal, Jesse Silver, and Roy Silver, *The Encyclopedia of Jews in Sports* (New York: Bloch Publishing Company , 1965), 32–33; Peter S. Horvitz and Joachim Horvitz, *The Big Book Of Jewish Baseball* (New York: SPI Books, 2001), 134.

2. *Ibid.*; Donald Dewey and Nicholas Acocella, *The Biographical History of Baseball* (New York: Carrol and Graf, 1995), 363.

3. Postal et al., *The Encyclopedia of Jews in Sports*, 35.

4. Mark Alvarez, *The Old Ball Game* (Alexandria, VA: Redefinition Books, 1990), 54.

5. Jon David Cash, *Before They Were Cardinals: Major League Baseball in Nineteenth-Century St. Louis* (Columbia: University of Missouri Press, 2002), 3; Thorn et al., *Total Baseball*, 1540–41.

6. Alvarez, *The Old Ball Game* , 54; material found on internet, *www.baseballlibrary.com/baseballchronology/1873*; James H. Bready, "Play Ball! The Legacy of Nineteenth-Century Baltimore Baseball," *Maryland Historical Magazine* (Summer 1992): 133.

7. Donald D. Jones, *Former Major League Teams: An Encyclopedia* (Jefferson, N.C.: McFarland, 1995), 98; Pete Palmer and Gary Gillette (eds.), *The 2006 ESPN Baseball Encyclopedia* (New York: Sterling Publishing Company, 2004), 529.

8. Horvitz and Horvitz, *The Big Book of Jewish Baseball*, 135.

9. Postal et al., *The Encyclopedia of Jewish Sports*, 34; www.jewsinsports.org/profile; *New York Times*, October 1, 1881; Irving A. Leitner, *Baseball: Diamond in the Rough* (New York: Abelard-Schuman, 1972), 128.

10. Horvitz and Horvitz, *The Big Book of Jewish Baseball*, 135.

11. *New York Clipper*, July 9, 1881.

12. *Brooklyn Eagle*, October 12, 1893.

13. *The Sporting News*, October 21, 1893.

14. Robert Slater, *Great Jews in Sports* (Middle Village, New York: Jonathan David, 1992), 197.

15. David Spaner, "From Greenberg to Green: Jewish Ballplayers," in *Total Baseball*, John Thorn et al. (eds.), 172; Horvitz and Horvitz, *The Big Book of Jewish Baseball*, 135; Steven A. Reiss, "From Pike to Green With Greenberg in Between: Jewish Americans and the National Pastime," in *The American Game: Baseball and Ethnicity*, Lawrence Baldassaro and Richard A. Johnson (eds.)

(Carbondale: Southern Illinois University Press, 2002), 117.

16. Horvitz and Horvitz, *The Big Book of Jewish Baseball*, 135; lip-pike.wikiverse.org.

17. *www.Jewsinsports.org/profile.asp.; www.baseballlibrary. com.; U S A Today Baseball Weekly*, December 2–15, 1962; William C. Ryczek, *When Johnny Came Sliding Home: The Post Civil War Baseball Boom, 1865–1870* (Jefferson, N.C.: McFarland, 1998) 87, 111.

18. *Ibid.*, 111.

19. *Philadelphia Independent*, February 24, 1900.

20. Horvitz and Horvitz, *The Big Book of Jewish Baseball*, 133.

21. *Ibid.*, 72–73.

22. Palmer and Gillette, *The 2006 ESPN Baseball Encyclopedia*, 253; www.baseball-reference.com.

23. Unnamed newspaper clipping, March 19, 1890, Jake Goodman Files, Baseball Hall of Fame, Cooperstown, New York.

24. Palmer and Gillette, *The 2006 ESPN Baseball Encyclopedia*, 581; Horvitz and Horvitz, *The Big Book of Jewish Baseball*, 159; Ike Samuels Statistics, www.baseball-reference.com.

25. Palmer and Gillette, *The 2006 ESPN Baseball Encyclopedia*, 888.

26. *New York Times*, June 20, 1931.

27. Leo Fishel Statistics, www.baseball-reference.com.

Chapter 3

1. Article on internet in *Cincinnati Enquirer*, by Julie Erwin found at www.enquirer.com/editions/1999.

2. Hertzberg, *The Jews in America*, 146.

3. Address by Joseph Dorinson "Jews and Baseball," reprinted in SABR Bulletin (July 2004): 10.

4. Article on internet in *Cincinnati Enquirer*, by Julie Erwin found at www.enquirer.com/editions/1999.

5. *The Kentucky Post*, July 12, 1894.

6. James Garfield Stewart, *They Build a City* (Cincinnati, 1938), 167.

7. *Daily Commonwealth*, September 19, 1892.

8. "Playthings," *Business and Industry* (December 1908): 119.

9. *Kentucky Post*, July 12, 1894.

10. *Ibid*; "Playthings," 120.

11. Sarah Sturman, "City's Past Now Part of Smithsonian," found on *www.cincypost.com.*, 1–2.

12. Postal et al., *Encyclopedia of Jews in Sports*, 32.

13. Thorn et al., *Total Baseball*, 36; Lahman, *A Brief History of Baseball*, 1.

14. Harry Ellard, *Baseball in Cincinnati: A History* (Jefferson, N.C.: McFarland, 2004), 169.

15. Greg Rhodes and John Snyder, *The Redleg Journal* (Cincinnati: Road West Publishers, 1983), 60.

16. *Washington Post*, October 22, 1886; David Nemec, *The Beer and Whiskey League: The Illustrated History of the American Association—Baseball's Renegade Major League* (Guilford, Connecticut, 2004), 66–67.

17. *The Sporting News*, October 25, 1886; December 19, 1886.

18. Dean A. Sullivan, "Faces in the Crowd: A Statistical Portrait of Baseball Spectators in Cincinnati, 1886–1888," *Journal of Sports History* (Winter 1990): 355.

19. Undated article in *Cincinnati Enquirer* by John Erardi (found on reds.enquirer.com)

20. Lonnie Wheeler and John Baskin, *The Cincinnati Game* (Wilmington, Ohio: Orange Frazer Press, Inc., 1988), 200.

21. Dewey and Acocella, *The Biographical History of Baseball*, 449.

22. Dan Holmes, "From Cooperstown: A History of Spring Training," February 28, 2002, found on *www.the* baseball page.com, 1; www.springtrainingonline.com.

23. The *Brooklyn Eagle*, Sept. 1889 and the *New York Sun*, August 1, 1887,both quoted in Postal et al., *The Encyclopedia of Sports*, 36; *The Sporting News*, November 13, 1886.

24. David Pietrusza, *Major Leagues: The Formation, Sometimes Absorption and Mostly Inevitable Demise of 18 Professional Baseball Organizations, 1871 to the Present*, (Jefferson, N.C.: McFarland, 1991), 111.

25. Lee Allen, *The Cincinnati Reds* (New York: G. P. Putnam's Sons, 1948), 36; Bruce Chadwick, *The Cincinnati Reds*, (New York: Abbeyville Press, 1994), n.p. (book unpaginated).

26. *New York Times*, November 15, 1889; www.cincysports.net.

27. Allen, *The Cincinnati Reds*, 36–37.

28. Palmer and Gillette, *The 2006 ESPN Baseball Encyclopedia*, 1386.

29. Allen, *The Cincinnati Reds*, 39; *The Boston Globe*, October 5, 1890; *Chicago Daily Tribune*, October 13, 1891.

30. Bryan DiSalvatore, *A Clever Base-Ballist: The Life and Times of John Montgomery Ward* (New York: Pantheon Books, 1999), 306.

31. www.cincys ports.net 1890–1899.

32. Postal et al., *The Encyclopedia of Jews In Sports*, 36.

33. Copy of contract between Aaron Stern and John Hauck, dated October 1886 in Aaron Stern File, Baseball Hall of Fame, Cooperstown, New York.; Nemec, *The Beer and Whiskey League*, 66.

34. *Los Angeles Times*, February 19, 1891.

35. Postal, *The Encyclopedia of Jews In Sports*, 32.

36. *The Sporting News*, August 29, 1891.

37. *The Cincinnati Enquirer*, August 20, 1922; *Cincinnati Times-Star*, August 19, 1922.

38. Palmer and Gillette, *The Baseball Encyclopedia*, 1389–1401.

39. Frederick G. Lieb, *The Baseball Story* (New York: G. P. Putnam's Sons, 1950), 160.

40. *Cincinnati: The Queen City, 1788–1912*, Vol. IV (Chicago, 1912), 199.

41. *Chicago Daily Tribune*, April 7, 1903; *New York Times*, June 21, 1903; *Cincinnati the Queen City, Vol. III*, (Chicago, 1912), 916–918.

42. It was very common for Americans of German heritage to favor the Republican Party and not necessarily for economic reasons. Since most Germans were opposed to slavery and the Republican Party was founded as an antislavery party, it would be only natural for these German Americans to gravitate to the Republican Party.

43. *Chicago Daily Tribune*, April 3, 1900.

44. Undated article *Cincinnati Times-Star*, clipping in Fleischmann Files, Baseball Hall of Fame, Cooperstown, New York.

45. *New York Times*, April 7, 1903.

46. *Chicago Daily Tribune*, April 7, 1903; *New York Times*, June 21, 1903.

47. *Cincinnati: The Queen City, Volume IV*, 199–200.

48. Noel Hynd, *The Giants of the Polo Grounds*, (New York: Doubleday, 1988), 117; *New York Times*, August 10, 1902.

49. *Chicago Daily Tribune*, March 6, 1903; *Washington Post*, March 6, 1903.

50. *New York Times*, December 10, 1914; *Washington Post*, December 10, 1914.

51. Lieb, *The Baseball Story*, 193.

52. *New York Times*, November 15, 1903; *Chicago Daily Tribune*, December 9, 1903; *Washington Post*, March 4, 1904.

53. Quoted in Postal et al., *The Encyclopedia of Jews in Sports*, 39.

54. *New York Times*, October 17, 1951.

55. *Chicago Daily Tribune*, October 7, 1912; *New York Times*, November 13, November 14, 1915.

56. Palmer and Gillette, *The Baseball Encyclopedia*, 1403–1430.

57. *New York Times*, February 22, 1925.

58. *The Sporting News*, October 24, 1951; *The Cincinnati Times-Star*, October 17, 1951.

Chapter 4

1. David L. Porter (ed.), *Biographical Directory of American Sports*, (New York: Greenwood Press, 1987), 198; Riess, "From Greenberg to Green," 116.

2. *Washington Post*, January 28, 1875; Porter, *Biographical Dictionary of American Sports*, 198–199; Alexander, *Our Game: An American Baseball History*, 69; *The Sporting News*, November 10, 1973.

3. Hynd, *The Giants of the Polo Grounds*, 89.

4. Seymour, *Baseball: The Early Years*, 297.

5. Hynd, *The Giants of the Polo Grounds*, 90; Seymour, *Baseball: The Early Years*, 90.

6. Hynd, *The Giants of the Polo Grounds*, 90; Dewey and Acocella, *The Biographical History of Baseball*, 152–153.

7. Alexander, *Our Game*, 70.

8. Mark Alvarez, "The Abominable Owner," *Sports Heritage* (November/December 1987): 43.

9. David Voigt, *The League That Failed* (Lanham, MD: Scarecrow, 1998), 220.

10. *The Sporting News*, December 30, 1899.

11. Seymour, *Baseball: The Early Years*, 296.

12. Dewey and Acocella, *The Biographical History of Baseball*, 152.

13. "Riess, "From Pike to Green with Greenberg in Between," 118.

14. Porter, *Biographical Directory of American Sports*, 199.

15. Alexander, *Our Game*, 70.

16. Frank Graham, *The New York Giants: An Informal History* (New York: G.P. Putnam's Sons, 1952), 20–22.

17. Dewey and Acocella, *The Biographical History of Baseball*, 153.

18. Graham, *The New York Giants*, 20–22.

19. http://cbs.sportsline.com/mlb/teams/history/SF

20. Palmer and Gillette, *The 2006 ESPN Baseball Encyclopedia*, 1158.

21. Glenn Dickey, *The History of National League Baseball Since 1876* (New York: Stein & Day, 1979), 34.

22. *Washington Post*, March 22, 1896.

23. *The Sporting News*, April 4, 1896.

24. Seymour, *Baseball: The Early Years*, 297.

25. Dickey, *The History of National League Baseball*, 34.

26. Hynd, *The Giants of the Polo Grounds*, 92.

27. Alvarez, "The Abominable Owner," 45.

28. Seymour, *Baseball: The Early Years*, 297; Voigt, *The League That Failed*, 220.

29. Voigt, *The League That Failed*, 220.

30. Dickey, *The History of National League Baseball*, 34; Palmer and Gillette, *The 2006 ESPN Baseball Encyclopedia*. 1158.

31. Robert F. Burk, *Never Just a Game: Players, Owners, and American Baseball to 1920* (Chapel Hill: University of North Carolina Press, 1994), 133.

32. Riess, "From Pike to Green with Greenberg in Between," 118; Horvitz and Horvitz, *The Big Book of Jewish Baseball*, 216.

33. Charles C. Alexander, *John McGraw*, (New York: Viking, 1988), 61.

34. Hynd, *The Giants of the Polo Grounds*, 92–93.; Seymour, *Baseball: The Early Years*, 298; Albert G. Spalding, *America's National Game: Historic Facts Concerning the Beginning, Evolution, Development and Popularity of Baseball With Personal Reminiscences of its Vicissitudes, Its Victories and its Votaries* (San Francisco: Halo Books, 1991), 193.

35. Hynd, *The Giants of the Polo Grounds*, 93.

36. *Boston Daily Globe*, April 9, 1898 quoted in David Voigt, *American Baseball: From Gentleman's Sport to the Commissioner System* (Norman: University of Oklahoma Press, 1966), 284.

37. Burke, *Never Just a Game*, 133.

38. James D. Hardy Jr., *The New York Giants Base Ball Club: The Growth of a Team and a Sport, 1870–1900* (Jefferson, N.C.: McFarland, 1996), 163.

39. Seymour, *Baseball: The Early Years*, 298.

40. Hardy, *The New York Giants Base Ball Club*, 165.

41. *Ibid.*

42. *Ibid.*, 305.

43. *New York Times*, March 9, 1900; Dean A. Sullivan (ed.), *Early Innings: A Documentary History of Baseball, 1825–1908* (Lincoln: University of Nebraska Press, 1995), 248–249.

44. Seymour, *Baseball: The Early Years*, 305–306.

45. Hardy, *The New York Giants Base Ball Club*, 169–170; Dewey and Acocella, 153; Voigt, *The League That Failed*, 221.

46. Hynd, *The Giants of the Polo Grounds*, 96.

47. Arthur Bartlett, *Baseball and Mr. Spalding: The History and Romance of Baseball* (New York: Farrar, Strauss, & Young, 1951), 271.

48. Voigt, *American Baseball*, 228.

49. Hynd, *The Giants of the Polo Grounds*, 97; Bartlett, *Baseball and Mr. Spalding*, 273.

50. *Chicago Daily Tribune*, December 14, 1901; *Washington Post*, December 14, 1901; Alvarez, "The Abominable Owner," 47.

51. Peter Levine, *A. G. Spalding and the Rise of Baseball: The Promise of American Sport* (New York: Oxford University Press, 1985), 66–67.

52. Frommer, *Primitive Baseball*, 26; *New York Times*, December 14, 1901.

53. Hynd, *The Giants of the Polo Grounds*, 97.

54. *New York Clipper*, December 21, 1903, quoted in Levine, *A. G. Spalding and The Rise of Baseball*, 69.

55. Voigt, *The League That Failed*, 222–223.

56. Dewey and Acocella, *The Biographical History of Baseball*, 153; Bartlett, *Baseball and Mr. Spalding*, 284.

57. *Chicago Daily Tribune*, September 30, 1932.

58. Graham, *The New York Giants*, 43.

59. Alvarez, "The Abominable Owner," 47; Voigt, *The League That Failed*, 223; Riess, "From Pike to Green with Greenberg in Between," 119; Joseph Durso, *The Days of Mr. McGraw* (Englewood Cliffs, N.J.: Prentice-Hall, Inc., 1969), 44.

60. Ray Robinson, *Matty: An American Hero* (New York: Oxford University Press, 1993), 35–36; Damon Rice, *Seasons Past* (New York: Praegers, 1976), 99.

61. Sullivan, *Early Innings*, 259.

62. Alexander, *John McGraw*, 98; Hynd, *The Giants of the Polo Grounds*, 117.

63. Voigt, *The League Than Failed*, 223–224.

64. Ban Johnson, "Making the American League," *Saturday Evening Post* (March 22, 1930): 121.

65. *New York Times*, December 5, 1915; December 9, 1915.

66. Mike Shatzkin (ed.), *The Ballplayers: Baseball's Ulti-*

mate Biographical Reference (New York: Arbor House, 1990), 360.

67. *The Sporting News*, November 10, 1973; *The Sporting News*, August 6, 1898, quoted in Voigt, *American Baseball*, 229.

68. Hynd, *The Giants of the Polo Grounds*, 98.

69. John McCormick Harris, "Pinhead Christy Mathewson," *National Pastime* (1990): 20; Robinson, *Matty*, 37.

70. Horvitz and Horvitz, *The Big Book of Jewish Baseball*, 216; Voigt, *American Baseball*, 229.

71. Voigt, *The League That Failed*, 220.

Chapter 5

1. Burton A. Boxerman and Benita W. Boxerman, *Ebbets to Veeck to Busch: Eight Owners Who Shaped Baseball* (Jefferson, N.C.: McFarland, 2003), 29.

2. Fred Wertenbech, *Barney Dreyfuss Was a Dreamer Who Made Visions Come True*, (unnamed, undated article Barney Dreyfuss file, *The Sporting News*, St. Louis, Missouri).

3. Robert Slater, *Great Jews in Sports* (Middle Village, New York: Jonathan David, 1992), 63.

4. Jeff Youngblood, *The Early Life and Times of Barney Dreyfuss, Paducah, and the World Series*—found on internet *www.strangecloud.com*, 1–8; David Pietrusza, Matthew Silverman, and Michael Gershman, *Baseball: The Biographical Encyclopedia* (Kingston, New York: Sports Illustrated, 2000), 308.

5. *The Sporting News*, March 14, 1941.

6. Boxerman and Boxerman, *Ebbets to Veeck to Busch*, 30.

7. Youngblood, *The Early Life and Times of Barney Dreyfuss*, 9.

8. Dewey and Acocella, *The Ball Clubs*, 456.

9. *The Sporting News*, September 14, 1960.

10. Slater, *Great Jews in Sports*, 64.

11. Bob Smizik, *The Pittsburgh Pirates: An Illustrated History* (New York: Walker, 1990), 13.

12. *The Sporting News*, June 22, 1916.

13. Dennis De Valeria and Jeanne Burke De Valeria, *Honus Wagner: A Biography* (New York: Henry Holt & Company, 1998), 97.

14. Pietrusza et al., *Baseball: The Biographical Encyclopedia*, 308.

15. Dewey and Acocella, *The Biographical History of Baseball*, 121–122.

16. *Ibid.*, 153; Bartlett, *Baseball and Mr. Spalding*, 284.

17. Boxerman and Boxerman, *Ebbets to Veeck to Busch*, 34.

18. Youngblood, *The Early Life and Times of Barney Dreyfuss*, 10.

19. Boxerman and Boxerman, *Ebbets to Veeck to Busch*, 35.

20. *Ibid.*

21. Dewey and Acocella, *The Biographical History of Baseball*, 121.

22. Pittsburgh *Post-Gazette*, October 6, 2004.

23. John G. Robertson, *Baseball's Greatest Controversy: Rhubarbs, Hoaxes, Blown Calls, Ruthian Myths, Managers; Miscues and Front-Office Flops* (Jefferson, N.C.: McFarland, 1995), 13–14.

24. *Ibid.*, 14.

25. Sullivan, *Early Innings*, 114.

26. Slater, *Great Jews in Sports*, 64; Pietrusza et al., *Baseball: The Biographical Encyclopedia*, 308.

27. Postal et al., *The Encyclopedia of Jews in Sports*, 28.

28. Undated excerpt from a work in progress by Roger I. Abrams, *Constructing Baseball: Boston and the First World Series*.

29. Glenn Dickey, *The History of the World Series Since 1903* (New York: Stein & Day, 1984), 21.

30. Frederick G. Lieb, *The Pittsburgh Pirates*, (New York: G. P. Putnam's Sons, 1948), 112–113.

31. Hynd, *The Giants of the Polo Grounds*, 131.

32. Seymour, *The Golden Age*, 25.

33. Hynd, *The Giants of the Polo Grounds*, 131.

34. Dewey and Acocella, *The Biographical History of Baseball*, 121; *Sporting Life*, June 3, 1905; June 10, 1905; Graham, *The New York Giants: An Informal History*, 53.

35. Dewey and Acocella, *The Biographical History of Baseball*, 121; Hynd, *The Giants of the Polo Grounds*, 132.

36. *Pittsburgh Press*, June 30, 1909, found on Internet www.cl.pgh.org/exhibit/neighborhoods/Oakland/oak.

37. Lieb, *The Pittsburgh Pirates*, 132.

38. Slater, *Great Jews in Sports*, 64; Pietrusza et al., *Baseball: The Biographical Encyclopedia*, 309.

39. Thorn et al., *Total Baseball*, 339.

40. DeValeria and DeValeria, *Honus Wagner*, 259.

41. *Ibid.*

42. Alexander, *Our Game*, 104; Jonathan Fraser Light, *The Cultural Encyclopedia of Baseball* (Jefferson, N.C.: McFarland, 1997), 153.

43. DeValeria and DeValeria, *Honus Wagner*, 264.

44. Light, *The Cultural Encyclopedia of Baseball*, 153.

45. Boxerman and Boxerman, *Ebbets to Veeck to Busch*, 46.

46. *Ibid.*, 47.

47. Seymour, *Baseball: The Golden Age*, 260.

48. Michael Santa Maria and James Costello, *In the Shadows of the Diamonds: Hard Times in the National Pastime* (Carmel, IN: William C. Brown Communications, 1992), 209.

49. Seymour, *Baseball: The Golden Age*, 261; Eugene Murdock, *Ban Johnson, Czar of Baseball* (Westport, C: Greenwood Press, 1984), 163.

50. *The Sporting News*, December 5, 1918.

51. www.fcb.com/index_main.html.

52. *New York Times*, May 31, 1952.

53. Alan Schwarz, "Uncle Albert," *National Pastime* (1997), 54.

54. John A. Garraty and Mark C. Carnes, *The American National Biography*, vol. 13 (New York: Oxford University Press, 1999), 221.

55. Short sketch of Albert Lasker in "Albert Lasker—Lord and Thomas" by American National Business Hall of Fame, Laureate Albert Lasker, *www.anbhf.org/laureates/lasker/html*, 3–4.

56. *New York Times*, May 31, 1952; Garraty and Carnes, *American National Biography*, 221–222; *Chicago Daily Tribune*, May 31, 1952.

57. John Gunther, *Taken at the Flood: The Story of Albert D. Lasker* (New York: Harper Brothers, 1960), 117.

58. Alan Schwarz, "Uncle Albert," 55.

59. Gunther, *Taken at the Flood*, 118–119.

60. In those days the World Series was the winner of five of nine games rather than four of seven.

61. Eliot Asinof, *Eight Men Out: The Black Sox and the 1919 World Series* (New York: Holt, Rinehart & Winston, 1963), 199.

62. Seymour, *Baseball: The Golden Age*, 312; Murdock, *Ban Johnson, Czar of Baseball*, 180.

63. Gunther, *Taken at the Flood*, 121; Schwarz, "Uncle Albert," 55; Seymour, *Baseball: The Golden Age*, 312; Lee Lowenfish, and Tony Lupien, *The Imperfect Diamond: The Story of Baseball's Reserve System and the Men Who Fought To Change It* (New York: Stein & Day, 1980) 98.

64. David Pietrusza, *Judge and Jury: The Life and Times of Judge Kenesaw Mountain Landis* (South Bend: Diamond Communication, 1998), 162; *New York Times*, October 17, 1920.

65. Schwarz, "Uncle Albert," 55; Seymour, *Baseball: The Golden Age*, 312.

66. *Washington Post*, November 9, 1920.

67. Youngblood, *The Early Life and Times of Barney Dreyfuss*, 11; Boxerman and Boxerman, *Ebbets to Veeck to Busch*, 46; Pietrusza, *Judge and Jury*, 162; Benjamin G. Rader, *Baseball: A History of America's Game* (Urbana: University of Illinois Press, 2002), 120.

68. Warren Brown, *The Chicago Cubs* (Carbondale: Southern Illinois University Press, 1946), 81; Burk, *Never Just a Game* , 235–236.

69. Frederick G. Lieb, *The Baseball Story* (New York: G. P. Putnam's Sons, 1950), 224–225.

70. Murdock, *Ban Johnson, Czar of Baseball*, 180; J. G. Taylor Spink, *Judge Landis and Twenty-Five Years of Baseball* (Garden City Park, NY: Thomas Y. Crowell1947), 67.

71. Frank G. Menke, *Sport Tales and Anecdotes* (New York: A. S. Barnes, 1953), 57; Brown, *The Chicago Cubs*, 81.

72. Schwarz, "Uncle Albert," 56.

73. Gunther, *"Taken at the Flood*, 123.

74. "The International Jew," www.adl.org.

75. *Dearborn Independent*, September 3, 1921.

76. *Ibid.*, September 10, 1921.

77. *www.jewishsports.net/BioPages/Barney Dreyfuss.htm.*

78. Thorn et al., *Total Baseball*, 2118.

79. Postal et al., *Encyclopedia of Jews in Sports*, 29.

80. *The Sporting News*, January 20, 1927.

81. *Press Sports*, April 27, 1961.

82. Smizik, *The Pittsburgh Pirates*, 49; Lieb, *The Pittsburgh Pirates*, 242; John McCollister, *The Bucs: The Story of the Pittsburgh Pirates* (Lenexa, KS: Addax Publishing,1998), 99; Slater, *Great Jews in Sports*, 64.

83. Rita J. Simon, *In the Golden Land: A Century of Russian and Soviet Jewish Immigration in America* (Westport, CT: Praegers, 1997), 112.

84. Lieb, *The Pittsburgh Pirates*, 243–244; Youngblood, *The Early Life and Times of Barney Dreyfuss*, 12.

85. Postal et al., *Encyclopedia of Jews in Sports*, 29; Slater, *Great Jews in Sports*, 64.

86. *The Sporting News*, December 9, 1985.

87. *Pittsburgh Post-Gazette*, May 29, 1932.

88. *The New York Times*, May 31, 1952.

89. Garraty & Carnes, *American National Biography*, 221; www.adage.com/century/people.

90. Gunther, *Taken at the Flood*, 80.

91. *The New York Times*, May 31, 1952.

Chapter 6

1. Hasia R. Diner, *A Time For Gathering; The Second Migration 1820-1880* (Baltimore: Johns Hopkins University Press,1992), 233.

2. Moses Rischin, *The Jews of North America* (Detroit: Wayne State University Press, 1987), 26–28; Milton M. Gordon, *Assimilation in American Life* (New York: Oxford University Press, 1964), 184–185.

3. Rischin, *The Jews of North America*, 26–28; Gordon, *Assimilation in American Life*, 184–185.

4. Hertzberg, *The Jews in America*, 175–176; "Riess, "From Pike to Green with Greenberg in Between," 119.

5. Steven A. Riess (ed.), *Sports and the American Jew* (Syracuse: Syracuse University Press, 1998), 14.

6. Higham, *Strangers in the Land*, 67, 93.

7. Edward J. Rielly, *Baseball: An Encyclopedia of Popular Culture* (Santa Barbara: ABC-CLIO, Inc., 2000), 148.

8. Steven A. Riess, *City Games: The Evolution of American Urban Society and the Rise of Sports* (Urbana: University of Illinois Press, 1989), 16, 104; Baldassaro and Johnson, *The American Game*, 123; Dann Halem, *Jews on First*, slate.msn.com, 3.

9. Riess, *Sports and the American Jew*, 15.

10. Riess, *City Games*, 104.

11. Irving Howe and Kenneth Libo, *How We Lived: A Documentary History of Immigrant Jews in America 1880-1930* (New York, 1979), 51–52.

12. Riess, "From Pike to Green with Greenberg in Between," 122.

13. John M. Hoberman, "Why Jews Play Sports: Do Sport and Jewish Values Conflict?" *Moment* (April 1991): 38.

14. Stephen A. Riess, *Touching Base: Professional Baseball and American Culture in the Progressive Era* (Westport, CT: Greenwood Press, 1980), 188; Hoberman, "Why Jews Play Sports" *Moment*, 38.

15. Riess, *Sports and the American Jew*, 16.

16. Riess, *City Games*, 104; Riess, "From Pike to Green with Greenberg in Between," 123; Dann Halem, *Jews on First*, slate.msn.com, 3; Riess, *Touching Base*, 190.

17. Frederic Cople Joher, "Anti-Semitism in American Athletics," *Shofar* (Fall 2001): 69; John E. Dreifort (ed.), *Baseball History From Outside the Lines: A Reader* (Lincoln: University of Nebraska Press, 2001), 41–42; Riess, *Touching Base*, 189.

Chapter 7

1. Peter Levine, *Ellis Island to Ebbets Field: Sport and the American Jewish Experience* (New York, 1992), 100.

2. Ira Berkow, "In David's Footsteps," *Forward* (February 6, 2004): 2.

3. Spaner, "From Greenberg to Green: Jewish Ballplayers," 172.

4. Burk, *Never Just a Game*, 171.

5. *Los Angeles Times*, May 2, 1902.

6. *San Francisco Chronicle*, undated clipping, files *The Sporting News*; Horvitz and Horvitz, *The Big Book of Jewish Baseball*, 92.

7. *The Sporting News* , July 26, 1902 quoted in Postal et al., *Encyclopedia of Jews in Sports*, 27.

8. www.stat-junkie.com/pitcher.

9. Sketch of Harry Kane, December 30, 1905, Harry Kane Files, Baseball Hall of Fame, Cooperstown, New York.

10. Palmer and Gillette, *The 2006 ESPN Baseball Encyclopedia*, 983; Horvith and Horvith, *The Big Book of Jewish Baseball*, 92.

11. Palmer and Gillette, *The 2006 ESPN Baseball Encyclopedia*, 983.

12. *Washington Post*, August 12, 1906.

13. Postal et al., *The Encyclopedia of Jews In Sports*, 41.

14. Unnamed, undated 1931 clipping, Harry Kane files, Hall of Fame, Cooperstown, New York.

15. Unnamed clipping, September 22, 1932, Harry Kane files, Baseball Hall of Fame, Cooperstown, New York.

16. *Ibid.*

17. *The Washington Post*, May 8, 1910.

18. *Los Angeles Times*, April 13, 1909.

19. Unnamed, undated clipping Phil Cooney Files, Baseball Hall of Fame, Cooperstown, New York.

20. Palmer and Gillette, *The 2006 ESPN Baseball Encyclopedia*, 139; Horvitz and Horvitz, *The Big Book of Jewish Baseball*, 51.

21. *www.baseball-reference.com*; sportsillustrated.cnn.com/baseball; Horvitz and Horvitz; *The Big Book of Jewish Baseball*, 38.

22. Dorothy Corey Pinager to Bill Haber, May 11, 1980, Ed Corey Files, Baseball Hall of Fame, Cooperstown, New York.

23. Unnamed, undated clipping, Ed Corey File, Baseball Hall of Fame, Cooperstown, New York.

24. *Kenosha News*, April 22, 1980.

25. Unnamed, undated clipping, Ed Corey Files, Baseball Hall of Fame, Cooperstown, New York.

26. *The Sporting News*, April 4, 1918.

27. Horvitz and Horvitz, *The Big Book of Jewish Baseball*, 51; *www.baseball-reference.com*; sportsillustrated.cnn.com/baseball; Palmer and Gillette, *The Encyclopedia of Baseball*, 835.

28. *Chicago Daily Tribune*, May 1, 1932.

29. *Kenosha News*, September 17, 1970.

30. Horvitz and Horvitz, *The Big Book of Jewish Baseball*, 23.

31. *The London Free Press*, November 12, 2003.

32. Horvitz and Horvitz, *The Big Book of Jewish Baseball*, 23.

33. Slater, *Great Jews in Sports*, 194; Thorn et al., *Total Baseball*, 2153.

34. Information provided by Christopher Williams and Robert W. Bigelow for part of a book on the Dead-ball Era. (Hereafter referred to as Williams and Bigelow).

35. Legends of the Game-Barney Pelty, *www.deadball.com/peltybar.htm*, 1.

36. *St. Louis Post-Dispatch*, May 25, 1939; Thorn et al., *Total Baseball*, 2153.

37. Barney Pelty Statistics www, baseball-reference.com.

38. *The Washington Post*, October 10, 1903.

39. Williams and Bigelow, *Barney Pelty*, 2.

40. *The Washington Post*, October 31, 1906.

41. Williams and Bigelow, *Barney Pelty*, 2.

42. Thorn et al., *Total Baseball*, 2153.

43. *Ibid.*

44. Comiskey Park Firsts—*www.retrosheet.org/ballparks/comiskey_park.htm*; *The Washington Times*, July 1, 1997.

45. *New York Times*, December 4, 1910; Thorn et al., *Total Baseball*, 2153.

46. *The Washington Post*, June 12, 1912.

47. *Ibid.*, August 14, 1912.

48. *Ibid.*, June 17, 1912.

49. Thorn et al., *Total Baseball*, 2153; Williams and Bigelow, *Barney Pelty*, 3; Slater, *Great Jews in Sports*, 195.

50. Barney Pelty to Garry Herrmann, September 6, 1912, Pelty Files, Baseball Hall of Fame, Cooperstown, New York.

51. Slater, *Great Jews in Sports*, 195.

52. Williams and Bigelow, *Bernard Pelty*, 4; Horvitz and Horvitz, *The Big Book of Jewish Baseball*, 131.

53. Postal et al., *Encyclopedia of Jews in Sports*, 44; Simon, *In the Golden Land*, 112; .Horvitz and Horvitz, *The Big Book of Jewish Baseball*, 116.

54. Lyle Spatz, *Erskine Mayer*, part of SABR's Baseball Biography Project, found on bioproj.sabr.org; Harold U. Ribalow and Meir Z. Ribalow, *Jewish Baseball Stars* (New York: Hippocrene Books, 1984), 22.

55. Postal et al., *The Encyclopedia of Jews in Sports*, 46; Ward Mason, "Alexander's Right Hand Man: Erskine Mayer, the Phillies' Second Best Bet—His Great Record and the Secret of His Success," *Baseball Magazine* (November 1915): 70.

56. *The Sporting News*, March 20, 1957; *Atlanta Constitution*, March 22, 1934.

57. Erskine Mayer, www.geocities.com; ESPN Classic—All Time Stats—Erskine Mayer—sports.espn.gocom., 1; Erskine Mayer Statistics, *www.baseball-reference.com.*, 1; cnn/si-Baseball-Erskine Mayer,sportsillustrated.cnn.com, 1.

58. Postal et al., *The Cyclopedia of Jews in Sports*, 46; Harold U. Ribalow and Meir Z. Ribalow, *Jewish Baseball Stars*, 213.

59. This Date in Baseball—June 9th.*www.nationalpastime.com*. (Wagner would also become the first player in the major leagues to reach the century mark in home runs and this feat would also be accomplished against Erskine Mayer).

60. Steve Gietschier (ed.), *The Sporting News Complete Baseball Record Book* (St. Louis: Sporting News, 2005), 44.

61. Postal et al., *Encyclopedia of Jews in Sports*, 46.

62. The Sporting News—Baseball History of the World Series, *www.sportingnews.com/archives*; www.mlb.com.

63. Thorn et al., *Total Baseball*, 345.

64. Postal et al., *Encyclopedia of Jews in Sports*, 46.

65. *Ibid.,.*

66. *Chicago Daily Tribune*, June 20, 1918.

67. Ribalow and Ribalow, *Jewish Baseball Stars*, 24–25.

68. *Ibid.*, 24.

69. Thorn et al., *Total Baseball*, 349; Horvitz and Horvitz, *The Big Book of Jewish Baseball*, 116.

70. H. L. Stallard, "Players Who Have Starred with Both Leagues in World's Series," *Baseball Magazine* (November 1926): 542.

71. B. P. Robert Stephen Silverman, *The 100 Greatest Jews in Sports: Ranked According to Achievement* (Lanham, MD: Scarecrow, 2003), 85.

72. Horvitz and Horvitz, *The Big Book of Jewish Baseball*, 116.

73. Ribalow and Ribalow, *Jewish Baseball Stars*, 25; Postal et al., *The Encyclopedia of Jews in Sports*, 47.

74. Thorn et al., *Total Baseball*, 2082.

75. *Atlanta Constitution*, March 15, 1934.

76. Horvitz and Horvitz, *The Big Book of Jewish Baseball*, 117; *Washington Post*, August 27, 1915.

77. Sportsillustrated.cnn.com; Palmer and Gillette, *The 2006 ESPN Baseball Encyclopedia*, 426.

78. Horvitz and Horvitz, *The Big Book of Jewish Baseball*, 117.

79. *Ibid.*

80. *Atlanta Constitution*, March 14, 1934; *Washington Post*, July 2, 1918.

81. Horvitz and Horvitz, *The Big Book of Jewish Baseball*, 118; *Atlanta Journal*, July 2, 1962.

82. *Atlanta Journal*, July 2, 1962.

83. *The Sporting News*, September 12,1935.

84. Postal et al., *The Encyclopedia of Jews In Sports*, 51.

85. Horvitz and Horvitz, *The Big Book of Jewish Baseball*, 136.

86. Postal et al., *The Encyclopedia of Jews in Sports*, 51.

87. *The New York Times*, May 23, 1917; *The Washington Post*, May 23, 1917.

88. Jake Pitler Statistics—*www.baseball-reference.com*; Palmer and Gillette, *The 2006 ESPN Baseball Encyclopedia*, 530.

89. *The Washington Post*, August 11, 1927; Horvitz, *The Big Book of Jewish Baseball*, 137.

90. *The Sporting News*, April 20, 1939.

91. *New York Times*, October 2, 1986; Jeff Merron, "Green, Koufax and Greenberg—same dilemma, different decisions, espn.go.com.

92. Postal et al., *The Encyclopedia of Jews in Sports*, 51.

93. Levine, *Ellis Island to Ebbets Field*, 124.

94. *New York Times*, February 4, 1968.

95. Copy of Manuel's statistics compiled by grandson Mark G. Manuel, Manuel Files, Baseball Hall of Fame, Cooperstown, New York.

96. John Manuel to John Duxbury, July 20, 1978, Moxie Manuel File, *The Sporting News*, St. Louis, Missouri.

97. Horvitz and Horvitz, *The Big Book of Jewish Baseball*, 111.

98. Letter John Manuel to Clifford Kachline, May 22, 1972, Moxie Manuel File, Baseball Hall of Fame, Cooperstown, New York.

99. *New Orleans States Item*, February 28, 1967; unnamed, undated newspaper clipping, Moxie Manuel File, Baseball Hall of Fame, Cooperstown, New York.

100. Horvitz and Horvitz, *The Big Book of Jewish Baseball*, 111.

101. Palmer and Gillette, *The 2006 ESPN Baseball Encyclopedia*, 1035.

102. Murdock, *Ban Johnson*, 90–91. (It is unclear if "Manuel Rule" was commonly used to refer to the rule or if it is simply the author's name for it); Mark Manuel, "That Ball's on the Queer!" *The Baseball Research Journal* (1997): 114.

103. Letter John Manuel to Clifford Kachline, May 22, 1972, Moxie Manuel File, Baseball Hall of Fame, Cooperstown, New York.

104. Thorn, *Total Baseball*, 1771, 2289, 2299.

105. Copy of Manuel's Statistics in Manuel Files, Baseball Hall of Fame.

106. Horvitz and Horvitz, *The Big Book of Jewish Baseball*, 112.

107. *Ibid.*, 191.

108. Guy Zinn's Professional Batting Record in Zinn File, Baseball Hall of Fame, Cooperstown, New York; *The Washington Post*, August 20, 1911.

109. Shatzkin, *The Ballplayers*, 1224.

110. Guy Zinn, www.jewsinsports.org, 1.

111. Unnamed clipping, dated October 24, 1912, Zinn File, Baseball Hall of Fame, Cooperstown, New York.

112. *New York Times*, January 16, 1914.

113. Terrapin Park Firsts, *www.retrosheet.org*, 1.

114. Federal League, *www.toyou.com*; Palmer and Gillette, *The 2006 ESPN Baseball Encyclopedia*, 734.

115. *The Washington Post*, July 13, 1914.

116. Palmer and Gillette, *The 2006 ESPN Baseball Encyclopedia*, 734.

117. Horvitz and Horvitz, *The Big Book of Jewish Baseball*, 192; Zinn Professional Batting Record, Zinn File, Baseball Hall of Fame, Cooperstown, New York.

118. *The Sporting News*, Oct. 12, 1949.

Chapter 8

1. 1880 United States Census, *www.family* search. org.

2. *The Weekly Sentinel*, October 2, 1912.

3. John Ackenbruck, *Twentieth Century History of Fort Wayne* (Fort Wayne, 1975), 176–177; Horvitz and Horvitz, *The Big Book of Jewish Baseball*, 83; Postal et al., *Encyclopedia of Jews in Sports*, 31. .

4. Rob Raines, *The St. Louis Cardinals: The 100th Anniversary History* (New York: 1992), 9; Boxerman and Boxerman, *Ebbets to Veeck to Busch*, 55.

5. Rains, *The St. Louis Cardinals*, 11; Horvitz and Horvitz, *The Big Book of Jewish Baseball*, 83.

6. Postal et al., *The Encyclopedia of Jews In Sports*, 31.

7. *Fort Wayne Journal Gazette*, December 24, 1933.

8. Unnamed clipping, December 28, 1933, Heilbroner File, Baseball Hall of Fame, Cooperstown, New York.

9. Palmer and Gillette, *The 2006 ESPN Baseball Encyclopedia*, 1283.

10. Horvitz and Horvitz, *The Big Book of Jewish Baseball*, 83; Postal et al., *The Encyclopedia of Jews in Sports*, 31.

11. *Atlanta Constitution*, May 2, 1911.

12. Horvitz and Horvitz, *The Big Book of Jewish Baseball*, 83; Postal et al., *The Encyclopedia of Jews in Sports*, 31.

13. *Fort Wayne Daily News*, January 26, 1907.

14. *Ibid.*, September 10, 1913.

15. *Fort Wayne Journal Gazette*, December 24, 1933.

16. Unnamed, undated clipping found in archives of Allen County Library, Fort Wayne, Indiana; *Fort Wayne News Sentinel, December 31, 1933*.

17. *New York Times*, May 20, 1948; *The Sporting News*, January 15, 1939.

18. *The Sporting News*, January 15, 1939.

19. Alan Schwarz, *The Numbers Game* (New York: St. Martin's Press, 2004), 39.

20. *The Sporting News*, January 5, 1939; Schwarz, *The Numbers Game*, 40.

21. August, 1939, *www.baseballlibrary.com*; Al Munro Elias, www.jewishsports.net.

22. Herbert Simons, "Counting the Hits That Count," *Baseball Magazine* (November 1942): 566.

23. Schwarz, *The Money Game*, 40.

24. Postal and Silver, *The Encyclopedia of Jews In Sports*, 39.

25. Harold (Speed) Johnson, *Who's Who in Major League Baseball* (Chicago, 1933), 512; *The Sporting News*, January 5, 1939.

26. F. C. Lane, "Why Baseball Statisticians Get Prematurely Gray Headed," *Baseball Magazine*, (March 1928), 469–470.

27. Rich Kenda, "*Where Do Those Crazy Statistics Come From?*" USA Today Baseball Weekly, found on *www.usatoday.com*, 12/12/2001.

28. Schwarz, *The Numbers Game*, 41; Kenda, "Where Do Those Crazy Statistics Come From?"

29. Schwarz, *The Numbers Game*, 40;

30. F. C. Lane, "The Wizard of the Dopes," *Baseball Magazine* (April 1923): 510.

31. Schwarz, *The Numbers Game*, 41.

32. Unnamed newspaper clipping, August 2, 1939, Elias Files, Baseball Hall of Fame, Cooperstown, New York.

33. *The Sporting News*, May 26, 1948.

Chapter 9

1. *Cleveland Jewish News.com*, April 29, 2005.

2. David Ewen, *The American Songwriters* (New York: H.W. Wilson, 1987), 409; "Albert Von Tilzer: His Life and Music," parlorsongs.com/2004.

3. "Albert Von Tilzer: His Life and Music"; *New York Times*, October 21, 1956; Albert Von Tilzer Biography, www.songwritershalloffame.org.

4. "Albert Von Tilzer: His Life and Music"; Kenneth Aaron Kanter, *The Jews on Tin Pan Alley: The Jewish Contribution to American Popular Music, 1830–1940* (New York, 1982), 117.

5. "Take Me Out to the Ballgame," from wikipedia, the free encyclopedia. enwikidipia.org; Eden, *American Songwriters*, 409

6. "Take Me Out to the Ballgame, en.wikipedia.org.

7. *New York Times*, October 21, 1956.

8. "Baseball's Anthem For All Ages," www.smithsonianmag.si.edu

9. "Albert Von Tilzer, Tin Pan Alley Pioneer,"parlorsongs.com., 4–5.

10. Eden, *American Songwriters*, 410.

11. *Christian Science Monitor*, April 2, 2004.

12. "Baseball's Anthem For All Ages." *www.smithsonian* mag. si.edu

Chapter 10

1. Riess, "From Pike to Green with Greenberg in Between," 134.

2. 1931 newspaper clipping in possession of authors.

3. George V. Touhey, *A History of the Boston Baseball Club*, 235.

4. Twentieth Anniversary Report of the Secretary of the Class of 1881 of Harvard College, (1906),98.

5. Tuohey, *A History of the Boston Baseball Club*, 235.

6. Undated issue *Boston Traveler*, files *Boston Traveler* newspapers, Boston, Massachusetts.

7. Untitled newspaper clipping, January 27, 1942, in possession of authors.

8. Shatzkin, *The Ballplayers*, 764; Palmer and Gillette, *The 2006 ESPN Baseball Encyclopedia*, 1641; Profile of Jacob Morse found in newspaper clipping dated October 1915; name of paper unknown; clipping in possession of authors; untitled newspaper clipping Jan. 27, 1942.

9. Untitled newspaper clipping January 27, 1942.

10. Post.gazette.com, June 2, 2003.

11. Harvard College Class of 1881 Fiftieth Anniversary (Printed for the Class) Cambridge, 1931).

12. Untitled newspaper clipping, January 27, 1942; Albert Nelson Marquis (ed.), *Who's Who in New England* (Chicago: A.N. Marquis & Co., 1916), 766.

13. Lee Lowenfish and Tony Lupien, *The Imperfect Diamond*, 74

14. Douglas Wallop, *Baseball: An Informal History* (New York: W.W. Norton, 1969), 21–22.

15. Postal et al., *The Encyclopedia of Jews in Sports*, 32.

16. Fortieth Annual Report of the Secretary of the Class of 1881 of Harvard College, 170.

17. Unnamed clipping dated October 31, 1915, in possession of authors; Kathryn Allamong Jacob and Bruce A. Ragsdale (Eds.), *Biographical Directory of the United States Congress, 1774–1989*, (Washington, D.C., 1989), 1540.

18. Unnamed clipping dated October 4, 1915, in possession of authors.

19. Unnamed clipping dated January 25, 1923, in possession of authors; Unnamed clipping, dated 1931; in possession of authors.

20. *Boston Traveler*, September 30, 1933; March 30, 1934.

21. *The Sporting News*, April 22, 1937; *Boston Traveler*, April 12, 1937.

22. *Boston Traveler*, undated clipping.

23. Jerome Holtzman, *No Cheering in the Press Box* (New York: Holt, Rinehart & Winston, 1974), 4.

24. Fred J. Cook, "Dan Daniel's Golden Years in Baseball," *World Telegram and Sun Saturday Magazine*, (September 24, 1955), 14.

25. *The Sporting News*, February 10, 1954.

26. *The Sporting News*, January 31, 1935 quoted in John A. Garraty and Mark C. Carnes, 85; Holtzman, *No Cheering in the Press Box*, 10–11.

27. *The Sporting News*, March 19, 1958; David Voigt, *The* League That Failed (Lanham, MD: Scarecrow, 1998), 257–258.

28. *New York Times*, July 5, 1981.

29. Dan Yates to authors, October 6, 2005; www.baseballlibrary.com.

30. Holtzman, *No Cheering in the Press Box*, 5.

31. Garraty and Carnes, *American National Biography*, 86.

32. *Ibid.*

33. *Ibid.*

34. Richard Ben Cramer, *Joe DiMaggio: The Hero's Life* (New York: Simon& Schuster, 2000), 80–81.

35. *Ibid.*, 81.

36. *New York Times*, July 5, 1981; Holtzman, *No Cheering in the Press Box*, 13.

37. Cook, "Dan Daniel's Golden Years in Baseball, 15.

38. Garraty and Carnes, *American National Biography*, 86.

39. Holtzman, *No Cheering in the Press Box*, 5.

40. Cramer, *Joe DiMaggio: The Hero's Life*, 81.

41. Roger Kahn, *The Era 1947-1957: When the Yankees, the Giants, and the Dodgers Ruled the World* (New York: Ticknor & Fields, 1993), 71; *The Sporting News*, March 5, 1952, quoted in Garaty and Carnes, *American National Biography*, 86.

42. Cramer, *Joe DiMaggio: The Hero's Life*, 83–84.

43. *Cincinnati Post*, June 24, 2002.

44. *The Sporting News*, December 18, 1941.

45. Holtzman, *No Cheering in the Press Box*, 12.

46. Levine, *Ellis Island to Ebbets Field*, 130.

47. Jules Tygiel, *Baseball's Great Experiment* (New York: Oxford University Press, 1997), 178.

48. *Ibid.*,295.

49. *Ibid.*, 335.

50. *The Sporting News*, January 21, 1959.

51. *Ibid.*, December 9, 1972.

52. Bob Broeg to authors, November 21, 2004.

53. Richard Orodenker (ed.), *Twentieth Century American Sportswriters* (Detroit: Gale Research, 1996), 275; *Washington Post*, June 5, 1998.

54. Orodenker, *Twentieth Century American Sportswriters*, 275; Holtzman, *No Cheering in the Press Box*, 116. Povich often stated that Shirley was a masculine name until the 1900s. He never thought of it as a feminine name until he read of Shirley Booth and Shirley Temple.

55. Orodenker, *Twentieth Century American Sportswriters*, 275; *Washington Post*, June 5, 1998; Ralph Berger, "Shirley Povich," 1, found in bioproj.sabr.cfm

56. *Washington Post*, April 1, 2003.

57. Holtzman, *No Cheering in the Press Box*, 122.

58. David A. Nathan, "Reading and Remembering Shirley Povich," paper delivered at the North American Society for Sports History, Penn State University, May 24, 1999.

59. Orodenker, *Twentieth Century American Sportswriters*, 276.

60. *Washington Post*, April 1, 2003.

61. Reilly, *Baseball: An Encyclopedia of Popular Culture*), 236; Berger, "Shirley Povich," 2; *Editor and Publisher*, (June 20, 1998), 75.

62. Berger, "Shirley Povich," 3; *Washington Post*, June 4, 1999.

63. *Washington Post*, June 4, 1999.

64. Berger, "Shirley Povich," 3.

65. *Washington Post*, October 15, 1997.

66. *Ibid.*

67. Bob Broeg to Authors, November 21, 2004.

68. Berger, "Povich," 5.

69. *Augusta Chronicle*, June 6, 1998.

70. *Washington Post*, June 5, 1998.

71. *New York Times*, June 7, 1998.

72. Stephen H. Norwood and Harold Brackman, "Going to Bat for Jackie Robinson: The Jewish Role in Breaking the Color Line," *Journal of Sport History* (Spring 1999): 122.

73. Lawrence S. Katz, *Baseball in 1939: The Watershed Season of the National Pastime* (Jefferson, N.C.: McFarland, 1995), 143; Glenn Dickey, *The History of the National League Baseball Since 1876* (New York, 1979), 155–156; Tygiel, *Baseball's Great Experiment*, 35.

74. *Washington Post*, October 15, 1997.

75. Orodenker, *Twentieth Century American Sportswriters*, 278.

76. Dale A. Evans, "Late in the Game: The Integration of the Washington Senators," *The National Pastime* (2002), 46. Povich was referring to the fact that Griffith hired many dark-skinned players from the Caribbean, but no African-Americans.

77. Evans, "Late in the Game," 46; Orodenker, *Twentieth Century American Sportswriters*, 279.

78. Nathan, "Reading and Remembering Shirley Povich"; Orodenker, *Twentieth Century American Sportswriters*, 279.

79. Nathan, "Reading and Remembering Shirley Povich."

80. *The Sporting News*, September 26, 1964.

81. *www.baseballhalloffame.org*; Orodenker, *Twentieth Century Sportswriters*, 1996.

82. *Washington Post*, June 4, 1999.

83. Reilly, *Baseball: An Encyclopedia of Popular Culture*, 236; Berger, "Shirley Povich," 2; *Editor and Publisher*, (June 20, 1998), 75.

84. *Washington Post*, June 5, 1999.

Chapter 11

1. Levine, *Ellis Island to Ebbets Field*, 106.

2. Higham, *Strangers in the Land*, 280.

3. *Ibid.*, 285–286.

4. Hasia R. Diner, *The Jews of the United States 1654 to 2000* (Berkeley: The University of California Press, 2004), 209.

5. Riess, "From Pike to Greenberg," 123.

6. Daniel A. Nathan, "Anti-Semitism and the Black Sox Scandal," *Nine* (December 1995): 94–99.

7. Levine, *Ellis Island to Ebbets Field*, 106–107.

8. G. Edward White, *Creating the National Pastime: Baseball Transforms Itself 1903–1953* (Princeton: Princeton University Press, 1996), 253.

9. Riess, "From Pike to Greenberg," 126.

10. *Ibid.*, 127; Palmer and Gillette, *The 2006 ESPN Baseball Encyclopedia*, 1060.

11. Horvitz and Horvitz, *The Big Book of Jewish Baseball*, 57.

12. *USA Today Weekly*, December 2–15, 1992; Palmer and Gillette, *The 2006 ESPN Baseball Encyclopedia*, 829.

13. *Asbury Park (NJ) Press*, July 15, 1987.

14. *Ibid.*

15. Joe Bennett, *www.jewsinsports.org.*, 1.

16. Horvitz and Horvitz, *The Big Book of Jewish Baseball*, 37.

17. *Ibid.*

18. Bohne's Statistical Sheet, Sam Bohne File, *The Sporting News* Archives, St. Louis, Missouri.

19. *The Sporting News*, September 9, 1920.

20. Palmer and Gillette, *The 2006 ESPN Baseball Encyclopedia*, 65; Sam Bohne, *www.jewsinsports.org.*, 1.; *New York Times*, December 12, 1921.

21. Palmer and Gillette, *The 2006 ESPN Baseball Encyclopedia*, 65; *San Francisco Sunday Evening and Chronicle*, December 4, 1966.

22. Palmer and Gillette, *The 2006 ESPN Baseball Encyclopedia*, 65; *San Francisco Sunday Evening and Chronicle*, December 4, 1966; Postal et al., *The Encyclopedia of Jews in Sports*, 37.

23. *Chicago Daily Tribune*, December 27, 1923; CNNSI.com.—Samuel Bohne Fieldfigstats. 1.

24. unnamed clipping, May 26, 1977, Bohne Files, Baseball Hall of Fame, Cooperstown, New York.

25. *The Sporting News*, December 6, 1923.

26. *Ibid.*, September 8, 1924.

27. F. C. Lane, "Why Not More Jewish Ball Players?" *Baseball Magazine* (January 1926), 341.

28. *Ibid.*

29. Palmer and Gillette, 65–66.

30. Horvitz and Horvitz, *The Big Book of Jewish Baseball*, 38.

31. Undated clipping, Bohne Files, Baseball Hall of Fame, Cooperstown, New York.

32. *The Sporting News*, July 15, 1994.

33. Postal et al., *Encyclopedia of Jews in Sports*, 70; James D. Smith III. "Jimmie Reese," *The Baseball Research Journal* (1995), 89

34. Jimmie Reese Statistical Sheet, Jimmie Reese Files, *The Sporting News Archives*, St. Louis, Missouri.

35. David Falkner, *The Short Season: The Hard Work and High Times of Baseball in the Spring* (New York, 1986), 43.

36. *Ibid. 43–44.*

37. Falkner, *The Short Season*, 44.

38. *Futility Infielder—The Clubhouse Lawyer,www.futili tyinfielder.com*, 1.

39. Horvitz and Horvitz, *The Big Book of Jewish Baseball*, 140.

40. *U.S.A. Today Baseball Weekly*, July 20–26, 1994.

41. Smith, " "Jimmie Reese," 90.

42. *St. Louis Star and Times*, September 1, 1932.

43. Thorn et al., *Total Baseball*, 1562.

44. A fungo is a ball hit for fielding practice by throwing it up in the air and hitting it as it comes down.

45. *New York Times*, April 8, 1980; *Staten Island Advance*, September 12, 2004; *www.jewishf.com;www.jewsweek.com*; untitled obit clipping, July 23, 1994, Jimmie Reese Files, Baseball Hall of Fame Files, Cooperstown, New York.

46. *Orange County Register*, July 14, 1979.

Chapter 12

1. Ron Berler, "Let's Hear It For the Rabbi of Swat," *Sports Illustrated* (October 21, 1991), 108A; Howard Lavelle, "Moses Solomon, the Rabbi of Swat," *Baseball Research Journal* (1976), 90.

2. Berler, "Let's Hear It for the Rabbi of Swat," 108A; Dewey and Acocella, *The Biographical History of Baseball*, 433.

3. Solomon's statistical sheet in Solomon Files, Baseball Hall of Fame, Cooperstown, New York.

4. *American Hebrew*, September 14, 1923, 462; *The Sporting News*, September 6, 1923; Levine, *Ellis Island to Ebbets Field*, 110.

5. White, *Creating the National Pastime*, 253.

6. Louis Jacobson, "Will the Real Rabbi of Swat Please Stand Up?" *Baseball Research Journal* (1989), 17.

7. Horvitz and Horvitz, *The Big Book of Jewish Baseball*, 178.

8. Jacobson, "Will the Real Rabbi of Swat Please Stand Up?" 18.

9. Joseph Solomon to Authors, February 16, 2005.

10. Statistical Data Mose Solomon File, Baseball Hall of Fame, Cooperstown, New York.

11. Joseph Solomon to Authors, February 16, 2005; Horvitz and Horvitz, *The Big Book of Jewish Baseball*, 178.

12. Horvitz and Horvitz, *The Big Book of Jewish Baseball*, 178.

13. Berler, " Let's Hear It For the Rabbi of Swat," 108A.

14. *Ibid.*

15. Lavelle, "Moses Solomon, the Rabbi of Swat," 91.

16. *New York Times*, September 30, 1923.

17. Berler, "Let's Hear It For the Rabbi of Swat," 109A.

18. Horvitz and Horvitz, *The Big Book of Jewish Baseball*, 178; Palmer and Gillette, *The 2006 ESPN Baseball Encyclopedia*, 624.

19. White, *Creating the National Pastime*, 253; Horvitz and Horvitz, *The Big Book of Jewish Baseball*, 178–179; *The Sporting News*, February 7, 1924.

20. Joseph Solomon to Authors, February 16, 2005.

21. *The Sporting News*, Feb 28, 1929.

22. Jacobson, "Will the Real Rabbi of Swat Please Stand Up?" 18.

23. *Miami Herald*, June 26, 1966.

24. Berler, "Let's Hear It for the Rabbi of Swat," 109A.

25. *Los Angeles Times*, April 11, 1926; *Washington Post*, May 16, 1926; *Chicago Daily Tribune*, May 17. 1926; Riess, "From Pike to Green with Greenberg in Between," 125.

26. Andy Cohen Interview, New York Public Library, American Jewish Committee Oral History (hereafter to be called the Andy Cohen Interview).

27. Andy Cohen Interview

28. Interview Marina Lee with Authors, March 28, 2005.

29. Andy Cohen Interview.

30. Ribalow and Ribalow, *Jewish Baseball Stars*, 31; Bill Simons, "Andy Cohen: Second Baseman As Ethnic Hero," *National Pastime* (1990): 84.

31. Bill Simons, "Andy Cohen: Second Baseman As Ethnic Hero," 86.

32. *Ibid.*, 84.

33. Levine, *Ellis Island to Ebbets Field*, 110; White, *Creating the National Pastime*, 254.

34. Horvitz and Horvitz, *The Big Book of Baseball*, 46.

35. Palmer and Gillette, *The 2006 ESPN Baseball Encyclopedia*, 129.

36. Andy Cohen Interview.

37. Postal et al., *The Encyclopedia of Jews in Sports*, 38; Ray Sanchez, *El Paso's Greatest Sports Heroes I Have Known* (El Paso: Senturiano Press, 1989), 46; Horvitz and Horvitz, *The Big Book of Baseball*, 46.

38. *The New York Times*, July 13, 1927.

39. Andy Cohen Interview.

40. Riess, "From Pike to Green with Greenberg in Between," 125.

41. Charles Alexander, *John McGraw* (New York: Viking, 1988), 283; Levine, *Ellis Island to Ebbets Field*, 111; *Time* (April 23, 1928): 26–27; Eugene C. Murdock, *Mighty Casey All-American* (Westport, CT: Greenwood, 1984), 105; "One Baseball Hour To Live, *Baseball Magazine* (March 1937), 448.

42. *Chicago Daily Tribune*, April 12, 1928; *New York Times*, April 12, 1928; Levine, *Ellis Island to Ebbets Field*, 111.

43. Andy Cohen Interview; Richard C. Crepau, *Baseball: America's Diamond Mine 1919-1941* (Orlando: University Press of Florida, 1980), 166; White, *National Pastime*, 254.

44. Andy Cohen Interview; Postal et al., *The Encyclopedia of Jews in Sports*, 38; Robert J. Slater, *Great Jews in Sports*, 51.

45. *Chicago Tribune*, April 13, 1928; *American Hebrew*, April 20, 1928 quoted in Levine, *Ellis Island to Ebbets Field*, 112.

46. Levine, *Ellis Island to Ebbets Field*, 112–113; Simons, "Andy Cohen: Second Baseman as Ethnic Hero," 85–86.

47. Simons, "Andy Cohen: Second Baseman as Ethnic Hero," 84–85; Marina Nickerson, "Andy Cohen: El Paso's 'Mr. Baseball,'" *Texas Country* (April 1981): 30.

48. Andy Cohen Interview; Ribalow and Ribalow, *Jewish Baseball Stars*, 33; Simons, "Andy Cohen: Second Baseman as Ethnic Hero," 85.

49. Thorn et al., *Total Baseball*, 1307.

50. Dewey and Acocella, *The Biographical History of Baseball*, 85; Slater, *Great Jews in Sports*, 52; Levine, *Ellis Island to Ebbets Field*, 113; Simon, *In the Golden Land*, 111; Palmer and Gillette, *The 2006 ESPN Baseball Encyclopedia*, 129.

51. Thorn et al., *Total Baseball*, 2421.

52. Andy Cohen Interview.

53. Telephone Interview with Marina Lee, March 28, 2005; Slater, *Great Jews in Sports*, 52; Simons, "Andy Cohen: Second Baseman As Ethnic Hero," 86; Ribalow and Ribalow, *Jewish Baseball Stars*, 33; Marina Lee to Authors, March 28, 2005; White, *Creating the National Pastime*, 255.

54. Ribalow and Ribalow, *Jewish Baseball Stars*, 33.

55. Andy Cohen Interview.

56. *The Sporting News*, November 23, 1929.

57. Andy Cohen Interview.

58. Levine, *Ellis Island to Ebbets Field*, 115.

59. *New York Times*, June 22, 1932; *The Sporting News*, April 5, 1934; April 2, 1936; Sanchez, *El Paso's Greatest Sports Heroes I Have Known*, 47.

60. Andy Cohen Interview; Sanchez, *El Paso's Greatest Sports Heroes I Have Known*, 47; Ribalow and Ribalow, *Jewish Baseball Stars*, 34.

61. Simons, "Andy Cohen: Second Baseman As Ethnic Hero," 87.

62. *Los Angeles Times*, November 30, 1954; November 3, 1955; November 9, 1956; *New York Times*, December 18, 1957.

63. *The Sporting News*, April 27, 1960.

64. Horvitz and Horvitz, *The Big Book of Baseball*, 47; Simons, "Andy Cohen: Second Baseman As Ethnic Hero," 87; Slater, *Great Jews in Sports*, 53.

65. Horvitz and Horvitz, *The Big Book of Baseball*, 47.

66. Andy Cohen Interview.

67. Horvitz and Horvitz, *The Big Book of Baseball*, 47.

68. Marina Nickerson "Andy Cohen: El Paso's 'Mr. Baseball,'" 29.

69. Andy Cohen Interview.

70. Levine, *Ellis Island to Ebbets Field*, 116.

71. Horvitz and Horvitz, *The Big Book of Baseball*, 150; Palmer and Gillette, *The 2006 ESPN Baseball Encyclopedia*, 572.

72. *Chicago Daily Tribune*, June 26, 1930.

73. Horvitz and Hovitz, *The Big Book of Baseball*, 149; Levine, *Ellis Island to Ebbets Field*, 120.

74. *Washington Post*, July 6, 1930; *Chicago Daily Tribune*, July 6, 1930; *Los Angeles Times*, July 6, 1930.

75. *New York Times*, April 24, 1931.

76. *The Sporting News*, August 20, 1931; November 28, 1935; unnamed, undated article, files of *The Sporting News*, St. Louis, Missouri; Horvitz and Horvitz, *The Big Book of Jewish Baseball*, 149.

77. *Los Angeles Times*, April 20, 1941.

78. *The Sporting News*, August 5, 1943
79. *Ibid.*, February 17, 1944.
80. Horvitz and Horvitz, *The Big Book of Jewish Baseball*, 149.

Chapter 13

1. Jack Kavanaugh, *Walter Johnson: A Life* (South Bend: Diamond Communication, 1995), 231.
2. David L. Porter (ed.), *Biographical Dictionary of American Sports* (New York: Greenwood Press, 1987), 413.
3. Levine, *Ellis Island to Ebbets Field*, 127.
4. Clifford Bloodgood, "Players You Ought To Know," *Baseball Magazine* (July 1926): 366; Postal et al., *The Encyclopedia of Jews in Sports*, 48; David Pietrusza, Matthew Silverman and Michael Gershman, *Baseball, The Biographical Encyclopedia* (Kingston, N.Y.: Sports Illustrated, 2000), 822; Buddy Myer, *www.jewsinsports.org*; Horvitz and Horvitz, *The Big Book of Jewish Baseball*, 124; Kavanaugh, *Walter Johnson, A Life*, 232.
5. Palmer and Gillette, *The 2006 ESPN Baseball Encyclopedia*, 481.
6. Horvitz and Horvitz, *The Big Book of Jewish Baseball*, 124; Postal et al., *The Encyclopedia of Jews in Sports*, 48; Pietrusza et al., *Baseball, The Biographical Encyclopedia*, 822; Thorn et al., *Total Baseball*, 355.
7. *The Washington Post*, June 13, 1926.
8. Kavanaugh, *Walter Johnson: A Life*, 232.
9. *The Washington Post*, March 22, 1927.
10. *Ibid.*, May 3, 1927.
11. *Ibid.*, May 4, 1927.
12. Shatzkin, *The Ballplayers*, 780; Buddy Myer, www.jewsinsports.org.
13. Horvitz and Horvitz, *The Big Book of Jewish Baseball*, 124; Palmer and Gillette, *The 2006 ESPN Baseball Encyclopedia*, 558.
14. *The Washington Post*, December 16, 1928; *Los Angeles Times*, December 16, 1928.
15. *The Sporting News*, July 30, 1952.
16. *Ibid.*, November 23, 1974.
17. Jonathan Mark, "Buddy, Can You Spare a Shrine," *The Jewish Week*, January 21, 2003.
18. Palmer and Gillette, *The 2006 ESPN Baseball Encyclopedia*, 481.
19. *The Washington Post*, March 28, 1932.
20. Thorn et al., *Total Baseball*, 363.
21. Burk, *Much More Than a Game*, 50.
22. Levine, *Ellis Island to Ebbets Field*, 126; Ribalow and Ribalow, *Jewish Baseball Stars*, 62; Horvitz and Horvitz, *The Big Book of Jewish Baseball*, 124–125; Postal et al., *The Encyclopedia of Jews in Sports*, 48; Ben Chapman, www.baseballpage.com. (Ironically, in the middle of the 1936 season, Ben Chapman would be Buddy Myer's teammate when the Yankees traded him to the Washington Senators in a straight exchange for Senator outfielder Jake Powell.)
23. Riess, "From Pike to Green with Greenberg in Between," 127.
24. Donald Honig, *Baseball Between the Lines: Baseball in the '40s and '50s As Told by the Men Who Played It* (New York: Coward-McCann, and Geoghegan, Inc., 1976), 69.
25. *Los Angeles Times*, October 1, 1935; Postal et al., *The Encyclopedia of Jews in Sports*, 48.
26. Horvitz and Horvitz, *The Big Book of Jewish Baseball*, 125.
27. Jonathan Eig, *Luckiest Man: The Life and Death of Lou Gehrig* (New York: Simon & Schuster, 2005), 206; *The Sporting News*, October 24, 1935.

28. Palmer and Gillette, *The 2006 ESPN Baseball Encyclopedia*, 481.
29. *New York Times*, October 8, 1941.
30. *The Washington Post*, October 8, 1941.
31. *The Sporting News*, November 16, 1974.
32. Shatzkin, *The Ballplayers*, 780; Buddy Myer, jewsinsports.org; Charles "Buddy" Myer, www.jewishsports.net.
33. Bill James, *The Bill James Historical Abstract* (New York: Free Press, 2001), 346 quoted in Horvitz and Horvitz, *The Big Book of Jewish Baseball*, 123.
34. Porter, *Biographical Dictionary of American Sports*, 414.

Chapter 14

1. "Al Schacht," baseballlibrary.com.
2. Ralph Berger, "Al Schacht," The Baseball Biography Project, bioproj.sabr.org, 1.
3. Levine, *Ellis Island to Ebbets Field*, 91.
4. Berger, "Al Schacht," 1.
5. Rich Marazzi, "Al Schacht, "The Clown Prince of Baseball," *Baseball History* (Winter 1986): 35.
6. *Ibid.*
7. John Vergara, "Baseball's Clown Prince," *Sunday News* (June 24, 1955): 4.
8. Ribalow and Ribalow, *Jewish Baseball Stars*, 141; Marazzi, "Al Schacht, The Clown Prince of Baseball," 36.
9. Marazzi, "Al Schacht, The Clown Prince of Baseball," 36.
10. Anna Rothe (ed.), *Current Biography, 1946* (New York: H.W. Wilson, 1946), 535.
11. Marazzi, "Al Schacht , The Clown Prince of Baseball," 3.
12. Berger, "Al Schacht," 2.
13. Marazzi, "Al Schacht, The Clown Prince of Baseball," 36.
14. Horvitz and Horvitz, *The Big Book of Jewish Baseball*, 161; Berger, "Al Schacht," 2.
15. Larry Amman, "The Clown Prince of Baseball," *Baseball Research Journal* (1982): 125.
16. Roger Lax and Frederick Smith, *The Great Song Thesaurus* (New York: Oxford University Press, 1989), 574.
17. Horvitz and Horvitz, *The Big Book of Jewish Baseball*, 161; Berger, *Al Schacht*, 2
18. Berger, *Al Schacht*, 3.
19. Marazzi, *Al Schacht*, "The Clown Prince of Baseball," 35–36.
20. Horvitz and Horvitz, *The Big Book of Jewish Baseball*, 161; "Al Schacht," jewsinsports.org.
21. Cunningham, "Clown Prince," *Colliers* (September 4, 1937): 38.
22. *Ibid.*
23. *Washington Post*, September 19, 1919.
24. Palmer and Gillette, *The 2006 ESPN Baseball Encyclopedia*, 1166; Al Schacht Statistics—www.baseball-reference.com.
25. Berger, *Al Schacht*, 4.
26. Palmer and Gillette, *The 2006 ESPN Baseball Encyclopedia*, 1166.
27. C. F. Sawyer, "Players You Ought to Get to Know," *Baseball Magazine* (March 1921): 476.
28. Palmer and Gillette, *The 2006 ESPN Baseball Encyclopedia*, 1166; Al Schacht Player Page—sportsillustrated.cnn.com.
29. Chronology of Al Schacht's Career in Al Schacht Papers, *The Sporting News*, St. Louis, Missouri; Rothe, *Cur-*

rent Biography, 535; Horvitz and Horvitz, *The Big Book of Jewish Baseball*, 162.

30. Shatzkin, *The Ballplayers*, 966.

31. Lawrence R. Ritter, "Remembering Al Schacht," *Oldtyme Baseball News* (1996): 14; Ribalow and Ribalow, *Jewish Baseball Stars*, 142–143; Dan Holmes, "Baseball's Clown Princes," baseballhalloffame.org. 1; "Beer Drinkers and Hell Raisers, Al Schacht," thedeadballera.com.1.

32. Henry W. Thomas, *Walter Johnson Baseball's Big Train* (Lincoln: University of Nebraska Press, 1995), 198.

33. *Ibid.*; Jim Blenko, "Nick Altrock," *National Pastime* (1998): 75; baseballhalloffame.org; Cunningham, "Clown Prince," 39.

34. Berger, "Al Schacht," 5.

35. *The Washington Post*, April 10, 1932.

36. Lawrence R. Ritter, "Remembering Al Schacht," *Oldtyme Baseball News* (1996): 14; Ribalow and Ribalow, *Jewish Baseball Stars*, 142–143; Holmes, "Baseball's Clown Princes," 2.

37. Blenko, "Nick Altrock," 75; Bill Heward, *Some Are Called Clowns: A Season with the Last of the Great Barnstorming Baseball Teams* (New York: Crowell, 1974), 241; *The Sporting News*, October 5, 1933.

38. Ritter, "Remembering Al Schacht," 14.

39. Thomas, *Walter Johnson*, 199.

40. *The Sporting News*, November 18, 1934; *The Washington Post*, November 18, 1934; Cunningham, "Clown Prince," 39.

41. Rothe, *Current Biography*, 536; www.baseball-reference.com (Berg's statistics).

42. Shatzkin, *The Ballplayers*, 966.

43. Horvitz and Horvitz, *The Big Book of Jewish Baseball*, 162.

44. Ritter, "Remembering Al Schacht," 14.

45. Berger, "Al Schacht," 5.

46. Rothe, *Current Biography*, 536.

47. Berger, *Al Schacht*, 5.

48. *Chicago Daily Tribune*, December 28, 1951.

49. Thomas, *Walter Johnson*, 199.

50. Berger, "Al Schacht," 6.

51. Rothe, *Current Biography*, 536.

52. *Ibid.*

53. Shatzkin, *The Ballplayers*, 71.

54. "Moe Berg Biography," www.biographybase.com.

55. Ralph Berg, "Moe Berg," The Baseball Biography Project, bioproj.sabr.org, 1.

56. "Moe Berg," from En.wikipedia.org., 1.

57. "Moe Berg's Remarkable Life," www.ajhs.org/publications.

58. Nicholas Dawidoff, *The Catcher Who Was a Spy* (New York: Pantheon Books, 1994), 27.

59. Louis Kaufman, Barbara Fitzgerald, and Tom Sewell, *Moe Berg: Athlete, Scholar, Spy* (Boston: Little Brown, 1974), 42.

60. Berger, "Moe Berg," 2.

61. Ribalow and Ribalow, *Jewish Baseball Stars*, 149.

62. The Brooklyn Dodgers were unofficially known as the Robins from 1914 to 1930 in honor of their long-time manager, Wilbert Robinson (www.ebbets-field.com/FAQ).

63. "Moe Berg," from En.wikipedia.org, 2.

64. Ribalow and Ribalow, *Jewish Baseball Stars*, 150.

65. Jim David, "Baseball's Valedictorian," *Beckett Monthly* (August 1989):75; Slater, *Great Jews in Sports*, 32.

66. Gillette and Palmer, *The Baseball Encyclopedia*, 53; "The Smartest Major Leaguer?' *Sports History* (March 1989): 61.

67. "Moe Berg," from En.wikipedia.org, 3.

68. Ribalow and Ribalow, *Jewish Baseball Stars*, 150–151; "Moe Berg's Remarkable Life," www.ajhs.org, 1; Postal et al.,

The Encyclopedia of Jews in Sports, 37; "Morris Moe Berg," www.jewishsports.net.

69. *The Sporting News*, September 24, 1925; "The Smartest Major-Leaguer?" *Sports History*, 61.

70. *Chicago Daily Tribune*, March 6, 1926; Nicholas Dawidoff, "Scholar, Lawyer, Catcher, Spy," *Sports Illustrated* (March 23, 1992): 80.

71. Palmer and Gillette, *The 2006 ESPN Baseball Encyclopedia*, 53; Baseball—Moe Berg, sportsillustrated.cnn.com.

72. Dawidoff, "Scholar, Lawyer, Catcher, Spy," 80.

73. *The Washington Post*, March 17, 1932.

74. Ribalow and Ribalow, *Jewish Baseball Stars*, 151–152; Dawidoff, "Scholar, Lawyer, Catcher, Spy," 81; Horvitz and Horvitz, *The Big Book of Jewish Baseball*, 30; Slater, *Great Jews in Sports*, 33; David, "Baseball's Valedictorian," 75.

75. Ribalow and Ribalow, *Jewish Baseball Stars*, 153; "Moe Berg's Remarkable Life," www.ajhs.org., 1.

76. Bill Werber and C. Paul Rogers III, *Memories of a Ballplayer: Bill Werber and Baseball in the 1930s* (Lincoln: University of Nebraska Press, 2001), 106.

77. Dawidloff, "Scholar, Lawyer, Catcher, Spy, 81; "Moe Berg's Remarkable Life," www.ajhs.org, 1; Ribalow and Ribalow, *Jewish Baseball Stars*, 152–152; Horvitz and Horvitz, *The Big Book of Jewish Baseball*, 30; Berger, "Moe Berg," 2.

78. Horvitz and Horvitz, *The Big Book of Jewish Baseball*, 30.

79. F. C. Lane, "He Can Talk Baseball in Ten Languages," *Baseball Magazine* (September 1927): 440.

80. Palmer and Gillette, *The 2006 ESPN Baseball Encyclopedia*, 53; Baseball—Moe Berg, sportsillustrated.cnn.com.

81. Palmer and Gillette, *The 2006 ESPN Baseball Encyclopedia*, 53; Horvitz and Horvitz, *The Big Book of Jewish Baseball*, 31; Ribalow and Ribalow, *Jewish Baseball Stars*, 153; David, "Baseball's Valedictorian," 75.

82. Horvitz and Horvitz, *The Big Book of Jewish Baseball*, 30.

83. Dawidoff, "Scholar, Lawyer, Catcher, Spy, 81; Palmer and Gillette, *The 2006 ESPN Baseball Encyclopedia*, 53; Horvitz and Horvitz, *The Big Book of Jewish Baseball*, 30; "Moe Berg," from En.wikipedia.org, 3; Palmer and Gillette, *The 2006 ESPN Baseball Encyclopedia*, 53.

84. "Moe Berg," from En.wikipedia.org, 3; Palmer and Gillette, *The 2006 ESPN Baseball Encyclopedia*, 53.

85. Dawidoff, "Scholar, Lawyer, Catcher, Spy," 81.

86. Horvitz and Horvitz, *The Big Book of Jewish Baseball*, 31.

87. "Morris Moe Berg," www.baseballreliquary.org; Shatzkin, *The Ballplayers*, 71; Marvin Olasky, "The Strangest Man Ever to Play Baseball," www.townhall.com; Dewey and Acocella, *The Biographical History of Baseball*, 33; Horvitz and Horvitz, *The Big Book of Jewish Baseball*, 30.

88. *The Washington Post*, July 29, 1934.

89. *Los Angeles Times*, February 26, 1939.

90. Palmer and Gillette, *The 2006 ESPN Baseball Encyclopedia*, 53.

91. "The Smartest Major Leaguer?" 62.

92. Werber and Rogers , *Memories of a Ballplayer*, 109.

93. "The Shrine of the Eternals 2000 Electees," www.baseballreliquary.org.

94. Ribalow and Ribalow, *Jewish Baseball Stars*, 157.

95. Katz, *Baseball in 1939*, 78; Ribalow and Ribalow, *Jewish Baseball Stars*, 157–158.

96. Dawidoff, "Scholar, Lawyer, Catcher, Spy," 84.

97. "Moe Berg," en.wikipedia.org.

98. Shatzkin, *The Ballplayers*, 71.

99. David, "Baseball's Valedictorian," 75.

100. Dawidoff, "Scholar, Lawyer, Catcher, Spy," 81.

101. *Ibid.*, May 21, 1939.

102. Ribalow and Ribalow, *Jewish Baseball Stars*, 161.

103. David, "Baseball's Valedictorian," 75.

104. Berger, "Moe Berg," 2.

105. *Chicago Daily Tribune*, January 15, 1942.

106. "Morris Moe Berg," www.baseballreliquary.org.

107. Kaufman et al., *Moe Berg*, 112.

108. Lawrence S. Katz, *Baseball in 1939:The Watershed Season of the National Pastime* (Jefferson, N.C.: McFarland, 1995), 76.

109. Dawidoff, "Scholar, Lawyer, Catcher, Spy, 82.

110. *Ibid.*, "Moe Berg," en.wikipedia.org., 4; "Moe Berg's Remarkable Life," www.ajhs.org/publications, 2; Dennis Casey, "Jack of All Trades," aia.lackland.af.mil, 3.

111. *The Washington Post*, February 25, 1942; "Moe Berg's Remarkable Life, www.ajhs.org., 2; C. Philip Francis, "Chatter From the Dugout," www.gladwinmi.com., 2.

112. Ribalow and Ribalow, *Jewish Baseball Stars*, 162.

113. Casey, "Jack of All Trades," 4.

114. Ribalow and Ribalow, *Jewish Ball Stars*, 164.

115. "Moe Berg's Remarkable Life, 2.

116. Casey, "Jack of All Trades," 4; C. Phillip Francis, "Chatter From the Dugout," 3.

117. Dawidoff, "Scholar, Lawyer, Catcher, Spy," 85.

118. Francis, "Chatter From the Dugout," 3.

119. Larry Merchant, "Moe Berg," June 1972, untitled newspaper clipping, Moe BergFiles, *The Sporting News*, St. Louis, Missouri.; David, "Baseball's Valedictorian," 76;" Moe Berg," en.wikipedia, 2; Francis, "Chatter From the Dugout," 2; Dawidoff, "Scholar, Lawyer, Catcher, Spy," 81

120. Dawidoff, "Scholar, Lawyer, Catcher, Spy," 86.

121. "Moe Berg," en.wikipedia.org, 6; "The Shrine of the Eternals," 2; Obituaries of Berg can be found in *Los Angeles Times*, June 1, 1972; *Chicago Tribune*, June 1, 1972; *New York Times*, June 1, 1972; *The Sporting News*, June 17, 1972.

122. "Moe Berg's Remarkable Life," 3; Ribalow and Ribalow, *Jewish Baseball Stars*, 170.

123. Casey, "Jack of All Trades," 5.

124. Ribalow and Ribalow, *Jewish Baseball Stars*, 170.

Chapter 15

1. Horvitz and Horvitz, *The Big Book of Jewish Baseball*, 211.

2. His real name was Albert, but he adopted his nickname "Dolly" from an old-time baseball player who played for Cleveland and Brooklyn from 1909–1912.

3. Ribalow and Ribalow, *Jewish Baseball Stars*, 106.

4. Postal et al., *The Encyclopedia of Jews in Sports*, 54; *The Sporting News*, February 26, 1942.

5. Harold C. Burr, "Fate Hounds This Ump," *Baseball Magazine* (1932): 310.

6. Undated letter from Harry Feeney to J. G. Taylor Spink, Dolly Stark Files, *The Sporting News*.

7. Postal et al., *The Encyclopedia of Jews in Sports*, 54.

8. Ernest L. Barcella, "'Dolly' Stark Calls Them Quick," *The American Magazine* (September 1932): 62; *New York Times*, February 3 and 4, 1928; *The Sporting News*, February 9, 1928.

9. February 3, 1928 www.baseballlibrary.com.

10. *The Sporting News*, November 16, 1928.

11. Horvitz and Horvitz, *The Big Book of Jewish Baseball*, 211.

12. Undated Letter from Harry Feeney to J.G. Taylor Spink, Dolly Stark Files, *The Sporting News*.

13. *The Sporting News*, October 18, 1934.

14. *Ibid.*, February 28, 1935; *The New York Times*, August 25, 1968.

15. *The Sporting News*, July 3, 1930.

16. *Washington Post*, September 28, 1931; *Chicago Daily Tribune*, September 28, 1931.

17. *The Sporting News*, February 26, 1942; *New York Journal-American*, March 9, 1949.

18. *Ibid; The Sporting News*, September 7, 1968.

19. *The Los Angeles Times*, July 10, 1934; Horvitz and Horvitz, *The Big Book of Jewish Baseball*, 212; *The Sporting News*, February 28, 1935, April 14, 1935; *Chicago Daily Tribune*, October 1, 1935; *The Sporting News*, January 6, 1936; Lee Allen, *The Hot Stove League* (New York: A.S. Barnes, 2000), 124–125.

20. Horvitz and Horvitz, *The Big Book of Jewish Baseball*, 212; *The New York Times*, August 24, 1935; Ribalow and Ribalow, *Jewish Baseball Stars*, 108–109.

21. Shatzkin, *The Ballplayers*, 1038.

22. Clifford Bloodgood, "Kill the Umpire," *Baseball Magazine* (May 1949): 410.

23. "Baseball Precedent, *Literary Digest* (February 8, 1936): 37; *The Washington Post*, January 29, 1936.

24. *The Sporting News*, May 11, 1968.

25. Joe Williams, "Umps," *The American Magazine* (October 1936): 68.

26. Ribalow and Ribalow, *Jewish Baseball Stars*, 109; *Chicago Daily Tribune*, January 28, 1936.

27. *The Washington Post*, January 29, 1936.

28. *Ibid.*, Washington Post, February 5, 1936.

29. *The Sporting News*, April 23, 1936.

30. *The Los Angeles Times*, April 28, 1936.

31. Letter from Harry Feeney to J. G. Taylor Spink, Dolly Stark Files, *The Sporting News*.

32. *The Washington Post*, April 30, 1930; Ribalow and Ribalow, *Jewish Baseball Stars*. 109.

33. *The Sporting News*, February 19, 1942.

34. *The Sporting News*, April 22, 1943; *The Washington Post*, September 8, 1945; *The Sporting News*, February 7, 1946.

35. *The Sporting News*, June 8, 1949.

36. *New York Times*, August 25, 1968.

Chapter 16

1. Horvitz and Horvitz, *The Big Book of Jewish Baseball*, 65; Robert S. Fuchs and Wayne Soini, *Judge Fuchs and the Boston Braves, 1923-1935* (Jefferson, N.C.: McFarland, 1998), 3, 6.

2. *The Sporting News*, December 13, 1961; Postal et al., *The Encyclopedia of Jews in Sports*, 40; Fuchs and Soini, *Judge Fuchs and the Boston Braves*, 3; *New York Times*, December 6, 1961.

3. Ray Robinson, *Matty: An American Hero—Christy Mathewson of the New York Giants* (New York: Oxford University Press, 1993), 210; Philip Seib, *The Player: Christy Mathewson, Baseball, and the America Century* (New York: Four Walls, Eight Windows, 2003), 164; Harold Kaese, *The Boston Braves* (New York: G.P. Putnam's Sons, 1948), 190.

4. *The Sporting News*, January 22, 1972.

5. Dewey and Acocella, *The Biographical History of Baseball*, 156.

6. Kaese, *The Boston Braves*, 192.

7. *Washington Post*, February 21, 1923; *New York Times*, February 21, 1923.

8. *Ibid.*, 212.

9. Palmer and Gillette, *The 2006 ESPN Baseball Ency-*

clopedia, *1446*; "Managers of the Boston Braves 1912–1935," www.baseball-almanac.com.

10. Robinson, *Matty: An American Hero*, 212; Kaese, *The Boston Braves*, 196.

11. Kaese, *The Boston Braves*, 196.

12. "Managers of the Boston Braves," *www.baseball-almanac.com*; Palmer and Gillette, *The 2006 ESPN Baseball Encyclopedia*, 1448.

13. Robinson, *Matty: An American Hero*, 212.

14. Palmer and Gillette, *The 2006 ESPN Baseball Encyclopedia*, 1450.

15. *The Sporting News*, January 22, 1972.

16. Palmer and Gillette, *The 2006 ESPN Baseball Encyclopedia*, 1452, 1454; "Managers of the Boston Braves," www.baseball-almanac.com.

17. Kaese, *The Boston Braves*, 207.

18. *Los Angeles Times*, January 3, 1929; *New York Times*, January 3, 1929;, January 18, 1929; January 24, 1929.

19. Kaese, *The Boston Braves*, 211.

20. *Ibid.*, 203.

21. Palmer and Gillette, *The 2006 ESPN Baseball Encyclopedia*, 1456

22. Horvitz and Horvitz, *The Big Book of Baseball*, 66.

23. Kaese, *The Boston Braves*, 205–206; Horvitz and Horvitz, *The Big Book of Jewish Baseball*, 66; "Managers of the Boston Braves," *www.baseball-almanac.com*; Palmer and Gillette, *The 2006 ESPN Baseball Encyclopedia*, 1456.

24. Kaese, *The Boston Braves*, 207.

25. *New York Times*, November 8, 1928.

26. Palmer and Gillette, *The 2006 ESPN Baseball Encyclopedia*, 311.

27. Rogers Hornsby, "I Always Kept My Bags Packed," *Sport* (September 1955): 79.

28. Kaese, *The Boston Braves*, 209; *The Sporting News*, December 13, 1961.

29. *The Sporting News*, May 28, 1977; Daniel Okrent, "The Eternal Spring: 18 Instant Replays," *Esquire* (April 24, 1979): 62.

30. Palmer and Gillette, *The 2006 ESPN Baseball Encyclopedia*, 1458.

31. Dewey and Acocella, *The Biographical History of Baseball*, 156.

32. *The Sporting News*, January 22, 1972.

33. Bob Addie, "The Honorable Judge," *Baseball Magazine* (March 1965): 38; Postal et al., *The Encyclopedia of Jews in Sports*, 40.

34. Postal et al., *The Encyclopedia of Jews in Sports*, 40; *The Sporting News*, December 13, 1961.

35. Horvitz and Horvitz, *The Big Book of Baseball*, 66.

36. Kaese, *The Boston Braves*, 212–213.

37. *The Sporting News*, May 12, 1932.

38. *Ibid.*, January 26, 1933.

39. Postal et al., *The Encyclopedia of Jews in Sports*, 40; Kaese, *The Boston Braves*, 193.

40. Dewey and Acocello, *The Biographical History of Baseball*, 156; *The Sporting News*, December 20, 1934.

41. Kaese, *The Boston Braves*, 228.

42. Marshall Smelser, *The Life That Ruth Built: A Biography* (Lincoln: University of Nebraska Press, 1993), 492; Ken Sobol, *Babe Ruth and the American Dream* (New York: Random House, 1974), 245.

43. *The Sporting News*, December 13, 1961.

44. Sobol, *Babe Ruth and the American Dream*, 246.

45. *The Sporting News*, February 28, 1935; Sandro Cozzi and James G. Robinson, "The Babe Calls It Quits," *www.baseballlibrary.com*, 1; Robert W. Creamer, *Babe: The Legend Comes to Life*, (New York: Simon & Schuster, 1974), 384; "George Herman Ruth: 'The Bambino,' 'The Sultan of Swat;'" *www.baseball-statistics.com*, 1.

46. Sobol, *Babe Ruth and the American Dream*, 246.

47. Palmer and Gillette, *The 2006 ESPN Baseball Encyclopedia*, 579; Kaese, *The Boston Braves*, 231.

48. Dewey and Acocello, *The Biographical History of Baseball*, 157.

49. Creamer, *Babe*, 400.

50. *The New York Times*, June 4, 1935.

51. The New York Mets lost more games (120) in 1962, but their winning percentage of .254 was higher; "Managers of the Boston Braves," www.baseball-almanac.com.

52. *Los Angeles Times*, July 28, 1935; *New York Times*, August 1, 1935, August 2, 1935; *Washington Post*, August 3, 1935; *The Sporting News*, December 13, 1961.

53. Horvitz and Horvitz, *The Big Book of Jewish Baseball*, 66; Postal et al., *The Encyclopedia of Jews in Sports*, 40; Kaese, *The Boston Braves*, 192.

54. Remarks from *The Sporting News*, quoted in Postal et al., *The Encyclopedia of Jews in Sports*, 40.

55. Irvin Weil Memoir, August 1991, February-March 1992, 1 (hereafter referred to as IW Memoir)

56. I.W. Memoir; Undated Sidney Weil Memoirs, 4 (Hereafter referred to as SW Memoirs).

57. *Ibid.*, 1.

58. IW Memoirs, 4.

59. *Ibid.*, 5.

60. *Ibid.*, 6–7.

61. *Chicago Daily Tribune*, September 26, 1929; *The Sporting News*, October 3, 1929.

62. "Sidney Weil, Owner of the Cincinnati Reds, 1929–1933, *Baseball in the Buckeye State* (2004): 30.

63. *The Cincinnati Enquirer*, December 15, 1966.

64. Letter, Irwin Weil to Authors, November 15, 2004.

65. "Cincinnati Reds 1919 to 1929," *www.geocities.com.*, 1.

66. Palmer and Gillette, *The 2006 ESPN Baseball Encyclopedia*, 1458.

67. *The New York Times*, October 16, 1929; Allen, *The Cincinnati Reds*, 206–207.

68. SM Memoirs, 27.

69. "Will the real "Lip" stand up," *www.astrodaily.com*, 1.

70. Gerald Eskenazi, *The Lip: A Biography of Leo Durocher* (New York: William Morrow, 1993), 55.

71. Leo Durocher, "I Come to Kill You," *Saturday Evening Post* (May 11, 1963): 30.

72. Thorn et al., *Total Baseball*, 2531.

73. Palmer and Gillette, *The 2006 ESPN Baseball Encyclopedia*, 574.

74. Allen, *The Cincinnati Reds*, 214.

75. Thorn et al., *Total Baseball*, 2532.

76. IW Memoirs, 11.

77. Allen, *The Cincinnati Reds*, 216.

78. Bruce Chadwick, *The Cincinnati Reds: Memories and Memorabilia of the Big Red Machine* (New York: Abbeyville Press, 1994), 58.

79. Thorn et al., *Total Baseball*, 1397.

80. Palmer and Gillette, *The 2006 ESPN Baseball Encyclopedia*, 1464.

81. *Los Angeles Times*, December 8, 1932.

82. Palmer and Gillette, *The 2006 ESPN Baseball Encyclopedia*, 1278.

83. Allen, *The Cincinnati Reds*, 217.

84. Palmer and Gillette, *The 2006 ESPN Baseball Encyclopedia*, 10, 1204.

85. Eskenazi, *The Lip*, 63.

86. Thorn et al., *Total Baseball*, 1884; *The Cincinnati Enquirer*, October 28, 2003.

87. Allen, *The Cincinnati Reds*, 220–221.

88. SW Memoirs, 34; Crespau, *Baseball: America's Diamond Mine 1919–1941*, 182.

89. Allen, *The Cincinnati Reds*, 220; *New York Times*, November 7, 1933.

90. "Sidney Weil, Owner of the Cincinnati Reds," 29; www.geocities.com.

91. *The Cincinnati Times-Star*, April 25, 1940.

92. *IW Memoirs*, 12–13.

93. *Cincinnati Post-Times Star*, January 15, 1966.

94. *SW Memoirs*, 42; *IW Memoirs*, 29.

95. *New York Times*, January 15, 1966.

96. Untitled paper, March 5, 1966.

97. *The Sporting News*, January 29, 1972.

98. Lieb, *The Pittsburgh Pirates*, 242.

99. Boxerman and Boxerman, *Ebbets to Veeck to Busch*, 53.

100. *The Sporting News*, November 25, 1943.

101. Untitled Sketch William Benswanger, March 1946, Benswanger Files, *St. Louis Sporting News*, St. Louis, Missouri.

102. *The Sporting News*, November 21, 1935.

103. *Ibid.*, January 29, 1972.

104. "The Views of Wm. E. Benswanger, President of the Pittsburgh Pirates, on Sunday Baseball," *Baseball Magazine* (December 2, 1933).

105. Clifton Blue Parker, *Big and Little Poison: Paul and Lloyd Waner, Baseball Brothers* (Jefferson, N.C.: McFarland, 2003), 162.

106. *The Sporting News*, July 8, 1959.

107. *New York Times*, January 31, 1940.

108. Arthur B. Hittner, *Honus Wagner: The Life of Baseball's "Flying Dutchman"* (Jefferson, N.C.: McFarland, 1996), 247.

109. *Ibid.*, 248.

110. *The Sporting News*, November 25, 1943.

111. Palmer and Gillette, *The 2006 ESPN Baseball Encyclopedia*, 242.

112. *The Sporting News*, January 29, 1972.

113. William Marshall, *Baseball's Pivotal Era 1945–1951* (Lexington: The University Press of Kentucky., 1999), 68.

114. Palmer and Gillette, *The 2006 ESPN Baseball Encyclopedia*, 1292.

115. "Pittsburgh Pirates—Baseball History," www.Sports-wired.com, 4.

116. *The Sporting News*, January 29, 1972; November 25, 1943.

117. *Ibid.*, July 8, 1959.

118. Robert Peterson, *Only the Ball Was White: A History of Legendary Black Players and All-Black Professional Teams* (Englewood Cliffs, NJ: Prentice Hall, 1970), 177.

119. Katz, *Baseball in the 1930s*, 145; David Falkner, *Great Time Coming: The Life of Jackie Robinson, From Baseball to Birmingham* (New York: Simon & Schuster, 1995), 96.

120. William Brashler, *Josh Gibson: A Life In the Negro League* (New York, 1978), 117.

121. Tygiel, *Baseball's Great Experiment*: 39–40; Peterson; *Only the Ball Was White*, 177.

122. Dickey, *The History of National League Baseball Since 1876*, 155.

123. Neil Lanctot, *Negro League Baseball: The Rise and Ruin of a Black Institution* (Philadelphia: University of Pennsylvania Press, 2004), 234.

124. Palmer and Gillette, *The 2006 ESPN Baseball Encyclopedia*, 1488.

125. Alexander, *Our Game*, 203.

126. Marshall, *Baseball's Pivotal Era*, 67.

127. *The Sporting News*, May 23, 1946; Lowenfish and Lupien, *The Imperfect Diamond*, 144.

128. *The Sporting News*, June 5, 1946.

129. *Ibid.*

130. Lowenfish and Lupien, *The Imperfect Diamond*, 145.

131. *Ibid.*

132. Marshall, *Baseball's Pivotal Era*, 68.

133. *Chicago Daily Tribune*, June 8, 1946.

134. Lowenfish and Lupien, *The Imperfect Diamond*, 151.

135. Marshall, *Baseball's Pivotal Era*, 194.

136. *The Sporting News*, August 7, 1946; Palmer and Gillette, *The 2006 ESPN Baseball Encyclopedia*, 1492.

137. Marshall, *Baseball's Pivotal Era*, 194.

138. *The Sporting News*, August 7, 1946; Marshall, *Baseball's Pivotal Era*, 194.

139. *The Sporting News*, August 14, 1946.

140. *Ibid.*, January 1, 1947, January 8, 1947.

141. *Ibid.*, July 8, 1959.

142. Hittner, *Honus Wagner*, 257.

143. *Ibid.*, July 8, 1959.

144. *New York Times*, January 17, 1972.

Chapter 17

1. Karp, *Haven and Home*, 272.

2. Diner, *The Jews of the United States*, 211–212.

3. Riess, "From Pike to Green with Greenberg in Between," 126.

4. Levine, *Ellis Island to Ebbets Field*, 117–118.

5. Riess, "From Pike to Green with Greenberg in Between," 127.

6. Levine, *Ellis Island to Ebbets Field*, 143.

7. *Washington Post*, January 24, 1928; *Chicago Daily Tribune*, April 22, 1928; *New York Times*, April 23, 1928.

8. Palmer and Gillette, *The 2006 ESPN Baseball Encyclopedia*, 249.

9. *New York Times*, April 21, 1929; *Washington Post*, May 14, 1930.

10. Palmer and Gillette, *The 2006 ESPN Baseball Encyclopedia*, 249; Jonah Goldman—Statistics, www.baseball-reference, com.

11. *Washington Post*, March 7, 1931.

12. Jonah Goldman—Statistics, www.baseball-reference.com.

13. *The Sporting News*, October 22, 1931; Horvitz and Horvitz, *The Big Book of Jews in Baseball*, 71.

14. *The Sporting News*, August 20, 1980.

15. *Ibid.,*, April 11, 1970.

16. Horvitz and Horvitz, *The Big Book of Jewish Baseball*, 103.

17. Undated 1932 article in *The Sporting News*, *Sporting News* Files, St. Louis, Missouri.

18. Palmer and Gillette, *The 2006 ESPN Baseball Encyclopedia*, 387.

19. *Chicago Daily Tribune*, April 19, 1931.

20. Palmer and Gillette, *The 2006 ESPN Baseball Encyclopedia*, 387; Jim Levey—*www.stat-junkie.com*; CNN/SI—Baseball—Jim Levey, sportsillustrated.cnn.com; Jim Levey—Statistics, www.baseball-reference.com

21. Levine, *Ellis Island to Ebbets Field*, 123.

22. Robert Milne, "One of the Players You Ought to Know," *Baseball Magazine* (November 1931): 562–563.

23. *The Sporting News*, May 12, 1932.

24. Thorn et al., *Total Baseball*, 1388.

25. F.C. Lane, "A New Batting Stance Made Him a Good Hitter," *Baseball Magazine* (October 6, 1932), 509.

26. Undated 1932 *Sporting News* Article.

27. MVP Votes, 1930s—www.baseball-statistics.com.

28. Palmer and Gillette, *The 2006 ESPN Baseball Encyclopedia*, 387; *The Sporting News*, October 5, 1933.

29. Horvitz and Horvitz, *The Big Book of Jewish Baseball*, 104; *The Sporting News*, April 11, 1970.

30. Galatzer Statistical Sheet, Galatzer Files, *The Sporting News*, St. Louis, Missouri.

31. Galatzer Statistical Sheet, Galatzer Files.

32. Palmer and Gillette, *The 2006 ESPN Baseball Encyclopedia*, 231.

33. Undated Article in Galatzer File, *The Sporting News*.

34. Horvitz and Horvitz, *The Big Book of Jewish Baseball*, 67.

35. *Ibid.*, 67.

36. Galatzer Statistical Sheet, Galatzer Files.

37. Horvitz and Horvitz, *The Big Book of Jewish Baseball*, 67.

38. Palmer and Gillette, *The 2006 ESPN Baseball Encyclopedia*, 633; Horvitz and Horvitz, *The Big Book of Jewish Baseball*, 180; Bill Starr—Statistics, baseball-reference.com; Baseball Prospectus Player Card for Bill Starr, www.baseballprospectus.com.

39. Bill Star interview with Jim Smith and Bill Ohler, January 2, 1990 found in www.sandiegohistory.org.

40. *Los Angeles Times*, April 21, 1938.

41. Horvitz and Horvitz, *The Big Book of Jewish Baseball*, 180; *Los Angeles Times*, September 16, 1944; interview with Jim Smith and Bill Ohler.

42. *Los Angeles Times*, November 17, 1948; May 28, 1949.

43. Horvitz and Horvitz, *The Big Book of Jewish Baseball*, 180.

44. *The Washington Post*, July 17, 1927; *Los Angeles Times*, July 31, 1927.

45. *El Paso Times*, January 31, 1938; Floyd S. Fierman, "Insights and Hindsights of Some El Paso Jewish Families," *The El Paso Jewish Historical Review* (Spring 1983).

46. Horvitz and Horvitz, *The Big Book of Jewish Baseball*, 49; Sanchez, *El Paso's Greatest Sports Heroes*, 42; Ribalow and Ribalow, *Jewish Baseball Stars*, 35–36.

47. *The Sporting News*, September 13, 1934; *El Paso Times*, January 31, 1938.

48. Untitled 1941 article, Sydney Cohen Files, *The Sporting News* Files, St. Louis, Missouri; Sanchez, *El Paso's Greatest Sports Heroes*, 43; Horvitz and Horvitz, *The Big Book of Jewish Baseball*, 49.

49. *El Paso Times*, January 31, 1938; Untitled Chattanooga news clipping, April 1, 1936, Sydney Cohen Files, *The Sporting News*, St. Louis, Missouri.

50. CNN/SI—Baseball Syd Cohen, Sportsillustrated.cnn.com; Syd Cohen—Statistics, www.baseball-reference.com.

51. Ira L. Smith, *Baseball's Famous First Basemen* (New York: A.S. Barnes, 1956), 201; Postal et al., *The Encyclopedia of Jews in Sports*, 58; *Los Angeles Times*, April 13, 1937.

52. *The Sporting News*, September 30, 1937; October 21, 1937; Fierman, "Insights and Hindsights of Some of El Paso Jewish Families," 66; Sanchez, *El Paso's Greatest Sports Heroes*, 44.

53. *El Paso Times*, April 10, 1988; Ray Sanchez to Authors, February 23, 2005.

54. *El Paso Times*, March 17, 1963; *El Paso Herald Post*, January 26, 1963.

55. Undated clipping, Sydney Cohen Files, Baseball Hall of Fame, Cooperstown, New York.

56. *El Paso Times*, April 10, 1988.

57. Horvitz and Horvitz, *The Big Book of Jewish Baseball*, 176–177; Tom Deveaux, *The Washington Senators: 1970–1971* (Jefferson, N.C.: McFarland, 2001), 139.

58. *New York Times*, March 18, 1934, March 25, 1934; Untitled newspaper clipping, January 31, 1935, Fred Sington Files, *The Sporting News*, St. Louis, Missouri.

59. *Ibid.*

60. Palmer and Gillette, *The 2006 ESPN Baseball Encyclopedia*, 611.

61. Thorn et al., *Total Baseball*, 1628.

62. *Chicago Daily Tribune*, September 19, 1936; *New York Times*, September 13, 1936; *The Sporting News*, September 19, 1936; December 10, 1936; Horvitz and Horvitz, *The Big Book of Jewish Baseball*, 177.

63. *The Sporting News*, October 20, 1936.

64. *The Washington Post*, October 5, 1936.

65. Palmer and Gillette, *The 2006 ESPN Baseball Encyclopedia*, 611.

66. *New York Times*, January 5, 1939; *The Washington Post*, June 18, 1939.

67. *Birmingham News-Herald*, April 17, 1949.

68. CNN/SI—College Football—Alabama's Sington Dead At 88, Sportsillustrated.cnn.com.

69. Horvitz and Horvitz, *The Big Book of Jewish Baseball*, 177.

70. CNN/SI—College Football—Alabama's Sington Deat At 88, Sportsillustrated.cnn.com.

71. *Los Angeles Times*, July 5, 1936; Ribalow and Ribalow, *Jewish Baseball Stars*, 65.

72. Katz, *Baseball in 1939*, 90.

73. Rick Van Blair, *Dugout to Foxhole: Interviews with Baseball Players Whose Careers Were Affected by World War II* (Jefferson, N.C.: McFarland, 1994), 39.

74. Horvitz and Horvitz, *The Big Book of Jewish Baseball*, 52; Ken Smith, "The Giants' Jewish Catcher," *Baseball Magazine* (March 1938): 444.

75. Quentin Reynolds, "Harry the Horse," *Colliers*, (July 23, 1938): 54.

76. Palmer and Gillette, *The 2006 ESPN Baseball Encyclopedia*, 159.

77. Smith, "The Giants Jewish Catcher," 444.

78. *The Sporting News*, July 11, 1940.

79. Van Blair, *Dugout to Foxhole*, 41–42.

80. Ribalow and Ribalow, *Jewish Baseball Stars*, 70–71; Horvitz and Horvitz, *The Big Book of Jewish Baseball*, 53.

81. *The Los Angeles Times*, August 21, 1937.

82. *Ibid.*, September 15, 1937; *The Sporting News*, September 30, 1937.

83. Ribalow and Ribalow, *Jewish Baseball Stars*, 71; Palmer and Gillette, *The 2006 ESPN Baseball Encyclopedia*, 159; Barry Schweid, "Harry the Horse Danning," *The Baseball Research Journal* (1998): 80; Encyclopedia of Baseball Catchers—Harry Danning—members.tripod.com.

84. Thorn et al., *Total Baseball*, 1144.

85. Schweid, "Harry the Horse Danning," 80.

86. Van Blair, *Dugout to Foxhole*, 51; Horvitz and Horvitz, *The Big Book of Jewish Baseball*, 53.

87. Katz, *Baseball in 1939*, 140; Deep South Jewish Voice online edition, October 4, 2004—www.deepsouthjewishvoice.com.

88. Harry Danning, 1930s Baseball Star on www.innogize.com.

89. Charles C. Alexander, *Breaking the Slump: Baseball in the Depression Era*, 10.

90. Undated letter, Harry Danning to authors; The Journal News.com on p. 2, www.nynews.com.

91. *Northwest Indiana News*, September 25, 2004.

92. Van Blair, *Dugout to Foxhole*, 51; *Chicago Daily Tribune*, April 28, 1925.

93. Al Smitley, "Straight from the Horse's Mouth: A Chat with Harry Danning," *Oldtyme Baseball News* (1995): 21.

94. *Boston Globe*, December 3, 2004.

95. Levine, "*Ellis Island to Ebbets Field*, 93.

96. Horvitz and Horvitz, *The Big Book of Jewish Baseball*, 187.

97. *The Sporting News*, August 24, 1933.

98. *Lowell Citizen*, April 5, 1934; *Washington Post*, August 30, 1933; Palmer and Gillette, *The 2006 ESPN Baseball Encyclopedia*, 700; *The New York Times*, September 8, 1933.

99. *The Sporting News*, June 28, 1934; Horitz and Horvitz, *The Big Book of Jewish Baseball*, 187.

100. *Chicago Daily Tribune*, July 29, 1934; Palmer and Gillette, *The 2006 ESPN Baseball Encyclopedia*, 700.

101. Dan Parker writing in *The Sporting News*, December 27, 1934.

102. Thorn et al., *Total Baseball*, 1724; *The Sporting News*, December 11, 1935; *The New York Times*, August 4, 1936; *The Los Angeles Times*, August 19, 1936.

103. Levine, *Ellis Island to Ebbets Field*, 93.

104. *The Chicago Daily Tribune*, December 6, 1936; *The Sporting News*, December 24, 1936.

105. *Chicago Daily Tribune*, May 4, 1937.

106. *Ibid.*, April 26, 1937.

107. *Los Angeles Times*, July 4, 1937; *The Sporting News*, September 23, 1937; Horvitz and Horvitz, *The Big Book of Jewish Baseball*, 187.

108. Shatzkin, *The Ball Players*, 1153; *Chicago Daily Tribune*, December 3, 1938.

109. Horvitz and Horvitz, *The Big Book of Jewish Baseball*, 187.

110. *The Sporting News*, December 22, 1939.

111. *Chicago Daily Tribune*, April 17, 1941; *Los Angeles Times*, April 20, 1941; *The Sporting News*, April 24, 1941, March 26, 1942; August 16, 1942; September 24, 1942.

112. Postal et al., *The Encyclopedia of Jews in Sports*, 74; Horvitz and Horvitz, *The Big Book of Jewish Baseball* 187.

113. Palmer and Gillette, *The 2006 ESPN Baseball Encyclopedia*, 700.

114. *The Sporting News*. Undated clipping file in Weintraub Files, *The Sporting News*, St. Louis, Missouri.

115. Horvitz and Horvitz, *The Big Book of Jewish Baseball*, 19.

116. Herman D. White, *An Informal History of the Northern Baseball League* (St. Paul: The Gryphon Press, 1982), 9.

117. Early sketch of Arnovich, undated, Arnovich Files, Baseball Hall of Fame, Cooperstown, New York.

118. *Hazelton Sentinel*, April 18, 1935; Ribalow and Ribalow, *Jewish Baseball Stars*, 77.

119. Westcott and Bilovsky, *The New Phillies Encyclopedia* (Philadelphia: Temple University Press, 1993), 176.

120. Clifford Bloodgood, "Arnovich, a Superior Lad from Superior," *Baseball Magazine* (July 1939): 347.

121. Palmer and Gillette, *The 2006 ESPN Baseball Encyclopedia*, 207.

122. John E. Dreifort (ed.), *Baseball History from Outside the Lines: A Reader* (Lincoln: University of Nebraska Press, 2001), 164.

123. Levine, *Ellis Island to Ebbets Field*, 122.

124. *The Chicago Daily News*, August 3, 1939.

125. Levine, *Ellis Island to Ebbets Field*, 123; untitled newspaper clipping, July 20, 1939, Arnovich File, *The Sporting News*, St. Louis, Missouri.

126. Palmer and Gillette, *The 2006 ESPN Baseball Encyclopedia*, 1478; Postal et al., *The Encyclopedia of Jews in Sports*, 57; Westcott and Bilovsky, *The New Phillies Encyclopedia*, 176.

127. Thorn et al., *Total Baseball*, 370; *Superior Evening Telegram*, October 5, 1940.

128. Westcott and Bilovsky, *The New Phillies Encyclopedia*, 176.

129. *Ibid.*

130. *Superior Evening Telegram*, February 6, 1947; July 31, 1947; December 10, 1948; *Washington Post*, February 5, 1950.

131. *Superior Evening Telegram*, November 6, 1957; August 2, 1958; Horvitz and Horvitz, *The Big Book of Jewish Baseball*, 21.

132. *Ibid.*

133. *The Sporting News*, July 22, 1959.

Chapter 18

1. Leo Fiorito, "Where Are They Now?" *Oldtyme Baseball* (1992): 24; www.sportsecyclopedia.com/nl/bdodgers/brooklyn.

2. Palmer and Gillette, *The 2006 ESPN Baseball Encyclopedia*, 53, 65, 611.

3. *The Sporting News*, April 21, 1933.

4. *Ibid.*, January 29, 1931.

5. *Ibid.*, March 12, 1931.

6. Roscoe McGowen, "Baseball As It Used to Be," *Sport* (June 1994): 92; Jack Kavanaugh and Norman Macht, *Uncle Robbie* (Cleveland: Society for American Baseball Research, 1999), 178–179; Postal et al., *The Encyclopedia of Jews in Sports*, 58.

7. Horvitz and Horvitz, *The Big Book of Jewish Baseball*, 44; Richard Goldstein, *Superstars and Screwballs: 100 Years of Brooklyn Baseball* (New York, 1991), 163–164.

8. Horvitz and Horvitz, *The Big Book of Jewish Baseball*, 44–45.

9. Alta Cohen—"Oldest Brooklyn Dodger Alumnus Cohen Dies at 94," on www.historicbaseball.com.

10. Horvitz and Horvitz, *The Big Book of Jewish Baseball*, 151.

11. *The Sporting News*, March 5, 1931.

12. *Ibid.*, April 9, 1931.

13. Max Rosenfield Statistics—www.baseballreference.com.

14. Horvitz and Horvitz, *The Big Book of Jewish Baseball*, 152; *The Sporting News*, January 14, 1934.

15. *The Sporting News*, January 8, 1934.

16. Horvitz and Hortivz, *The Big Book of Jewish Baseball*, 152; *The Sporting News*, March 14, 1937.

17. Horvitz and Horvitz, *The Big Book of Jewish Baseball*, 151–152; *The Sporting News*, January 24, 1946.

18. Horvitz and Horvitz, *The Big Book of Jewish Baseball*, 152.

19. Mrs. Evelyn Eisenstat to Authors, May 23, 2005.

20. Unnamed clipping, May 1, 1935, Eisenstat Files, *The Sporting News*, St. Louis, Missouri.

21. Mrs. Evelyn Eisenstat to Authors, May 23, 2005.

22. Undated, and unpaginated sketch of Eisenstat, Harry Eisenstat Files, Baseball Hall of Fame Files, Cooperstown, New York.

23. Newspaper Clipping, February 27, 1936, Harry Eisenstat Files, *The Sporting News*, St. Louis, Missouri.

24. Hall of Fame clipping, undated and unnamed, Harry Eisenstat Files, Cooperstown, New York; Palmer and Gillette, *Total Baseball*, 874.

25. Levine, *Ellis Island to Ebbets Field*, 141.

26. Horvitz and Horvitz, *The Big Book of Jewish Baseball*, 874.

27. Mrs. Evelyn Eisenstat to Authors, May 23, 2005; "Harry Eisenstat," *Baseball Magazine* (August 1939), 395.

28. Brent Kelley, *In the Shadow of the Babe: Interviews with Baseball Players Who Played With or Against Babe Ruth* (Jefferson, N.C.,1995), 169; unmarked clipping, February 10, 1938, Eisenstat Files, *The Sporting News*, St. Louis, Missouri; Katz, *Baseball in 1939*, 44.

29. White, *Creating the National Pastime*, 263.
30. "Harry Eisenstat," 395.
31. Katz, *Baseball in 1939*, 140–141.
32. Evelyn Eisenstat to Authors, May 23, 2005.
33. "Harry Eisenstat," 395.
34. Horvitz and Horvitz, *The Big Book of Jewish Baseball*, 55; Katz, *Baseball in 1939*, 44; Ira Berkow, *Hank Greenberg: The Story of My Life* (New York: Times Books, 1989), 104.
35. Unmarked, undated clipping, Eisenstat Files, Baseball Hall of Fame, Cooperstown, New York.
36. Palmer and Gillette, *The 2006 ESPN Baseball Encyclopedia*, 874; *The Washington Post*, June 15, 1939.
37. Katz, *Baseball in 1939*, 44, 92.
38. Thorn et al., *Total Baseball*, 1904.
39. Henry Eisenstat Statistics—*www.baseball-reference. com*; Palmer and Gillette, *The 2006 ESPN Baseball Encyclopedia*, 874; Kelly, *In the Shadow of the Babe*, 172.
40. Katz, *Baseball in 1939*, 44, 92.
41. *Cleveland Plain Dealer*, March 23, 2003; MLB Baseball Eisenstat Dies at 87—cbs.sportsline.com; Detroit Free Press, March 24, 2003 on *www.freep.com/*
42. Dan Turner, *Heroes, Bums and Ordinary Men: Profiles in Canadian Baseball* (Toronto, 1988), 93.
43. Horvitz and Horvitz, *The Big Book of Jewish Baseball*, 147.
44. *Ibid*. 147; Van Blair, *Dugout to Foxhole*, 171.
45. Turner, *Heroes, Bums and Ordinary Men*, 96.
46. *Ibid*.
47. *Ibid.*,97.
48. Levine, *Ellis Island to Ebbets Field*, 128–129.
49. Ribalow and Ribalow, *Jewish Baseball Stars*, 85; Van Blair, *Dugout to Foxhole*, 172; *The Sporting News*, September 23, 1937.
50. Fiorito, "Where Are They Now?" *Oldtyme Baseball* 4 (1992): 24.
51. David Spaner, "From Greenberg to Green: Jewish Ballplayers," found in John Thorn et al., *Total Baseball*, 173, 1997 edition.
52. Horvitz and Horvitz, *The Big Book of Jewish Baseball*, 147–148; Thorn et al., *Total Baseball*, 1587.
53. *The New York Times*, March 2, 1939.
54. *New York Times*, June 15, 1939; Van Blair, *Dugout to Foxhole*, 172; Ribalow and Ribalow, *Jewish Baseball Stars*, 86.
55. *The Washington Post*, August 29, 1939; Palmer and Gillette, *The 2006 ESPN Baseball Encyclopedia*, 572.
56. *Chicago Daily Tribune*, February 11, 1940; *The Washington Post*, February 11, 1940.
57. Turner, *Heroes, Bums and Ordinary Men*, 98.
58. Ribalow and Ribalow, *Jewish Baseball Stars*, 86.
59. *Los Angeles Times*, May 31, 1944.
60. Palmer and Gillette, *The 2006 ESPN Baseball Encyclopedia*, 572; Ribalow and Ribalow, *Jewish Baseball Stars*, 86.
61. *The Sporting News*, June 28, 1945.
62. Horvitz and Horvitz, *The Big Book of Baseball*, 148; Turner, *Heroes, Bums and Ordinary Men*, 100–101; Unnamed, undated article from American Jewish Archives, Cincinnati, Ohio.
63. Roscoe McGowen, "Little 'Bum' With the Big Bat," *Baseball Magazine* (November 1945): 416.
64. *Chicago Daily Tribune* April 28, 1946; *New York Times*, April 28, 1946; *The Sporting News*, May 2, 1946.
65. Postal et al., *Encyclopedia of Jews in Sports*, 72; Horvitz and Horvitz, *The Big Book of Jewish Baseball*, 148; Van Blair, *Dugout to Foxhole*.
66. *The Sporting News*, February 16, 1955.
67. Goody Rosen Statistics—www.baseball-reference. com.

68. Turner, *Heroes, Bums and Ordinary Men*, 101; *The Sporting News*, February 5, 1947; Horvitz and Horvitz, *The Big Book of Jewish Baseball*, 149; 1965 clipping in Goody Rosen Files, *The Sporting News*, St. Louis, Missouri.
69. Van Blair, *Dugout to Foxhole*, 175, 177.
70. Levine, *Ellis Island to Ebbets Field*, 128–129.
71. *The New York Times*, April 8, 1994.
72. Palmer and Gillette, *The 2006 ESPN Baseball Encyclopedia*, 1084.
73. Horvitz and Horvitz, *The Big Book of Jewish Baseball*, 125–126.
74. *The Sporting News*, May 25, 1941.
75. *Ibid*.
76. *The Jewish News Weekly*, April 23, 2004.
77. Unnamed clipping, May 7, 1941, Sam Nahem Files, *The Sporting News*, St. Louis, Missouri.
78. *The Jewish News Weekly*, April 23, 2004.
79. Horvitz and Horvitz, *The Big Book of Jewish Baseball*, 126; Palmer and Gillette, *The 2006 ESPN Baseball Encyclopedia*, 1084.
80. *The Jewish News Weekly*, April 23, 2004.
81. *The Sporting News*, May 24, 1941.
82. Horvitz and Horvitz, *The Big Book of Jewish Baseball*, 126.
83. Unmarked clipping, May 7, 1941, Nahem Files, *St. Louis Sporting News*.
84. Palmer and Gillette, *The 2006 ESPN Baseball Encyclopedia*, 1084.
85. *The Washington Post*, February 19, 1942.
86. Palmer and Gillette, *The 2006 ESPN Baseball Encyclopedia*, 1484.
87. Sam Nahem MLB +Minor League Batting Statistics—Baseball Cube on www.sports-wired.com.
88. Sam Nahem debuted with Dodgers in 1938, *www. historicbaseball.com*.
89. Stan Isaacs, "Major Leaguer Sam Nahem Was One-Of-a-Kind, *www.thecolumnists.com*; www.jewishf.com.
90. Jewishmajorleaguers.org.

Chapter 19

1. Levine, *Ellis Island to Ebbets Field*, 130.
2. White, *Creating the National Pastime*, 249.
3. Horvitz and Horvitz, *The Big Book of Jewish Baseball*, 64; *The Los Angeles Times*, February 5, 1939; *New York Times*, February 5, 1939.
4. *The Washington Post*, September 8, 1940; Horvitz and Horvitz, *The Big Book of Jewish Baseball*, 65.
5. *The Washington Post*, July 29, 1942; Palmer and Gillette, *The 2006 ESPN Baseball Encyclopedia*, 224.
6. *The Sporting News*, October 16, 1946.
7. *The Sporting News*, May 16, 1946; Alexander, *Our Game*, 204.
8. Horvitz and Horvitz, *The Big Book of Jewish Baseball*, 65.
9. Brief Sketch on Feldman by Frederick H. Lieb, in Feldman Files, *The Baseball Hall of Fame*, St. Louis, Missouri.
10. *Ibid*.
11. Horvitz and Horvitz, *The Big Book of Jewish Baseball*, 59–60; unnamed, undated sheet Harry Feldman Files, *The Sporting News*, St. Louis, Missouri; *The Sporting News*, March 28, 1962.
12. Lieb Sketch of Harry Feldman.
13. *New York Times*, May 14, 1940; *The Washington Post*, September 22, 1941; Horvitz and Horvitz, *The Big Book of Jewish Baseball*, 60.

14. *Ibid.*

15. *The Sporting News,* December 17, 1942.

16. Horvitz and Horvitz, *The Big Book of Jews in Baseball,* 60.

17. Palmer and Gillette, *The 2006 ESPN Baseball Encyclopedia,* 883.

18. Marvin A. Cohen, *The Dodgers–Giants Rivalry 1900 1957: A Year By Year Retrospective,* (Kearney, NE: Morris Publishing, 1999), 149.

19. Horvitz and Horvitz, *The Big Book of Jews in Baseball,* 60; Palmer and Gillette, *The 2006 ESPN Baseball Encyclopedia,* 883.

20. Cohen, *The Dodgers-Giants Rivalry,* 155, 157.

21. Palmer and Gillette, *The 2006 ESPN Baseball Encyclopedia,* 883.

22. Harry Feldman Statistics—www.baseball-reference.com.

23. *The New York Times,* April 27, 1946; *Chicago Daily Tribune,* April 27, 1946

24. *New York Times,* May 10, 1946; *Chicago Daily Tribune,* September 24, 1946.

25. *The Washington Post,* June 20, 1949.

26. Undated Statistical Sheet on Harry Feldman, Feldman Files, *The Sporting News,* St. Louis, Missouri.

27. Horvitz and Horvitz, *The Big Book of Jewish Baseball,* 61; *The Sporting News,* March 28, 1962; *New York Times,* March 18, 1962.

28. Thorn et al., *Total Baseball,* 375.

29. Horvitz and Horvitz, *The Big Book of Jewish Baseball,* 33.

30. Harriet Block to Authors, May 2, 2005.

31. "The Cy Block Story," undated draft of story in Cy Block Files, *The Sporting News,* St. Louis, Missouri.

32. "Minor Portrait: Cy Block," *Baseball Magazine* (July 1949): 270.

33. Horvitz and Horvitz, *The Big Book of Jewish Baseball,* 33.

34. *The Sporting News,* November 14, 1940; "Minor Portrait: Cy Block," 270; Cy Block's Statistical Sheet, Cy Block Files, *St. Louis Sporting News,* St. Louis, Missouri; Horvitz and Horvitz, *The Big Book of Jewish Baseball,* 34.

35. Levine, *Ellis Island to Ebbets Field,* 125–126.

36. Harriet Block to Authors, May 2, 2005.

37. *The Sporting News,* November 14, 1940; "Minor Portrait: Cy Block," 270; Cy Block's Statistical Sheet, Cy Block Files, *St. Louis Sporting News,* St. Louis, Missouri; Horvitz and Horvitz, *The Big Book of Jewish Baseball,* 34.

38. *Long Island Press,* June 6, 1967; *The Chicago Daily Tribune,* September 14, 1945.

39. Horvitz and Horvitz, *The Big Book of Jews in Baseball,* 34.

40. "The Cy Block Story;" Harriet Block Interview with Authors.

41. Palmer and Gillette, *The 2006 ESPN Baseball Encyclopedia,* 63; *The Sporting News,* September 18, 1946.

42. *The Sporting News,* February 24, 1968.

43. Harriet Block interview with authors, March 22, 2006.

44. *New York Times,* September 28, 1984.

45. Harriet Block Interview with Authors, May 2, 2005; *Great Neck Record,* November 19, 2004.

46. *Chicago Tribune,* October 17, 2004.

47. Tom Meany, "Sid Gordon—The Answer to a Giant Prayer?" *Sport* (July 1949): 32.

48. Ribalow and Ribalow, *Jewish Baseball Stars,* 93.

49. Charles Dexter, "Braves Coal, Coal Heart," *Baseball Digest* (March 1952): 6.

50. Ralph Berger, "Sid Gordon," *Baseball Biography Project,* 1; Slater, *Great Jews in Sports,* 97.

51. Slater, *Great Jews in Sports,* 97; Milton Richman, "The Kid From Brooklyn—New Giants' Hero," *Sport Life* (March 1949): 80; Clifford Bloodgood, "The Gordon Across the River," *Baseball Magazine* (February 1944): 315; Jack Newcombe, "Old Pro of the Braves," *Sport* (July 1953): 84.

52. Newcombe, "Old Pro of the Braves," 85; Ribalow and Ribalow, *Jewish Baseball Stars,* 94.

53. Palmer and Gillette, *The 2006 ESPN Baseball Encyclopedia,* 254.

54. Berger, "Sid Gordon," 1; Ribalow and Ribalow, *Jewish Baseball Stars,* 95.

55. Sid Gordon Statistics—www.baseball-reference.com; Berger, "Sid Gordon," 2.

56. Palmer and Gillette, *The 2006 ESPN Baseball Encyclopedia,* 1486; Newcombe, "Old Pro of the Braves," 85.

57. *The Washington Post,* April 14, 1943.

58. *New York Times,* September 17, 1943; *The Washington Post,* September 30, 1943; *New York Times,* December 1, 1945.

59. Palmer and Gillette, *The 2006 ESPN Baseball Encyclopedia,* 1492.

60. Thorn et al., *Total Baseball,* 2551.

61. Newcombe, "Old Pro of the Braves," 85; Slater, *Great Jews in Sports,* 97.

62. Meany, "Sid Gordon: The Answer to a Giant Prayer?" 98.

63. *The Sporting News,* December 1, 1948.

64. Palmer and Gillette, *The 2006 ESPN Baseball Encyclopedia,* 254; Berger, "Sid Gordon," 2; Newcombe, "O ld Pro of the Braves," 85; Dexter, "Braves' Coal, Coal Heart," 7.

65. Postal et al., *The Encyclopedia of Jews in Sports,* 60; Horvitz and Horvitz, *The Big Book of Jewish Baseball,* 76; Newcombe, "Old Pro of the Braves," 85; Richman, "The Kid from Brooklyn," 81.

66. *New York Times,* February 10, 1949.

67. Slater, *Great Jews in Sports,* 98; Pietrusza et al., *Baseball: The Biographical Encyclopedia,* 423; Ribalow and Ribalow, *Jewish Baseball Stars,* 99.

68. Berger, "Sid Gordon," 2; Ribalow and Ribalow, *Jewish Baseball Stars,* 101.

69. Dexter, "Braves' Coal, Coal Heart," 7.

70. Postal et al., *The Encyclopedia of Jews in Sports,* 61.

71. Ribalow and Ribalow, *Jewish Baseball Stars,* 102.

72. *Ibid.,* 99.

73. Dexter, "Braves' Coal, Coal Heart," 8.

74. Palmer and Gillette, *The 2006 ESPN Baseball Encyclopedia,* 254, 1506.

75. Baseball—Sid Gordon—Sportsillustrated.cnn.com.

76. Jane Leavy, *Sandy Koufax: A Lefty's Legacy* (New York: Harper Collins, 2002), 65.

77. Ribalow and Ribalow, *Jewish Baseball Stars,* 102.

78. Meany, "Sid Gordon: The Answer to a Giant Prayer?" 99.

79. Horvitz and Horvitz, *The Big Book of Jewish Baseball,* 76; Berger, "Sid Gordon," 3.

80. Jewishmajorleaguers.org.; www.baseball-almanac.com/players.

Chapter 20

1. www.jewishvirtuallibrary.org.

2. Shatzkin, *The Ballplayers,* 410.

3. Ralph Berger, "Hank Greenberg," bioproj.sabr.org, 1; unnamed newspaper clipping, August 6, 1934, Greenberg Files, *St. Louis Sporting News,* St. Louis, Missouri.

4. Ed Fitzgerald, "Hank Greenberg: A Study in Success," *Sport Magazine* (March 1951): 29.

5. Clifford Bloodgood, "A Star Rookie of 1933," *Baseball Magazine* (February 1934): 407.

6. Lee Allen, *The Hot Stove League* (New York: A. S. Barnes, 2000), 21–22; Lawrence S. Ritter, *The Glory of Their Times: The Story of the Early Days of Baseball Told by the Men Who Played It* (New York: William Morrow, 1984), 308; Berler, "Let's Hear it For the Rabbi of Swat," 109A.

7. Pietrusza et al., *Baseball: The Biographical Encyclopedia*, 432.

8. *The Sporting News*, October 3, 1970.

9. Jack Drees and James C. Mullen, *Where is He Now?* (Middle Village, N.Y.: Jonathan David, 1973), 37; John A Garaty and Mark C. Carnes (eds.), *American National Biography* (New York: Oxford University Press, 1999), 515.

10. Ritter, *The Glory of Their Times*, 311.

11. *Ibid.*

12. Palmer and Gillette, *The 2006 ESPN Baseball Encyclopedia*, 260.

13. Werber and Rogers, *Memoirs of a Ballplayer*, 151.

14. Hank Greenberg Statistics—*www.baseballlibrary.com*; Palmer and Gillette, *The 2006 ESPN Baseball Encyclopedia*, 260; Ritter, *The Glory of Their Times*, 313.

15. Palmer and Gillette, *The 2006 ESPN Baseball Encyclopedia*, 1417.

16. Thorn et al., *Total Baseball*, 364.

17. Brian Moynahan, *The Player Nobody Wanted*, 2003, appearing on Baseball Almanac, 5.

18. William M. Simons, "The Athlete as Jewish Standard Bearer: Media Images of Hank Greenberg," *Jewish Social Studies* (Spring 1982): 100.

19. Brian Moynahan, *The Player Nobody Wanted*, 5.

20. Ira Berkow, *Hank Greenberg: The Story of My Life* (New York: Times Books, 1989), 58.

21. Jeff Merron, "Green, Koufax and Greenberg—same dilemma, different decisions," September 20, 2001, found on Espn.go.com; Michael Feldberg, *Hank Greenberg: Baseball's First Jewish Superstar*, found on www.uja.org.

22. Ronnie Friedland, *A Jewish Baseball Hero Who Gave Up Hope and Inspiration to Jews Across the Nation*, found on *www.Jewishsports.com*, 1.

23. Unnamed clipping, May 2, 1935, Hank Greenberg Files, *The St. Louis Sporting News*, St. Louis, Missouri.

24. Moynahan, *The Player Nobody Wanted*, 6; Berkow, *Hank Greenberg: The Story of My Life*, 60.

25. Ritter, *The Glory of Their Times*, 314; www.baseballibrary.com.

26. Thorn et al., *Total Baseball*, 365.

27. Postal et al., *The Encyclopedia of Jews in Sports*, 62.

28. Ritter, *The Glory of Their Times*, 317.

29. Ritter, *The Glory of Their Times*, 316; Rielly, *Baseball: An Encyclopedia of Popular Culture*, 122.

30. Palmer and Gillette, *The 2006 ESPN Baseball Encyclopedia*, 223.

31. www.baseballibrary.com.

32. Ritter, *The Glory of Their Times*, 317.

33. Kates, 'Of Horsehides and Hexagrams," *The National Pastime* (May 2004): 122; Dorinson and Warmund, *Jackie Robinson*, 114; Berkow, *Hank Greenberg: The Story of My Life*, 102–103.

34. Stanley Frank, "Hank Made Greenberg," *Saturday Evening Post* (March 15, 1941): 46.

35. Palmer and Gillette, *The 2006 ESPN Baseball Encyclopedia*, 260.

36. *The Sporting News*, November 17, 1940.

37. Thorn et al., *Total Baseball*, 2543.

38. *Ibid.*, 370.

39. Garaty and Carnes, *American National Biography*, 515.

40. Thorn et al., *Total Baseball*, 374.

41. Ritter, *Glory of Their Times*, 325; Tom Meany, "The Great Greenberg Mystery," *Sport* (June 1947): 18; Daniel M. Daniel, "Hank Greenberg's Shift to Pirates Presents Case Without Any Preceded," *Baseball Magazine*: (May 1947): 415.

42. Pietrusza, *Baseball: The Biographical Encyclopedia*, 434; *The Sporting News*, October 3, 1970.

43. Slater, *Great Jews in Sports*, 64; Pietrusza et al., *Baseball: The Biographical Encyclopedia*,

44. Berger, "Hank Greenberg," 7.

45. Ritter, *The Glory of Their Times*, 325–326.

46. *www.baseballibrary.com*, 3.

47. Garaty and Carnes, *American National Biography*, 515; Palmer and Gillette, *The 2006 ESPN Baseball Encyclopedia*, 260.

48. *The Sporting News* February 8, 1956.

49. Slater, *Great Jews in Sports*, 105; www,jewishvirtuallibrary.org, 3.

50. Berger, "Hank Greenberg," 9.

51. *The Washington Post*, March 28, 1948; *The New York Times*, March 28, 1948; The *Sporting News*, April 7, 1948, May 5, 1948.

52. Boxerman and Boxerman, *Ebbets to Veeck to Busch*, 134; Garaty and Carnes, *American National Biography*, 516.

53. Ira Berkow, *Hank Greenberg: The Story of My Life* (New York: Times Books, 1989), 213.

54. Berkow, *Hank Greenberg: The Story of My Life*, 207–208.

55. "Going to Bat," *Journal of Sport History* (Spring 1999): 133–134.

56. Boxerman and Boxerman, *Ebbets to Veeck to Busch*, 134; Garaty and Carnes, *American National Biography*, 516; *The Sporting News*, October 30, 1957.

57. Berger, "Hank Greenberg," 9.

58. *Ibid.*

59. Ritter, *The Glory of Their Times*, 328.

60. Bob Broeg, "Hank Greenberg: He Was a Self-Made Hall of Famer," *Baseball Digest*, (December 1986): 69–70; www. Thedeadballera.com, 2; Berger, "Hank Greenberg," 9.

61. *The Detroit News*, November 24, 2004.

62. Maxwell Kates, "Of Horsehides and Hexagrams," 120–121; Joseph Dorinson and Joram Warmund, *Jackie Robinson: Race, Sports, and the American Dream* (Armonk, N.Y.: M. E. Sharpe, 1998), 114.

63. Riess, "From Pike to Green with Greenberg in Between," 127.

64. Benjamin G. Rader, *Baseball, A History of America's Game* (Urbana: University of Illinois Press, 2002), 139.

65. Jaher, "Anti-Semitism in American Athletics," 68; Berkow, *Hank Greenberg: The Story of My Life*, 103.

66. Alexander, *Breaking the Slump*, 194–195; Berkow, *Hank Greenberg: The Story of My Life*, 41–42.

67. Berkow, *Hank Greenberg: The Story of My Life*, 62; Ritter, *The Glory of Their Times*, 330.

68. Brad Zellar, *Baseball Moses*, found in *www.citypages. com*, 4.

69. David Spaner, "From Greenberg to Green: Jewish Ballplayers," 174.

70. Friedland, *A Jewish Baseball Hero*, *www.Jewish sports.com*, 2.; Simons, *In the Golden Land*, 110; Garaty and Carnes, *American National Biography*, 516; White, *Creating the National Pastime*, 263, 266.

71. Zellar, *Baseball Moses*, 2–3.

72. Riess, *Sports and the American Jew*, 205.

73. Simons, "The Athlete as Jewish Standard Bearer," 107.

74. White, *Creating the National Pastime*, 265.

Epilogue

1. Riess, "From Pike to Green with Greenberg in Between," pp. 134–135.

2. Ron Kaplan, "Literary Hitters," www.njjewishnews.com

3. Brian Heyman, "Quality, but not quantity," www.ny news.com.

4. www.baseball-reference.com.

5. Al Rosen, interview with authors, January 14, 2005.

6. Brian Heyman, "Quality, but not quantity," www.ny news.com.

7. Ross Baumgarten, e-mail to authors, January 5, 2005.

Bibliography

Personal

Alexander, Charles C. E-mail correspondence, November 29, 2005.

Baumgarten, Ross. E-mail correspondence, January 5, 2005.

Block, Harriet (Mrs. Cy). Telephone interview, May 2, 2005.

Danning, Harry. Letter, undated.

Eisenstat, Evelyn (Mrs. Harry). Telephone interview, May 23, 2005; March 22, 2006.

Halstead, Larry. E-mail correspondence, February 24, 2005.

Lee, Marina. Telephone interview, March 28, 2005.

Rosen, Al. Telephone interview, January 14, 2005.

Ross, Neal. E-Mail correspondence, February 24, 2005; February 25, 2005; March 1, 2005; March 5, 2005.

Sanchez, Ray. Telephone interview, February 23, 2005.

Solomon, Joseph M. Telephone interview, February 16, 2005.

Weil, Professor Irwin. Letter, November 14, 2004.

Yates, Dan. E-mail correspondence, October 6, 2005.

Libraries

Allen County Historical Society, Ft. Wayne, IN
American Jewish Archives, Cincinnati, OH
Boston Herald Archives, Boston, MA
Boston Public Library, Boston, MA
Cincinnati Historical Society, Cincinnati, OH
Cincinnati Public Library, Cincinnati, OH
Douglas County Historical Society, Superior, WI
El Paso Museum of History, El Paso, TX
El Paso Texas Times Archives, El Paso, TX
Elias Sports Bureau, New York, NY
Farmington Public Library, Farmington, MO
Ft. Wayne Journal-Gazette Archives, Ft. Wayne, IN
Ft. Wayne Public Library, Ft. Wayne, IN
John Olin Library, St. Louis, MO
Kenton County Public Library, Covington, KY
New York City Public Library, New York, NY
Philadelphia Phillies Baseball Club Archives, Philadelphia, PA
Pope Pius XII Library, St. Louis, MO
Saul Brodsky Jewish Community Library, St. Louis, MO
Society for American Baseball Research, Cleveland, OH
St. Louis County Library, St. Louis, MO
St. Louis Public Library, St. Louis, MO
The National Baseball Hall of Fame, Cooperstown, NY
The News-Sentinel Archives, Ft. Wayne, IN
The Sporting News Archives, St. Louis, MO
Thomas Jefferson Library, St. Louis, MO
University of Cincinnati Library, Cincinnati, OH

Books

Adelman, Melvin L. *Sporting Time: New York City and the Rise of Modern Athletics 1820–1870.* Urbana: University of Illinois Press, 1986.

Alexander, Charles C. *Breaking the Slump: Baseball in the Depression Era.* New York: Columbia University Press, 2002.

_____. *John McGraw.* New York: Viking, 1988.

_____. *Our Game: An American Baseball History.* New York: Henry Holt & Company, 1991.

_____. *Rogers Hornsby.* New York: Henry Holt & Company, 1995.

Allen, Lee. *The American League Story.* New York: Hill & Wang, 1995.

_____. *Cincinnati Reds.* New York: G. P. Putnam's Sons, 1948.

_____. *The Hot Stove League.* New York: A. S. Barnes, 2000.

_____, and Tom Meany. *Kings of the Diamond.* New York: G. P. Putnam's Sons, 1965.

Alvarez, Mark. *The Old Ball Game.* Alexandria, VA: Redefinition Book, 1990.

Andreano, Ralph. *The Dilemma of Major League Baseball.* Rochester, VT: Schenkman Books, 1965.

Ankenbruck, John. *Twentieth Century History of Fort Wayne.* Ft. Wayne: Twentieth Century Historical, Inc., 1975.

Asinof, Eliot. *Eight Men Out: The Black Sox and the 1919 World Series.* New York: Holt, Rinehart & Winston, 1963.

Astor, Gerald, and Joe Falls. *The Detroit Tigers.* New York: Walker, 1989.

Axelson. Gustav. *Commy: The Life Story of Charles Comiskey.* Jefferson, N.C.: McFarland, 2003.

Baldassaro, Lawrence, and Richard A. Johnson, eds. *The American Game—Baseball and Ethnicity.* Carbondale: Southern Illinois University Press, 2002.

Barth, Gunther. *City People: The Rise of Modern City Culture in 19th Century America.* New York: Oxford University Press, 1980.

Bartlett, Arthur. *Baseball and Mr. Spalding: History and Romance of Baseball.* New York: Farrar, Strauss, & Young, 1951.

Berke, Arthur, and Paul Schmitt. *This Date in Chicago History.* New York: Stein & Day, 1982.

Berkow, Ira. *Hank Greenberg: The Story of My Life.* New York: Times Books, 1989.

Bernheimer, Charles S. *Russian Jews in the United States.* New York: Young Peoples Missionary, 1905.

Biale, David. *Power and Powerlessness in Jewish History.* New York: Schocken Books, 1986.

Block, David. *Baseball Before We Knew It: A Search for the Roots of the Game.* Lincoln: University of Nebraska Press, 2005.

Boxerman, Burton A., and Benita W. Boxerman. *Ebbets to Veeck to Busch: Eight Owners Who Shaped Baseball.* Jefferson, N.C.: McFarland, 2003.

Brashler, William. *Josh Gibson: A Life in the Negro Leagues.* New York: Harper & Row, 1978.

Broeg, Bob, and William Miller, Jr. *Baseball from a Different Angle.* South Bend: Diamond Communication, 1988.

Brown, Warren. *The Chicago Cubs.* Carbondale: Southern Illinois University Press, 1946.

Burk, Robert F. *Much More Than a Game: Players, Owners, and American Baseball Since 1921.* Chapel Hill: University of North Carolina Press, 2001.

_____. *Never Just a Game: Players, Owners, and American Baseball to 1920.* Chapel Hill: University of North Carolina Press, 1994.

Cash, Jon David. *Before They Were Cardinals.* Columbia: University of Missouri Press, 2002.

Chadwick, Bruce. *The Cincinnati Reds: Memories and Memorabilia of the Big Red Machines.* New York: Abbeyville Press, 1994.

Cohen, Marvin A. *The Dodgers-Giants Rivalry 1900–1957: A Year by Year Retrospective.* Kearny, NE: Morris Publishing, 1999.

Cohen, Stanley. *The Dodgers: First 100 Years.* New York: Carol Publishing Group, 1990.

_____. *The Game They Played.* New York: Farrar, Strauss, Giroux, 1977.

Cohen, Steven M. *American Modernity and Jewish Identity.* New York: Tavistock Publications, 1983.

_____. *Jewish Assimilation or Jewish Revival.* Bloomington: Indiana University Press, 1988.

Condit, Carl W. *Chicago 1910–1929.* Chicago: University of Chicago Press, 1973.

Condon, Dave. *The Go-Go Chicago White Sox.* New York: Coward-McCann, 1960.

Cramer, Richard Ben. *Joe DiMaggio: The Hero's Life.* New York: Simon & Schuster, 2000.

Creamer, Robert W. *Babe. The Legend Comes to Life.* New York: Simon & Schuster, 1974.

Crepau, Richard C. *Baseball: America's Diamond Mine 1919–1941.* Orlando: University Press of Florida, 1980.

Davis, Mac. *Lore and Legends of Baseball.* New York: Lantern Press, 1953.

Dawidoff, Nicholas. *The Catcher Was a Spy: The Mysterious Life of Moe Berg.* New York: Pantheon Books, 1994.

DeValeria, Dennis, and Jeanne Burke DeValeria. *Honus Wagner: A Biography.* New York: Henry Holt & Company, 1998.

Deveaux, Tom. *The Washington Senators 1901–1971.* Jefferson, N.C.: McFarland, 2001.

Dewey, Donald, and Nicholas Acocella. *The Biographical History of Baseball.* New York: Carrol and Graf, 1955.

Dickey, Glenn. *The History of American League Baseball Since 1901.* New York: Stein & Day, 1980.

_____. *The History of National League Baseball Since 1876.* New York: Stein & Day, 1979.

_____. *The History of the World Series Since 1903.* New York: Stein & Day, 1984.

Diner, Hasia R. *The Jews of the United States 1654–2000.* Berkeley: The University of California Press, 2004.

_____. *A Time for Gathering: The Second Migration 1820–1860.* Baltimore: Johns Hopkins University Press, 1992.

DiSalvatore, Bryan. *A Clever Base Ballist. The Life and Times of John Montgomery Ward.* New York: Pantheon Books, 1999.

Dorinson, Joseph, and Joram Warmund, eds. *Jackie Robinson: Race, Sports & the American Dream.* Armonk, NY: M.E. Sharpe, 1998.

Drees, Jack, and James Mueller. *Where Is He Now?* Middle Village, NY: Jonathan David, 1973.

Dreifort, John E., ed., *Baseball History From Outside the Lines: A Reader.* Lincoln: University of Nebraska Press, 2001.

Durso, Joseph. *Baseball and the American Dream.* St. Louis: Sporting News, 1986.

_____. *Days of Mr. McGraw.* Englewood Cliffs, NJ: Prentice-Hall, Inc., 1969.

Eig, Jonathan. *Luckiest Man: The Life and Death of Lou Gehrig.* New York: Simon & Schuster, 2005.

Eisen, George, and David Wiggins, eds. *Ethnicity and Sport in North American History.* Westport, CT: Greenwood Press, 1994.

Ellard, Harry. *Baseball in Cincinnati.* Jefferson, N.C.: McFarland, 2004.

Eskenazi, Gerald. *The Lip: A Biography of Leo Durocher.* New York: William Morrow, 1993.

Ewen, David, ed. *American Songwriters.* New York: H. W. Wilson, 1987.

Falkner, David. *Great Time Coming. The Life of Jackie Robinson from Baseball to Birmingham.* New York: Simon & Schuster, 1995.

_____. *Nine Sides of the Diamond.* New York: Times Books, 1990.

_____. *The Short Season.* New York: Times Books, 1986.

Feingold, Henry. *A Time for Searching—Entering the Main Stream.* Baltimore: Johns Hopkins University Press, 1992.

Feldstein, Stanley. *The Land That I Show You: Three Centuries of Jewish Life in America.* Garden City, NY: Doubleday, 1978.

Frank, Stanley. *The Jew in Sports.* New York: Miles Publishing, 1936.

Frick, Ford. *Games, Asterisks, and People.* New York: Crown, 1973.

Frommer, Harvey. *Baseball's Greatest Rivalry.* New York: Atheneum, 1982.

_____. *Primitive Baseball.* New York: Atheneum, 1988.

_____. *Shoeless Joe Jackson and Ragtime Baseball.* Dallas: Taylor Publishing, 1992.

Fuchs, Robert S. *Judge Fuchs and the Boston Braves 1923-1935.* Jefferson, N.C.: McFarland, 1998.

Garraty, John, and Mark C. Carnes, eds. *The American National Biography,* Vol. 13. New York: Oxford University Press, 1999.

Gietschier, Steve, ed. *Sporting News Complete Baseball Record Book.* St. Louis: Sporting News, 2005.

Goldstein, Richard. *Superstars and Screwballs: 100 Years of Brooklyn Baseball.* New York: Dutton, 1991.

Goldstein, Warren. *Playing for Keeps: History of Early Baseball.* Ithaca, NY: Cornell University Press, 1989.

Gordon, Milton M. *Assimilation in American Life.* New York: Oxford University Press, 1964.

Graham, Frank. *McGraw of the Giants.* New York: G. P. Putnam's Sons, 1944. 89.*The Washington Post,* August 11, 1927. Horvitz, *The Big Book of Jewish Baseball,* 137.

_____. *The New York Giants.* New York: G.P. Putnam's Sons, 1952.

_____. *The New York Giants—An Informal History.* New York: G. P. Putnam's Sons, 1952. Reprint: Carbondale: Southern Illinois University Press, 2002.

Grayson, Harry. *They Played the Game: The Story of Baseball Greats.* New York: A. S. Barnes, 1944.

Gropman, Donald. *Say It Ain't So, Joe.* Boston: Little Brown, 1979.

Gunther, John. *Taken at the Flood: The Story of Albert Lasker.* New York: Harper Brothers, 1960.

Guttmann, Allen. *From Ritual to Record—The Nature of Modern Sports.* New York: Columbia University Press, 1978.

Hardy, James D. Jr. *The New York Giants Baseball Club 1870-1900.* Jefferson, N.C.: McFarland, 1996.

Helyer, John. *Lords of the Realm: The Real History of Baseball.* New York: Villard Books, 1994

Henderson. Robert. *Ball, Bat & Bishop: Origin of Ball Games.* Urbana: University of Illinois Press, 2001.

Hertzberg, Arthur. *Jews in America: Four Centuries of an Uneasy Encounter.* New York: Simon & Schuster, 1989.

Heward, Bill. *Some Are Called Clowns. A Season with the Last of the Great Barnstorming Baseball Teams.* New York: Crowell, 1974.

Higham, John. *Strangers in the Land: Patterns of American Nativism 1860-1925.* New York: Atheneum, 1966.

Hittner, Arthur D. *Honus Wagner: The Life of Baseball's "Flying Dutchman."* Jefferson, N.C.: McFarland, 1996.

Holtzman, Jerome. *No Cheering in the Press Box* New York: Holt, Rinehart & Winston, 1974.

Honig, Donald. *Baseball America: The Heroes of the Game and the Times of Their Glory.* New York: Macmillan, 1985.

_____. *Baseball Between the Lines: Baseball in the '40s and '50s as Told by the Men Who Played It.* New York: Coward-McCann, and Geoghegan, Inc., 1976.

Horvitz, Peter S., and Joachim Horvitz. *The Big Book of Jewish Baseball.* New York: SPI Books, 2001.

Howe, Irving. *World of Our Fathers.* New York: Harcourt Brace, 1976.

_____, and Kenneth Libo. *How We Lived 1880-1930.* New York: Richard Marek Publishing, 1979.

Hynd. Neil. *The Giants of the Polo Grounds.* New York: Doubleday, 1988.

Jacob, Kathryn Allamong, and Bruce A. Ragsdale, eds. *Biographical Dictionary of United States Congress 1774-1989.* Washington, D.C.: Superintendent of Documents, U.S. Government Printing Office, 1989.

James, Bill. *The Bill James Historical Abstract.* New York: Free Press, 2001.

_____. *Politics of Glory: How the Baseball Hall of Fame Really Works.* New York: Macmillan, 1994

Johnson, Harold. *Who's Who in Major League Baseball.* Chicago: Buxton Publishing Company, 1933.

Jones, Donald D. *Former Major League Teams: An Encyclopedia.* Jefferson, N.C.: McFarland, 1995.

Kaese, Harold. *The Boston Braves.* New York: G P. Putnam's Sons, 1948.

Kahn, Roger. *The Era 1947 to 1957: When the Yankees, the Giants, and the Dodgers Ruled the World.* New York: Ticknor & Fields, 1993.

Kanter, Kenneth Aaron. *The Jews on Tin Pan Alley. The Jewish Contribution to American Popular Music 1830-1940.* New York: KTAV, 1982.

Karp, Abraham J. *Haven and Home: A History of Jews in America.* New York: Schocken Books, 1985.

Katz, Lawrence. *Baseball in 1939.* Jefferson, N.C.: McFarland, 1995.

Kaufman, Louis, Barbara Fitzgerald, and Tom Sewell. *Moe Berg: Athlete, Scholar, Spy.* Boston: Little Brown, 1974.

Kavanaugh, Jack. *Walter Johnson: A Life.* South Bend: Diamond Communication, 1995.

_____, and Norman Macht. *Uncle Robbie.* Cleveland: Society for American Baseball Research, 1999.

Kelley, Brent. *In the Shadow of the Babe. Interviews with Baseball Players Who Played With or Against Babe Ruth.* Jefferson, N.C.: McFarland, 1995.

Kirsch, George B. *The Creation of American Team Sports 1838-1872.* Urbana: University of Illinois Press, 1989.

Lanctot, Neil. *Negro League Baseball: The Rise and Ruin of a Black Institution.* Philadelphia: University of Pennsylvania Press, 2004.

Langford, Jim. *The Game Is Never Over.* South Bend: Icarus Press, 1980.

Lansche, Jerry. *Forgotten Championships—Postseason Baseball 1882-1981.* Jefferson, N.C.: McFarland, 1989.

Lax, Roger, and Frederick Smith. *The Great Song Book Thesaurus.* New York: Oxford University Press, 1989.

Leavy, Jane. *Sandy Koufax: A Lefty's Legacy.* New York: Harper Collins, 2002.

Leitner, Irving. *Baseball Diamond in the Rough.* New York: Abelard-Schuman, 1972.

Levine, Peter. *A. G. Spalding and the Rise of Baseball. The Promise of American Sport.* New York: Oxford University Press, 1985.

_____. *Ellis Island to Ebbets Field: Sport and the American Jewish Experience.* New York: Oxford University Press, 1992.

Lewis. Franklin. *The Cleveland Indians.* New York: G. P. Putnam's Sons, 1949.

Lieb, Frederick G. *The Baseball Story.* New York: G. P. Putnam's Sons, 1950.

_____. *The Pittsburgh Pirates.* New York: G. P. Putnam's Sons, 1948.

_____. *The St. Louis Cardinals.* Carbondale: Southern Illinois University Press, 2001.

Light, Jonathan Fraser. *The Cultural Encyclopedia of Baseball.* Jefferson, N.C.: McFarland, 1997.

Lindbergh, Richard. *Stealing First in a Two-Team Town.* Champaign, IL: Sagamore, 1994.

_____. *Who's on Third?—The Chicago White Sox Story.* South Bend: Icarus Press, 1983.

Lowenfish, Lee, and Tony Lupien. *The Imperfect Diamond—The Story of Baseball's Reserve System and the Men Who Fought to Change It.* New York: Stein & Day, 1980.

Mansch, Larry D. *Rube Marquard: The Life and Times of a Baseball Hall of Famer.* Jefferson, N.C.: McFarland, 1998.

Marquis, Albert Nelson, ed. *Who's Who in New England.* Chicago: A. N. Marquis & Company, 1916.

Marshall, William. *Baseball's Pivotal Era 1945–1951.* Lexington: The University Press of Kentucky, 1999.

McCollister, John. *The Bucs: The Story of Pittsburgh Pirates.* Lenexa, KS: Addax Publishing, 1998.

Mead, William B. *Even the Browns.* Chicago: Contemporary Group Books, 1978.

Meany, Tom. *The Artful Dodgers.* New York: A. S. Barnes, 1953.

Menke, Frank. *Sports Tales and Anecdotes.* New York: A. S. Barnes, 1953.

Moore, Deborah Dash. *At Home in America.* New York: Columbia University Press, 1981.

Moore, Jack B. *Joe DiMaggio: A Bio-Bibliography.* New York: Greenwood Press, 1986.

Mrozck, Donald J. *Sport and American Mentality 1880–1910.* Knoxville: University of Tennessee Press, 1983.

Murdock, Eugene. *Ban Johnson: Czar of Baseball.* Westport, CT: Greenwood Press, 1982.

_____. *Mighty Casey All American.* Westport, CT: Greenwood Press, 1984.

Nash, Roderick. *The Nervous Generation 1917–1930.* Chicago: Rand McNally, 1970.

Nathan, Daniel. *Saying It's So: A Cultural History of the Black Sox Scandal.* Urbana: University of Illinois Press, 2003.

Nemec, David. *The Beer & Whiskey League: The Illustrated History of the American Association Baseball's Renegade Major League.* Guilford, CT: Lyons Press, 2004.

Orodenker, Richard, ed. *Dictionary of Literary Biography* V. 171. Detroit: Gale Research, 1996.

_____. *Twentieth-Century American Sports Writers.* Detroit: Gale Research, 1996.

Palmer, Pete, and Gary Gillette, eds. *The 2006 ESPN Baseball Encyclopedia.* New York: Sterling Publishing Company, 2005.

Parker, Clifton Blue. *Big and Little Poison—Paul and Lloyd Waner, Brothers.* Jefferson, N.C.: McFarland, 2003.

Peterson, Harold. *Only the Ball Was White.* Englewood Cliffs, NJ: Prentice-Hall, Inc., 1970.

Pietrusza, David. *Major Leagues: The Formation, Sometimes Absorption and Mostly Inevitable Demise of 18 Professional Baseball Organizations 1871–Present.* Jefferson, N.C.: McFarland, 1991.

_____. *Judge & Jury: Life and Times of Kenesaw Mountain Landis.* South Bend: Diamond Communication, 1998.

_____, Matthew Silverman, and Michael Gershman, eds. *Baseball. The Biographical Encyclopedia.* Kingston, NY: *Sports Illustrated,* 2002.

Porter, David, ed. *The Biographical Directory of American Sports.* New York: Greenwood Press, 1987.

Postal, Bernard, Jesse Silver, and Roy Silver. *The Encyclopedia of Jews in Sports.* New York: Bloch Publishing Company, 1965.

Povich, Shirley. *All These Mornings.* New York: Prentice-Hall, Inc., 1969.

_____. *The Washington Senators.* New York: G. P. Putnam's Sons, 1954.

Quirk, James, and Rodney Furt. *Pay Dirt: The Business of Professional Team Sports.* Princeton: Princeton University Press, 1993.

Rader, Benjamin G. *Baseball: A History of America's National Game.* Urbana: University of Illinois Press, 1992.

Rains, Rob. *The St. Louis Cardinals: The 100th Anniversary History.* New York: St. Martin's Press, 1992.

Rhodes, Greg, and John Snyder. *The Redleg Journal.* Cincinnati: Road West Publishers, 1983.

Ribalow, Harold U. and Meir Z. Ribalow. *Jewish Baseball Stars.* New York: Hippocrene Books, 1984.

Rice, Damon. *Seasons Past.* New York: Praeger, 1776.

Rielly, Edward J. *Baseball—An Encyclopedia of Popular Culture.* Santa Barbara: ABC-CLIO, Inc., 2000.

Riess, Stephen A. *City Games: Evolution of American Urban Society.* Urbana: University of Illinois Press, 1989.

_____. *Sports and the American Jew.* Syracuse: Syracuse University Press, 1998.

_____. *Touching Base: Professional Baseball and American Culture in the Progressive Era.* Westport, CT: Greenwood Press, 1980.

Rischin, Moses, ed. *The Jews of North America.* Detroit: Wayne State University Press, 1987.

_____. *The Promised City: New York City's Jews: 1870 to 1914* Cambridge: Harvard University Press, 1962.

Ritter, Lawrence. *The Glory of Their Times—The Story of the Early Days of Baseball Told by Men Who Played It.* New York: William Morrow, 1984.

Robertson, John. *Baseball's Greatest Controversies: Rhubarbs, Hoaxes, Blown Calls, Ruthian Myths, Managers Miscues, and Front Office Flops.* Jefferson, N.C.: McFarland, 1995.

Robinson, Ray. *Matty—An American Hero—Christy Mathewson of the New York Giants.* New York: Oxford University Press, 1993.

Rosenberg, John M. *The Story of Baseball.* New York: Random House, 1962.

Rosenthal, Harold. *Baseball Is Their Business.* New York: Random House, 1952.

Rothe, Anna, ed. *Current Biography, 1946.* New York: H. W. Wilson, 1947.

Ryczek, William J. *When Johnny Came Sliding Home: The Post-Civil War Baseball Boom 1865–1870.* Jefferson, N.C.: McFarland, 1998.

Sachar, Howard M. *A History of the Jews in America.* New York: Alfred A. Knopf, 1992.

Sanchez, Helen, and Hawley Richeson, eds. *El Paso's Greatest Sports Heroes.* El Paso: Mesa Publishing Corp., 1989.

Sanchez, Ray. *El Paso's Greatest Sports Heroes I Have Known.* El Paso: Senturiano Press, 1989.

Sanders, Ronald. *The Downtown Jews: Portraits of an Immigrant Generation.* New York: Harper & Row, 1969.

_____. *Shores of Refuge: One Hundred Years of Jewish Emigration*. New York: Henry Holt & Company, 1988.

Santa Maria, Michael, and James Costello. *In the Shadows of the Diamonds: Hard Times in the National Pastime*. Carmel, IN: William C. Brown Communications, 1992.

Schacht, Al. *Clowning Through Baseball*. New York: A. S. Barnes, 1941.

Schwarz, Alan. *The Numbers Game*. New York: St. Martin's Press, 2004.

Scully, Gerald W. *The Business of Major League Baseball*. Chicago: University of Chicago Press, 1989.

Seib, Philip. *The Player—Christy Mathewson, Baseball, and the American Century*. New York: Four Walls, Eight Windows, 2003.

Seymour, Harold. *Baseball: The Early Years*. New York: Oxford University Press, 1960.

_____. *Baseball: The Golden Age*. New York: Oxford University Press, 1989.

_____. *Baseball: The People's Game*. New York: Oxford University Press, 1990.

Shapiro, Edward S. *A Time for Healing—American Jewry Since World War II*. Baltimore: Johns Hopkins University Press, 1992.

Shatzkin, Mike, ed. *The Ballplayers—Baseball's Ultimate Biographical Reference*. New York: Arbor House, 1998.

Silverman, B. P. Robert Stephen. *The 100 Greatest Jews in Sports Rated According to Achievement*. Lanham, MD: Scarecrow, 2003.

Simon, Rita J. *In the Golden Land. A Century of Russian and Soviet Jewish Immigration in America*. Westport, CT: Praeger, 1997.

Singer, Isidore (ed). Jewish Encyclopedia 1964. New York: Funk and Wagnall's, 1964.

Slater, Robert. *Great Jews in Sports*. Middle Village, NY: Jonathan David, 1992.

Smelser, Marshall. *The Life That Ruth Built*. Lincoln: University of Nebraska Press, 1975.

Smith, Ira. *Baseball's Famous First Basemen*. New York: A. S. Barnes, 1956.

Smith, Leverett, Jr. *The American Dream and the National Game*. Bowling Green, OH: Bowling Green University Popular Press, 1975.

Smith, Robert. *Baseball in the Afternoon*. New York: Simon & Schuster, 1993.

Smith, William C. *Americans in the Making*. New York: Simon & Schuster, 1993.

Smizik, Bob. *The Pittsburgh Pirates: An Illustrated History*. New York: Walker, 1990.

Sobol, Ken. *Babe Ruth and the American Dream*. New York: Random House, 1974.

Spalding A. G. *Baseball: America's National Game*. San Francisco: Halo Books, 1991.

Spink, Alfred E. *The National Game*. Carbondale: Southern Illinois University Press, 2000:

Spink, J. G. Taylor. *In the Shadows of the Diamonds: Hard Times in the National Pastime*. New York: Thomas Y. Crowell, 1947.

Sullivan, Dean A., ed. *Early Innings—A Documentary History of Baseball 1825-1908*. Lincoln: University of Nebraska Press, 1995.

Thomas, Henry W. *Walter Johnson Baseball's Big Train*. Lincoln: University of Nebraska Press, 1995.

Thorn, John, Phil Birnbaum, and Bill Dean, eds. *Total Baseball* Wilmington, DE: Sports Media Publishing, Inc., 2004.

Torry, Jack. *Endless Summers: The Fall and Rise of the Cleveland Indians*. South Bend: Diamond Communication, 1996.

Turner, Dan. *Heroes, Bums, and Ordinary Men: Profiles in Canadian Baseball*. Toronto: Doubleday, 1988.

Tygiel, Jules. *Baseball's Great Experiment—Jackie Robinson and His Legacy*. New York: Oxford University Press, 1997.

Van Blair, Rick. *Dugout to Foxhole: Interviews with Baseball Players Whose Careers Were Affected by World War II*. Jefferson, N.C.: McFarland, 1994.

Voigt, David. *America Through Baseball*. Chicago: Nelson-Hall, 1976.

_____. *American Baseball—From Gentleman Sport to Commissioner Reform*. Norman: University of Oklahoma Press, 1996.

_____. *The League That Failed*. Lanham, Maryland: Scarecrow, 1998.

Wallop, Douglas. *Baseball: An Informal History*. New York: W. W. Norton, 1969.

Werber, Bill, and C. Paul Rogers. *Memoirs of a Ball Player*. Lincoln: University of Nebraska Press, 2001.

Westcott, Rich, and Frank Bilovsky. *The New Phillies Encyclopedia*. Philadelphia: Temple University Press, 1993.

Wheeler, Lonnie, and John Baskin. *The Cincinnati Game*. Wilmington, OH: Orange Frazer Press, Inc., 1988.

White, G. Edward. *Creating the National Pastime: Baseball Transforms Itself*. Princeton: Princeton University Press, 1996.

White, Herman D. *An Informal History of the Northern Baseball League*. St. Paul: The Gryphon Press, 1982.

Wiebe, Robert H. *The Search for Order 1877-1920*. New York: Hill & Wang, 1967.

Zoss, Joel, and John Bowman. *Diamonds in the Rough: The Untold History of Baseball*. New York: Macmillan, 1989.

Magazines

Addie, Bob. "Honorable Judge." *Baseball Digest* 24 (March 1965): 38.

Alvarez, Mark. "Abominable Owner." *Sports Heritage* 1 (November/December 1987): 43–45.

Amman, Larry. "The Clown Prince of Baseball." *Baseball Research Journal* (1982): 119–126.

Barcella, Earnest. "Dolly Stark Calls 'Em Quick." *American Magazine* 114 (September 1932): 62.

"Baseball Precedent." *Literary Digest* 121 (February 8, 1936): 37.

Batsmen." *Time* 11 (April 23, 1928): 26.

Berler, Ron. "Let's Hear It for the Rabbi of Swat." *Sports Illustrated* 75 (October 21, 1921): 108a–109a.

Bern, Harold. "One Baseball Hour to Live." *Baseball Magazine* 58 (March 1937): 448, 470.

Blanko, Jim. "Nick Altrock." *National Pastime* (1998): 73–75.

Block, Seymour (Cy) "Selling Life Insurance Is Like Playing Baseball." *Life Insurance Selling* (June 1953).

Bloodgood, Clifford. "Arnovich Superior Lad from Superior." *Baseball Magazine* 63 (July 1939): 347.

_____. "The Gordon Across the River." *Baseball Magazine* 73 (February 1944): 315.

_____. "Kill the Umpire." *Baseball Magazine* 82 (May 1949): 410.

_____. "Players You Ought to Get to Know." *Baseball Magazine* 37 (July 1926): 366.

_____. "A Star Rookie of 1933." *Baseball Magazine* 52 (February 1934): 407–408.

Bready, James H. "Play Ball: The Legacy of 19th Century Baltimore Baseball." *Maryland Historical Magazine* 87 (Summer 1992): 127–133.

Broeg, Bob. "Hank Greenberg Self-Made Hall of Famer." *Baseball Digest* 45 (December 1986): 69–71.

Burr, Harold. "Fate Hounds This Ump." *Baseball Magazine* 69 (June 1942): 309–310.

Cunningham, Bill. "Clown Prince." *Colliers* 100 (September 4, 1937): 24, 38–39.

Daniel, Dan. "Hank Greenberg's Shift to Pirates Presents Case Without Any Precedent." *Baseball Magazine* 78 (May 1947): 415–417.

_____. "Looks Soft, But Oh My." *Baseball Magazine* 60 (March 1938): 449.

David, Jim. "Baseball's Valedictorian." *Beckett Monthly* (August 1989): 75–76.

_____. "The Smartest Major Leaguer." *Sports History* 2 (March 1989): 61–63.

Dawidoff, Nicholas. "Scholar, Lawyer, Catcher, Spy—Moe Berg, Baseball's Renaissance Man of the 1920s and '30s Was a US Atomic Spy in World War II." *Sports Illustrated* 76 (March 23, 1992): 78–86.

Dexter, Charles. "Braves' Cool, Cool Heart." *Baseball Digest* 11 (March 1952): 5–8.

"Doll Making in America." *Playthings* (December 1908): 118–120.

Dorinson, Joe. "Jews and Baseball." *Society for American Baseball Research* 5 (July 2004): 10–11.

Durocher, Leo. "I Come to Kill You." *Saturday Evening Post* 236 (May 11, 1963): 30.

Edelstein, Tilden G. "Cohen at the Bat." *Commentary* (November 1953): 53–56.

Eisenstat, Harry. *Baseball Magazine* 63 (August 1939): 395.

Evans, David A. "Late in the Game." *National Pastime* (2002): 45–46.

Fierman, Floyd. "Insights and Hindsights of Some El Paso Jewish Families." *The El Paso Jewish Historical Review* 1 (Spring 1983): 64–67.

Fiorito, Lou. "Where Are They Now?" *Old Tyme Baseball News* 4 (1992): 24.

Fitzgerald, Ed. "Hank Greenberg: A Study in Success." *Sport* 10 (March 1951): 25–27, 85–89.

Frank, Stanley. "Hank Made Greenberg." *Saturday Evening Post* 213 (March 15, 1941): 35–37, 43–48.

Graham, Frank. "The Little Napoleon." *Sport* 28 (May 1959): 46, 87–88.

_____. "The New York Giants." *Sport* 10 (July 1951): 29–30, 80.

Harris, John. "Pinhead Christy Mathewson." *National Pastime* (1990): 17–20.

Harrison, Walter Lee. "Six Pointed Diamond." *Journal of Pop Culture* 15 (September 15, 1981): 112–118.

Hoberman, John M. "Why Jews Played Sports: Do Sports and Jewish Values Conflict?" *Moment* 16 (April 1991): 34–42.

"Home Run Slugger Is Bought by Giants." *American Hebrew* 113 (September 14, 1923): 462.

Hornsby, Roger. "I Always Kept My Bag Packed." *Sport* 20 (September 1955): 16, 79.

Jacobson, Louis. "Will the Real Rabbi of Swat Please Stand Up.?" *Baseball Research Journal* (1989): 17–18.

Jaher, Frederic Cople. "Anti-Semitism in American Athletics." *Shofar* 24 (Fall 2001): 61–69.

Johnson, Ban. "Making the American League." *Saturday Evening Post* 202 (March 22, 1930): 12, 121–122, 125.

Kates, Maxwell, "Of Horsehides and Hexagrams." *National Pastime* (2004): 118–126.

Lane, F. C. "The Crime of Baseball Pools." *Baseball Magazine* 15 (September 1915): 29.

_____. "He Can Talk Baseball in Ten Languages." *Baseball Magazine* 39 (September 27): 439–440.

_____. "How Much Is a Star Worth?" *Baseball Magazine* 10 (April 1913): 54.

_____. "A New Batting Stance Made Him a Good Hitter." *Baseball Magazine* 49 (October 1932): 509.

_____. "Shall Certain Magnates Defy the Public?" *Baseball Magazine* 10 (May 1913): 25.

_____. "Why Baseball Statisticians Get Prematurely Gray-Headed." *Baseball Magazine* 40 (March 1928): 442, 469–470.

_____. "Why Not More Jewish Ball Players?" *Baseball Magazine* 36 (January 1926): 341, 372.

_____. "The Wizard of Dope." *Baseball Magazine* 30 (April 1923): 509–510.

Lavelle, Howard. "Moses Solomon, Rabbi of Swat." *Baseball Research Journal* (1976): 90–92.

Manuel, Mark. "That Ball's on the Queer." *Baseball Research Journal* (1997): 114–118.

Marozzi, Rich. "Al Schacht—Clown Prince of Baseball." *Baseball History* 1 (Winter 1986): 34–45.

Mason, Ward. "Alexander's Right Hand Man—Erskine Mayer, the Phillies Second Best Bet—His Great Record and the Secret of His Success." *Baseball Magazine* 16 (November 1915): 68–70.

McGowen, Roscoe. "Baseball As It Used to Be." *Sport* 37 (June 1964): 64, 92.

_____. "Little Bum with the Big Bat." *Baseball Magazine* 72 (November 1943): 415–417.

Meany, Tom. "The Great Greenberg Mystery." *Sport* 2 (June 1947): 16–18.

_____. "Syd Gordon—The Answer to a Giant Prayer?" *Sport* (July 1949): 30–32, 98–99.

Milne, Robert. "One of the Players You Ought to Know." *Baseball Magazine* 47 (November 1931): 562–563.

"Minor Portrait—Cy Block." *Baseball Magazine* 83 (July 1949): 270.

Nathan, Daniel. "Anti-Semitism in the Black Sox Scandal." *Nine* (December 1995): 94–100.

Newcombe, Jack. "Old Pro of the Braves." *Sport* (July 1953): 35, 83–85.

Nickerson, Marina. "Andy Cohen: El Paso's Mr. Baseball." *Texas Country* (April 1981): 29–31.

Norwood, Stephen H. and Harold Brackman. "Going to Bat for Jackie Robinson: The Jewish Role in

Breaking Baseball's Color Line." *Journal of Sport History* 26, (Spring 1999): 115–141.

"Obit." *Baseball Magazine* 48 (April 1932): 482.

Okrent, Daniel. "The Eternal Spring." *Esquire* 91 (April 24, 1979): 62–63.

Phelan, William A. "Great American Magnate." *Baseball Magazine* 10 (January 1913): 17.

_____. "Shall Baseball Cease?" *Baseball Magazine* 22 (December 1919): 101.

Reynolds, Quentin. "Harry the Horse." *Colliers* 102 (July 23, 1938): 18, 54.

Richman, Milton. "The Kid from Brooklyn." *Sport Life* (March 1949): 28–29, 80–81.

Ritter, L. S. "Remembering Al Schacht." *Old Tyme Baseball News* 8 (1996): 14.

Sanborn, Irving E. "Problems of a Big League Club Owner." *Baseball Magazine* 32 (February 1924): 391.

Sawyer, C. F. "Players You Ought to Get to Know." *Baseball Magazine* 46 (March 1921): 475–476.

Schwarz, Alan. "Uncle Albert." *National Pastime* (1997): 54–56.

Schweid, Barry. "Harry the Horse Danning." *Baseball Research Journal* (1998): 79–80.

"Shirley Povitch, Hall of Fame Sportswriter, 92" *Editor and Publisher* (June 20, 1998): 75.

Simmons, Herbert. "Counting the Hits That Count." *Baseball Magazine* 69 (November 1942): 541–542, 566.

Simons, William M. "Andy Cohen: Baseman as Ethnic Hero." *National Pastime* (1990): 83–87.

_____. "The Athlete As Jewish Standard Bearers: Media Image of Hank Greenberg." *Jewish Social Studies* 44 (Spring 1982): 95–108.

Smith, James D., III. "Jimmie Reese." *Baseball Research Journal* (1995): 89–91.

Smith, Ken. "The Giants' Jewish Catcher." *Baseball Magazine* 60 (March 1938): 444, 473–474.

_____. "Over Age Destroyer." *Baseball Magazine* 73 (September 1944): 341–343.

Smitley, Al. "Straight from the Horse's Mouth—A Chat with Harry Danning." *Old Tyme Baseball News* 7 (1995): 20–21.

Solomon, Eric. "Jews, Baseball, and the American Novel." *Arete* 1 (Spring 1984): 44–46.

Stallard, H. L. "Players Who Have Starred with Both Leagues in World Series." *Baseball Magazine* 37 (November 1926): 542.

Sullivan, Dean A. "Faces in the Crowd: A Statistical Portrait of Baseball Spectators in Cincinnati 1886–1888." *Journal of Sport History* 17 (Winter 1990): 354–365.

Williams, Joe. "Umps." *American Magazine* 122 (October 1936): 66.

Newspapers

Asbury Park (NJ) *Press*
Atlanta Constitution
Atlanta Jewish Times
Atlanta Journal
Augusta (Ga.) *Chronicle*
Baltimore Sun
Birmingham News-Age-Herald

Boston Evening Transcript
Boston Globe
Boston Traveler
The Brooklyn Citizen
Chicago Daily News
Chicago Daily Tribune
Christian Science Monitor
Cincinnati Enquirer
Cincinnati Post
Cincinnati Times Star
Cleveland Jewish News
Dearborn Independent
Deep South Jewish Voice
Detroit Free Press
El Paso Herald-Post
El Paso Times
Ft. Wayne Daily News
Ft. Wayne Journal Gazette
Ft. Wayne News Sentinel
The Gladwin County (Gladwin, MI) *Record*
Great Neck Record
Hazelton (WI) *Sentinel*
Jewish News of Greater Phoenix
Kenosha News
Kentucky Post
Leader-Call (Laurel, MS)
Long Island Press
Los Angeles Times
Lowell Citizen
Miami Sunday Herald
New Jersey Jewish News
New Orleans States Item
New York Herald Tribune
New York Journal-American
New York Post
New York Times
New York World Telegram
The Northwest Indiana News
Orange County Register
The Philadelphia Inquirer
Pittsburgh Post-Gazette
St. Louis Post-Dispatch
St. Louis Star and Times
San Francisco Chronicle
The Scrantonian
The Seattle Times
The Sporting News
Staten Island Advance
Superior Evening Telegram
Today's Sports
USA Today Baseball Weekly
The Washington Post

Internet

Ajhs.org
Americanhistory.si.edu
Angelfire.com
Astrodaily.com
Baseball.almanac.com
Baseball.com
Baseballhalloffame.org
Baseballist.com

Baseballlibrary.com
Baseball-reference.com
Baseball-statistics.com
Biographybase.com
Biojproj.sabr.org
Blackbetsy.com
Blogofdeath.com
CBS.sportsline.com
Cincysports.net
Citypages.com
Cloverdalesoftball.com
Diamondtide.tidefans.com
Dickiethon.com
Dodgersscout.com
Encarat.msn.com
En.wikipedia.org
Espn.go.com
Forward.com
Futilityinfielder.com
Geocities.com
Historicalbaseball.com
Innogize.com
Ivyleaguesports.com
Jewishf.com
Jewishsports.net
Jewishvirtuallibrary.com
Jewsinsports.org

Jewsweek.com
Jrbook.sonline.com
Jta.org
Members.tripod.com
Nationalpastime.com
Neworleansbaseball.com
Paperofrecord.com
Parlorsongs.com
Redsoxconnection.com
Retrosheet.org
Searchancestry.com
Smithsonianmag.si.edu
Songwritershalloffame.org
Sportingnews.com
Sportsillustrated.cnn.com
Sports-wired.com
Springtrainingonline.com
Stargazettenews.com
Stat-junkie.com
Thebaseballpage.com
Thebaseballreliquary.org
Thecolumnists.com
Thedeadball.com
Thornpricks.blogspot.com
Townhall.com
Toyou.com

Index